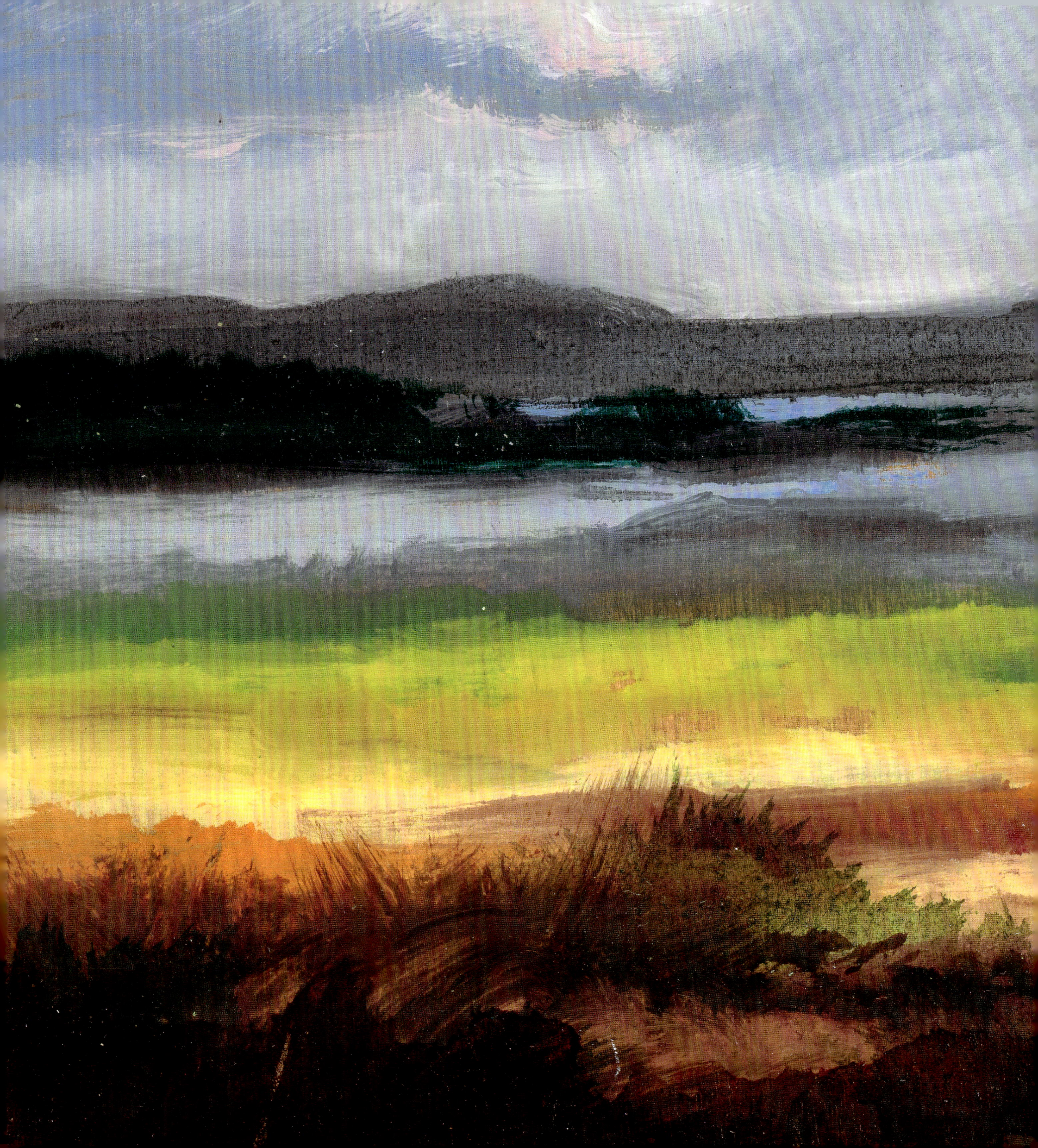

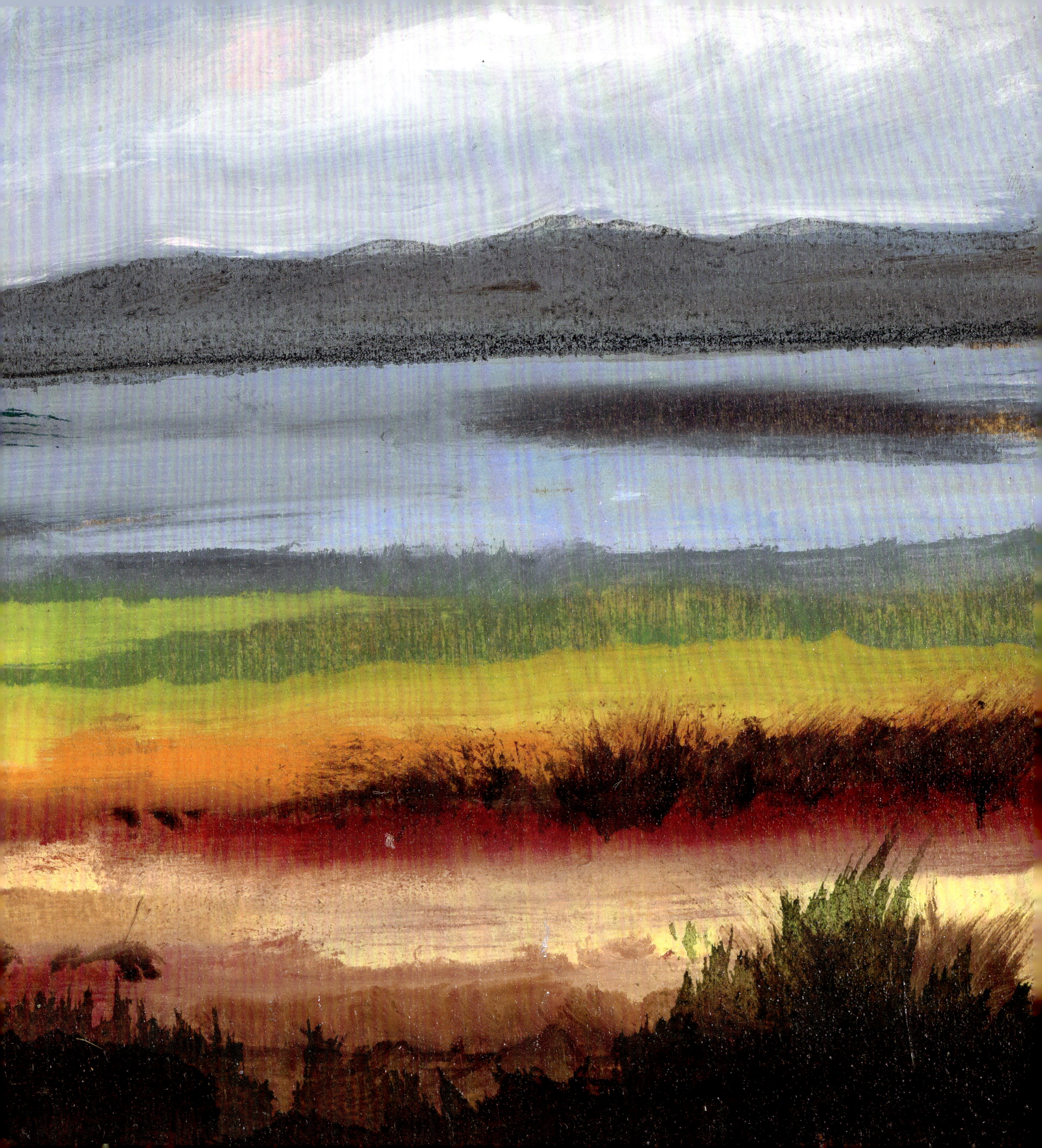

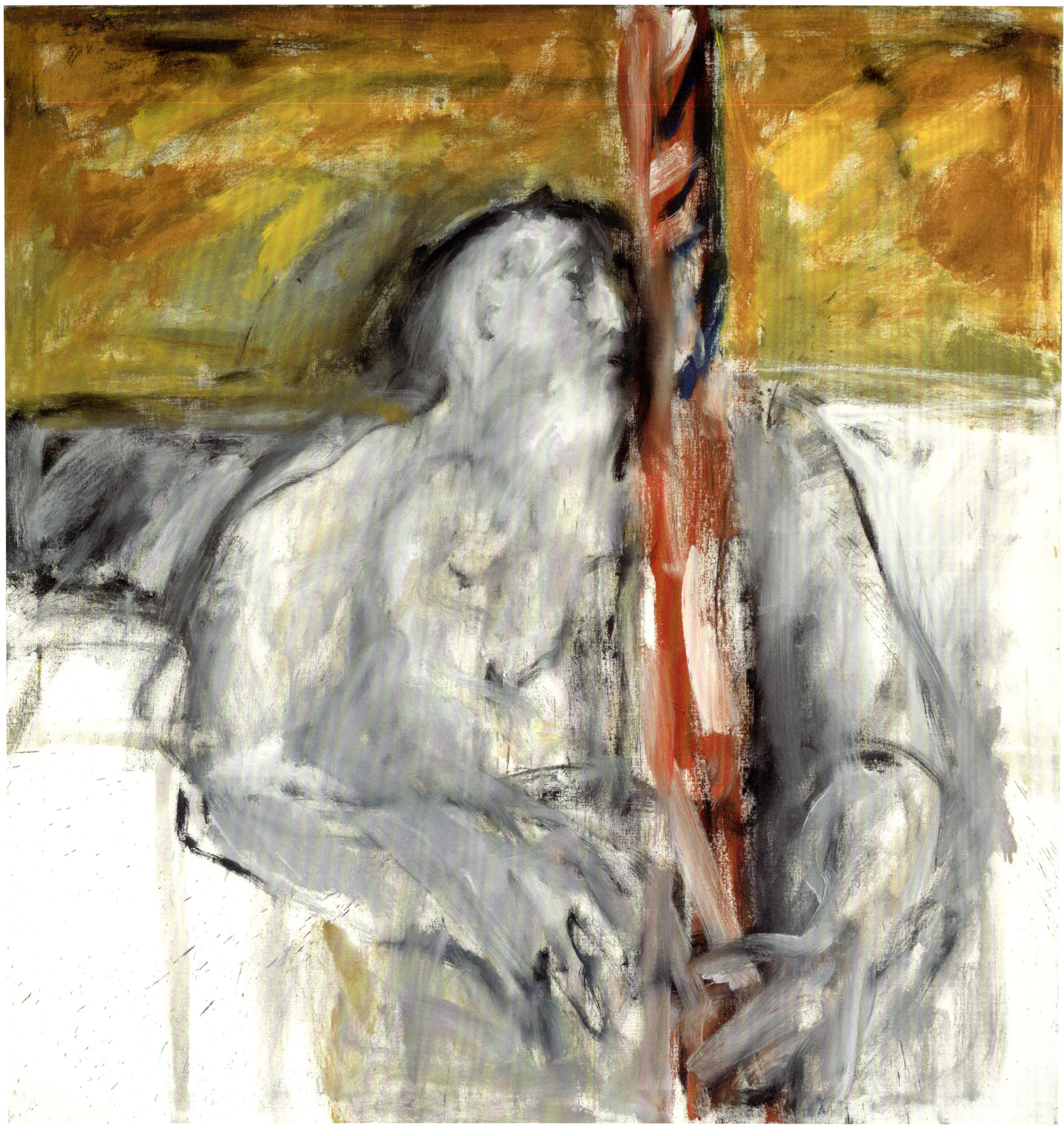

Hodermarsky

FOREWORD BY
Duncan Christy

ESSAYS BY
Allison Rudnick, MPhil
Kat Lee, MA, RDT-BCT, LCAT

ARTIST INTERVIEWS BY
Anna Hammond

The Artist Book Foundation
North Adams, Massachusetts

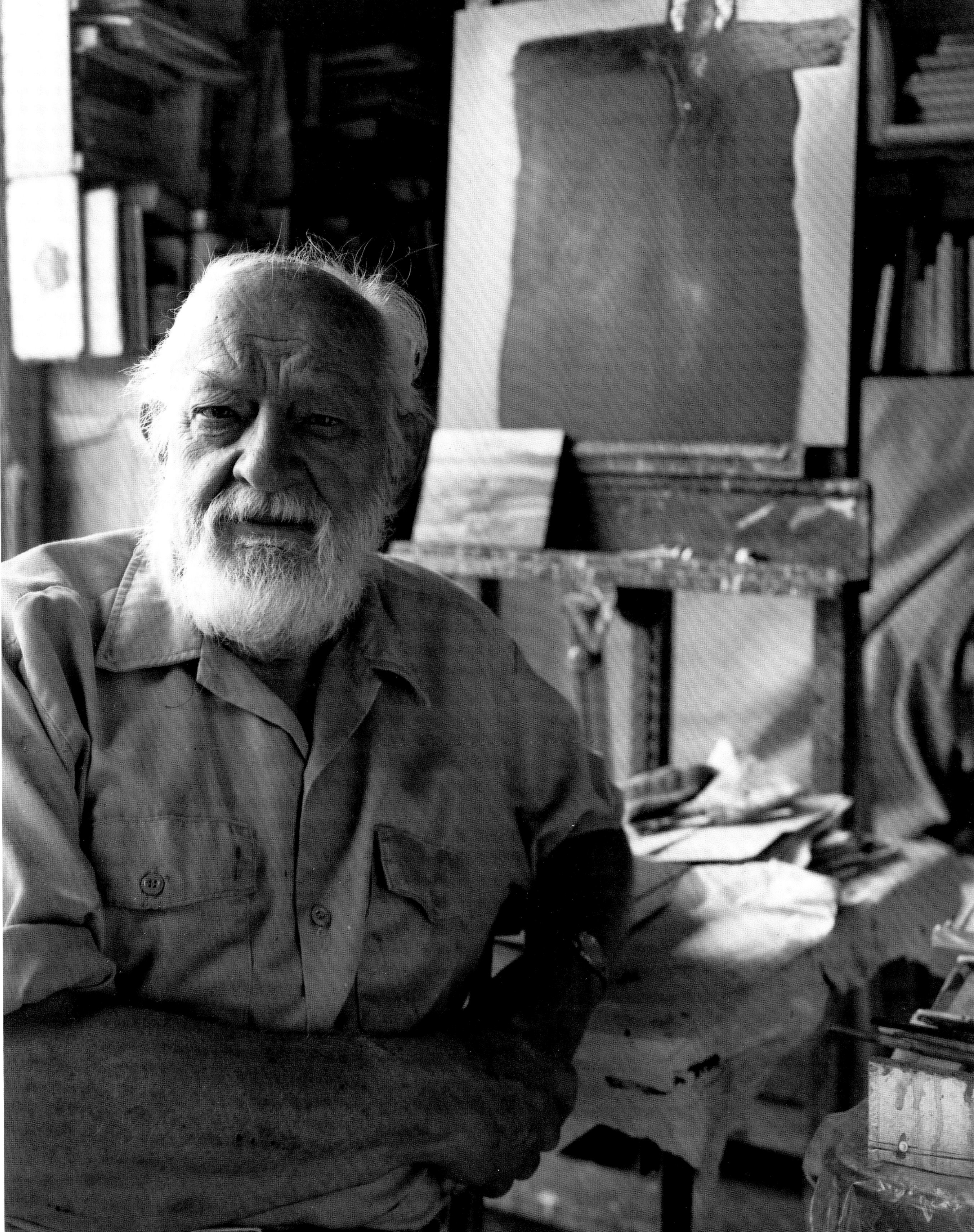

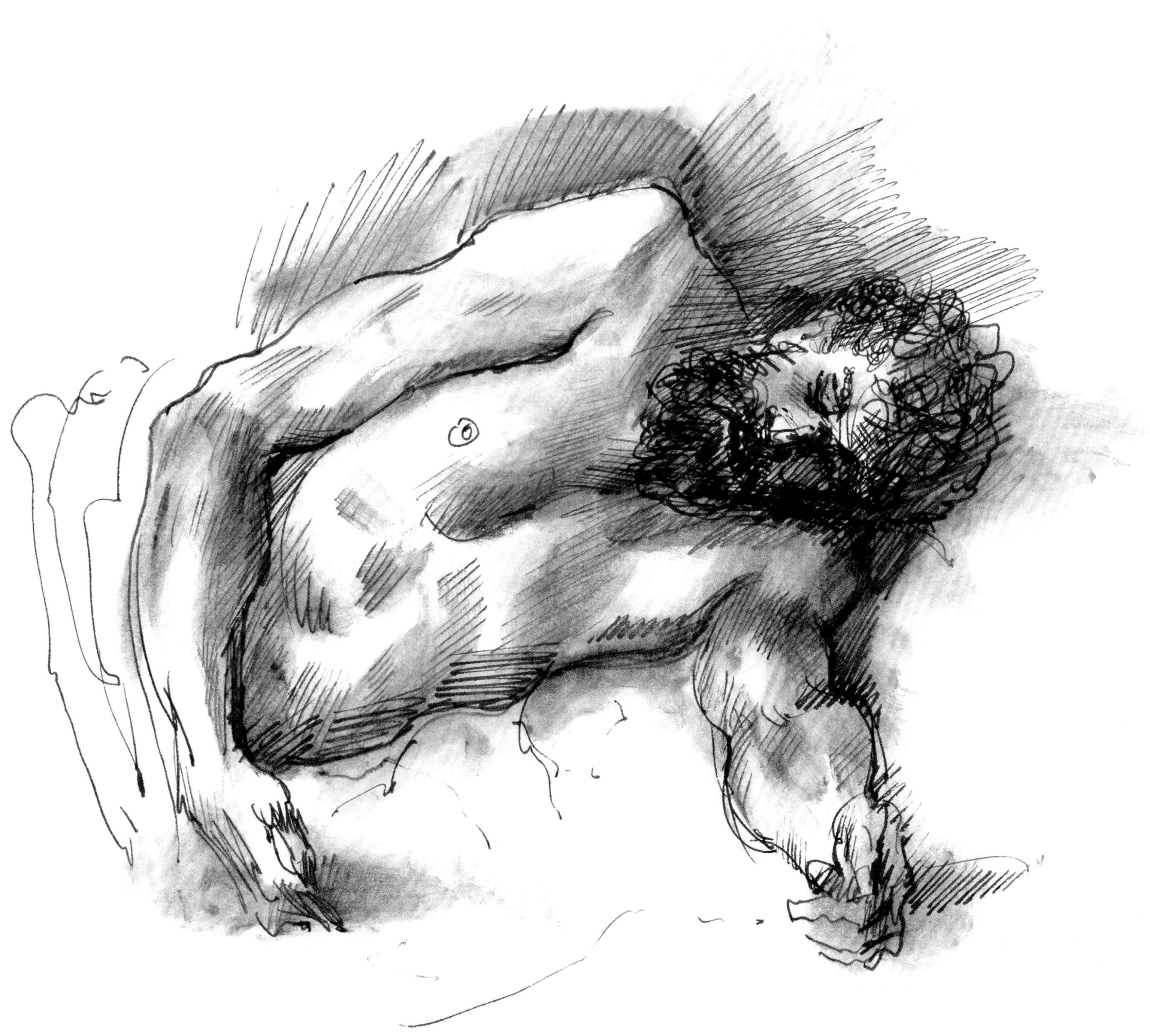

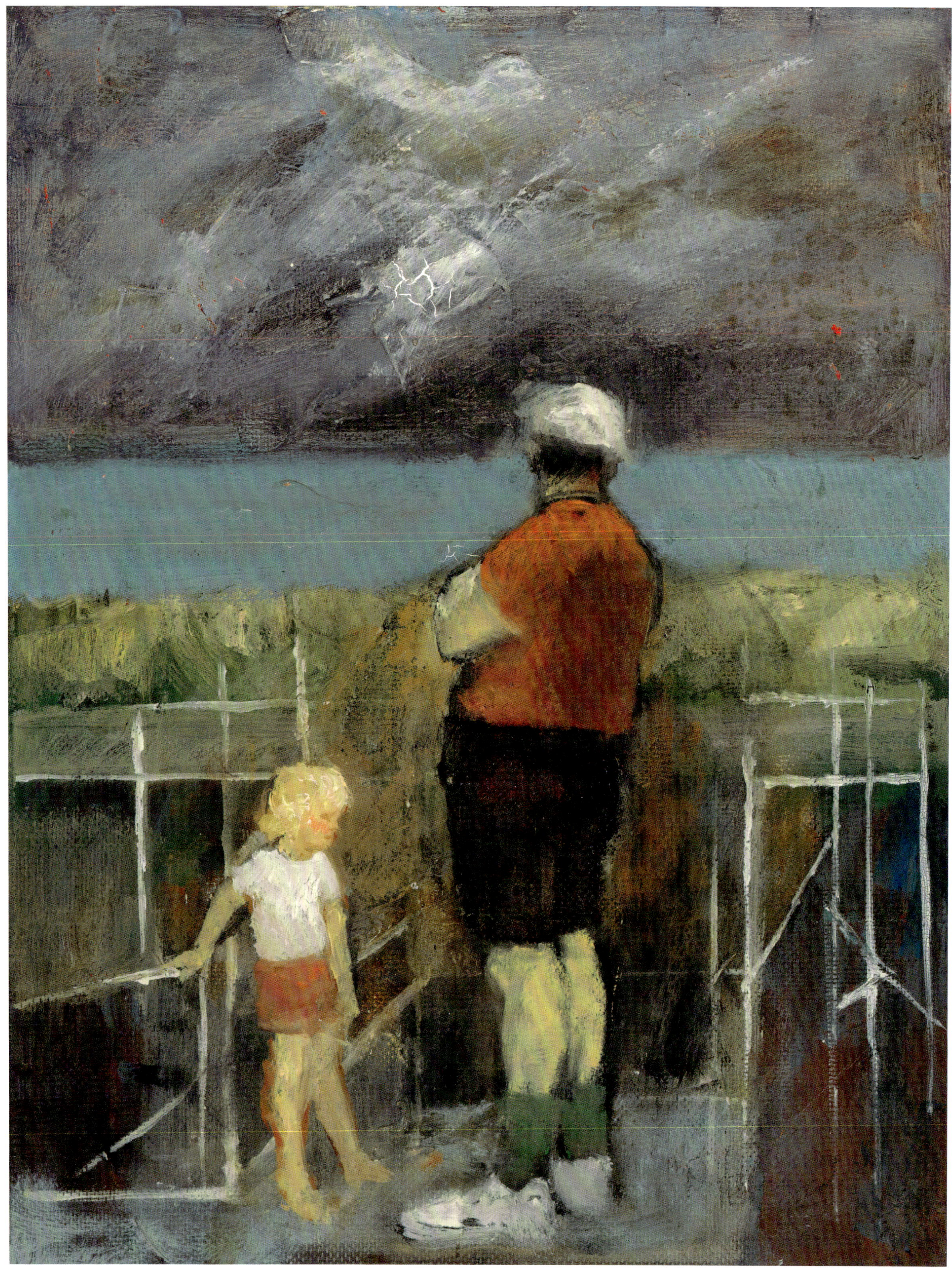

How He Hovers in
Our Consciousness

THOSE OF US WHO KNEW HIM, those of us fortunate to have known him—how he hovers in our consciousness. How some 20 or more years after his death, Dan Hodermarsky is still what he always was to us: a force of nature. A force of art. A force of life.

And what a life!

This volume brings together a life in art, and even a quick and cursory glance reveals his range in every sense of the term: subject, technique, theme, meaning, execution, inspiration. He was fond of painting in series, and here is only a partial list of them: *Peasants Series*, *Penobscot Nation Series*, *Paradise Tree Series*, *Chautauqua Series*, *Ambergris Series*, *De Profundis Series*, *Mexican Series*, *Gold at the Shore Series*. And each series is a true exploration of different nuances and facets of the subject at hand.

But how did he get there, this marvelous, Slavic-derived bear of a man?

In overview it looks like this: Artist. Student. Soldier. Teacher. Husband. Artist. Mentor. Father. Artist. Always an artist, that is, up and down the many slopes of life, of which the most profound experience was World War II. Assigned to an Allied unit dubbed the "Bastard Battalion" for their unrelenting exposure to battle, he more than saw war at first-hand—he lived it. And it would touch him as no other experience would, leaving him for decades afterward with PTSD, post-traumatic stress disorder, and always with pills for anxiety safely in a pocket.

The evidence of that is here in the graphic paintings that depict dismembered subjects and recall Francis Bacon's similar, horrifying ectoplasms, which Kat Lee explores in the powerful essay, "Painting the Unspeakable."

"He painted because he had to," his daughter Maria says of her father. "It was his way of taking in the world, of responding. . . , of processing, of valuing. . . . His art allowed his many unspoken,

Dan and Maria, 1963–1964
Oil on canvas
13½ x 17 in. (34.3 x 43.2 cm)
Collection of Maria Hodermarska
and Penn Rhodeen

unspeakable experiences to be metabolized and rendered on canvas. Through making art he could step away from those experiences—physical, existential, emotional—and move the experiences from formlessness to form."[1]

She offers a powerful clue to his story as, relevantly, it also lies in the profession that he embraced and that enabled him to embrace life directly: teaching.

That career began in 1955 in his native Cleveland, Ohio, at institutions including the Cleveland Institute of Art. Notably, it featured an involvement with the Bussed-in Arts Program for the Cleveland Supplementary Educational Center. "He ran a Title III inner-city arts program for poor kids who had no art in their schools," Maria explains. "They would be bussed to the converted factory where he worked for art lessons. He was committed to bringing art to people who wouldn't have access to it."

Then, in 1969, he accepted an appointment to Deerfield Academy in Massachusetts. Today it is considered one of the world's finest coeducational preparatory schools, excelling in every area of student life and opportunity. But at the end of the sixties, it was something of a refined backwater, catering mainly to the sons of affluent New England families, and it had no arts program. That it is what it is today owes credit to many. But its greatest credit belongs to Dan Hodermarsky, who started not so much a renaissance as a new beginning. Put simply, he hit Deerfield like a bomb going off.

And he did it simply by being what he was: an artist and teacher who loved life in all its earthy, earthly manifestations, which he shared openly, unlike the other buttoned-down, longtime faculty quietly going about their chosen existences. Here's what "Hodo" wasn't: quiet.

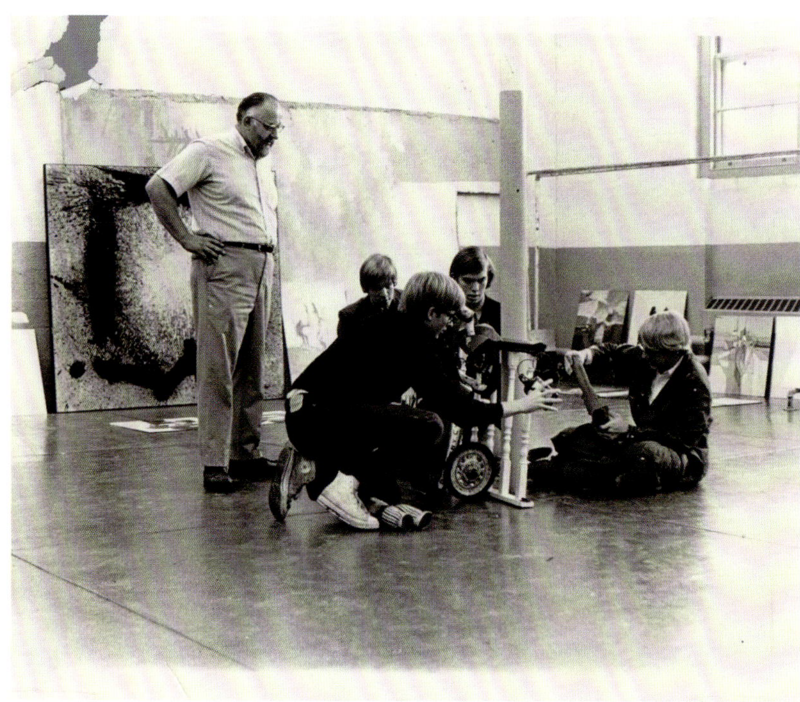

Dan in his Deerfield classroom studio;
estate of the artist

"I remember seeing Hodo for the very first time," Tom Henry recalls of the new teacher's arrival, "and how differently he carried himself compared to all the other teachers I had at Deerfield. In his presence he made me feel different, too. As soon as you walked into the art room, anything seemed possible, and every creative exploration was encouraged without hesitation. I always felt like he was on a mission to unleash everyone's creative talents in whatever way they chose to express them."[2]

Under Dan's guidance, Henry created a sculpture, *Connections*, in a Minimalist style and it still stands outside Deerfield's main library. He remembers his mentor in action: "Beyond the art room was Hodo's studio, filled with easels holding paintings in progress and canvases leaning against every wall. And then came the inner sanctum where the world of his haunted figures came to mind and then appeared across his studio."[3]

The haunted figures would only eventually leave him or at least ebb in importance. Deerfield, where he taught for 25 years, offered stability in all important respects. "He resisted getting a gallery in New York and could have easily," Maria explains. "He was offered jobs at other institutions and universities running art education programs, but chose to stay at Deerfield because he had a comfortable rhythm there and the summers free. He could spend as much time as he wanted in the studio. And that beautiful valley to ride through on his bike."

He retired in 1989. There were 10 halcyon years of painting-infused retirement on Deer Isle, Maine, before he died of a heart attack in his studio—as he probably would have wished if he'd had a choice. Reflecting his Slavic heritage, he would have enjoyed, and laughed heartily, that kielbasa was served at his memorial service.

"He made everyone he loved feel safe and secure in his love," Maria recalls tenderly. "He loved his large family without exception. He loved people. He was a good human being, good to the bone." And a very good and ambitious artist as you will savor in these pages with their incisive essays that paint him and his work in large and fair dimensions.

A decade or more ago, I stood with Dan's widow, Nancy, in the living room of the home they had shared on Deer Isle. Dan's paintings dominated, principally bright still lifes of the nearby sea. Like her husband, she is robust and outgoing, both cheerful and candid; she said firmly, "His work will be recognized." Yes, it will. Deservedly.

Duncan Christy
New York, New York
January 2, 2023

1. All statements from Maria Hodermarska are from an email interview with the author, December 25, 2022.

2. Tom Henry in an email correspondence with the author, December 25, 2022.

3. Ibid.

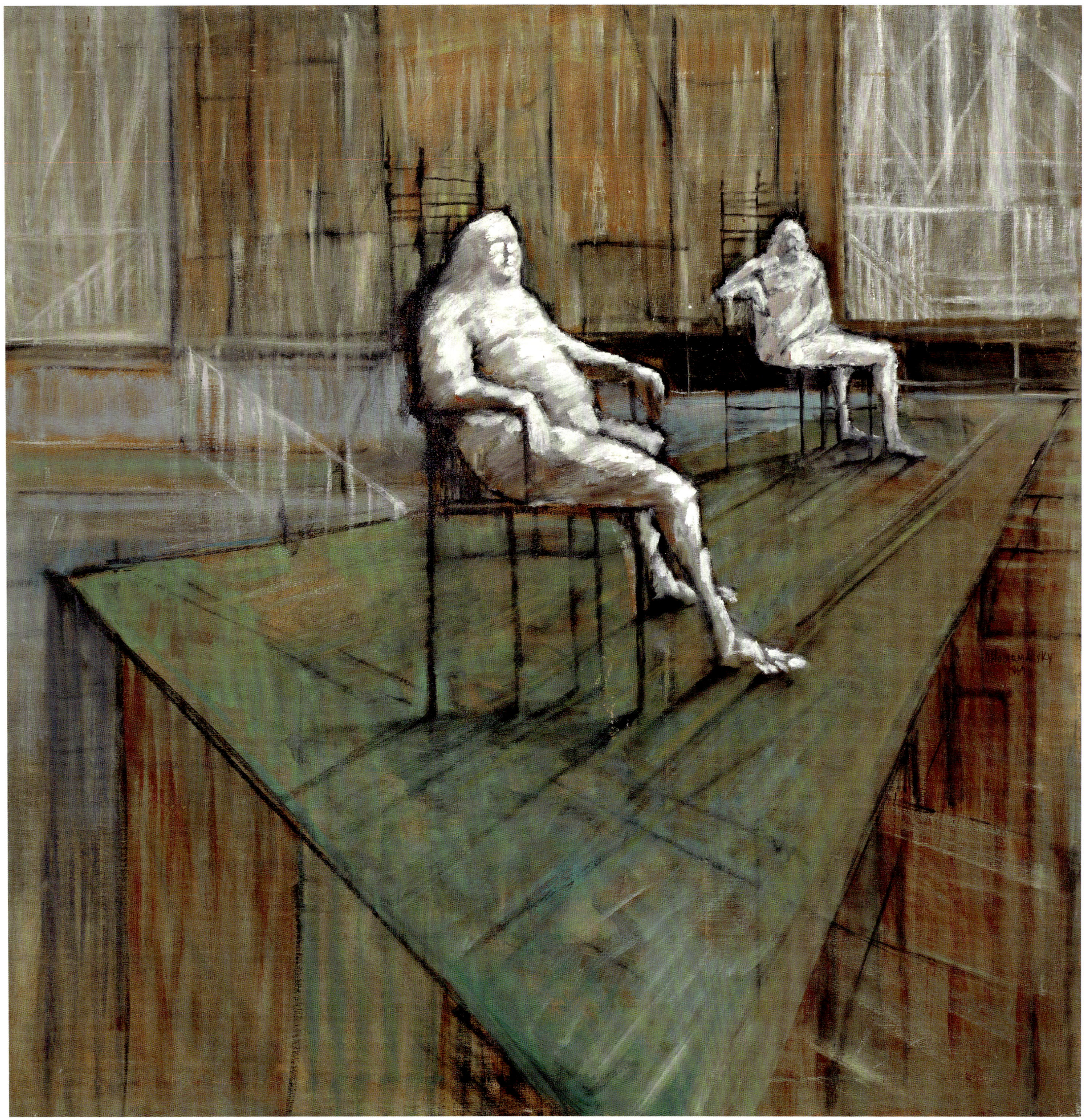

A Humanist Vision:
The Art of Daniel Hodermarsky

ALLISON RUDNICK, MPHIL

As the son of working-class slovakian immigrants, Daniel Hodermarsky's navigation of social contexts—from corporate settings to educational institutions to the art world—was shaped by his identity as a blue-collar, second-generation American. While aspects of Hodermarsky's identity enabled him to achieve professional stability and, to some degree, be assimilated into predominantly white elite environments, his ethnic and socioeconomic background simultaneously cast him as "other." The complexities embedded in his life experience endowed him with an acute sensitivity to societal behaviors and structures that he deployed as an artistic tool, and the time he spent on the front lines during World War II only augmented his empathetic disposition. In 1975, nearly fifteen years before Deerfield Academy transitioned from an all-boys student body to a coeducational academy, Hodermarsky, who had recently become the founding chair of the art department, wrote a letter to the school's newspaper addressing troubling behavior on the part of a few male students.[1] One had abandoned his date at a social affair while another had mocked a fellow student for his homosexuality. Hodermarsky's letter is an incisive social commentary on sexism, bigotry, and "manliness" that, according to him, should not be measured by one's sexuality or physical strength but by one's character. The letter ends with an appeal: "Your humanity is the most important function in life. Nurture it. Be a human being."[2]

As his former students have attested, Hodermarsky applied this philosophy to his egalitarian style of teaching. But the statement also reveals his approach to his own artistic practice. Despite the diversity of media, genres, and styles that marks Hodermarsky's decades-spanning oeuvre, a common thread that runs throughout is the artist's propensity for probing the depths of the human condition.

Palace of Men (Seated and Standing Women and Men Series), 1969
Oil on canvas
42 x 42 in. (106.7 x 106.7 cm)
Estate of the artist

His works' engagement with big themes such as power, violence, and vulnerability were informed by his early encounters with poverty and warfare. As he wrote in his letter to the Deerfield paper, "A man has tender feelings. The lives of men everywhere is [*sic*] clear evidence of that. One of the most moving photographs of the war had a medic embracing a horribly wounded soldier."[3] Hodermarsky brought the full spectrum of his own tender feelings to bear on a body of work that grapples with the cataclysm of war and the resulting societal rebuilding that characterized the second half of the twentieth century.

Daniel Hodermarsky was born in 1924 in Horning, Pennsylvania. He was the youngest of twelve children born to Daniel and Mary, who had immigrated from Slovakia to the United States in the early years of the century. Daniel senior worked as a coal miner, but miners' strikes in Pennsylvania's coalfields during the 1920s prompted the family to move to Cleveland, Ohio, around 1927 where he found work as a janitor at a car manufacturing company.[4] Like his siblings, young Dan worked from an early age to help support his family during the years of the Depression. One of only three students in his graduating class of 750 to attend college, Hodermarsky was awarded a full scholarship to the Cleveland Institute of Art, but his studies were interrupted by World War II after just one semester.

In the spring of 1943, at the age of nineteen, Hodermarsky was drafted into the United States Army, where he served with the 400th Armored Artillery Battalion—the so-called "Bastard Battalion" that was sent wherever artillery was needed. The battalion landed at Utah Beach shortly after D-Day and proceeded to fight in every major battle of the European theater, including Saint-Lô, Remagen Bridge, the Battle of the Bulge, and the Battle of Hürtgen Forest. Hodermarsky was in active combat for over ninety percent of the two and a half years he spent with the battalion. He received an honorable discharge in December 1945 and later earned a Presidential Citation, the French and Belgium Croix de Guerre, and a Silver Combat Star for his service.

Following the war, Hodermarsky resumed his studies at the Cleveland Institute, where he received his BFA with honors in painting in 1949. He took advantage of the tuition aid offered to veterans by the GI Bill, earning a degree in education from Kent State University in 1950 and an MFA in art history from Case Western Reserve University in in 1960. From 1950 to 1955, he worked as a graphic designer for the Cleveland Diesel Engine Division of General Motors. The graphic design profession acted as a launchpad for many artists' careers at mid-century, enabling them to hone the drawing skills that form the backbone of artistic practice. A well-known example is Andy Warhol, who had a successful career as a graphic designer creating illustrations for magazines and fashion brands in the 1940s and 1950s. Like Warhol, Hodermarsky was a naturally gifted draftsman. His playful illustrations for General Motors flyers possess an economy of line that attests to the artist's confident handling of pen and ink, and his keen sense of humor (figs. 1, 2).[5]

Shortly after leaving GM, Hodermarsky began his lifelong career as an educator when he was invited to teach evening courses at the Cleveland Institute. Over the next fifteen years, he taught studio art and art history classes at high schools and universities in Cleveland, and he coordinated the art program at the Supplementary Educational Center of the Cleveland Public Schools. During this period,

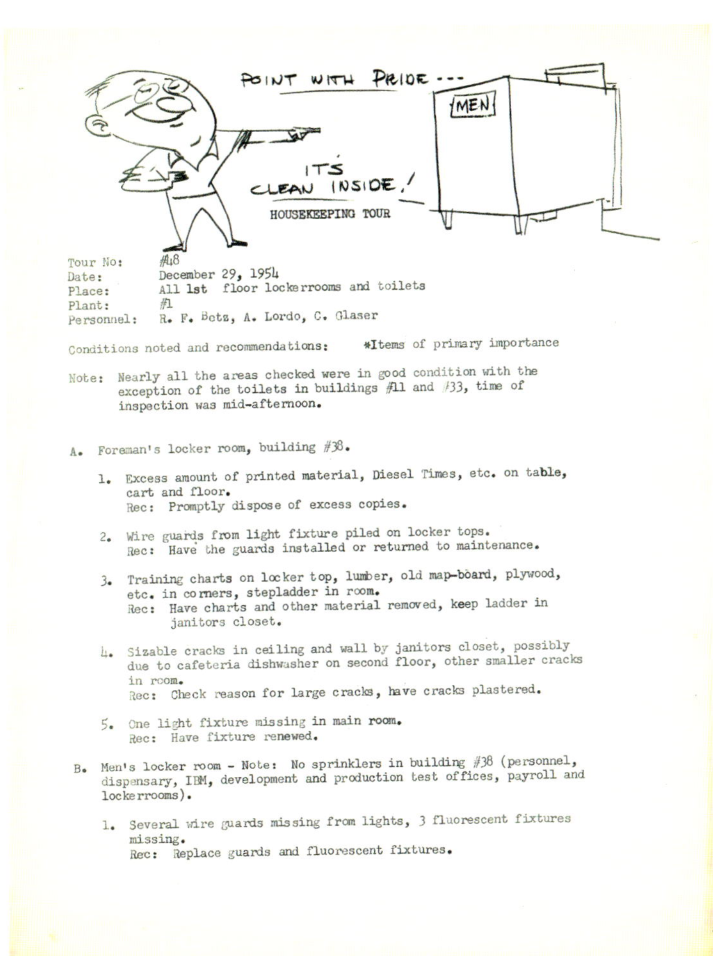

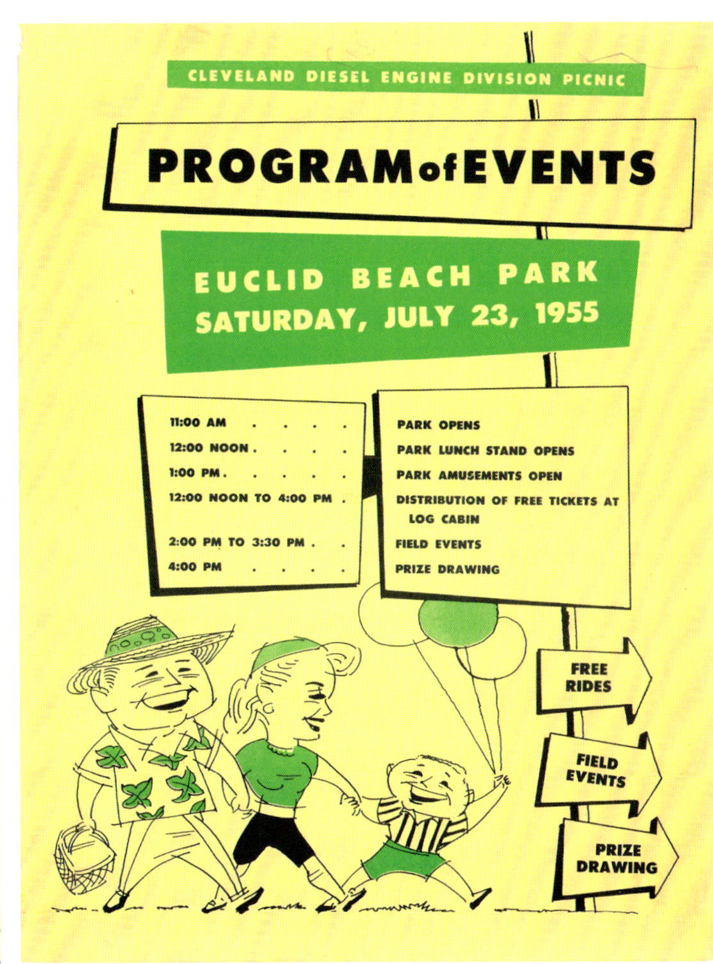

above, left: FIG. 1.

Daniel Hodermarsky, illustration General Motors Cleveland Diesel Engine Division, housekeeping tour flyer, 1954
Mimeograph
8½ x 11 in. (21.6 x 27.9 cm)
Estate of the artist

above, right: FIG. 2.

Daniel Hodermarsky, General Motors Cleveland Diesel Engine Division, picnic announcement, 1955
Two-color offset lithographic flyer on yellow paper
8½ x 6½ in. (21.6 x 16.5 cm)
Estate of the artist

he exhibited his work at museums and art galleries throughout the city, including at the Cleveland Museum of Art, where his work was shown in six annual May Shows, earning him a Juror's Mention in 1968 and a Special Jury Mention in 1969. It was during these years that he developed the themes and compositional strategies that he would engage in his work for the duration of his career as an artist.

In *Engine Charlie*, a man in a black suit and red tie sits in a schematically rendered chair whose long, thin legs and spindles echo the structure of the scaffolding that surrounds it (fig. 3). The figure leans back uncomfortably, his feat dangling above the ground. His blank stare is directed beyond the confines of the canvas, and he sits before a landscape composed of a flesh-toned pink sky and a lurid brown ground that engender an air of unsettling isolation. The painting's title indicates that he is Charlie Wilson, who was nicknamed "Engine Charlie" for his years as the president and CEO of GM from 1941 to 1953, after which he became secretary of defense in the Eisenhower administration. *Engine Charlie* was the first of numerous paintings by Hodermarsky to feature the motif of a seated figure in an abstracted setting, with the early works depicting historic men and women in positions of power and authority.

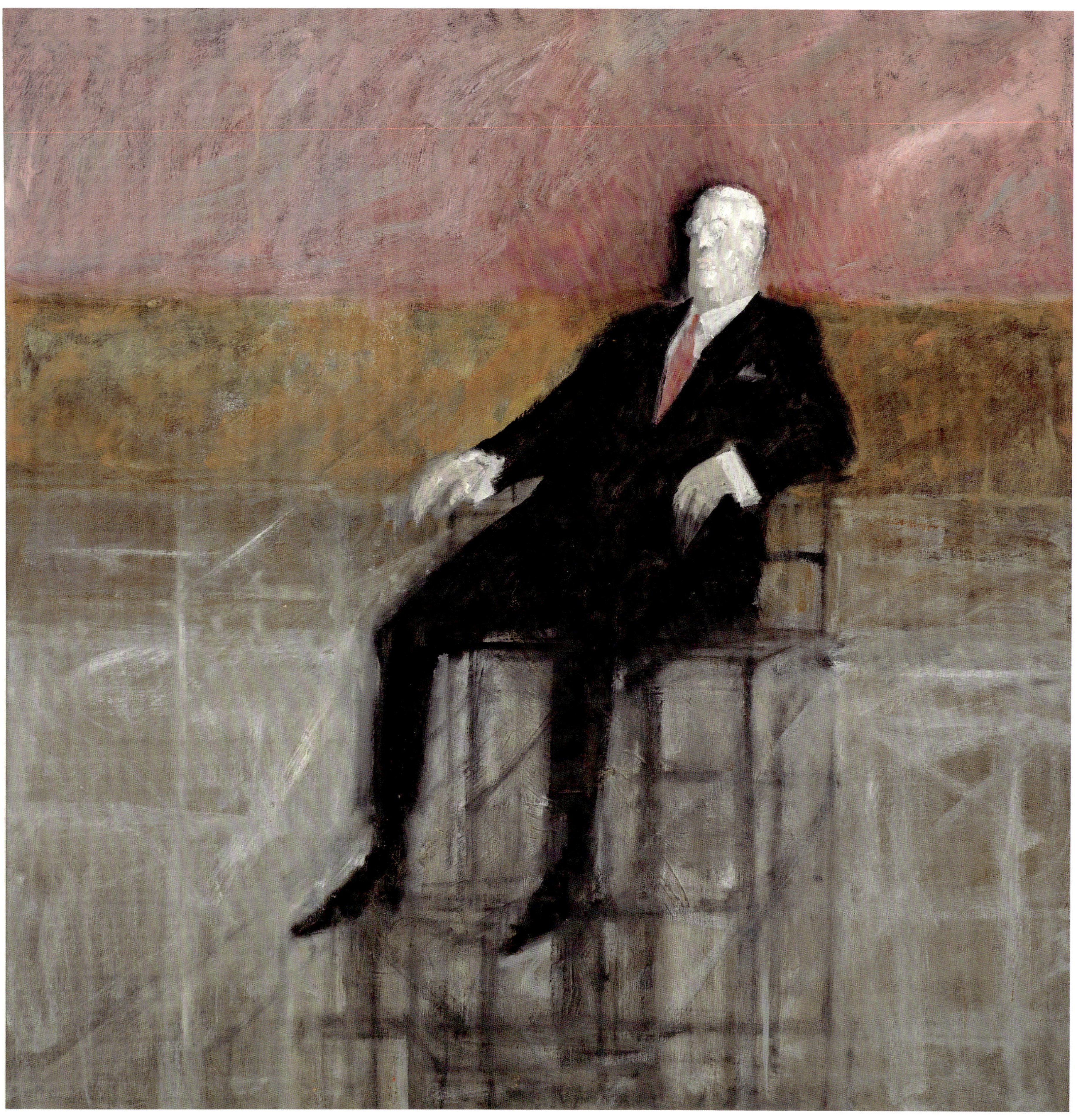

As a second-generation American from a working-class background, Hodermarsky was often placed in situations whose circumstances were determined by men like Wilson, men who were responsible for waging wars in which boys from blue-collar families were sent to fight; these men ran the corporations that employed—and often exploited—those boys if they survived the war and returned home needing jobs. Hodermarsky's decision to depict the former CEO of a car manufacturer speaks to the particularly weighty resonance that the automotive industry held for Hodermarsky, and not only because he was employed by GM during Wilson's tenure there. Several of his family members also worked in car manufacturing: four of his siblings including a brother who, like him, worked as a graphic designer, and his father, who worked in maintenance. The family's relationship to the industry was defined by generational upward mobility, which was reflected in the progression from the menial position held by Daniel senior to the skilled trades taken up by his children.

Nonetheless, there existed a massive gap in the levels of the corporate ladder between Hodermarsky and Wilson, and the loneliness that pervades *Engine Charlie* reveals that Hodermarsky regarded Wilson with sympathy rather than resentment. Indeed, the artist once described his paintings of authority figures from the period (the *Historic Women and Men Series*) as being about certain men who have "risen to the top of corporate structures" and who, in their isolation, found "a great melancholy and sadness" there.[6] And while the painting's title indicates the specificity of its subject, Wilson's indistinct, monochrome facial features and bland suit suggest a generalized representation of a corporate leader, thus positioning the paintings in the series as a broad commentary on people in power.

The eerie stillness of *Engine Charlie* also marks both *The Suit (Robert McNamara)*, a painting of the former secretary of defense during the Kennedy and Johnson administrations (fig. 4), who, like Wilson, transitioned from the automotive industry to politics, and *Palace of Men* (p. 14), an image of two nondescript corporate leaders seated in a cavernous interior. The paintings demonstrate the influence of Francis Bacon, whose work Hodermarsky encountered on a visit to the Cleveland Museum in the early 1960s.[7] While the postwar art world was saturated with works in abstraction, in *Painting*, for example, Bacon centered the figure in his works, depicting mutilated bodies in comfortless spaces electrified by an uncanny energy (fig. 5). Bacon offered Hodermarsky a visual vocabulary for representing the human form after the horrors of the Holocaust, the atomic bomb, and the atrocities that he witnessed on the front lines.

When Theodore Adorno wrote in 1949 that "to write poetry after Auschwitz is barbaric," he articulated what Bacon had already internalized: that the aesthetic strategies of prewar Modernism were no longer sufficient, particularly for treatments of the figure.[8] Hodermarsky's grasp of the relationship between Bacon's work and the war is attested to by his handwritten notes on the artist, which state: "The record of this century is a perfect analogy to the compounded disasters of all western history—its violence, fear, its living death, an acute anxiety syndrome. One feels the cold sweat of terror—or of a heroin detoxification."[9] In the same text, Hodermarsky described Bacon's "grotesque" figures as "flayed, pink-like mutton, freshly skinned."[10] While *Engine Charlie* invokes a Baconesque palette, it is *Palace of Men* whose figures most demonstrate Bacon's influence. They are rendered in staccato strokes of bright white paint, implying a lightness to their apparition-like forms that belies the weightiness of their solid frames.

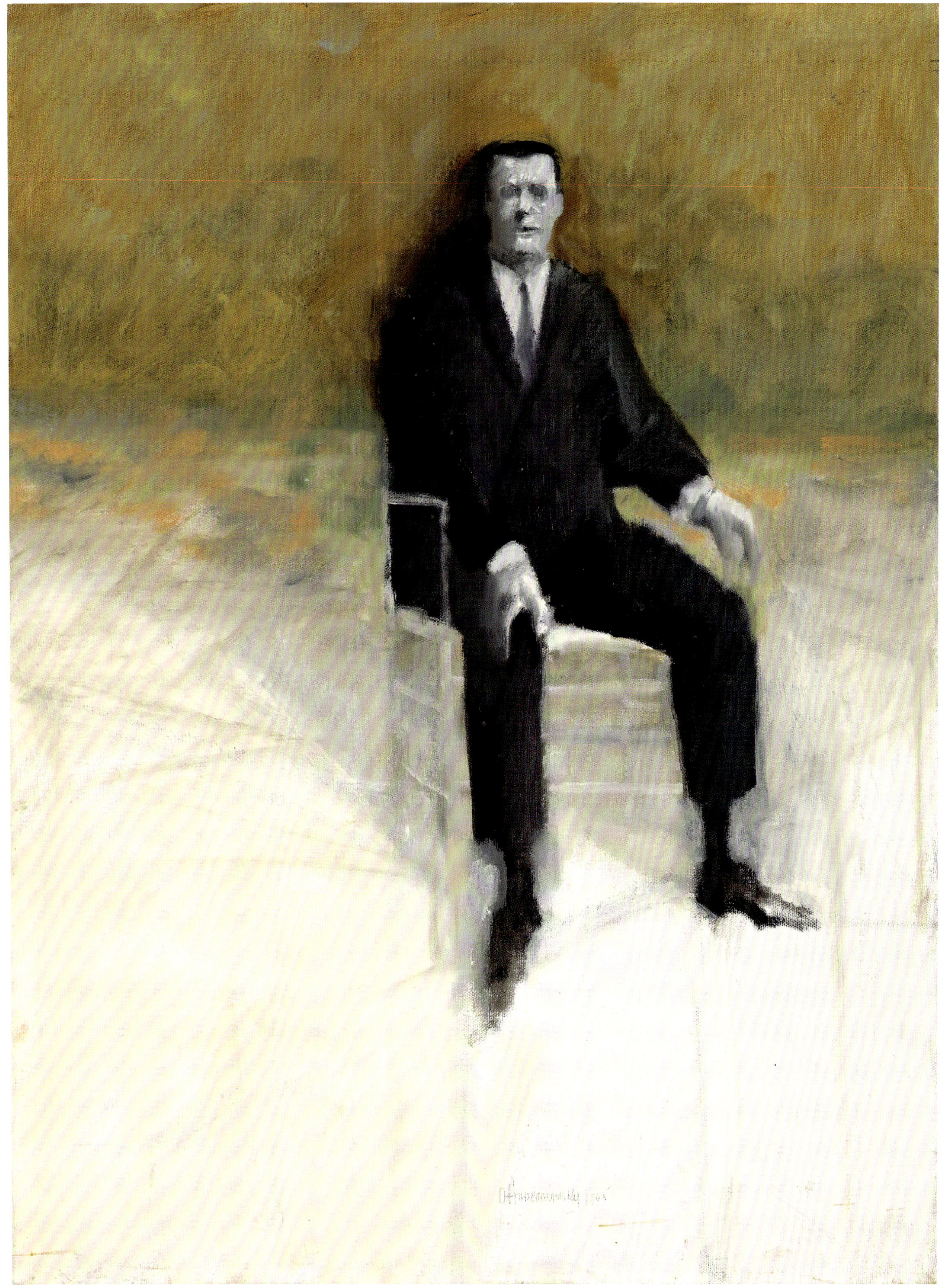

The massive upper arms, torso, and thighs of the figure in the foreground are out of proportion with other parts of his elongated body; the engorged mass of his neck connects directly to the back of his head. Whereas Bacon's men are disembodied and wispy, the deformed figures in *Palace of Men* appear as though they've been fossilized, on the verge of disintegrating at any moment. Applying such a stylistic approach to the depiction of corporate administrators suggests a universality to the effects of violence and war—elements of the human condition that impact those in power as well as the disenfranchised.

In the mid-1960s, as media coverage of the Vietnam War began to ramp up, Hodermarsky embarked on a series of war paintings drawn from his own combat experience. Working in the tradition of Francisco Goya, Käthe Kollwitz, and Otto Dix, whose images of war count among the most powerful and haunting artworks in the Western canon, Hodermarsky confronted his suppressed trauma in

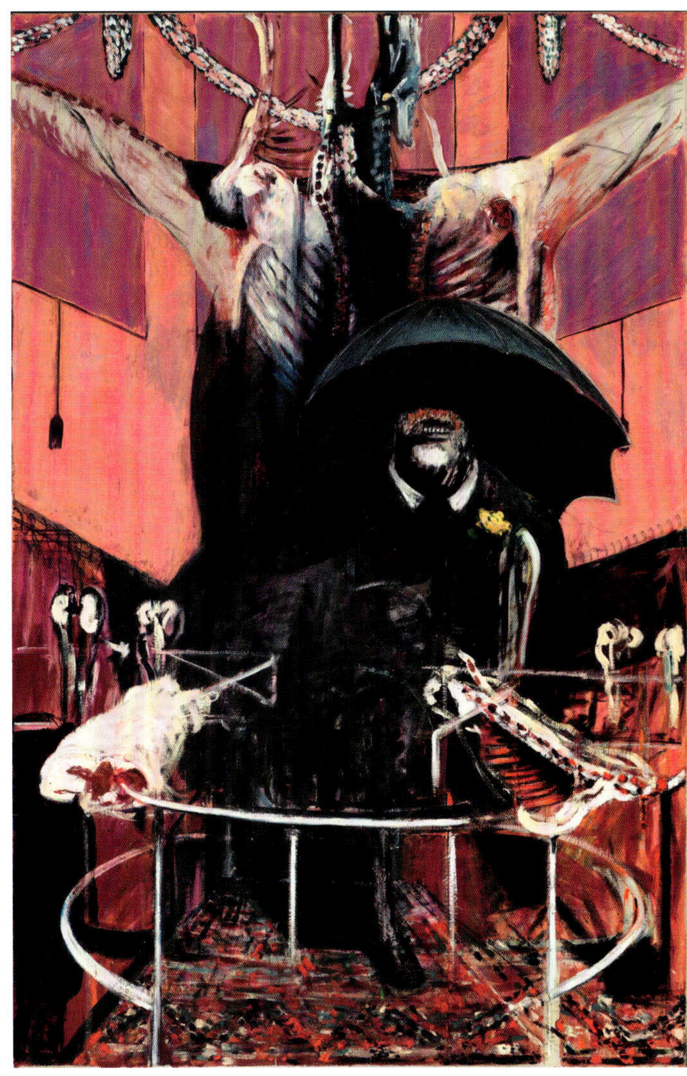

response to the inescapable influx of images of Vietnam that were part and parcel of American visual culture for almost the next decade. He created works that were informed by, but not literal representations of, things he witnessed on the front. A group of paintings depicting dismembered bodies conjures the disfigured soldiers in Dix's portfolio of etchings entitled *The War* (fig. 6). Its seated figure motif reappears in *Gestapo*, a black, white, and gray image of an abstractly rendered figure sitting on a table in a stark, cold setting (fig. 7). The painting's palette and the inclusion of a table at its center place it in dialogue with Gerhard Richter's early painting, *Table* (fig. 8). In Richter's work, a naturalistically rendered table, which the artist painted from an ad in the Italian design magazine *Domus*, is obscured by a second layer of paint applied in frenetic circular motions.[11] The comparison between *Gestapo* and *Table* highlights the differences in approach to figuration between postwar American and German artists. Richter's table eschews the subject of war and any direct reference to German culture or history altogether, instead engaging international trends at three registers: that of Modernist design (at the level of content), mass media and consumerism (at the level of source imagery), and abstraction (at the level of style). Indeed, *Table* is emphatic in its allegiance to abstraction, as its painterly blur literally conceals the figuratively rendered table.

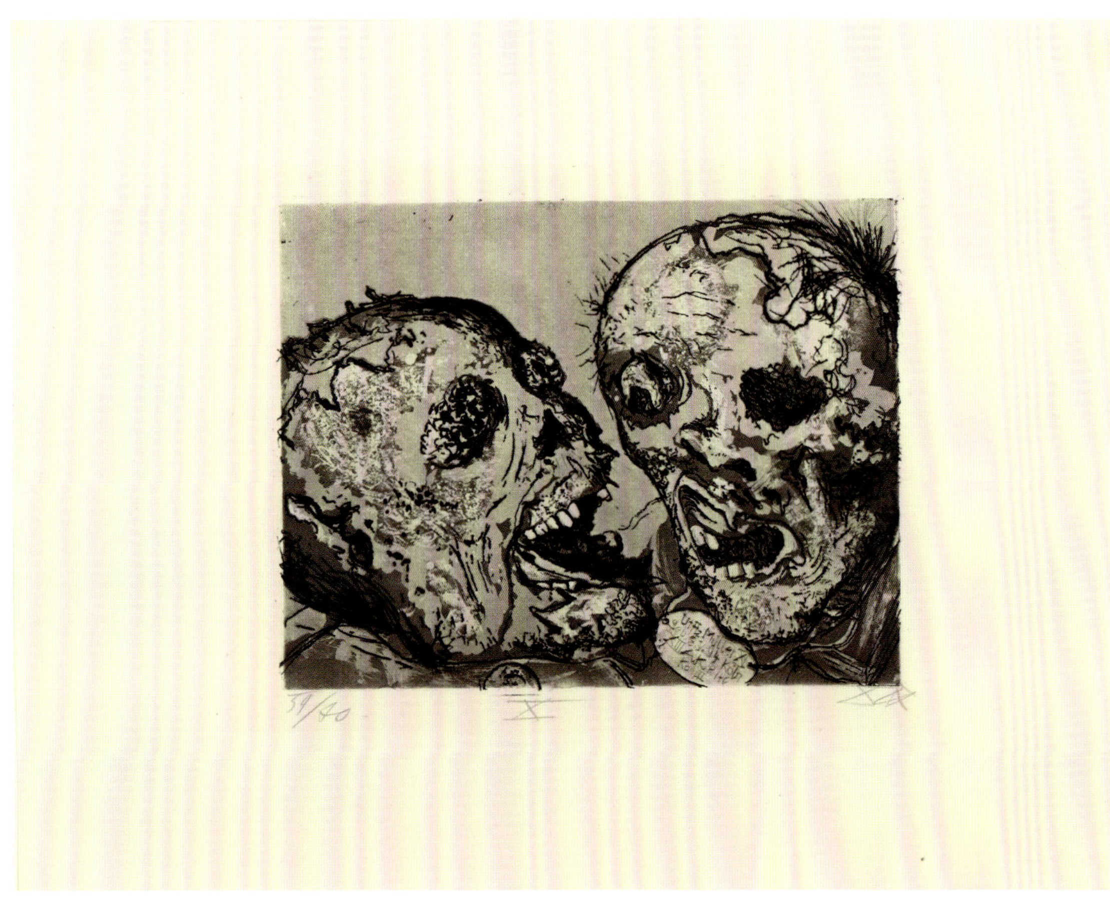

Gestapo (War Series), 1965
Oil on Masonite
24 x 30 in. (61 x 76.2 cm)
Estate of the artist

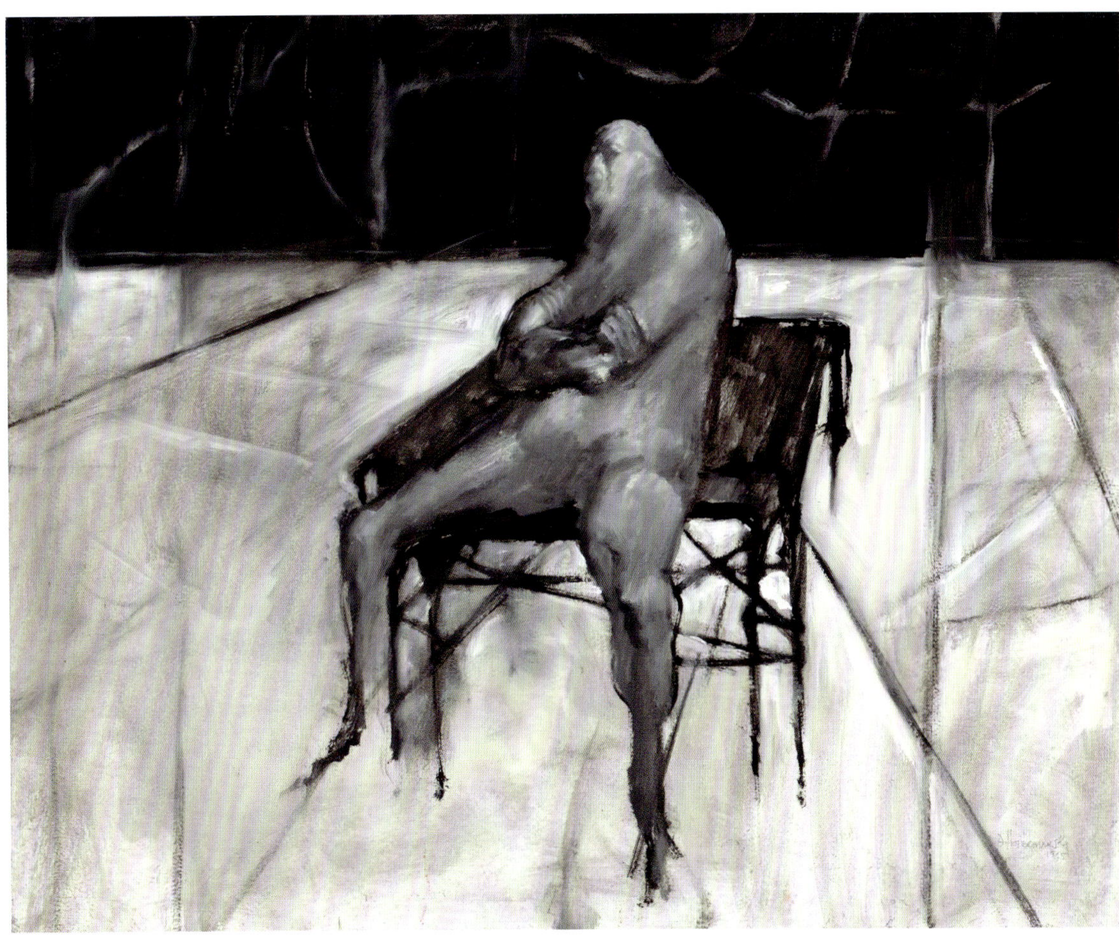

Gerhard Richter (German, 1932–),
Table (Tisch), 1962
Oil on canvas
35½ x 44½ in. (90 x 113 cm)
Private collection
© Gerhard Richter 2023
(02052023)
Photograph: Jennifer Bornstein

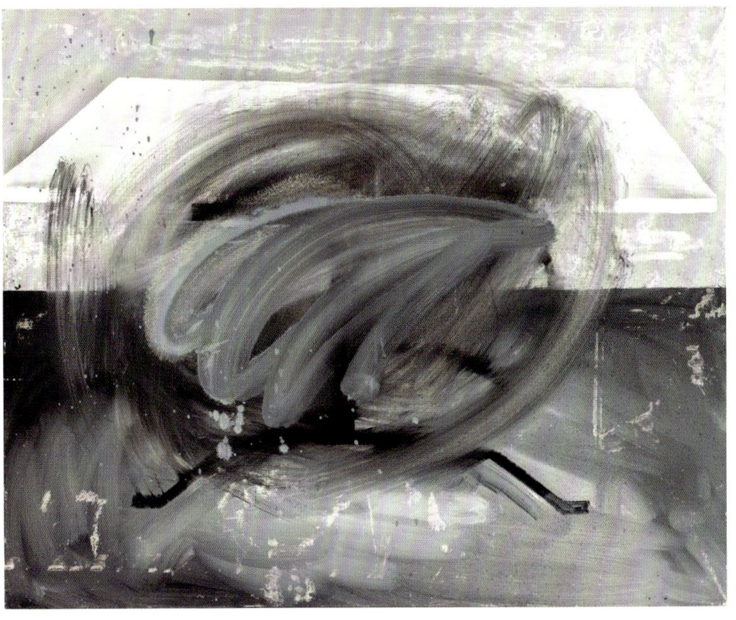

By contrast, Hodermarsky's *Gestapo* confronts the war directly in its representation of a member of the Nazi party's political police. While Germans had yet to fully reckon with their country's recent history, the dominating presence of the Vietnam War in the United States prompted Americans to face their own relationship to World War II twenty years after it ended. And though *Gestapo* engages abstraction in its painterly technique and pared-down, two-tone background, unlike *Table* there is no mistaking the subject for anything but a human figure leaning on a table. It thus falls squarely within the category of figuration rather than abstraction, invoking once again the broken bodies of Bacon's oeuvre. As with Hodermarsky's images of corporate and political leaders, *Gestapo* is characterized by a sense of isolation and melancholy—a remarkable fact when one considers that these attributes require a degree of empathy on the part of the artist.

In 1970, Hodermarsky created what he would later call one of the most important paintings of his career. It is a monumental black-and-white portrait of Adolf Hitler who, depicted with a stout body in a casual pose, resembles an average person rather than one of the most consequential leaders in Western history (fig. 9). Hodermarsky stated that in the portrait, Hitler is represented in the jail cell from which he wrote *Mein Kampf* in the early 1920s, as is suggested by a barred window at the top-left corner of the canvas.[12] This is an image of Hitler prior to his rise to power, at a moment when the events that would transpire a decade later seemed unfathomable. Hodermarsky's representation of Hitler as a common man brings to mind Hannah Arendt's term "the banality of evil."[13] In *Eichmann in Jerusalem*, Arendt uses the term to describe Nazi bureaucrats who were "simply following orders"—Hitler's orders—when committing atrocities. In its evocation of an average-looking person before his rise to power, the portrait illustrates the irony of humankind's astonishing ability to cloak violence and destruction beneath the guise of a seemingly ordinary individual.

The banality of *Hitler* is also subversive. Propagandistic portraits of *Der Führer* made by his followers while he was in power represent him in heroic terms, as seen in Hubert Lanzinger's painting, *Der Bannerträger* (*The Standard Bearer*, 1934–1936), which casts Hitler as a chivalric knight in shining armor. With his idealized facial features and a perfectly straight posture, Lanzinger depicts Hitler as a picture of health, strength, and resolve. Hodermarsky's portrait functions by countering Lanzinger's idolizing view, undercutting the mythic status that characterizes celebratory representations of the leader. Further emphasizing the subject's mortality, Hodermarsky described throwing water at the wet paint he applied to articulate Hitler's face, thereby "making him suffer" in "an adolescent, almost childish . . . kind of mythic way."[14] The performative act of throwing water at the painting recalls Jackson Pollock's method of flinging paint at his canvases, which Harold Rosenberg famously interpreted as a means for Pollock to release his inner feelings, whereby the canvas functioned as a repository for his angst.[15] Like Pollock's action painting, Hodermarsky's technique may be interpreted in psychological terms: throwing water at the face of the ultimate perpetrator constituted an attempt at catharsis.

In the late 1960s, Hodermarsky created a body of work whose lightheartedness stands in stark contrast to his paintings of historic figures and the war. In an artist's statement on *Industrials*, one in a series of exhibitions of Hodermarsky's work that were organized between 1967 and 1968, the artist wrote: "This exhibition reveals the art hidden in the machines that surround us. In complex engines,

FIG. 9.
The Leader (Hitler, War Series),
1970
Oil on canvas
70 x 46 in. (177.8 x 116.8 cm)
Estate of the artist

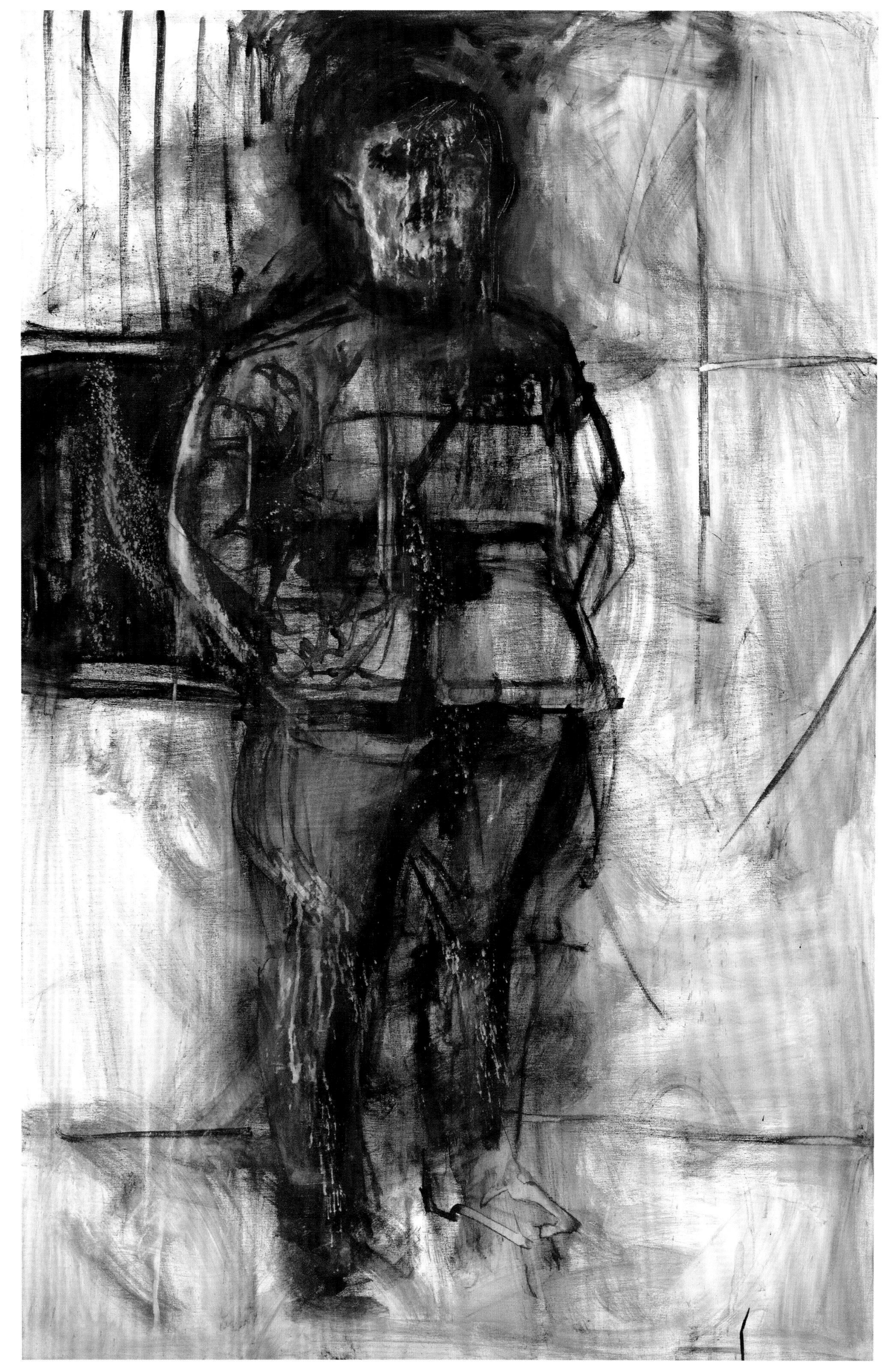

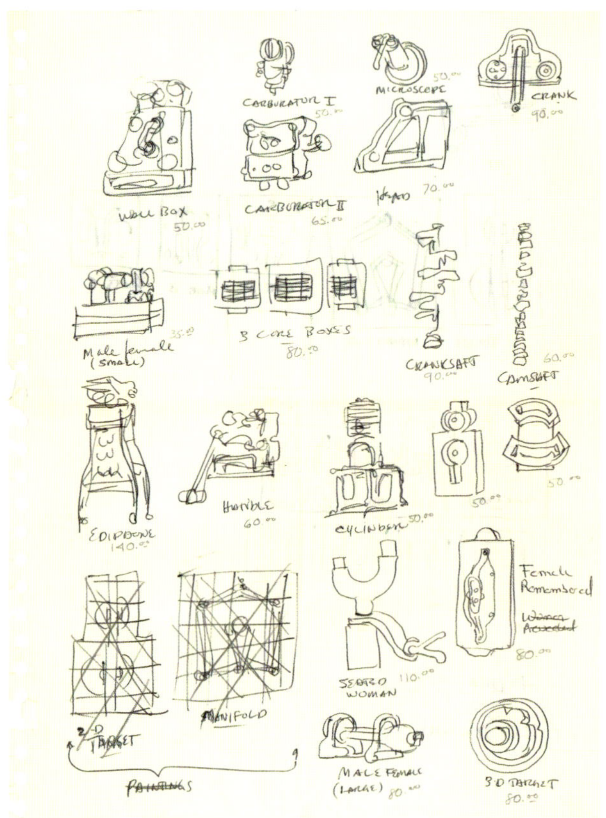

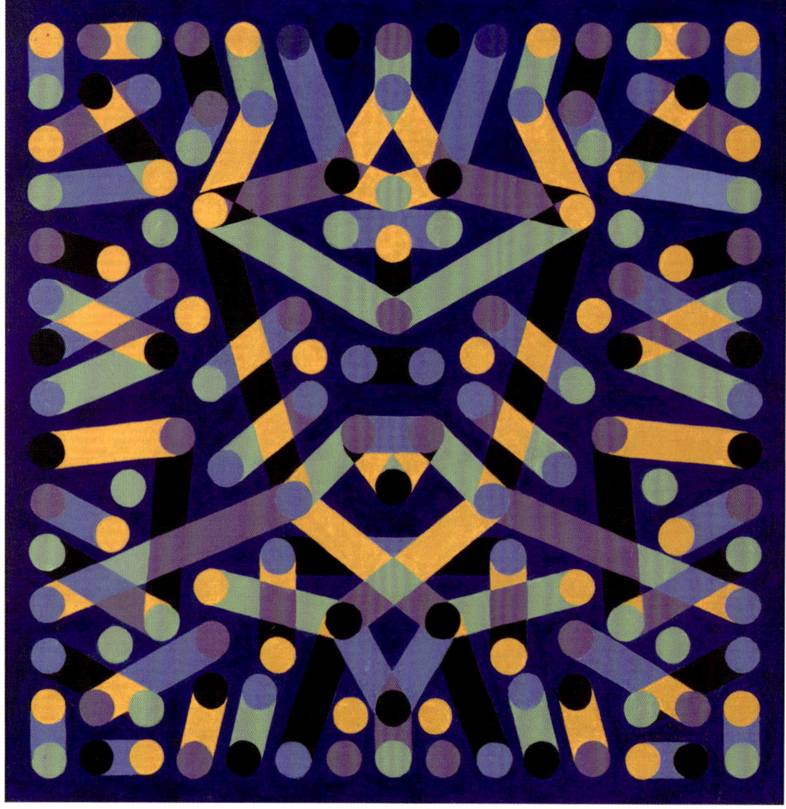

pumps, and generators, exciting forms wait to be disclosed. To discover, to alter, to assemble these components into a new reality is the artist's challenge."[16] The sculptures, paintings, and prints that comprise the *Industrials Series* were inspired by the compositions of industrial parts—everyday objects whose aesthetic merit Hodermarsky revealed through modifications, in the spirit of Marcel Duchamp's readymades. In a profile for a 1967 issue of the *Cleveland Press*, Hodermarsky described sourcing car parts from scrap yards that "were made to be functional—that were engineered for a purpose, not things that were styled for looks (fig. 10)."[17] He manipulated the carburetors, crankshafts, and camshafts by combining forms and, on occasion, painting their surfaces. He also produced prints by dissecting the car parts and rolling ink onto their surfaces, creating a set of brilliantly colored abstract paintings, such as *Blue Ballgame* (fig. 11) and *Illumination* (plate 7), that were inspired by the retina-stimulating works of the Op Art movement and whose real-world referents are circuit boards.[18]

The sculptures in the *Industrials Series* relate to a broader trend in American postwar sculpture toward constructed found objects, which marked a departure from conventional methods of casting, carving, and modeling using traditional materials. In her book *Passages in Modern Sculpture*, Rosalind Krauss identifies a tension between figuration and abstraction, and between artisanship and industrial processes in the work of David Smith, one of the first practitioners of constructed sculpture in the United States.[19] There is a similar ambivalence at play in the sculptures in Hodermarsky's *Industrials*

FIG. 10.
Sketches of industrial
sculptures, 1967
Pen and ink
11 x 8½ in. (27.9 x 21.6 cm)
Estate of the artist

FIG. 11.
*Blue Ballgame
(Industrials Series)*, 1967
Dayglo acrylic on Masonite
24 x 24 in. (61 x 61 cm)
Estate of the artist

Series that extends to the works' reception, as is attested to by the conflicting interpretations offered by critics. One critic described the series as "fun," writing that "Hodermarsky began this whole idea . . . easily, casually, being *amused* by shapes in abandoned machinery, in the loot of junkyards."[20] Another, by contrast, understood the artist's process to be a means of "overcoming a revulsion of the Machine Age by placing parts in a new perspective."[21] The opposing readings speak to the complex relationship that the work has to the subject of industry, one which also characterizes the artist's own nuanced view. In the *Cleveland Press* profile on Hodermarsky, the artist spoke of having "warm memories" of working at GM during the previous decade.[22] While the positive associations he had with his employment at the automobile manufacturer and the familiarity with car parts that it offered him might explain the ease, casualness, and amusement that one critic ascribed to his sculptures, a passage from the graduation address that Hodermarsky presented at Deerfield Academy in the late 1980s suggests a more urgent and somber relationship to industry, technology, and science. He stated:

> Forty-five years ago, in June of 1942, six months after the United States had declared war on Germany and Japan, I sat with *my* high school graduating class on the stage of the Music Hall, a civic auditorium in Cleveland, Ohio. . . . Ironically that night Harry Merger gave a long valedictory speech on how science was going to help mankind and all we, the children of blue-collar workers, could think about that night was that we were going to war. We were going to use, and possibly be killed by, some of the most incredible weaponry ever created by science.[23]

For Hodermarsky, the stuff of industry acted as a slate on which to experiment with cutting-edge methods, but the association between his work and the war persisted.

Hodermarsky's adoption of avant-garde approaches extended to a series of performances on which he collaborated with the influential musician Donald Erb and choreographer Lawrence Berger, both of Cleveland. The performances were staged at Cain Park in Cleveland and at the 92nd Street Y and Hunter College in New York between the late 1960s and early 1970s. They signal Hodermarsky's engagement with the experimental, multimedia productions of the Fluxus movement, an international group of artists, poets, and musicians whose shared goal was to use found objects, sounds, and events to integrate art into everyday life in order to bring social and economic change to the art world. Hodermarsky designed the sets, costumes, and lighting for the performances, Erb composed the music using electronic recordings and live instruments, and Berger provided choreography performed by dance students at Cuyahoga Community College, where he held an artist residency.

In *Pipe Dream* (fig. 12), the dancers wear white shirts and tights with colored helmets that mirror the painted mannequin busts that Hodermarsky placed on the stage along with his Op Art paintings such as *Dizzy* (plate 11). In her review of *Fission*, a related performance staged in Cain Park, Wilma Salisbury wrote that the dancers' movements became increasingly "animated and angular until the frantic climax of the piece. . . [when] light projections of lines and patterns are flashed on their mobile bodies. The effect of slowly rotating bodies moving through stationary light pattern [*sic*] is eerie, like watching a man walk through an X-ray of himself. The lines of light, which periodically change color,

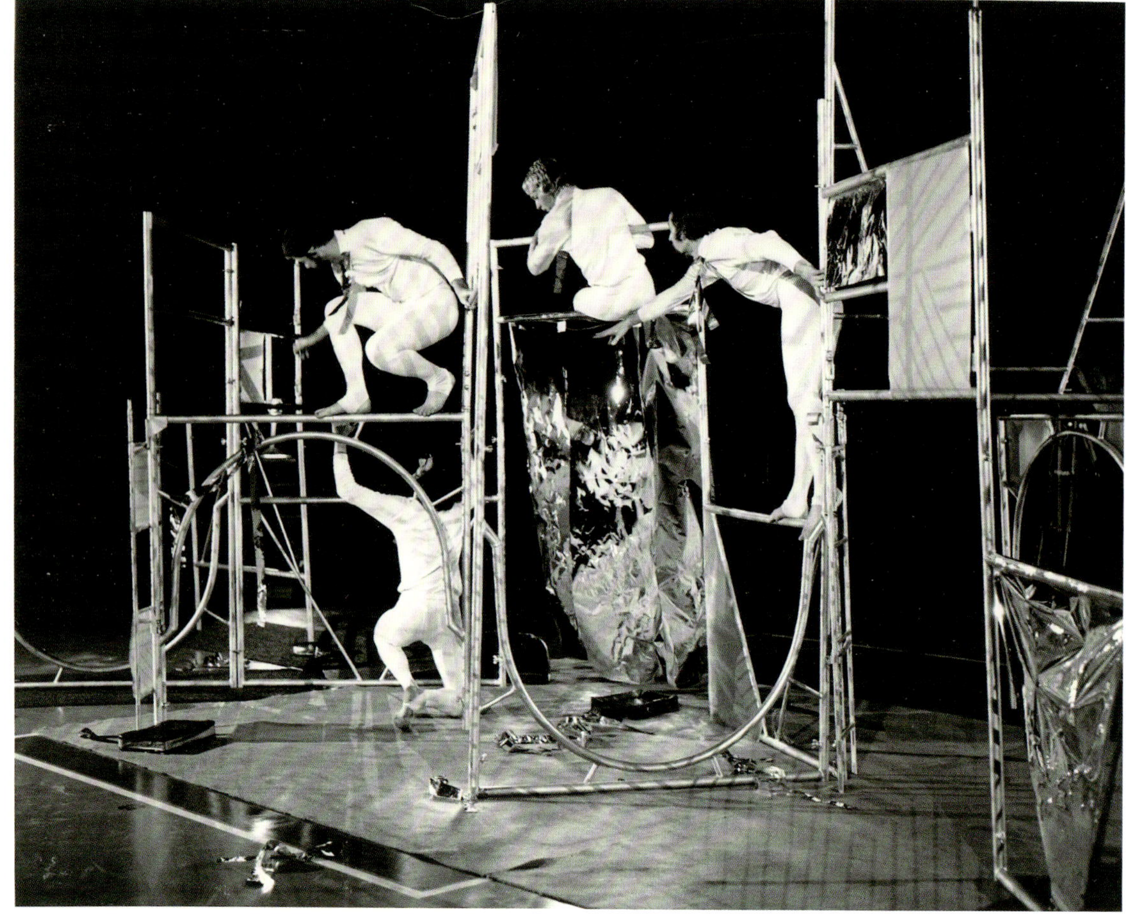

transform the dancers into boneless, oozing creatures."[24] To create the psychedelic effect of swirling
vivid colors, Hodermarsky churned acrylic paints between two glass dishes and projected them onto
the dancers' bodies as well as the screens that were part of the stage set. By integrating projections and
strobe lights into the performances, Hodermarsky expanded his interest in phenomenology and the
sensory arousal on view in his Op Art paintings to a durational, multimedia experience. In her explana-
tion of the performance, Dorita Berger, who was the pianist for several performances, aptly described
the "close involvements of people with one another, with their surroundings, and with new technological
developments" as "being interpreted . . . through experimentation with total theater, audience participa-
tion, and fusion of artistic media."[25]

A grant application that Hodermarsky wrote seeking support for the interdisciplinary collaborations attests to his enduring commitment to art education, even with regard to the most esoteric of
contexts. Despite—or perhaps because of—the avant-garde nature of the performances, Hodermarsky
identified "promoting awareness and insight of contemporary trends in the community" as one of the
project's key objectives, and outlined a series of educational programming for children and adults in
an effort to rectify what he identified as an enduring difficulty students encountered in "defining what

contemporary art is, and how to identify themselves with it."[26] The grant application dates to 1968, one year before he moved his family to northwest Massachusetts to establish and run the studio art program at Deerfield, where he would remain chairman of the department for the next eleven years. Hired on the basis of his extensive teaching experience and effective management of the art program at the Cleveland public schools' Supplementary Educational Center, Hodermarsky was tasked with developing an arts curriculum at the height of the anti-war movement—a time of social unrest at the all-boys preparatory school.

The teaching philosophy that Hodermarsky applied during his tenure at Deerfield was informed by aspects of his personal identity. At the first faculty cookout he attended, he arrived wearing a necklace made of kielbasa—a playful declaration of the pride he had for his status as the son of working-class immigrants.[27] His embrace of his own otherness within the upper-class, Anglo-American context of the New England prep school was reflected in the inclusive environment that he fostered as a teacher. In a catalogue essay on Hodermarsky's work, his former student Arthur Hardigg wrote that "everyone mattered equally to Mr. Hodermarsky," which related to "an attitude gained through experience as a teacher and artist."[28] Stephen Hannock similarly recollected Hodermarsky's classrooms at the high-pressure school as being "such non-judgmental havens that everybody flocked to them."[29] The dynamic, lively environment of the open-studio plan promoted community and interdependence—elements that Hodermarsky learned to value during his experience as a soldier at war, where "mutual trust, mutual respect, mutual regard for each other's lives and well-being" were key to survival.[30] The contrast between Hodermarsky's teaching style and that of other instructors at Deerfield is attested to by Duncan Christy, another alumnus of the school, who remarked that Hodermarsky "wasn't just a breath of fresh air. He was a gale of fresh air. He really was this new wind, this new current, the avant-garde" (fig. 13).[31]

Shortly after joining the Deerfield faculty, Hodermarsky and his wife Nancy traveled to Hačava, the small Slovakian village in the foothills of the Carpathian Mountains where his parents were born. Before the trip, he made a series of small oils on wood, the *Peasants Series*, that anticipated his visit to the village, then part of the Soviet Union. With titles such as *Aunt Mary*, *"The Dirty," The Landowner*, and *The Mayor* (plates 34, 35, 37) the whimsical paintings evoke the characters in a nineteenth-century Russian novel. In *Mama* (plate 36), a stout woman wearing a babushka recalls Nancy's observation, as told to her daughters, that the people of Hačava still dressed in the traditional clothes worn by Hodermarsky's parents before they emigrated to the United States.[32] Pencil-drawn lines articulate the contours of the figure, whose face, hands, and top are described using a brushy, semitransparent application of paint, while her babushka and skirt are left bare. Hodermarsky dragged a pencil across the upper quadrant of the white background, creating a jagged horizon line suggestive of a snowy landscape. The surface of *Mama* and other paintings in the *Peasants Series* are textured and their subjects are placed off-center, investing them with a feeling of a casual encounter. With its overall sketchy quality and translucent figural depiction, *Mama* possesses a dreamlike quality, as if the *Peasants* paintings represented what Hodermarsky's ancestors looked like in his imagination.

Because teaching at Deerfield Academy provided housing for faculty members and their families during the school year, the artist and his wife were able to purchase a property on Deer Isle, Maine, following a number of years of vacationing there. They bought an old farmhouse just outside the coastal town, where Hodermarksy set up a studio and spent every summer on the island until he moved there

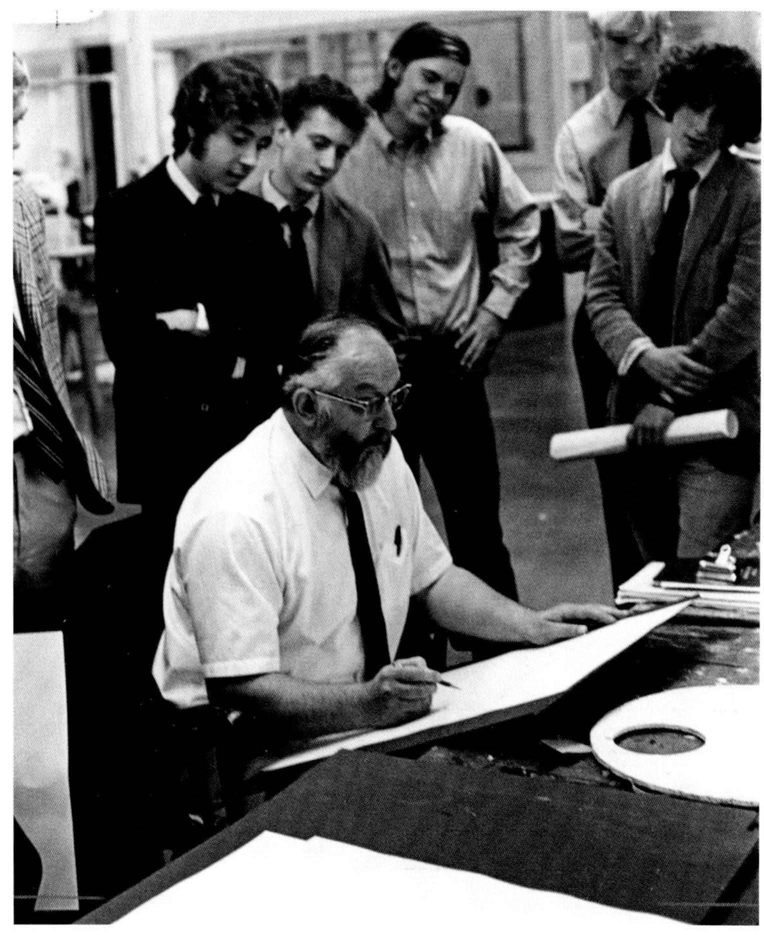

FIG. 13.
Daniel Hodermarsky and his
students at Deerfield Academy

permanently upon his retirement from teaching. The *Penobscot Nation Legend Series* of 1974 continues the experiments with the painting techniques he used in the *Peasants Series* and relates to the oral traditions passed down by generations of the Penobscot tribe who have lived in Maine since before European colonization.

To create the *Penobscot Nation Legend* works, Hodermarsky applied paint to wooden planks sourced from a woodworker who lived down the street from him on Deer Isle. He left the bulk of the wooden supports' surfaces raw, harnessing their naturally occurring elements in his compositions. In *Blue Jay Rising from Fire* (plate 39), an ovoid knot in the wood acts as a springboard for an image of the bird. The structure of its spectacularly colored tail feathers is informed by the wood grain's curved striations. The people and animals that populate the series allude to ancient Penobscot legends, while the appreciation and respect for nature that characterizes Hodermarsky's technique is aligned with traditional Penobscot values.[33]

The coastal landscape of Maine served as an inspiration for Hodermarsky over the next two decades. There, he found "perfect liberty" where he was "free of imitation and easy familiarity."[34] Just as Winslow Homer and Marsden Hartley had experienced the natural surroundings of this northern-most region of New England, the area served as a *tabula rasa* on which Hodermarsky could explore different mediums and techniques.[35] Among his earliest Maine landscapes are a series of watercolors that demonstrate Hodermarsky's mastery of the medium. In *Beauty at the Shore* (plate 73), a group of rock formations are painted different colors; some are natural grays and browns, one is emerald green, another is depicted in a gradient that transitions from blue to orange, and the largest, at center, contains charcoal blacks, soft purples, and vibrant reds. Additional rocks seen in the distance are painted a soft gray that fades into the atmospheric background. In *Early Morning at the Shore* (plate 84), the rock at center is comprised of muted blues, grays, and ochers set against a moody gray sky. The rock's horizontal bands of earthy tones and firmly planted base evince its ability to withstand the effects of weathering over the course of millions of years. Read as a metaphor for life, the ancient rock seems to possess the dual human elements of strength and endurance as it weathers both wind and waves.

In depicting the Maine coast in varying weather conditions, Hodermarsky followed in the footsteps of Winslow Homer, whose fascination with the shore in front of his home in Prouts Neck is recorded in the numerous paintings he made during the last three decades of his life.[36] His *Early Morning After a Storm at Sea* (fig. 14) captures the restless Atlantic at dawn in the aftermath of a storm, the water and sky glinting with sunlight that emerges from the clouds. In his *Gold at the Shore Series*, Hodermarsky applied gold leaf to the foreground landscape of the compositions to augment the effect of light hitting the area where the land meets the sea. Like Homer, Hodermarsky depicted the coastline at different times of day and in various seasons, as is demonstrated by *Gold at the Shore #2* (plate 63), whose clear blue sky evokes a midday atmosphere, and *Gold at the Shore #5* (plate 65), whose brilliantly illuminated clouds suffuse a sunset scene.

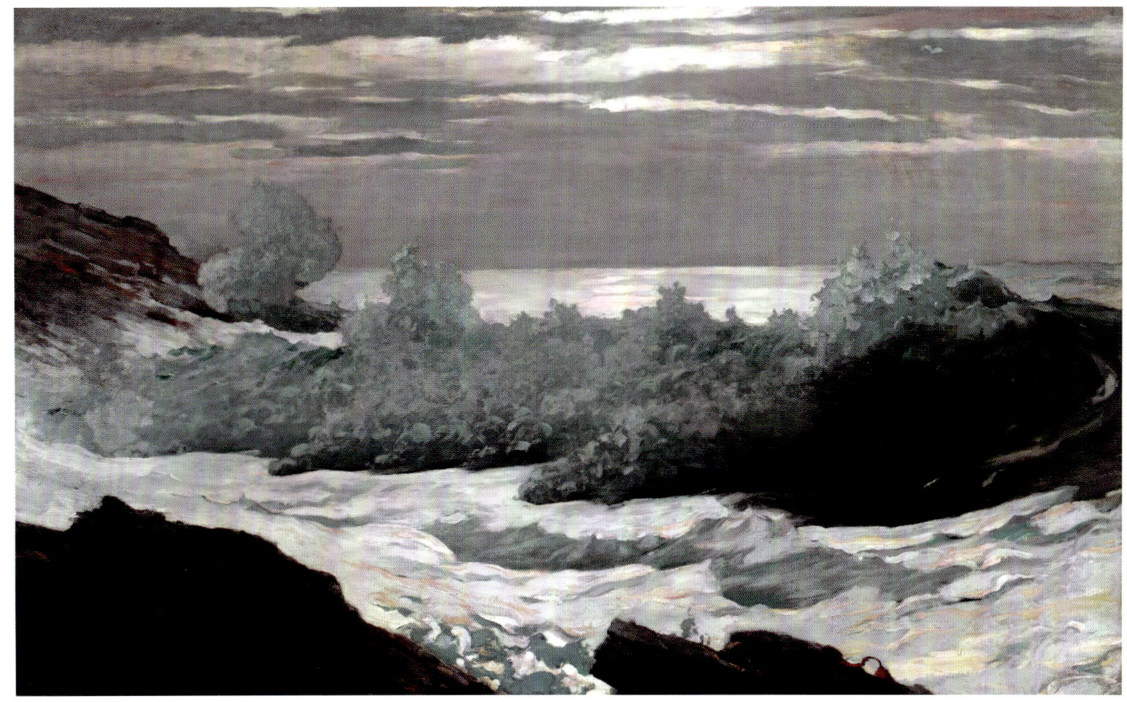

FIG. 14.

Winslow Homer (American, 1836–1910), *Early Morning After a Storm at Sea*, 1900–1903
Oil on canvas
30¼ x 50 in. (76.8 x 127 cm)
The Cleveland Museum of Art, Cleveland, OH
Gift of J. H. Wade, 1924.195

The paintings of the *Chautauqua Series* of the early 1990s take their inspiration not from the New England seascape, but from the expansive fields and bodies of water that Hodermarsky encountered on a road trip taken from Cleveland to Chautauqua, a town on Lake Erie in western New York (plates 45–47). In this series, an incandescent palette of bold, saturated colors is coupled with exaggerated perspectival lines to create dynamic landscapes suggestive of scenes observed from a moving car, "viewed at high speed."[37] While the paintings variously contain vegetation, mountains, and other elements that are abstractly rendered but clear in their referents, the land and water that comprise their foregrounds are made up of strokes of unmodulated color reminiscent of the abstracted grids of Wayne Thiebaud's farmlands seen as from a bird's-eye view (fig. 15). Like Thiebaud's work, the *Chautauqua Series* offers seductive views of the postwar American landscape that buzz with a lively energy.

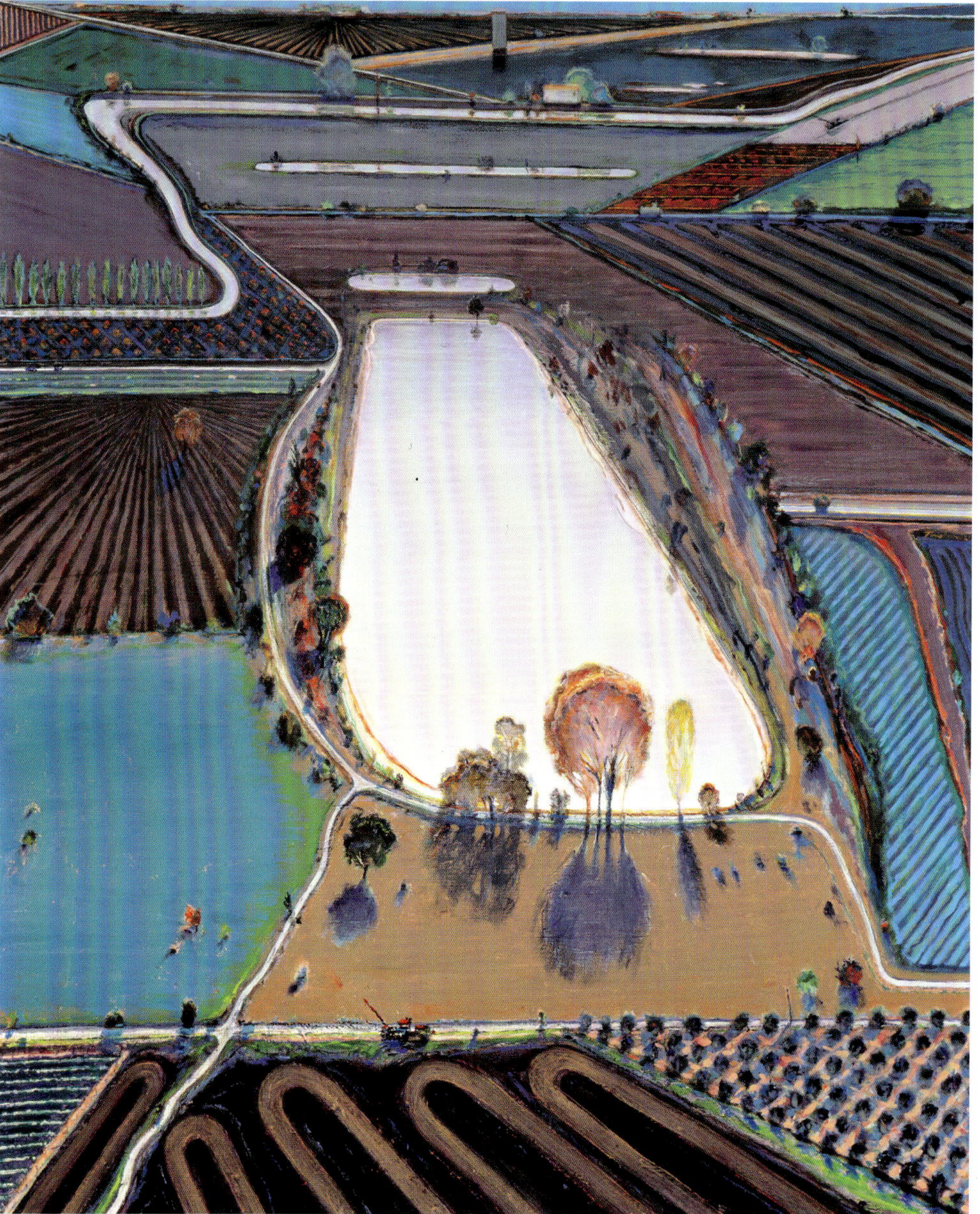

FIG. 15.
Wayne Thiebaud (American, 1920–), *Ponds and Streams*, 2001
Acrylic on canvas
72 x 60 in. (182.9 x 152.4 cm)
Fine Arts Museums of San Francisco, San Francisco, CA
Museum purchase, gift of Richard N. Goldman, 2001.168
© 2023 Wayne Thiebaud Foundation / Licensed by VAGA at Artists Rights Society (ARS), New York, NY
Photograph by Joseph McDonald, courtesy of the Fine Arts Museums of San Francisco

opposite: FIG. 16.
Adolph Gottlieb (American, 1903–1974), *Blast, I*, 1957
Oil on canvas
90 x 45⅛ in. (228.7 x 114.4 cm)
The Museum of Modern Art, New York, NY
Philip Johnson Fund, 6.1958
© 2023 Adolph and Esther Gottlieb Foundation/Licensed by VAGA at Artists Rights Society (ARS), New York, NY
Digital Image © The Museum of Modern Art / Licensed by SCALA / Art Resource, NY

At the center of the *Chautauqua* painting *To the Edge of the Sea* (plate 45) is a mass of overlapping strokes of color, a compositional device reminiscent of a number of Hodermarsky's early career paintings. *Earth, Sea, and Sky*, a series of abstractions that contain horizon lines intimating the separation of elements suggested by their titles, are the earliest works to contain a concentration of layered paint at their centers (plates 22–26). This composition recurs in the *Paradise Trees Series* paintings (plates 48, 49) and later in two related series entitled *Ambergris* (plates 50–55) and *De Profundis* (plates 56, 57). According to an artist's statement, Hodermarsky drew his inspiration for the latter two series from the "forms and colors that the sea provides." The large forms that rise "from the deep, jeweled and animated with color" evoke ambergris, as indicated by the series' title.[38] A substance found in the digestive system of sperm whales that is used in perfumes and spices, ambergris acquires its value only after it is harvested from the sea and subjected to an alchemical transformation—a process that is suggested by the colorful, tantalizing masses that emerge from the water. In an artist's statement, Hodermarsky also references the Bikini and Eniwetok atolls in the South Pacific, where the United States government performed dozens of nuclear tests during the Cold War. This allusion brings the paintings—their centers "boiling with atoms in fission"—into dialogue with Adolph Gottleib's mature works, such as *Blast, I* (fig. 16), which feature a circle floating above a gestural mass and have often been interpreted as referencing the atomic bomb. As with Hodermarsky's *War* paintings, the works in the *Ambergris* and *De Profundis* series evoke the spectacle of warfare; unlike them, however, the later paintings seem to offer hope, insinuating that, just as alluring substances may be contrived from the fecal matter of ambergris, societies may be rebuilt from rubble.[39]

While Hodermarsky experimented with abstraction in his final years, he never abandoned the figure. He engaged the motif of seated men and women that made an early appearance in his work through the end of his career. While the figures that populate these works variously represent specific people as well as generalized types, the psychological dimension that they share begs the question of whether they can convincingly be read as a collective self-portrait of sorts. Two professed self-portraits provide hints. In *Self-Portrait in Helmet* (plate 66), Hodermarsky presents himself as

a muscular nude figure donning a bronze helmet. It stands
in stark contrast to another self-portrait of the same year in
which his naked body appears fleshy and vulnerable (plate
70). These drawings present two versions of the artist: one
as an immortal, idealized Greek god; the other as an earth-
bound, flawed human being.

The dichotomous representations on view in
Hodermarsky's self-portraits converge in *Seated Man in
Laddered Chair* (fig. 17), from the *Seated and Standing
Women and Men Series*, in which a figure appears to sit in
an invisible chair, his feet firmly planted on the ground that
is painted in the same purple tones as his body. In place of
a chair is a ladder whose thin white rungs evaporate just
above the horizon line where the earth meets the sky. At
the top edge of the composition is a row of fragmented,
rectangular gold forms suggestive of a celestial realm.
Combining figuration, landscape, and abstraction, *Seated
Man in Laddered Chair* is a culmination of Hodermarsky's
sustained work in all three genres. Read as a self-portrait
in which its lone, hulking figure stands in for the artist, it
is also a culmination of the themes Hodermarsky wrestled
with throughout his career. The figure appears weighted
but buoyant, solid but precarious, powerful but fragile. He
occupies a liminal space between earth and heaven reserved for those as deeply in touch with their own
mortality as Hodermarsky was. It is a portrait of an artist toward the end of his life, painted toward the
end of a century scarred by war. The elements of gold at top, torn but intact, offer the hope of redemption.

New York, New York
October 14, 2022

FIG. 17.
*Seated Man in Laddered Chair
(Seated and Standing Women
and Men Series)*, 1988
Oil on Masonite
24 x 24 in. (61 x 61 cm)
Estate of the artist

1. I'd like to thank Maria Hodermarska and Elisabeth
Hodermarsky for providing invaluable information on
their father's biography and insightful interpretations
of his work. The content of our conversations helped
shape this essay.

2. Daniel Hodermarsky, "Letter to the Editor," *The
Deerfield Scroll*," March 1, 1975, Deerfield Academy,
Deerfield, MA.

3. Ibid.

4. Daniel Hodermarsky on the Hodermarsky family
history. Unpublished document from the Daniel
Hodermarsky Family Trust.

5. Maria Hodermarska and Elisabeth Hodermarsky
recalled that their father opted to work the nightshift
due to the post-traumatic stress disorder he suffered
as a consequence of his wartime experience. Maria
Hodermarska and Elisabeth Hodermarsky, virtual
meeting with the author, July 15, 2022.

6. Daniel Hodermarsky, in discussion with Rob Potter,
Deerfield, Massachusetts, winter 1988, video record-
ing, "A Year in the Life: Mr. Hodermarsky," directed
by Rob Potter; camerawork and production by Ed
Can, Ravi Dahiya, Paul Lyle, and Rob Potter; the
Hodermarsky family archives.

7. Interview with Michael Tracy conducted by Anna Hammond at the artist's studio in San Ygnacio, Texas, June 2022.

8. Theodor Adorno, "Cultural Criticism and Society," in *Prisms* (London: Neville Spearman, 1967), 34.

9. Daniel Hodermarsky, "Francis Bacon." Unpublished document from the Daniel Hodermarsky Family Trust.

10. Ibid.

11. Gerhard Richter, "Comments on Some Works, 1991," in *Gerhard Richter: Writings, 1961–2007*, ed. Dietmar Elger and Hans Ulrich Obrist (New York: Distributed Art Publishers, 2009), 259.

12. Daniel Hodermarsky, in discussion with Rob Potter, "A Year in the Life: Mr. Hodermarsky."

13. Hannah Arendt, *Eichmann in Jerusalem: A Report on the Banality of Evil*, rev. ed. (New York: Viking, 1965).

14. Daniel Hodermarsky, in discussion with Rob Potter, "A Year in the Life: Mr. Hodermarsky."

15. Harold Rosenberg, "The American Action Painters," in *Reading Abstract Expressionism: Context and Critique*, edited by Ellen G. Landau (New Haven: Yale University Press, 2005), 189–198.

16. Daniel Hodermarsky on "Industrials," an exhibition of his work, 1967; unpublished document from the Daniel Hodermarsky Family Trust.

17. Dick Wootten, "Dan and His Works," *Cleveland (OH) Press*, January 28, 1967.

18. Ibid.

19. Rosalind Krauss, "Tanktotem: Welded Images," in *Passages in Modern Sculpture* (New York: The Viking Press, 1977), 147–200.

20. Katherine White, "The New Hodermarsky Gallery," *Fine Arts: A Weekly Guide*, February 20, 1967.

21. Helen Borsick, "Art and Artists," *Plain Dealer* (Cleveland), February 5, 1967.

22. Wootten, "Dan and His Works."

23. Daniel Hodermarsky, "Looking Backward to the Future." Graduation address, Deerfield Academy, Deerfield, MA, ca. 1988; unpublished transcript from the Daniel Hodermarsky Family Trust.

24. Wilma Salisbury, "Cain Park's Avant-Garde Offering, 'Fission,' Excites," *Plain Dealer* (Cleveland), August 13, 1968.

25. Dorita Berger, "Multi-Media," *Fine Arts: A Weekly Guide* 15, August 12, 1968.

26. Daniel Hodermarsky, "Project in Multi-Media," 1969; unpublished grant application from the Daniel Hodermarsky Family Trust.

27. Maria Hodermarska, "For My Father," *Island Ad-Vantages* (Stonington, ME), May 24, 2007.

28. Arthur Hardigg, "Steps to the Shore" in *Daniel Hodermarsky: Landscapes*, exh. cat. (Deer Isle, ME: Turtle Gallery, 2008), 5.

29. Interview with Stephen Hannock by Anna Hammond, conducted via Zoom, May 2022.

30. Daniel Hodermarsky, "Looking Backward to the Future."

31. Duncan Christy quoted in Alicia Anstead, "Deer Isle Artist Brings Love of Life to Palette," *Bangor (ME) Daily News*, October 10–11, 1998.

32. As told to the author by Maria Hodermarska and Elisabeth Hodermarsky in a virtual meeting, July 15, 2022.

33. For more on Penobscot history, see Pauleena MacDougall, *The Penobscot Dance of Resistance: Tradition in the History of a People* (Durham, NH: University of New Hampshire Press, 2004).

34. Daniel Hodermarsky, artist's statement, June, 1995. Unpublished document from the Daniel Hodermarsky Family Trust.

35. Donna M. Cassidy, et. al., "Introduction: Marsden Hartley's Maine" in Donna M. Cassidy, et. al., *Marsden Hartley's Maine*, exh. cat. (New York: The Metropolitan Museum of Art, 2017), 33–34.

36. For more on Homer's landscapes, see Stephanie L. Herdrich, "Crosscurrents: Conflict, Nature, and Mortality in Winslow Homer's Art" in Stephanie L. Herdrich and Sylvia Yount, *Winslow Homer: Crosscurrents*, exh. cat. (New York: Metropolitan Museum of Art, 2022), 132–154.

37. Hardigg, "Steps to the Shore," 6.

38. Daniel Hodermarsky, "Statement on *De Profundis* Paintings; unpublished document from the Daniel Hodermarsky Family Trust.

39. See also Kate McNamara, "Above and Below," in *Daniel Hodermarsky: Abstraction Paintings*, exh. cat. (Deer Isle, ME: Turtle Gallery, 2009), 5–7.

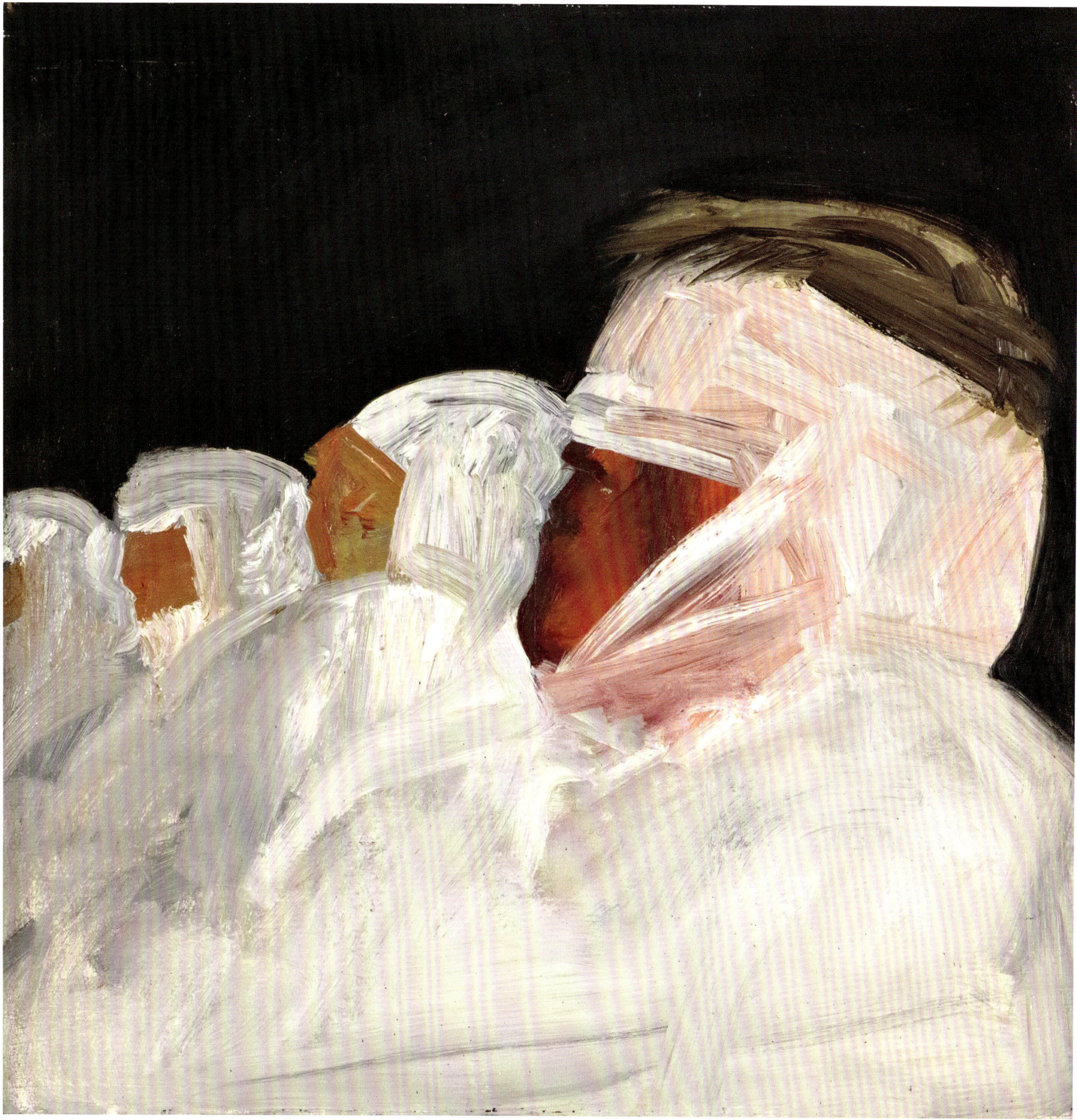

Painting the Unspeakable

KAT LEE, MA, RDT-BCT, LCAT

"PTSD is, in a manner of speaking, a way of institutionalizing moral outrage. Trauma transcends the individual. Trauma is symbolic. Trauma is history made manifest in the flesh. Trauma, when heard by society, is a form of testimony."
David J. Morris, *The Evil Hours: A Biography of Post-Traumatic Stress Disorder*[1]

While dan hodermarsky rarely, if ever, spoke of his combat experiences, he offered his testimony in images.[2] Holding a dialectic between horror and relentless optimism, his paintings convey the phenomenological, unspeakable experience of combat through a heightened aesthetic that transcends words. Hodermarsky's visceral depictions offer a counterpoint to Western psychology's medicalization of trauma.

Beginning in the American Civil War, men who returned broken from battle were said to have "soldier's heart." Despite its romantic ring, the term literally referred to an observed phenomenon: veterans' cardiovascular systems were changed by their combat experience.[3] After World War I, Western psychology offered "combat fatigue" and "shell shock" as descriptors.[4] These presentations of "male hysteria" were considered a result of purely physical—not psychic—trauma.

Hodermarsky entered World War II at age 19. The treatment *du jour* for combat trauma was a quick-fix intervention done on the sidelines of battle, aiming to send minimally functional soldiers back into the field within a week.[5] Hodermarsky left the battlefield twice for these "quick fixes" for physical ailments that he understood to have potential psychological origins.[6] Such band-aid approaches discouraged soldiers' truth-telling about their experiences. Instead, the United States military institutionalized a notion of combat trauma as a deficit of moral character: cowardice meriting dishonorable

War Casualties in Ambulance, 1970
Oil on Masonite
24 x 24 in. (61 x 61 cm)
Estate of the artist

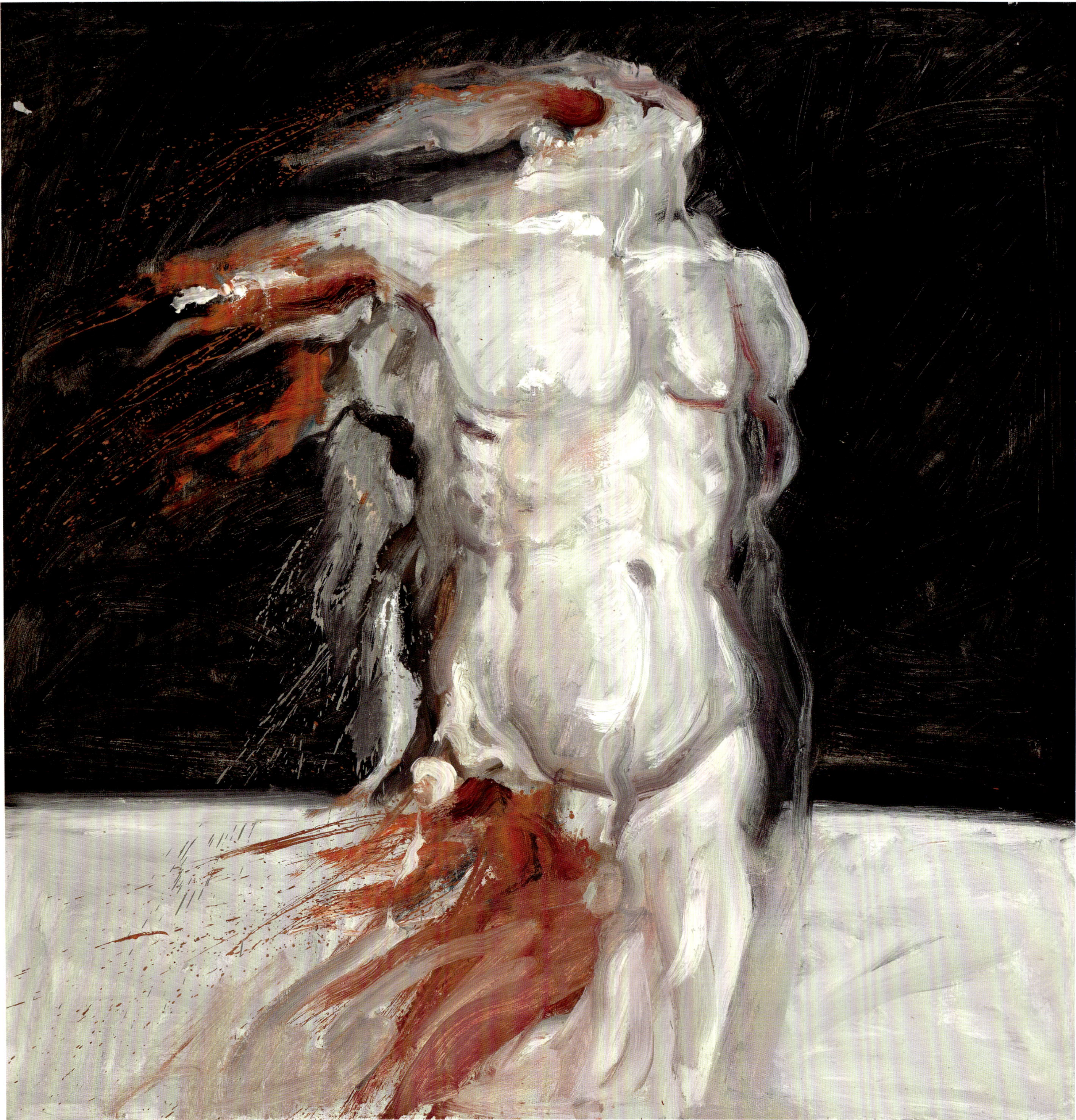

discharge. It was not until the Vietnam War that the concept of post-traumatic stress disorder (PTSD) emerged thanks to the activism of veterans' groups.[7] It was also during this period that Hodermarsky began engaging directly with his wartime trauma experiences through his work.

Current traumatology describes PTSD in clusters of symptoms: intrusive experiences, avoidance of memories, negative changes in cognition and mood, and changes in arousal or reactivity.[8] But the *Diagnostic and Statistical Manual of Mental Disorders* (DSM) defined these experiences in a vacuum, neglecting to contextualize them in a political or social framework. Critics of the biomedical model offered, instead, that trauma is "an experience or series of experiences, rooted in past and present state-produced and colonial conditions, that break or betray the inherent need for safety, belonging, dignity, agency, and 'enough-ness.'"[9]

Such a break manifested in Hodermarsky's behavior immediately after returning from the war. He avoided open spaces; preferred night work to avoid daytime travel; and carried an "unnamed pill" (most likely a tranquilizer) in his pocket for many years.[10] He compartmentalized and sublimated his distress through art and teaching.[11] Hodermarsky "educated his heart" on canvas; through painting, he "kept his demons at bay."[12] He began to show what he could not tell.

Annihilation and the Phenomenological Experience of War

Between 1943 and 1944, Hodermarsky's battalion experienced combat 95% of the time during its 9-month tour across Europe. His comrades died by accident, by bullets, by grenades, by land mines, by mortar, by artillery fire. They were shot down in planes and suffocated in collapsed fox holes.[13] By December of 1944, at least two members of the battalion were evacuated with "combat fatigue." The ubiquity of dead, wounded, and debilitated comrades surrounding Hodermarsky is unimaginable, even before accounting for enemy deaths he witnessed or perpetrated.

"Moral injury" describes the phenomenon of distress from committing acts that go against one's values.[14] In a Memorial Day address, Hodermarsky himself said, "Once a soldier had been committed to the battlefield that soldier's fear of his own death was somehow lessened by his killing of an enemy. Imagine the fact that a man's survival is dependent upon his killing of another human being. Can there be anything as deeply and psychologically damaging as that terrible fact upon the human spirit?"[15]

War correspondent David Morris described the traumatized mind as a "mad curator of the grotesque" that "adheres to the visions of the extinction of others, as if to collect clues to its own demise."[16] Hodermarsky was the "mad curator" of his war memories; in his own words, the pieces in his *War Series* are "startling and brutal."[17] This psychic purge also served as his therapy: "In the privacy of the creative act, and in the exploration of ideas and forms, the artist has experiences which rise farther, plunging deeper into the greatest pleasures of self-revelation, challenging any insight revealed in any form of therapy."[18]

Dismembered Bleeding Man (fig. 18) throws us into the grotesque liminal space between survival and annihilation. Having just been alive, the figure is now mid-dissolution. Hodermarsky did not paint corpses; rather, he focused on the horror that characterized the suspended moment before death.

His frantic brush strokes, leaving splatters of blood and flesh at the edges, make the figure look almost as if he moves on the canvas. The dismembered man's face is blown off, his jaw ripped apart as if in mid-scream. He is at once a man, still standing, and what used to be a man. He is amputated not only at his arm but also at his leg and groin, his penis decimated along with the rest of him.

These artistic depictions of violent death as a slow-motion nightmare contain elements of what Freud referred to as *the uncanny*: a grotesque subject that evokes an uneasy feeling, where ambiguity between reality and fantasy emerges. It is "that class of the terrifying which leads back to something long known to us, once very familiar."[19] It is a primal terror that taps into an ancient fear—fear at its most base, like a Neanderthal running from a panther without being able to rationally explain why. This hair-on-the-back-of-the-neck feeling involves balancing the real and not-real on a razor's edge. The impossibility of *Dismembered Bleeding Man*, overlaid with the knowledge of its historical reality, leaves us unsettled, not only because we weren't there, but because Hodermarsky distorts time and reality to elicit a specific feeling of horror. The experience is different than if we were to witness this man in the moments before his death (when he is a whole man) or after being shot (when he is a maimed corpse). Hodermarsky expressed hope that his paintings "will effect a change, however obscure, in the viewer."[20] He wanted to deepen the viewer's understanding of humanity and the human condition, to bring the viewer further in touch with what it means viscerally to be human by trying to bring us into the phenomenological experience of combat, death, slaughter, violent loss—the parts of war most of us do not witness. Whether that informs our relationship to our own aggressive impulses, or political ideas, is left up to us. The uncanny quality of his imagery defies the witness to remain unchanged, unaffected, confronting us with the same questions he posed in his Memorial Day address: "What is this terrible dark aspect of human beings, this need to resolve issues of power through warfare? Is there something in the genes of mankind, something base, animal, and primitive that needs to ignite into armed conflict, into hatred and death?"[21]

Raw Meat (plate 18) depicts another moment of annihilation in freeze frame, this time less ghostly and arguably more violent. Rather than brush strokes smoothly tracing the dissipation of flesh, blood splashes across the canvas, as though literally combusting before our eyes. "I felt the splatter of someone's loss of life as it exploded across my face," wrote Vietnam War veteran John Ketwig, "and no matter how many times I have washed my face in the past 47 years I cannot wash away that horrible stain."[22] *Raw Meat* makes us complicit in the scene, asking us to feel the splatter. The body (no longer titled *Man*, but *Meat*) becomes a grotesque chaos of cells, tissue, blood, ribs, and pelvis. Christopher Dixon described how Hodermarsky "sees the obscenity of war: the shattered bodies, transformed from that harmony of sense and touch we call 'life' into a miasma of mud, blood, and feces; the melting faces, losing in an instant that tenuous hold on reality which we salute as 'courage.'"[23]

Detonated Man (plate 17) is even further disintegrated. As if witnessing an atomic blast, we catch a microsecond freeze-frame of a person evaporating. His limbs evoke movement, as though still engaged in the futile act of survival, running but not escaping. The frozen animation captures a singular experience of soldiers: "Every second could either save you or kill you, where even the smallest gesture took on a certain weight because you knew it might be your last."[24] Like Hodermarsky's figures, which exist between living and dying, Victor Turner described the returning veteran as "not alive, not dead, but somehow both and neither."[25] We might witness Hodermarsky's *War Series* not only as haunting images from the past, but also as symbols of the "enigma of homecoming, the frustrating transit between worlds" that soldiers experience.[26]

This fraught journey between fragmented wholeness and obliteration is perhaps best epitomized by *War Triptych*. The gesture of arms being swept away, blurring into motion, repeats throughout the series: "something discreet, but always moving."[27] Yet unlike the other war paintings, the triptych begins with the distinct imprint of a face (plate 19). The figure's mouth opens as if surprised. We cannot know what he sees, or if he sees, as his eyes are scarcely visible. In the second panel (plate 20), the mouth is drawn more into a groan or scream, intimating that the figure is aware of his annihilation as it is happening, but unable to stop it. The final panel (plate 21) is the most abstract and disintegrated of any in the series. The figure, no longer recognizable as human, is swept away into molecules, "dust to dust." Tim O'Brien recounted a similar revelation of altered reality: "As if in slow motion, frame by frame, the world would take on the old logic—absolute silence, then the wind, then sunlight, then voices. It was the burden of being alive."[28]

Unlike Hodermarsky's other war figures, the *Limbless Man* (fig. 19) sees with one large, open eye. He appears alive and stationary in contrast to the bloody, explosive motion of other paintings. Yet this piece is among the most horrifying in the series. He has survived—but to what end? His glazed eye, ratcheted wide open, appears dissociated from its present reality while re-experiencing the horror of his dismemberment that is frozen in time. Even after his wounds have healed, he remains stuck, frozen in that moment of violence. His expression, open-mouthed and staring, is pleading. He is naked and vulnerable, mutilated by war. Juxtaposed with Hodermarsky's paintings of the dying, *Limbless Man* seems to ask: Is this better than death?

War Casualties in Ambulance (p. 36) finds men after battle. They seem to go on and on past the confines of the canvas, swaddled in bandages with only their mouths and noses free. They do not see. Their mouths are not open to plead, or scream, or even speak. They seem to be waiting in stillness. Like an unresolved chord, the "wrapped up" image intimates with hesitation, "Is the worst over?"

Winter March (fig. 20) leaves the macro experience of the battlefield, zooming out so far as to depersonalize the soldiers completely. Their walk appears infinite, their humanity decreasing over time and space until each speck is indistinguishable from another. Yet the muted colors of the scene betray none of the violence of Hodermarsky's other war paintings. Christopher Dixon reflected on the tension in this piece between anonymity and "peculiar beauty." For Dixon, Hodermarsky "presents the total scene as it might be observed with the impersonal rectitude of the eye of God: each individual personally caught in that violent web which is modern history."[29]

We can feel O'Brien's words: "It was not battle, it was just the endless march, village to village, without purpose, nothing won or lost. They marched for the sake of the march."[30] Yet unlike O'Brien's description, which emphasizes inertia, emptiness, and automation, Hodermarsky's winter scene wrestles with the beauty, even calm, overlaying the anonymous procession.

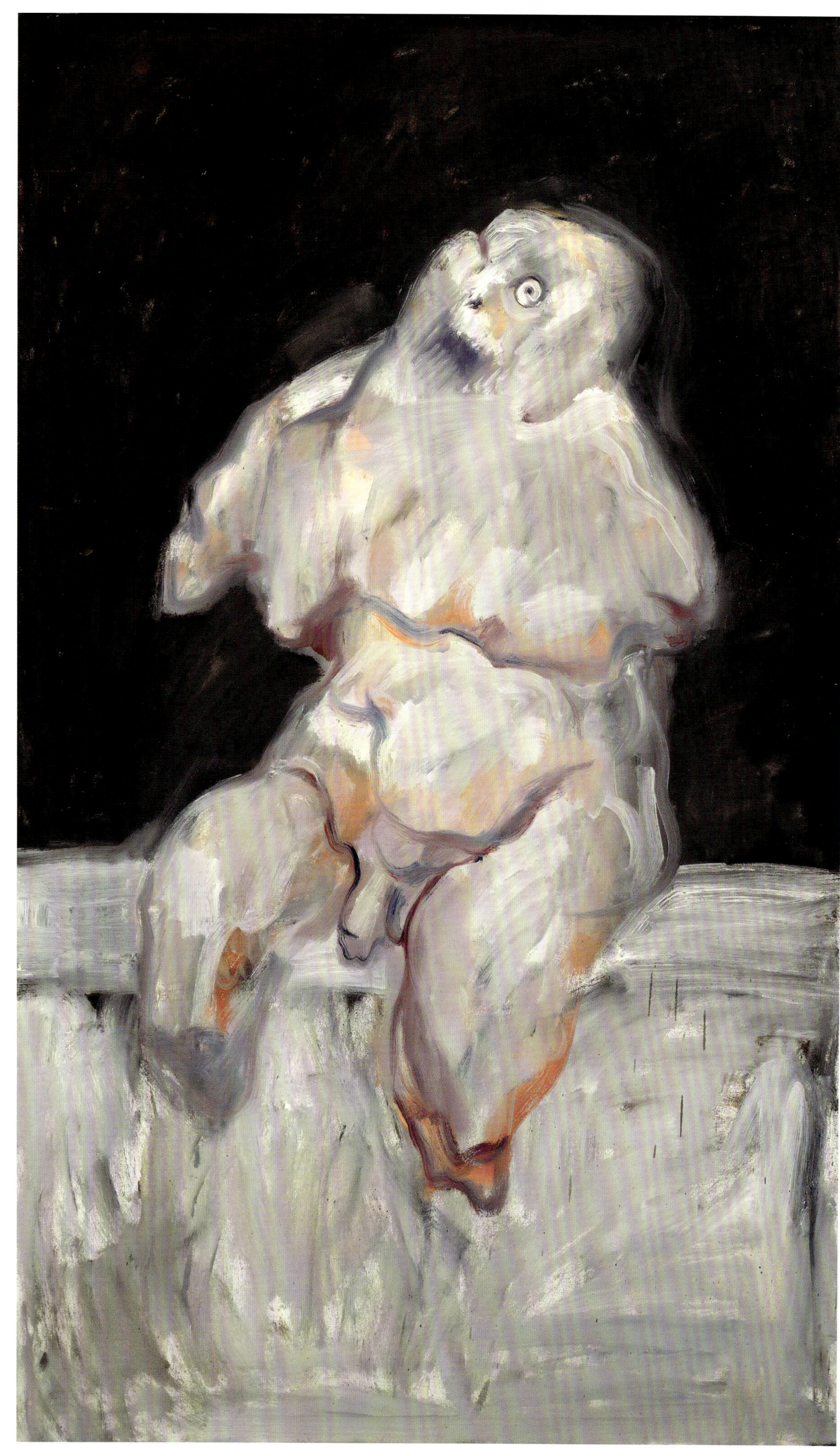

FIG. 19.
Limbless Man (War Series), 1970
Oil on canvas
64 x 39¼ in. (162.6 x 99.7 cm)
Estate of the artist

opposite: FIG. 20.
Winter March (War Series), 1970
Oil on Masonite
24 x 24 in. (61 x 61 cm)
Estate of the artist

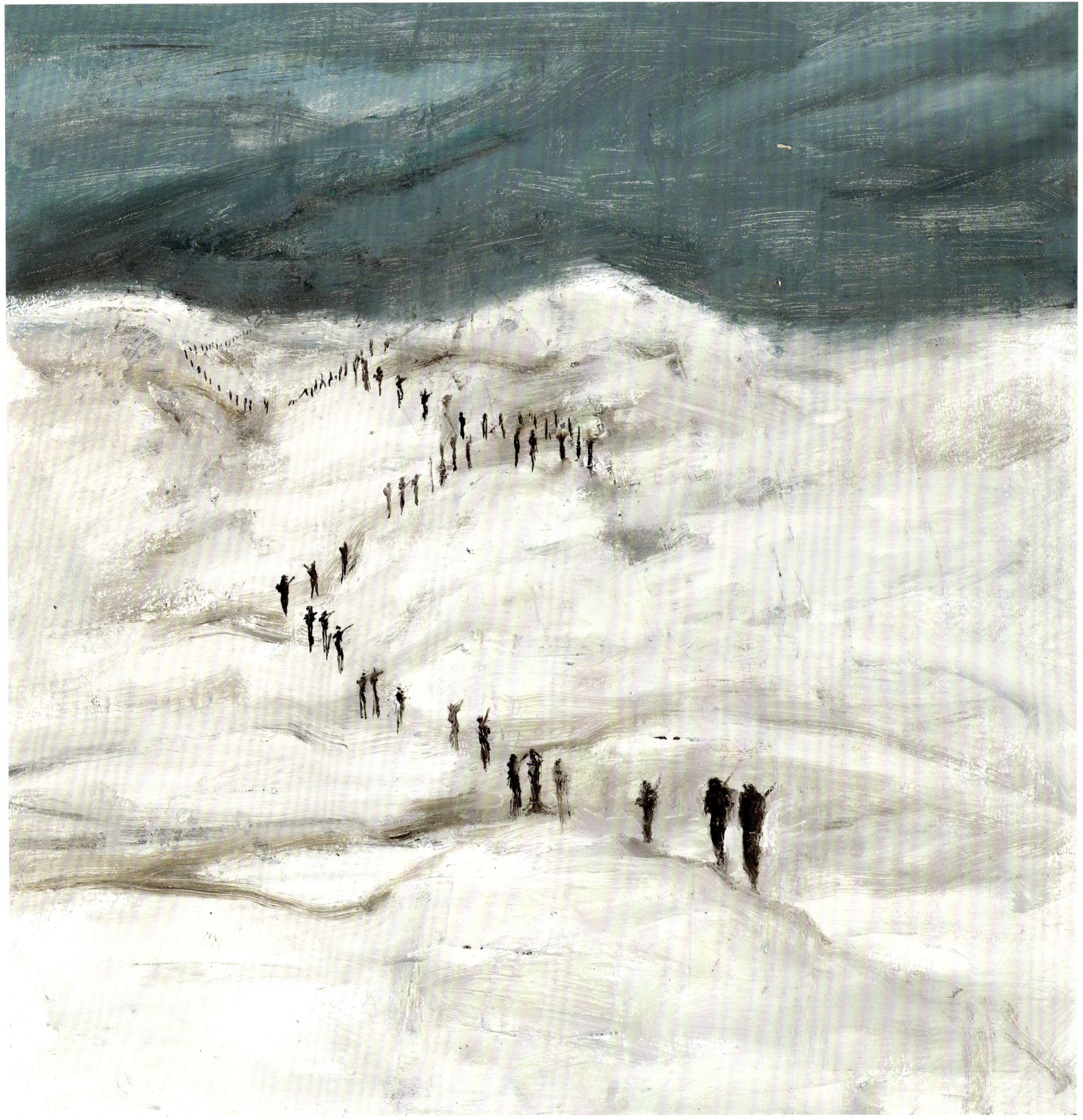

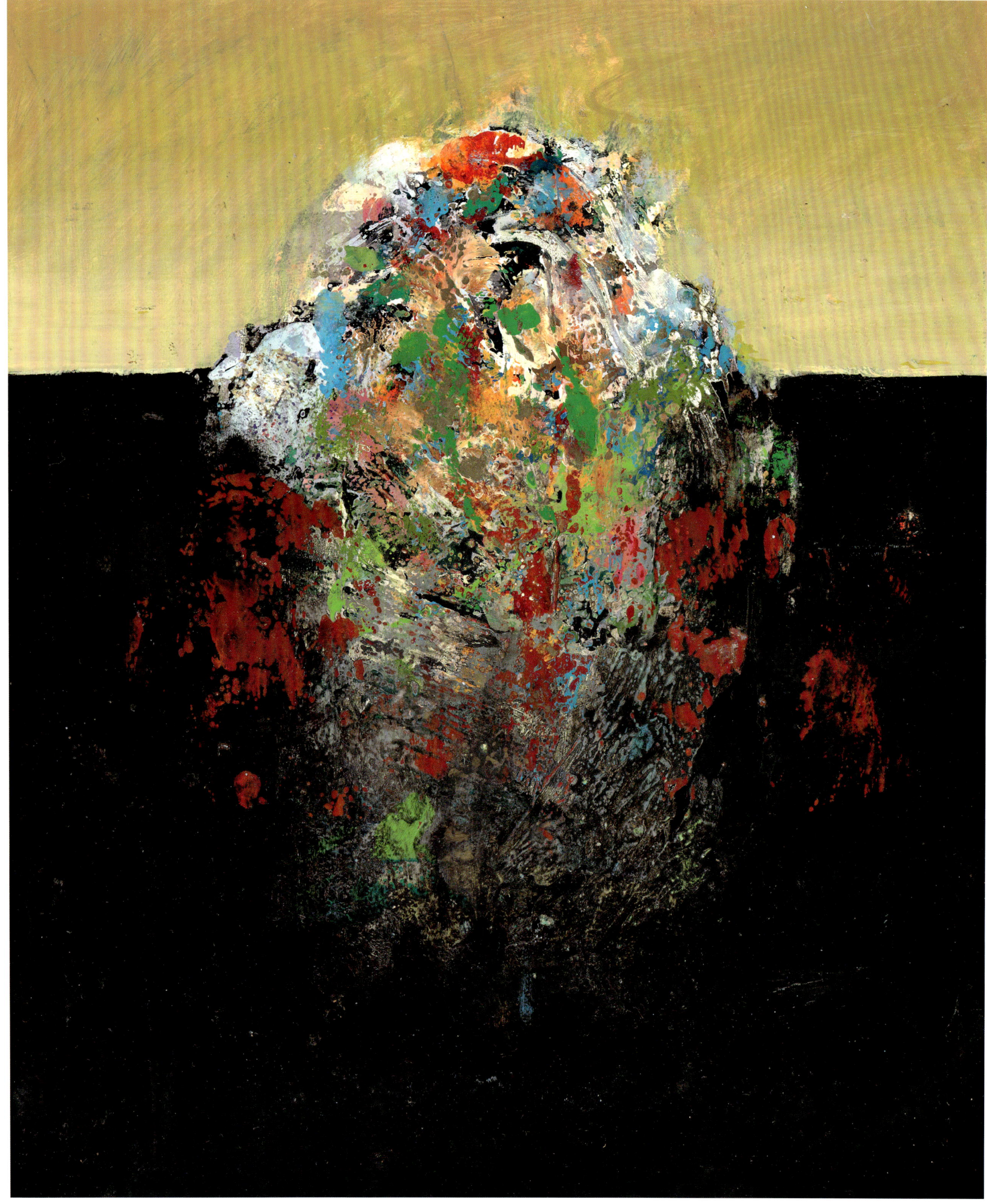

Metamorphosis and Meaning Making

Although painted earlier than most of the other works in the *War Series*, *Veterans Day* (p. 4) reckons with the realities of post-war life: how Hodermarsky's experiences of massacre are celebrated by his country. He colors this figure similarly to the man in *War Triptych*, yet here is the one who survived—more formed, yet still ghostly. Hodermarsky considered this one of his more important paintings,[31] and the body within it is recognizable as a self-portrait. The figure stands alone, holding what appears to be a flag that, rather than unfurling in the breeze, is rolled up tightly. He holds it close to his body as if holding a rifle. The expression is difficult to discern, but its pale, flat visage evokes stoic melancholy. Indeed, during a Veterans Day or Memorial Day parade, Hodermarsky would be found on the sidelines, watching but not participating.[32] For him "the thing we call courage often came not from nobility but having your humanity stripped away."[33] This painting, focused on Veterans Day, places our national narrative of the courageous hero in dialogue with this real, fleshy man who was flung into a war at 19.

In the 1990s, war reverberated through Hodermarsky's work more abstractly. In his *Ambergris* (plates 50–55) and *De Profundis* series (plates 56, 57), mushroom clouds burst forth as if from atomic blasts—yet carry with them "the ghost residue of a recently ignited firework at that perfect moment when everything becomes static and the colorful sparks separate and are held in the air."[34] They depict a metamorphosis from a dark expulsion into a stunning kaleidoscope. In *Ambergris 11 (Ambergris Series)*, the muddy ochre above the horizon in *Veterans Day* here transforms into radiant, crisp gold (fig. 21). These works represent what Viktor Frankl called *tragic optimism*: optimism in the face of the "tragic triad" of pain, guilt, and death.[35] From the Latin, *de profundis* means "from the depths" (fig. 22). From deep within a whale, ambergris begins as intestinal waste that becomes transmuted, over years, into a substance coveted for its rarity and scent. By the time Hodermarsky produced his *Ambergris* and *De Profundis* paintings, he had been digesting the war for 45 years.

Trauma shatters one's basic understanding of reality. Deeply held convictions about morality and justice are thrown into question. *Meaning-making* is the post-traumatic process of reducing the discrepancy between one's shattered view of the world and the meaning of the trauma itself.[36] Having confronted trauma directly in his *War Series*, Hodermarsky's *Ambergris* and *De Profundis* series turn toward meaning making as he explores beauty erupting from destruction. The trauma itself cannot be separated from a fervent celebration of life. The series demonstrate integration by "fusing the sublime and monstrous."[37]

Humor and Humanity

Kurt Vonnegut noted that "the kindest and funniest [veterans], the ones who hated war the most, were the ones who'd really fought."[38] Hodermarsky, like many survivors of atrocities, seemed buoyed back to life by humor. In Frankl's account of surviving concentration camps during World War II, he wrote, "Quite unexpectedly, most of us were overcome by a grim sense of humor. We knew that we had nothing to lose except our so ridiculously naked lives."[39] Hodermarsky "answered fear with an

*Ambergris 11
(Ambergris Series)*, 1991
Oil on wood
14 x 12 in. (35.6 x 30.5 cm)
Estate of the artist

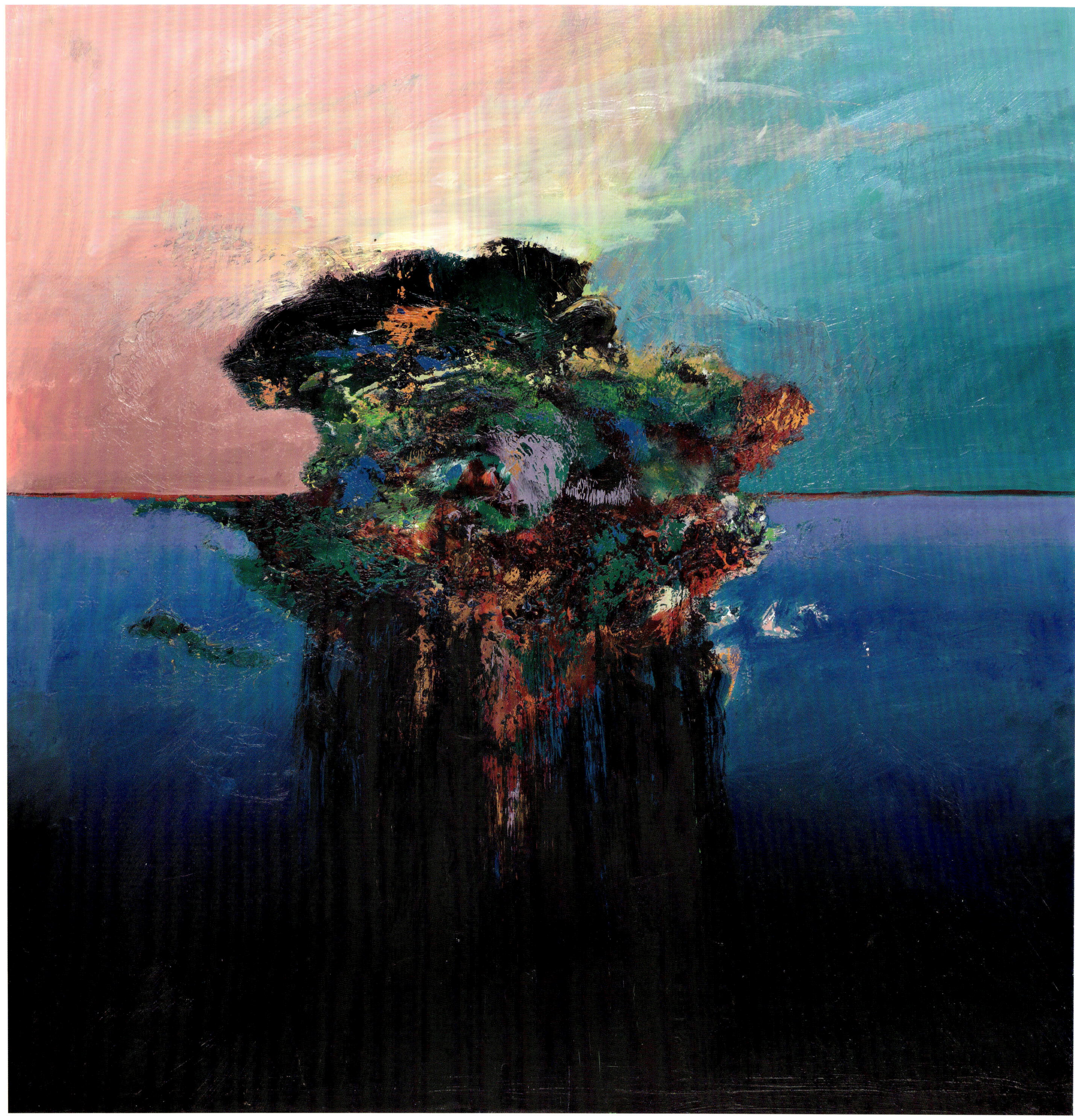

outrageous sense of humor, deep compassion, and a radiant ability to love."[40] Through his painting, he maintained an optimistic view of life despite all evidence to the contrary. "It is often heathen, sensual, and profane," he wrote, "but it is optimistic."[41]

Following the war, Hodermarsky appeared to walk alongside death with a profound sense of acceptance and humor. His daughter Elisabeth reflected, "He was one of these people who deeply wanted to live, but what the war taught him was that you can never program when, where, or how you're going to die."[42] He was not afraid to die. His only fear was encountering his "demons" again. "After all those years he put into getting them onto canvases, he dreaded a return to the horror that was so hard to talk about—the sight of his dead buddies, especially the sight of a dead German soldier at Utah beach with the belt buckle that read 'Gott mit uns'—God with us."[43]

We will never know the reality of Hodermarsky's final moments and whether his demons followed him there. What we do know is that he died painting in his studio. Transmogrified by trauma like ambergris in the belly of the whale, he lives on in his family, students, and friends. "I have loved people, the sea, sky, land, animals," he scrawled in his long cursive. "I have avoided success and tried hard to recognize what love really is."[44]

Cheshire, Connecticut
December 7, 2022

FIG. 22.
*From Out of the Deep
(De Profundis Series)*, 1991
Oil on Masonite
24 x 24 in. (61 x 61 cm)
Estate of the artist

1. David J. Morris, *The Evil Hours: A Biography of Post-Traumatic Stress Disorder* (Boston: Houghton Mifflin Harcourt, 2015), 221.

2. Anna Hammond, "Memorial Lecture for Dan" (lecture, Deerfield Academy, Deerfield, MA, 1999); Maria Hodermarska and Elisabeth Hodermarsky in discussion with the author, November, 2022.

3. , Matthew Friedman, "The Soldier's Heart. Pbs.org. October 7, 2004, http s://www.pbs.org/wgbh/pages/frontline/shows/heart/interviews/friedman.html (accessed March 22, 2023).

4. Judith Herman, *Trauma and Recovery* (New York: BasicBooks, 1992), 20.

5. Ibid, 25.

6. Maria Hodermarska, email message to author, December 2, 2022.

7. Herman, *Trauma and Recovery*, 27; Morris, *The Evil Hours: A Biography of Post-Traumatic Stress Disorder*, 17.

8. American Psychiatric Association, *Diagnostic and Statistical Manual of Mental Disorders*, 5th ed. (Arlington, VA: American Psychiatric Association, 2013), 271–272.

9. Christine Mayor, "Trauma as White Property and the Erasure of Black Victims: The Critical Trauma, Anti-Black Racism, and Whiteness," PhD diss. (Wilfrid Laurier University, 2022), 66.

10. Maria Hodermarska, "For My Father," *Island Ad-Vantages* (Stonington, ME), May 24, 2007.

11. Maria Hodermarska and Elisabeth Hodermarsky in discussions with the author, November, 2022.

12. Hammond, "Memorial Lecture for Dan."

13. "400th Armored Field Artillery Battalion Statistical Summary." Unpublished document from the Daniel Hodermarsky Family Trust.

14. Sonya B. Norman and Shira Maguen, "Moral Injury," United States Department of Veterans Affairs, https://www.ptsd.va.gov/professional/treat/cooc-curring/moral_injury.asp (accessed November 29, 2022).

15. "Dan Hodermarsky May 30, 1989." Unpublished document from the Daniel Hodermarsky Family Trust.

16. Morris, *The Evil Hours*, 44–45.

17. Daniel Hodermarsky, artist's statement, June, 1995. Unpublished document from the Daniel Hodermarsky Family Trust.

18. Ibid.

19. Sigmund Freud, "The Uncanny," in *On Creativity and the Unconscious*, trans. Alix Strachey (Vienna: Imago, 1919; reis., New York: Harper & Row, 1958), 123–124.

20. Daniel Hodermarsky, artist's statement, June, 1995.

21. "Dan Hodermarsky May 30, 1989." Unpublished document from the Daniel Hodermarsky Family Trust.

22. John Ketwig, *Vietnam Reconsidered: The War, the Times, and Why They Matter*. (Walterville, OR: Trine Day, 2018), 329.

23. Christopher Dixon, "An Exhibition of Paintings in the Hilson Gallery of Art at Deerfield Academy: October 28 through December 6, 1970." Unpublished document from the Daniel Hodermarsky Family Trust.

24. Morris, *The Evil Hours*, 5.

25. Victor W. Turner, "Betwixt and Between: The Liminal Period in *Rites de Passage*," in *Reader in Comparative Religion*, ed. Evon Z. Lessa (New York: Harper & Row, 1979), quoted in Morris, *The Evil Hours*, 7.

26. Morris, *The Evil Hours*, 74.

27. Daniel Hodermarsky, artist's statement, June, 1995.

28. Tim O'Brien, *The Things They Carried* (Boston: Mariner Books, 2015), 14.

29. Dixon, "An Exhibition of Paintings in the Hilson Gallery of Art at Deerfield Academy."

30. O'Brien, *The Things They Carried*, 14.

31. Maria Hodermarska in discussion with the author, November, 2022.

32. Ibid.

33. Hodermarska, "For My Father."

34. Kate McNamara, "Above and Below," in *Daniel Hodermarsky: Abstraction Paintings*, exh. cat. (Deer Isle, ME: Turtle Gallery, 2009), 5–6.

35. Viktor E. Frankl, *Man's Search for Meaning* (Boston: Beacon Press, 1959; reissued 2014), 125.

36. Crystal L. Park, "Trauma and Meaning Making: Converging Conceptualizations and Emerging Evidence," in *The Experience of Meaning in Life: Classical Perspectives, Emerging Themes, and Controversies*, eds. J.A. Hicks and C. Routledge (New York: Springer, 2013), 64–65.

37. McNamara, "Above and Below," 7.

38. Kurt Vonnegut, *Slaughterhouse Five* (New York: Dial Press, 1969; reissued 2009), 13.

39. Frankl, *Man's Search for Meaning*, 15.

40. Hodermarska, "For My Father."

41. Daniel Hodermarsky, artist's statement, June, 1995.

42. Elisabeth Hodermarsky in discussion with the author, November, 2022.

43. Hodermarska, "For My Father."

44. Daniel Hodermarsky, artist's statement, June, 1995.

Hodermarsky

PLATES

The Leader (Seated Churchill), 1964

Oil on Masonite
24 x 24 in. (61 x 61 cm)
Estate of the artist

Paintings

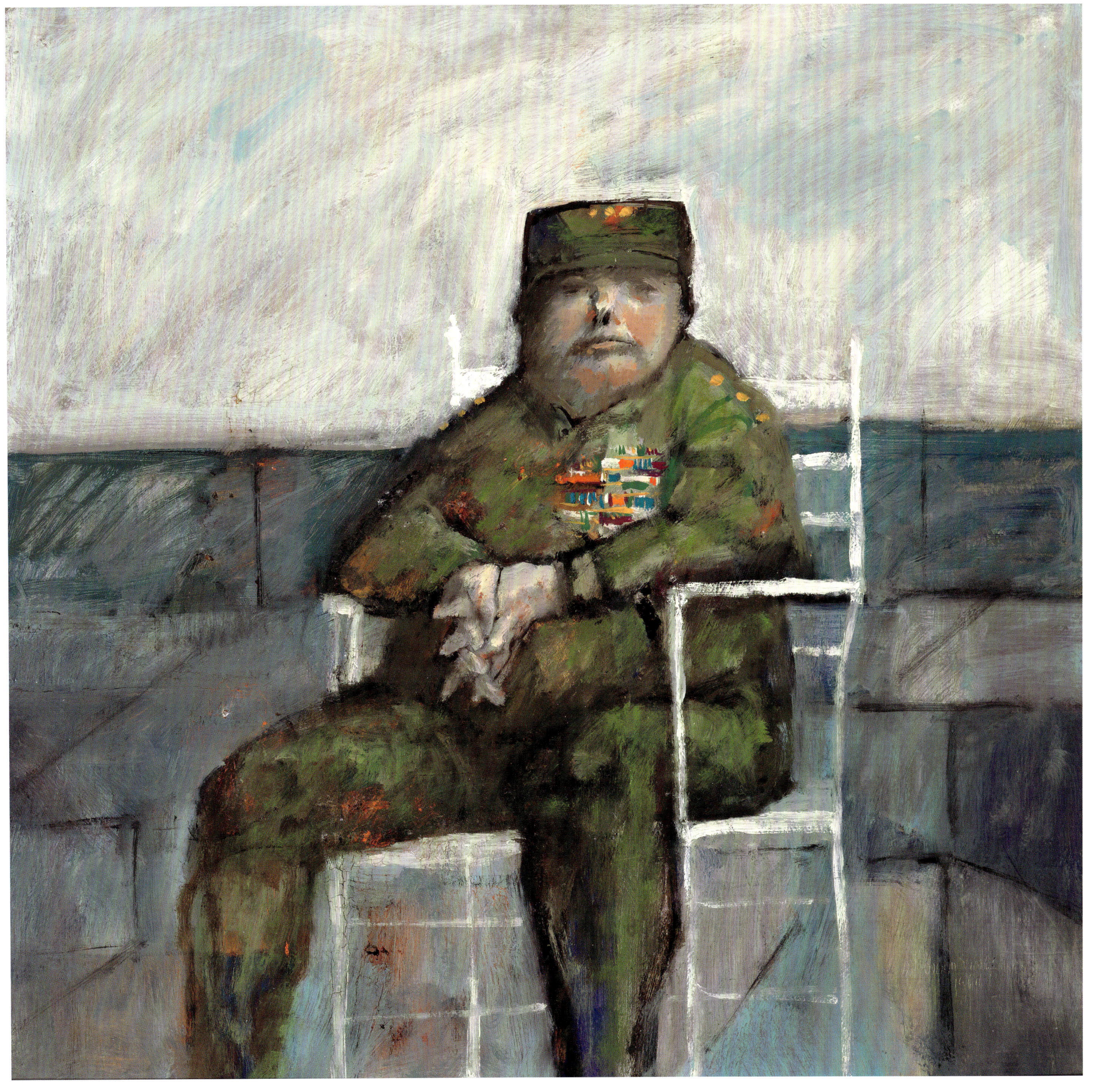

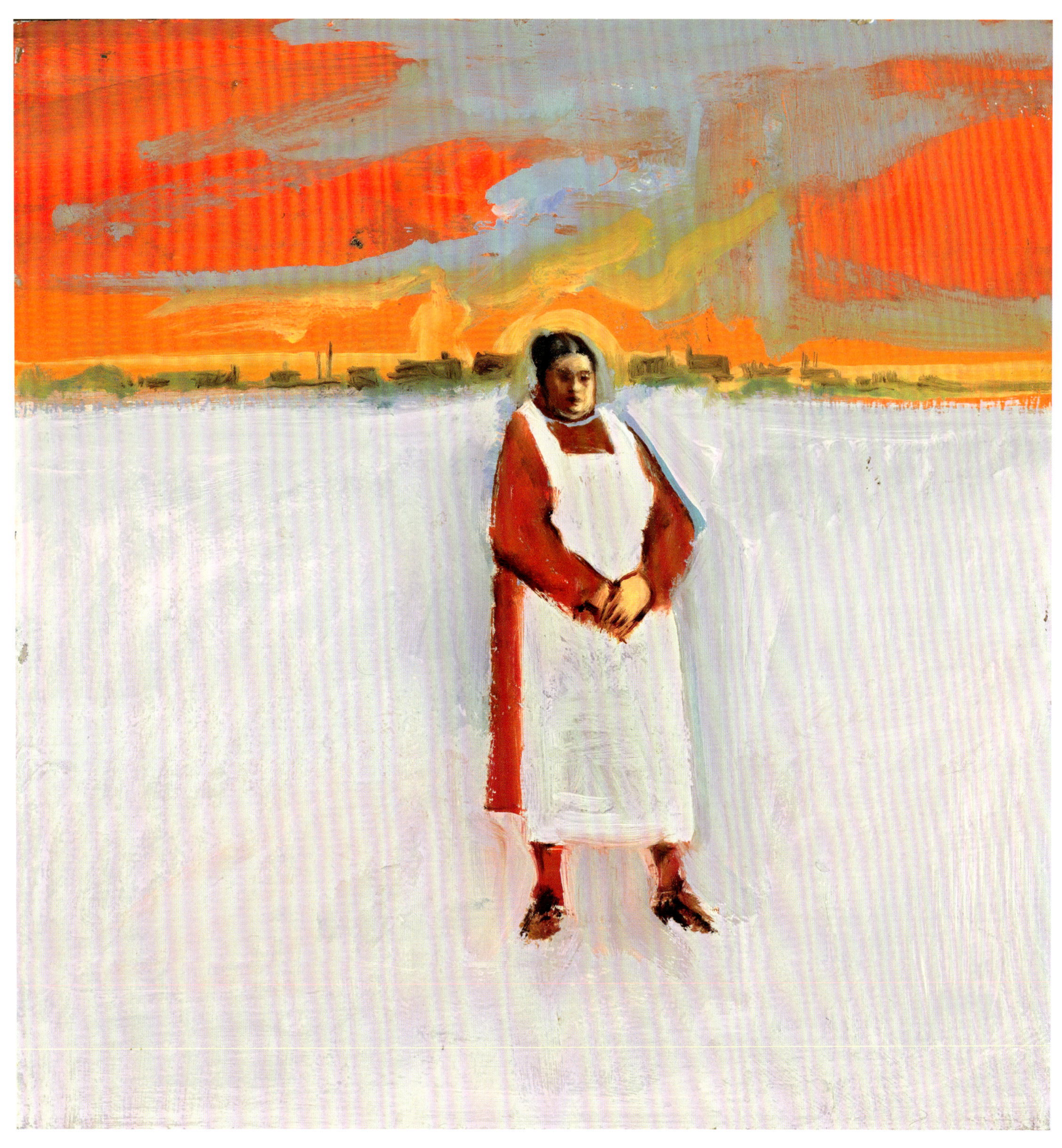

The Anarchist (Emma Goldman), 1965

Oil on wood
12 x 12 in. (30.5 x 30.5 cm)
Estate of the artist

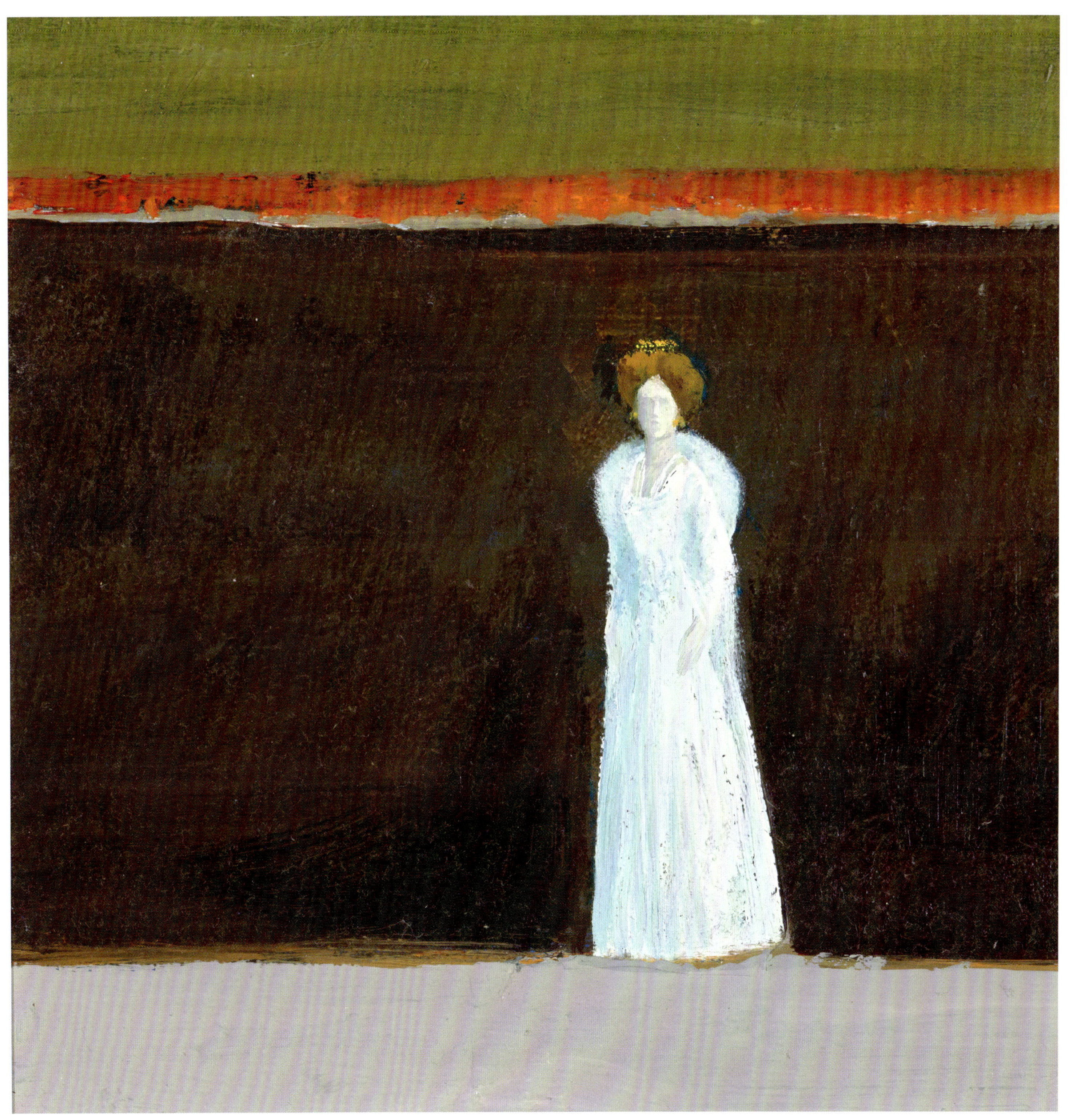

PLATE 3

Czarina, 1973

Oil on wood
12 x 12 in. (30.5 x 30.5 cm)
Collection of Maria Hodermarska and Penn Rhodeen

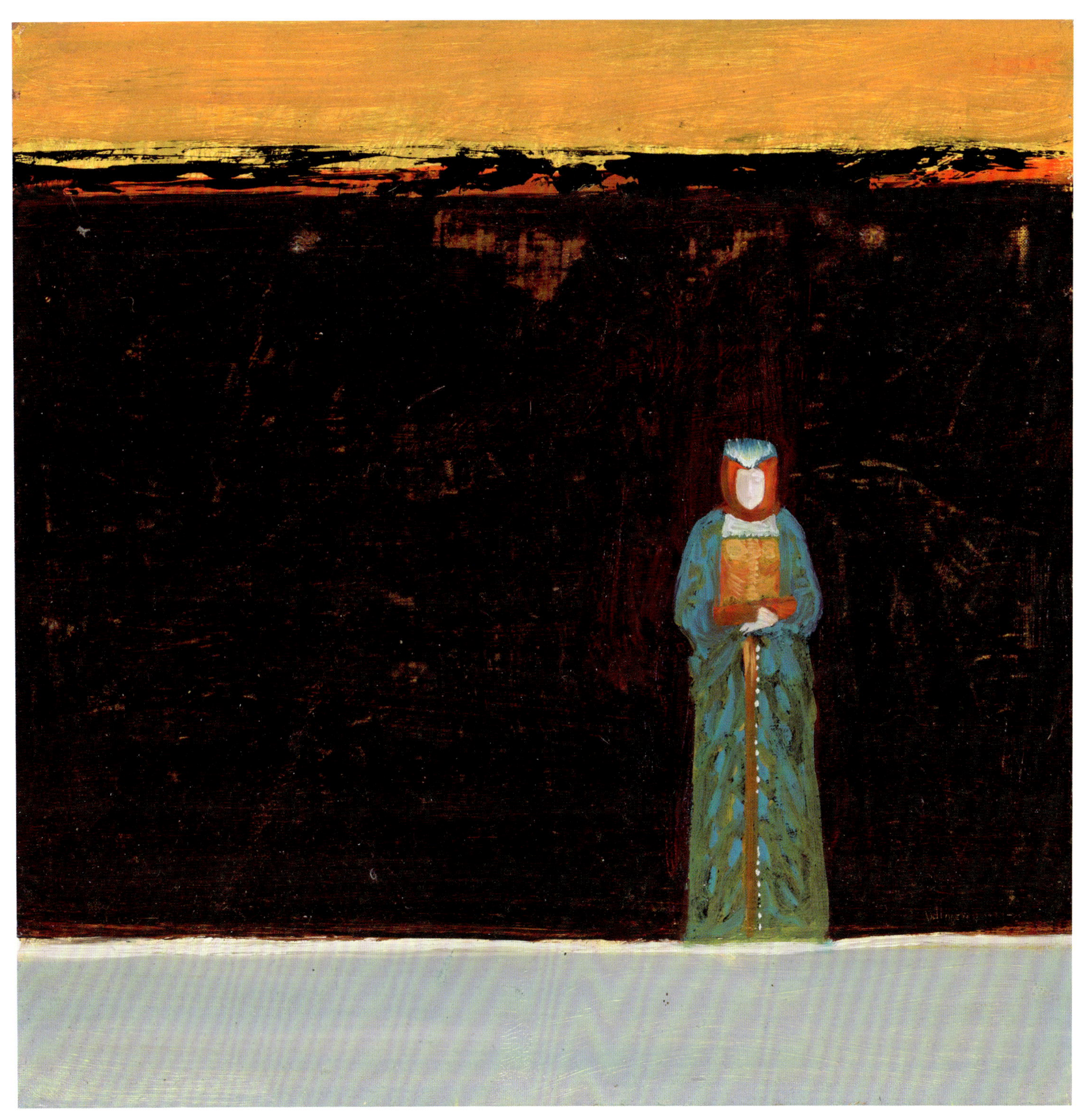

PLATE 4

Heloise, 1973

Oil on wood

12 x 12 in. (30.5 x 30.5 cm)

Collection of Liz and Joe Haberstroh

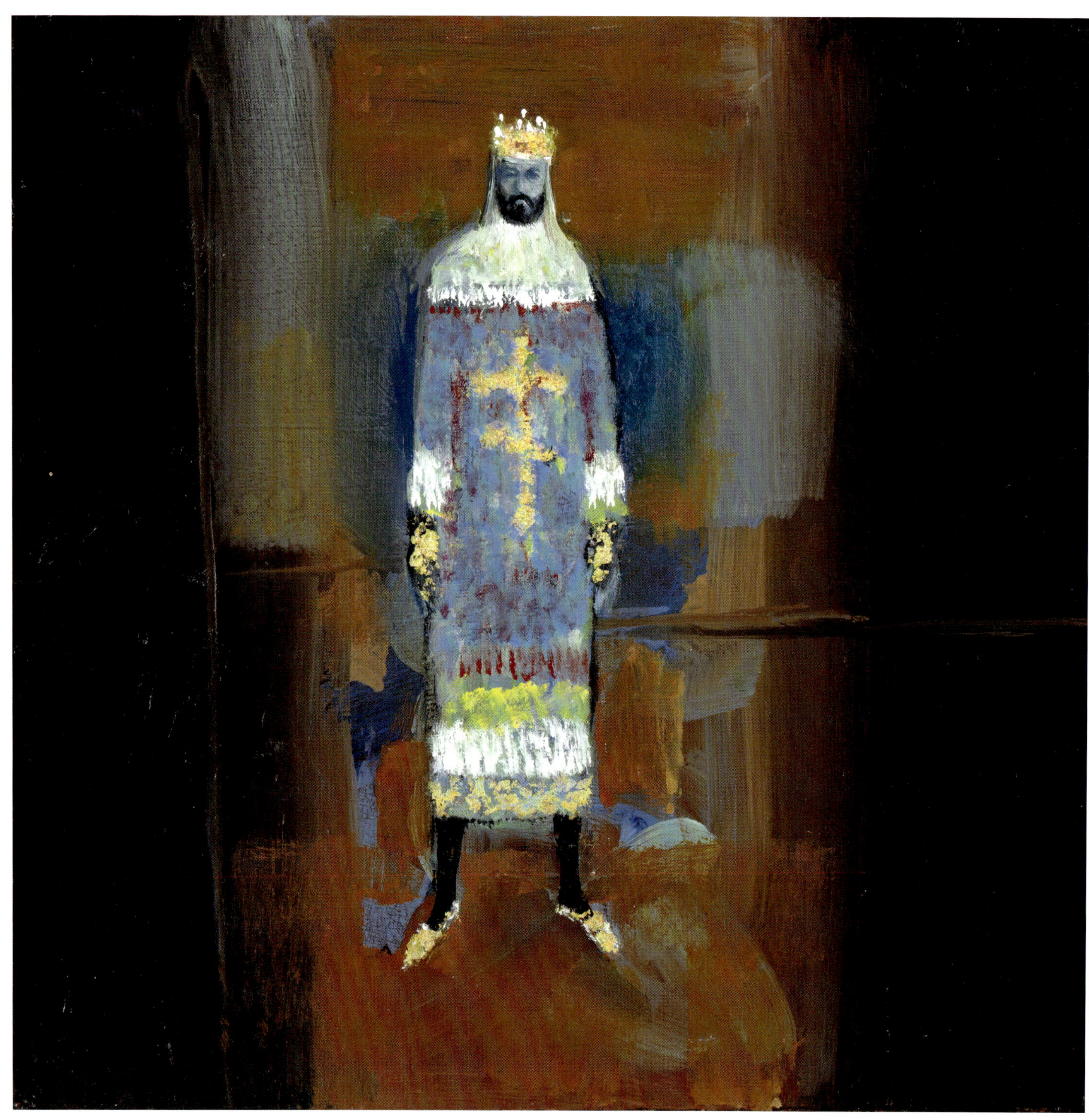

Medieval Slovak King, 1973
Oil on board
12 x 12 in. (30.5 x 30.5 cm)
Collection of Stephen Hannock

Important Person in Doorway, 1997
Oil on canvas
28 x 24 in. (71.1 x 61 cm)
Estate of the artist

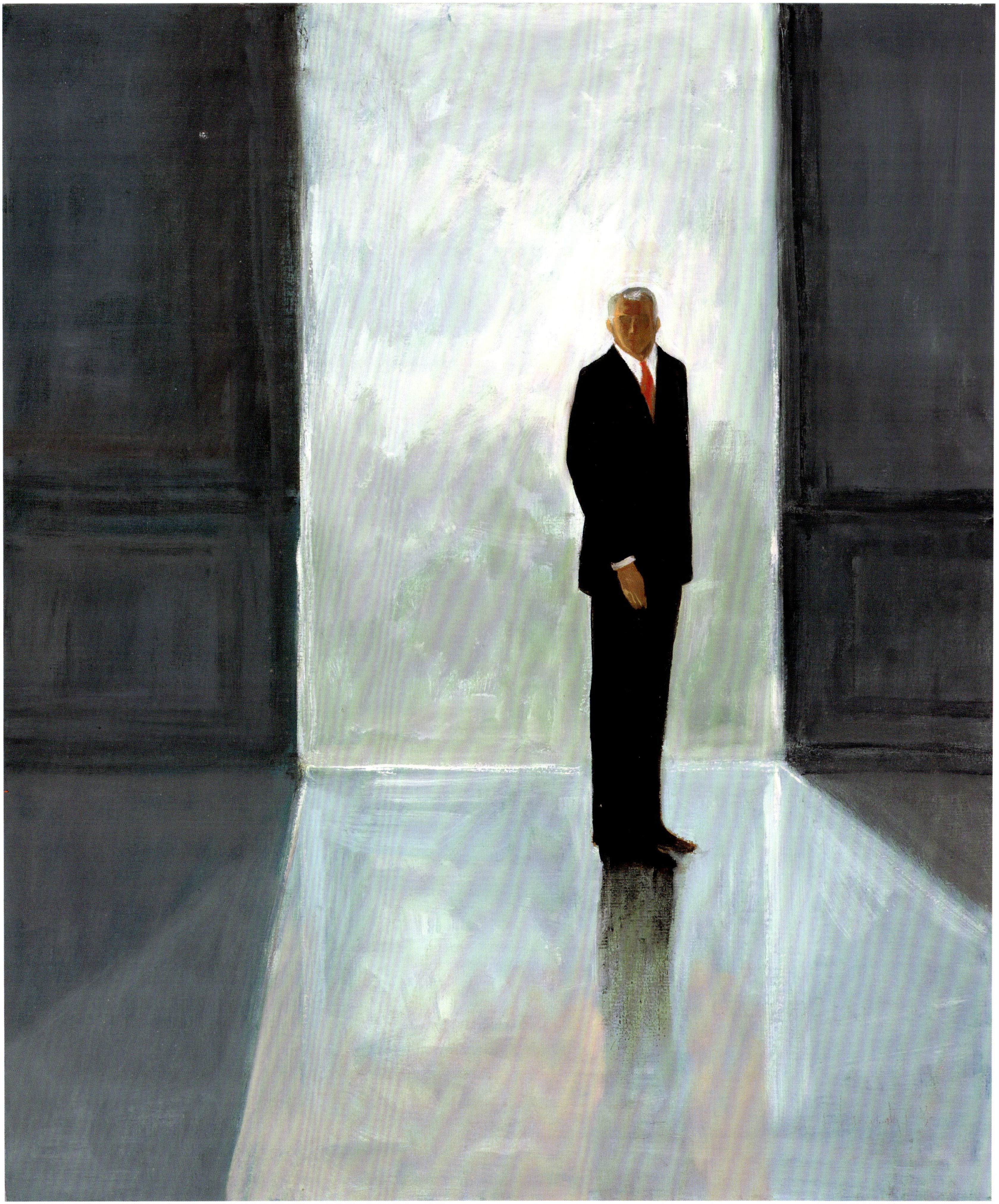

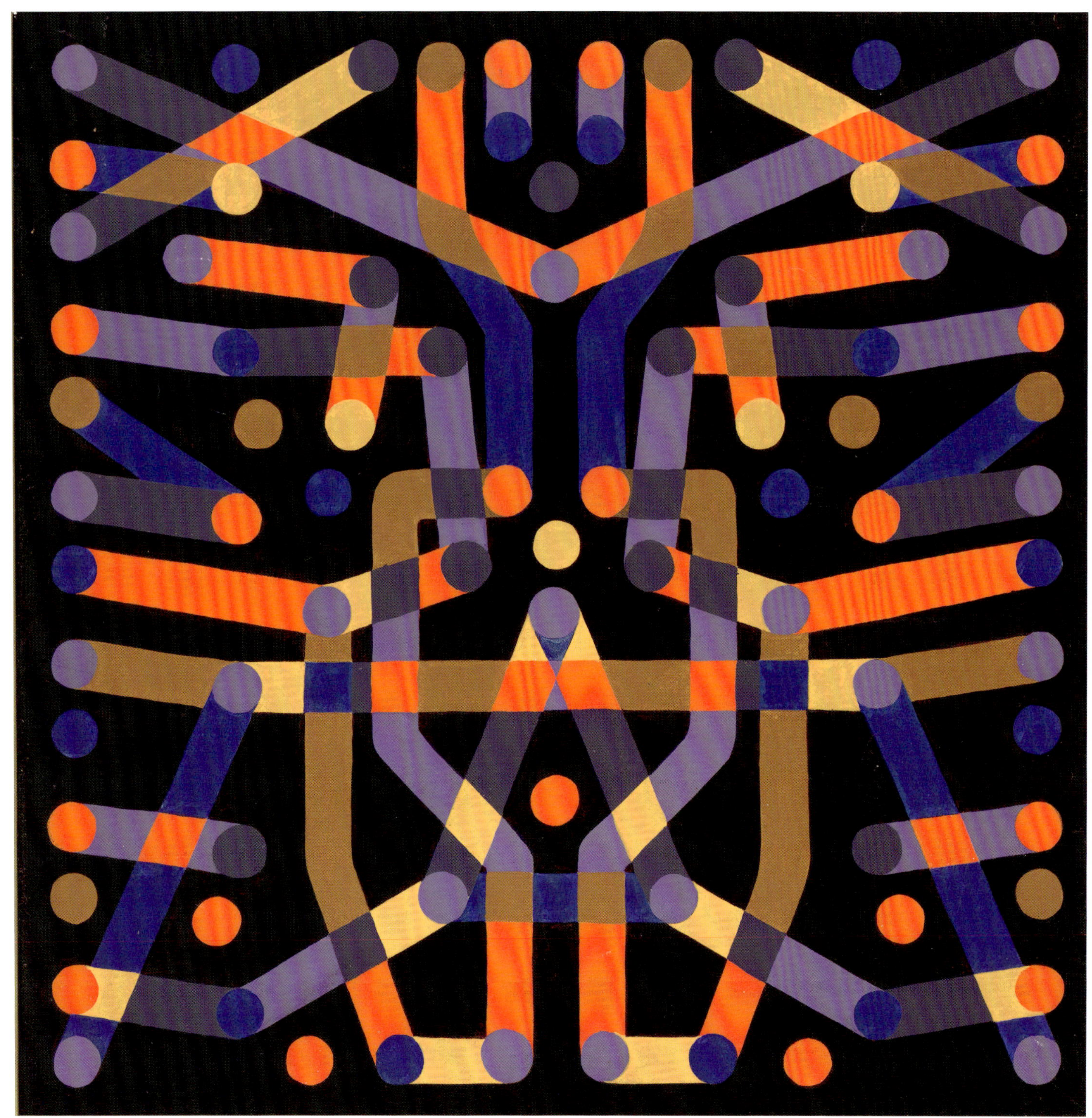

PLATE 7

Illumination, 1967

Acrylic on Masonite
24 x 24 in. (61 x 61 cm)
Estate of the artist

opposite: PLATE 8

Mill Blue, 1967

Acrylic on Masonite
36 x 36 in. (91.4 x 91.4 cm)
Estate of the artist

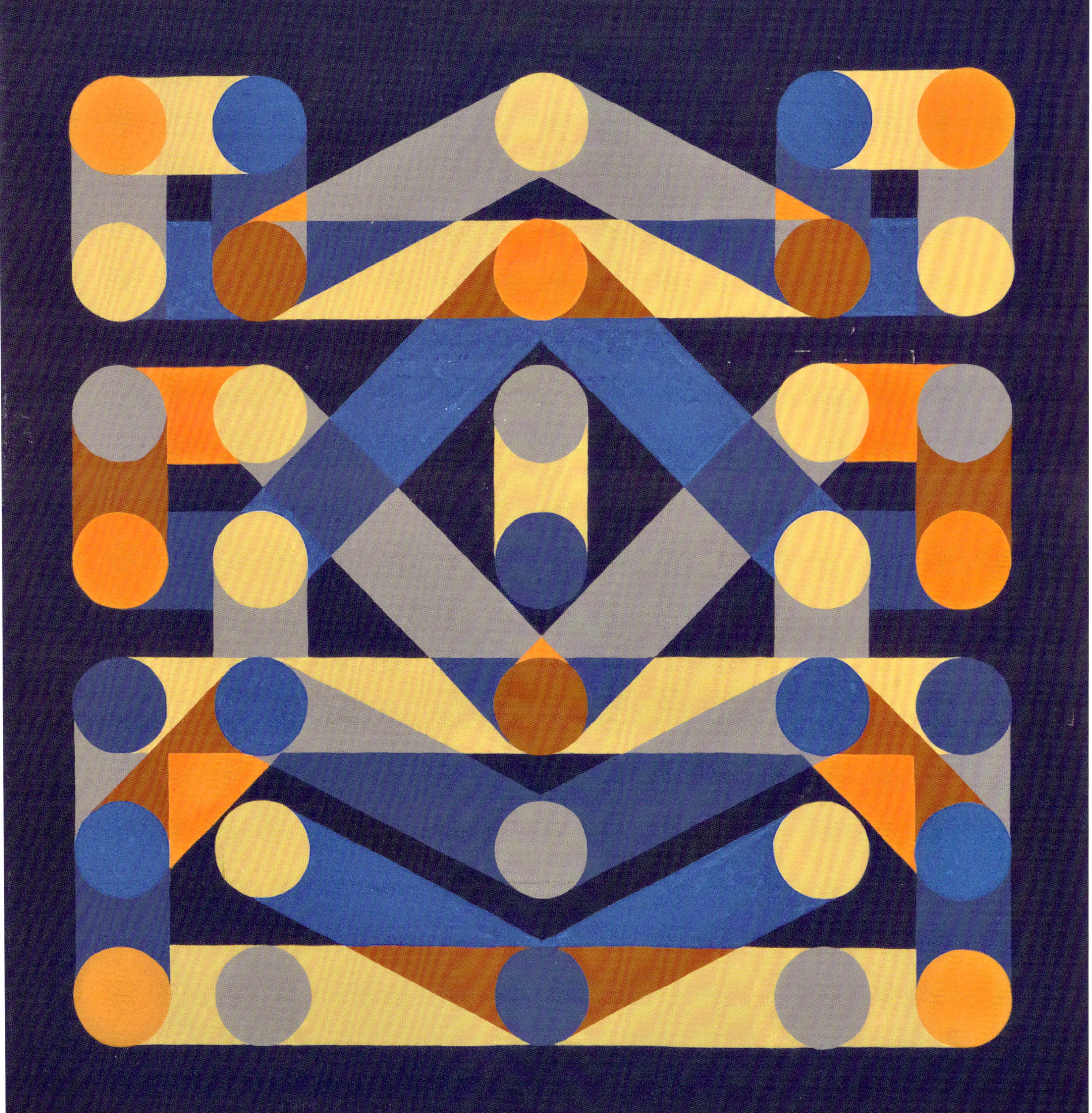

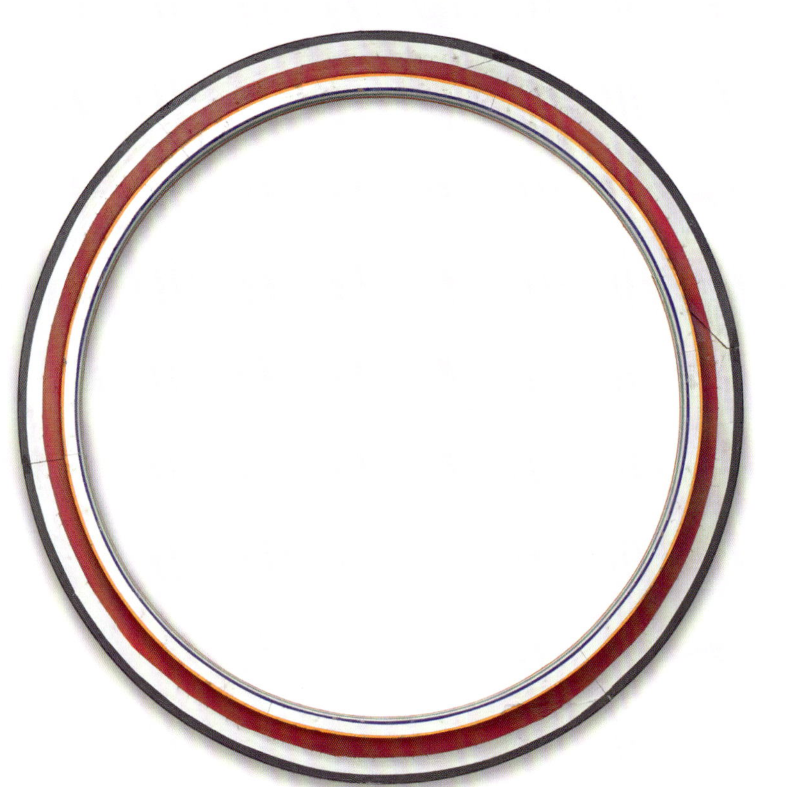

Circular Industrial, late 1960s

Acrylic on wood
34⅝ in. diameter (87.9 cm)
Collection of Elisabeth Hodermarsky
and Sloan Wilson

Dayglo Industrial, late 1960s

Dayglo oil on wood
57 x 5½ in. (144.8 x 14 cm)
Estate of the artist

Dizzy, late 1960s

Acrylic on wood
25½ x 23 x 34 in. (64.8 x 58.4 x 86.4 cm)
Collection of Maria Hodermarska and Penn Rhodeen

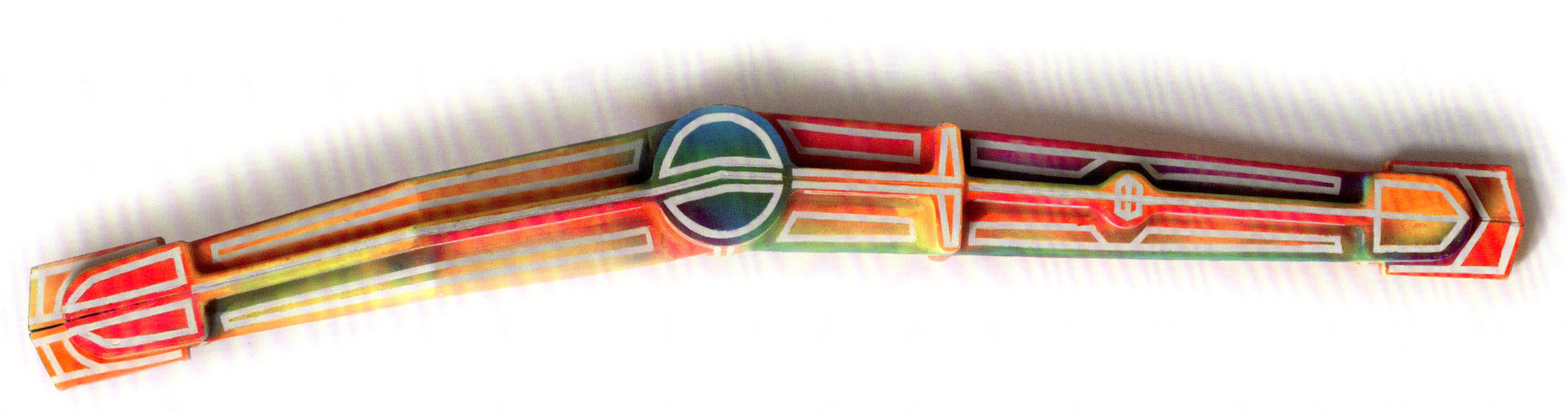

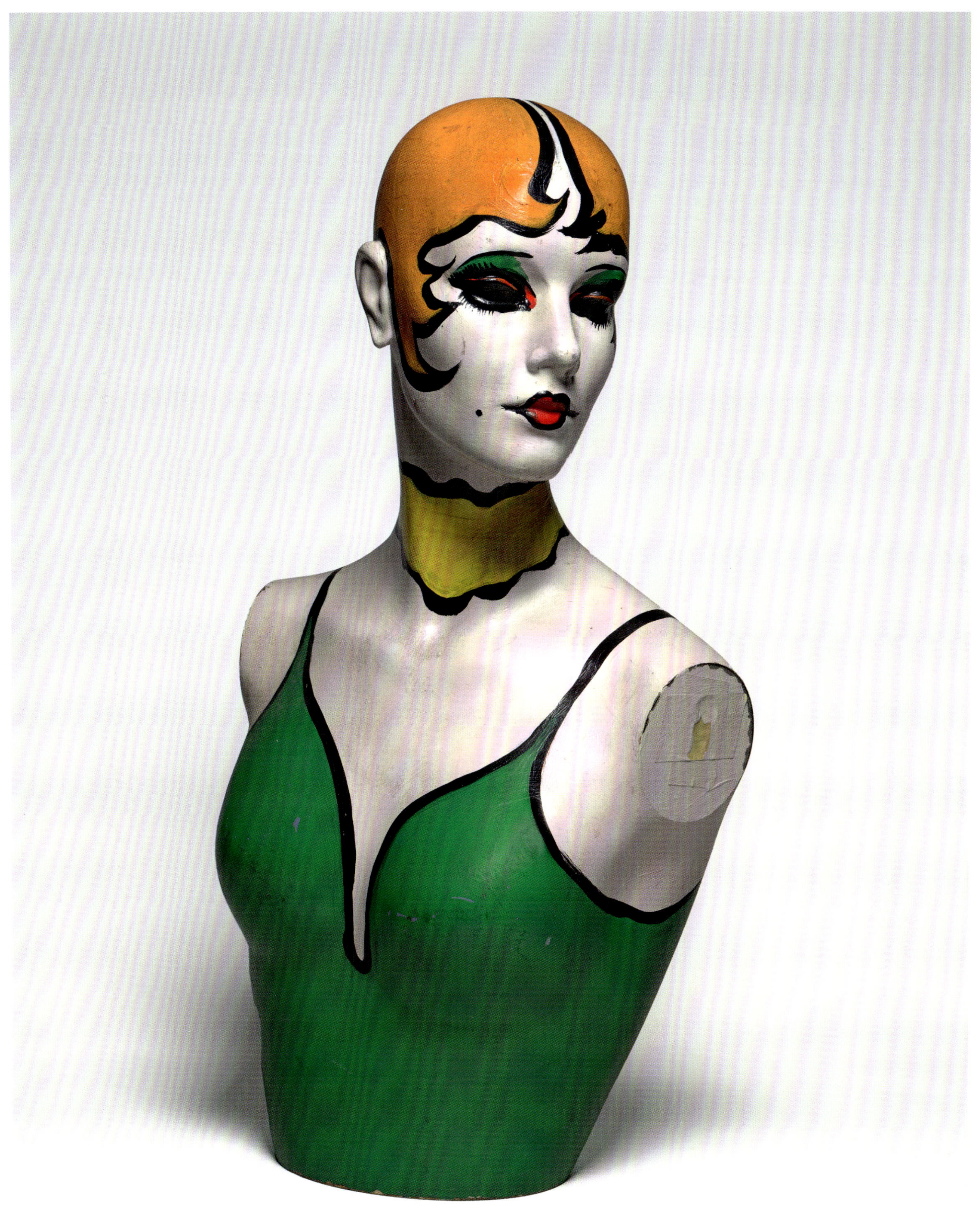

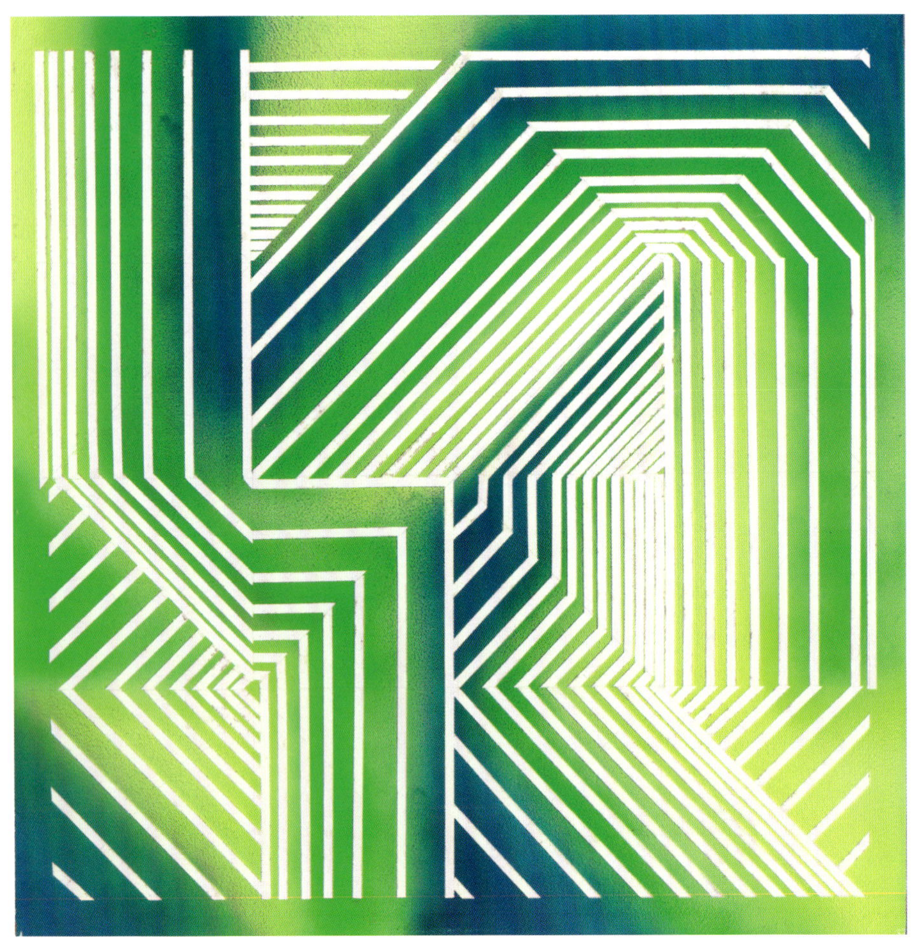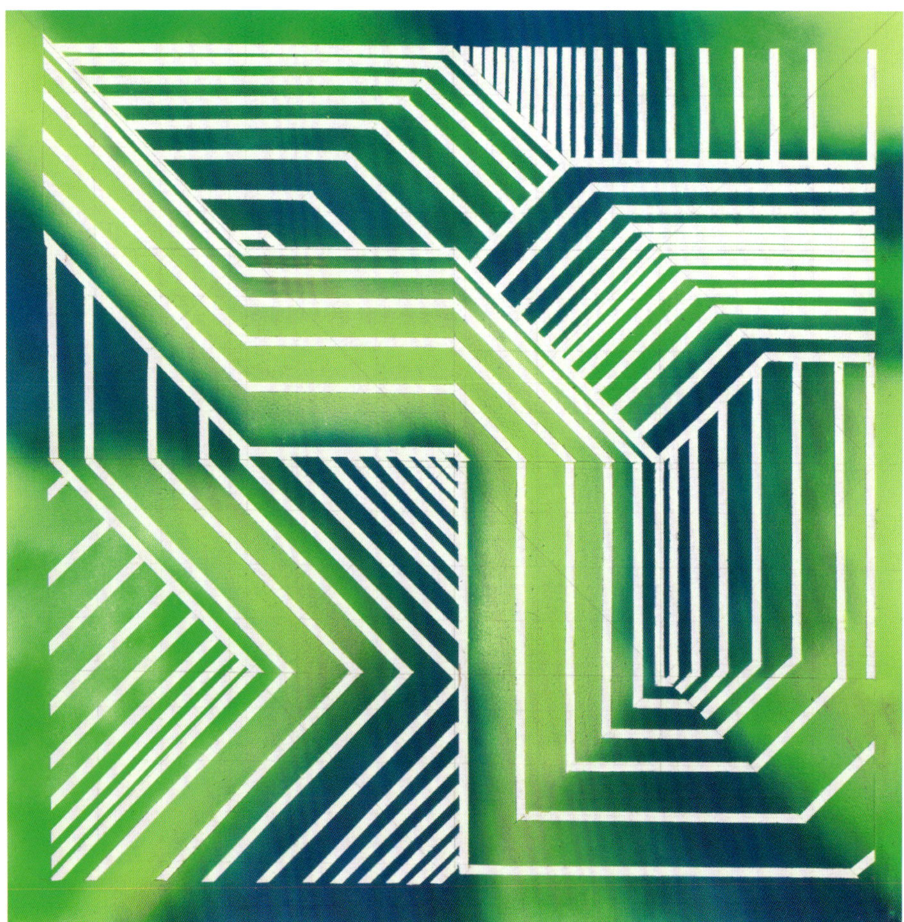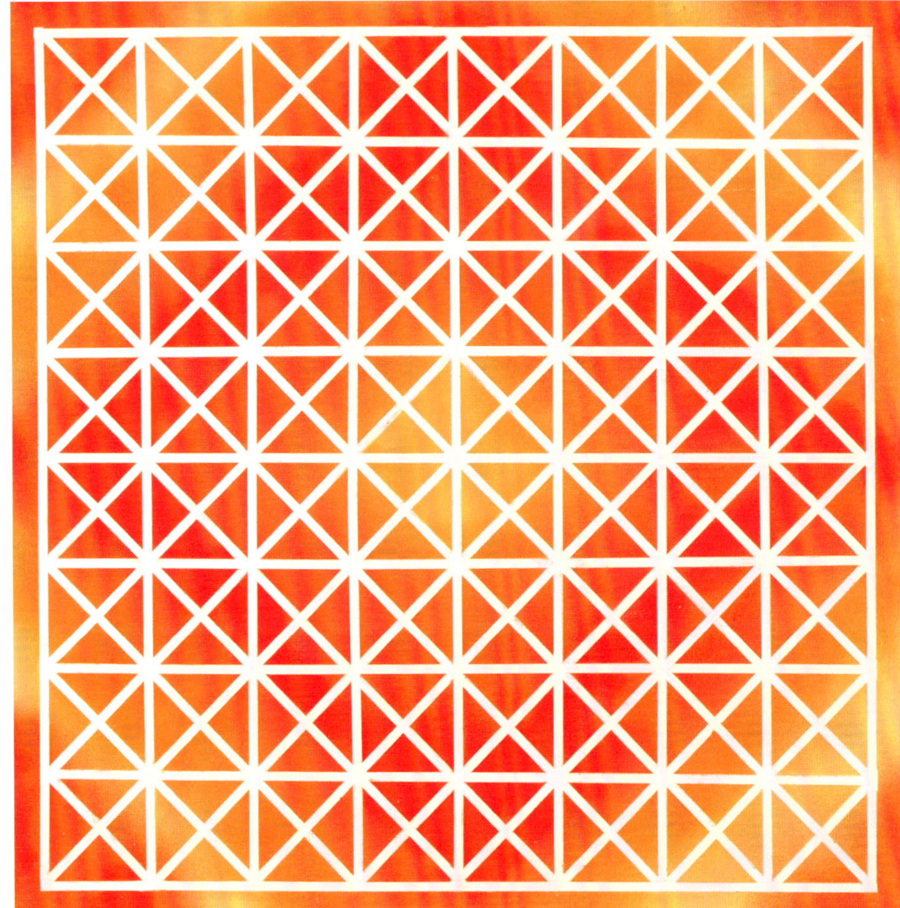

above: PLATES 12, 13

Dayglo Blue & Green Intersections, 1970

Dayglo acrylic on Masonite
Each 24 x 24 in. (61 x 61 cm)
Estate of the artist

left: PLATE 14

Dayglo Red & Orange, ca. 1970

Dayglo acrylic on Masonite
24 x 24 in. (61 x 61 cm)
Estate of the artist

opposite: PLATE 15

Robot Man, 1970

Dayglo oil on Masonite
44 x 44 in. (111.8 x 111.8 cm)
Estate of the artist

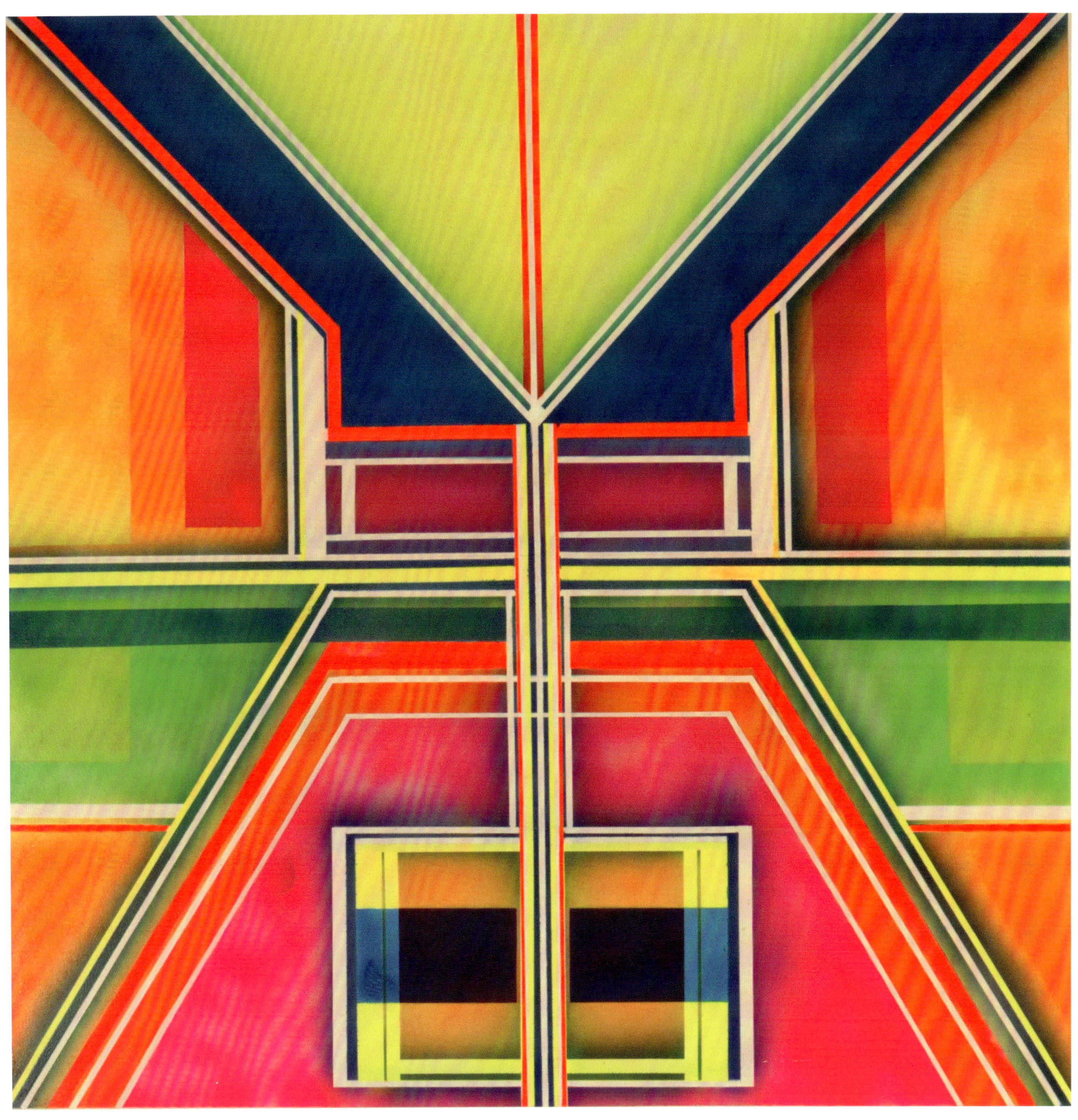

PLATE 16

Plugged-In Man #1, 1966

Oil on Masonite
29½ x 29½ in. (74.9 x 74.9 cm)
Estate of the artist

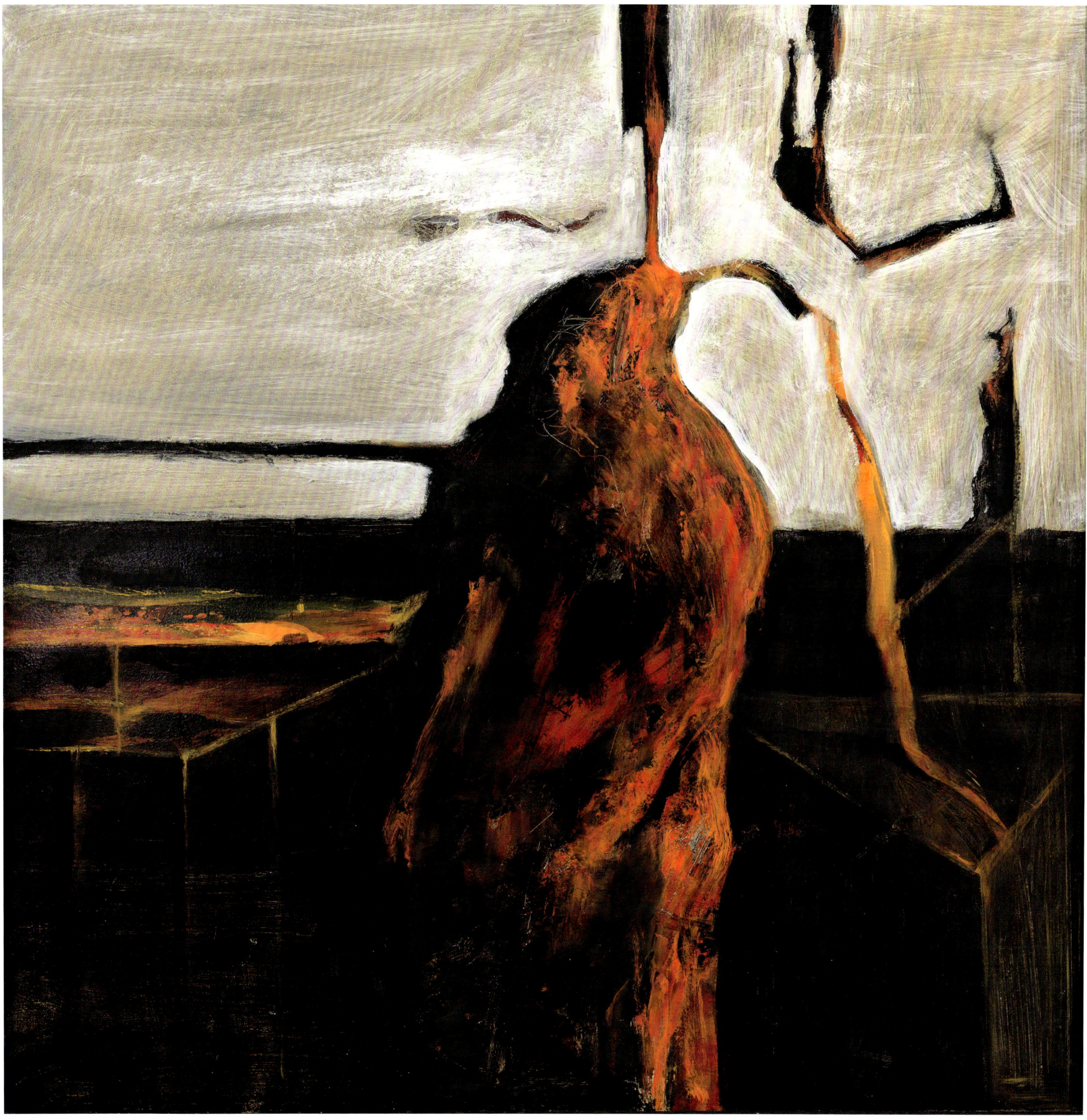

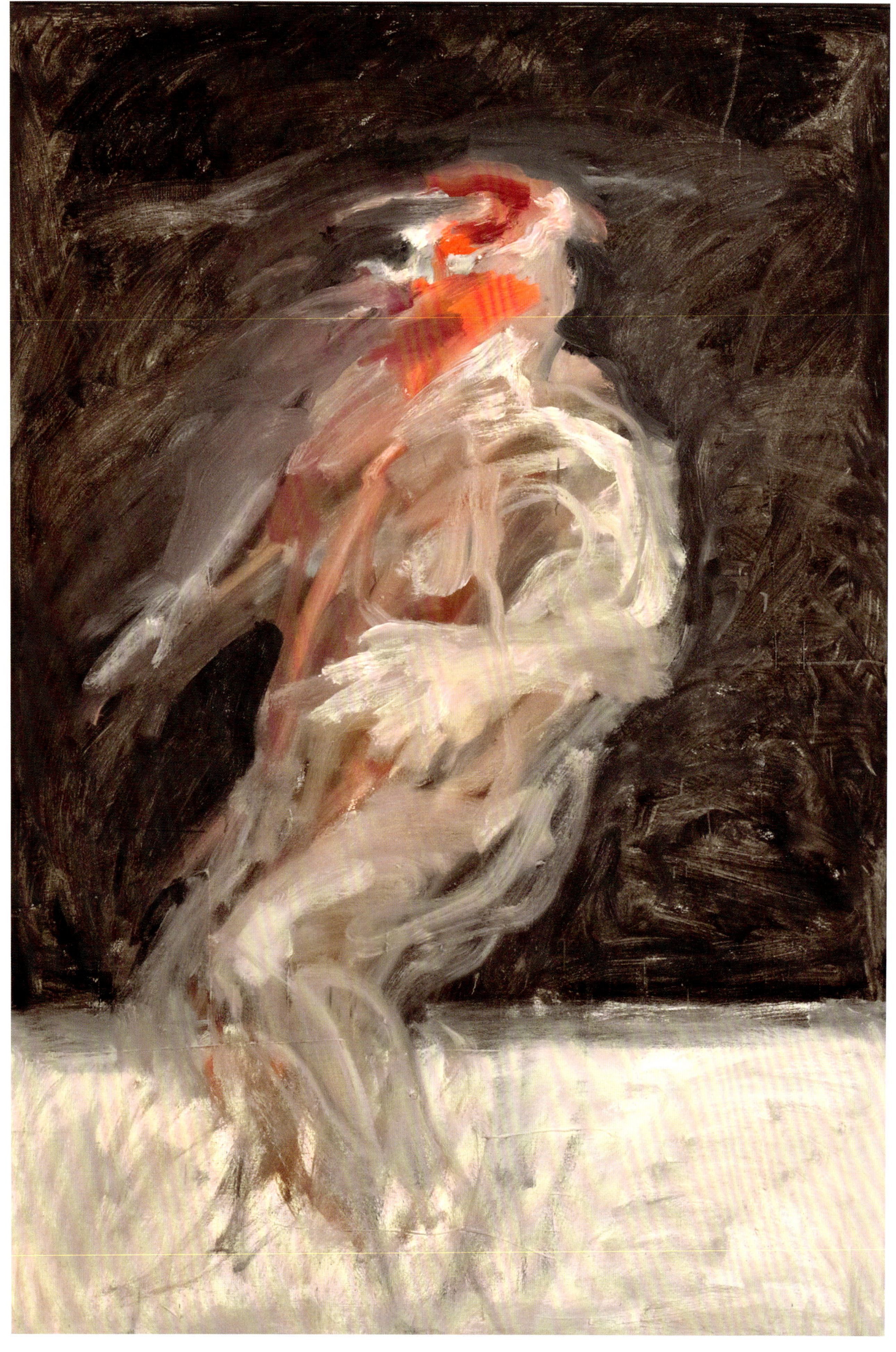

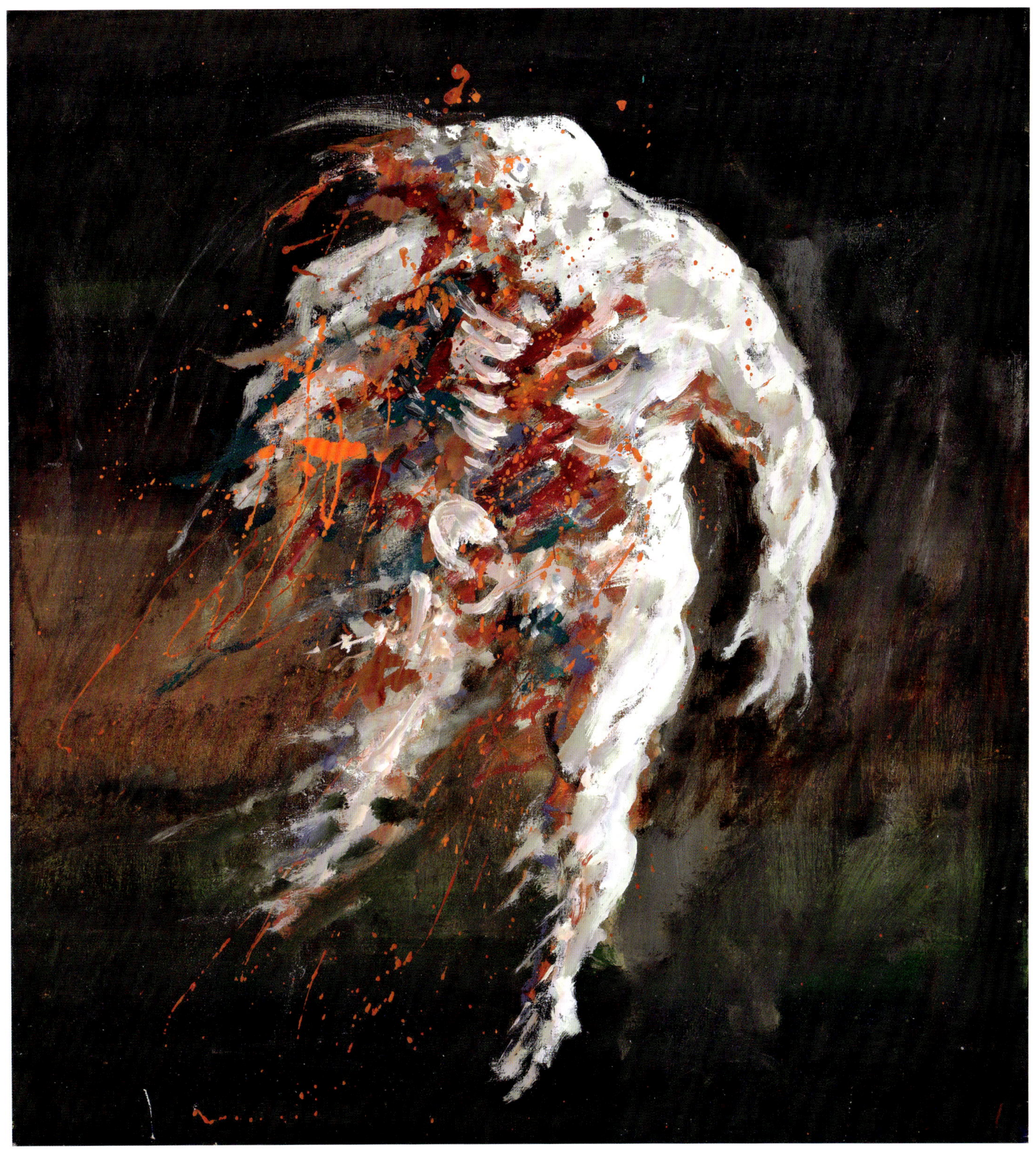

Detonated Man, 1970

Oil on canvas
70 x 46 in. (177.8 x 116.8 cm)
Estate of the artist

PLATE 18

Raw Meat, 1970

Oil on wood
24 x 24 in. (61 x 61 cm)
Estate of the artist

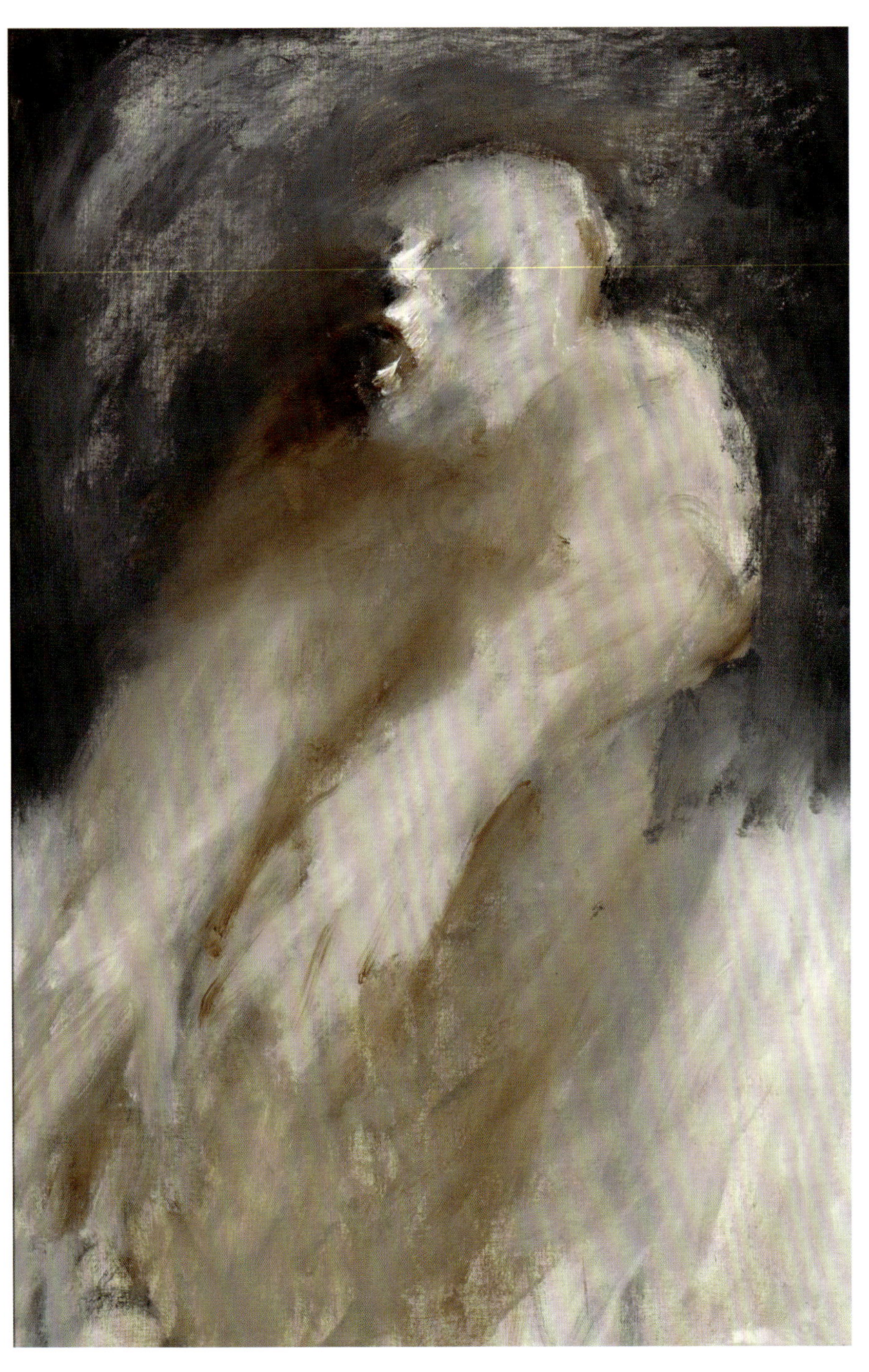

PLATE 19

War Triptych, 1970

Oil on canvas
48 x 36 in. (122 x 91.4 cm)
Estate of the artist

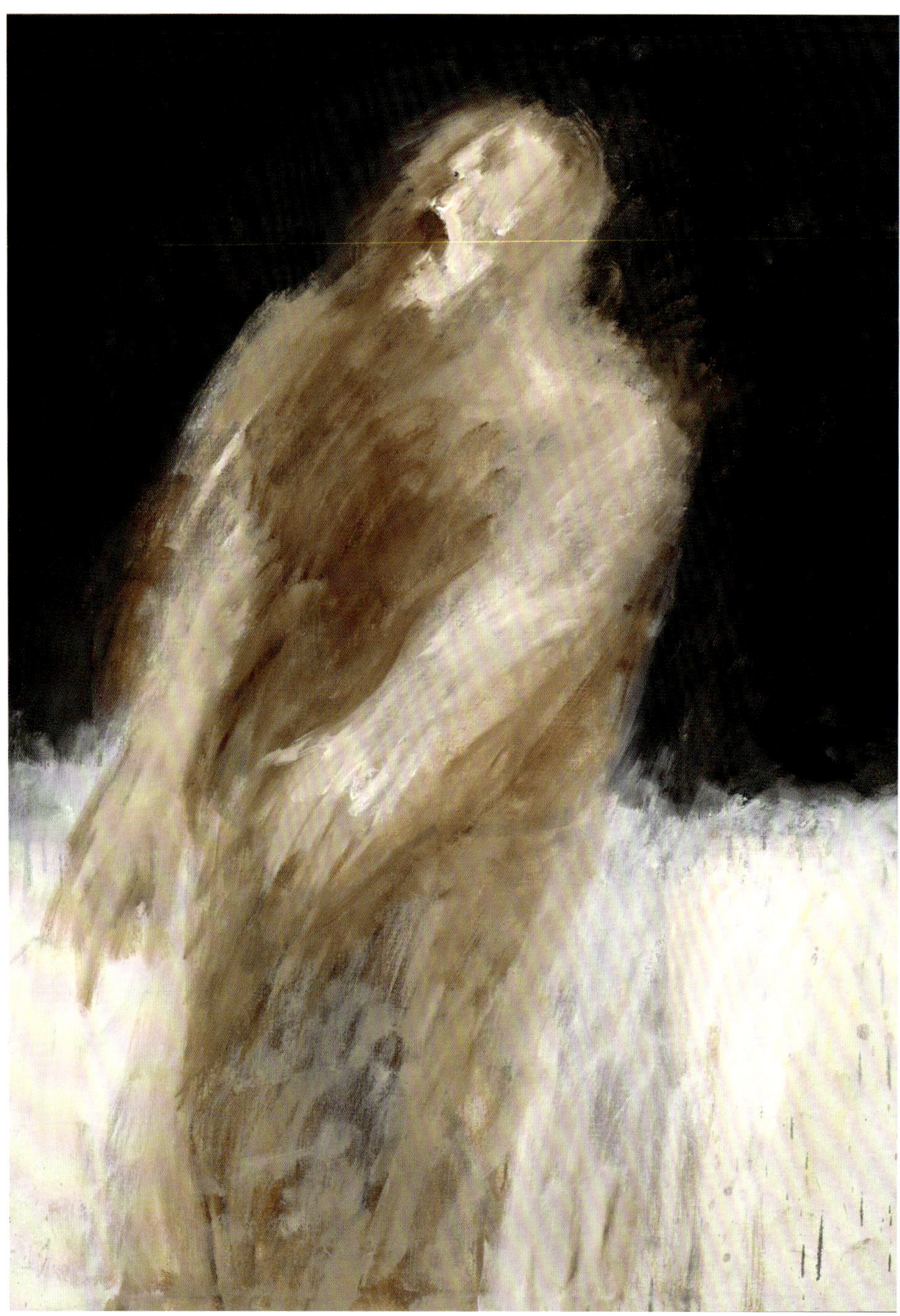

PLATE 20

War Triptych, 1970

Oil on canvas
48 x 36 in. (122 x 91.4 cm)
Estate of the artist

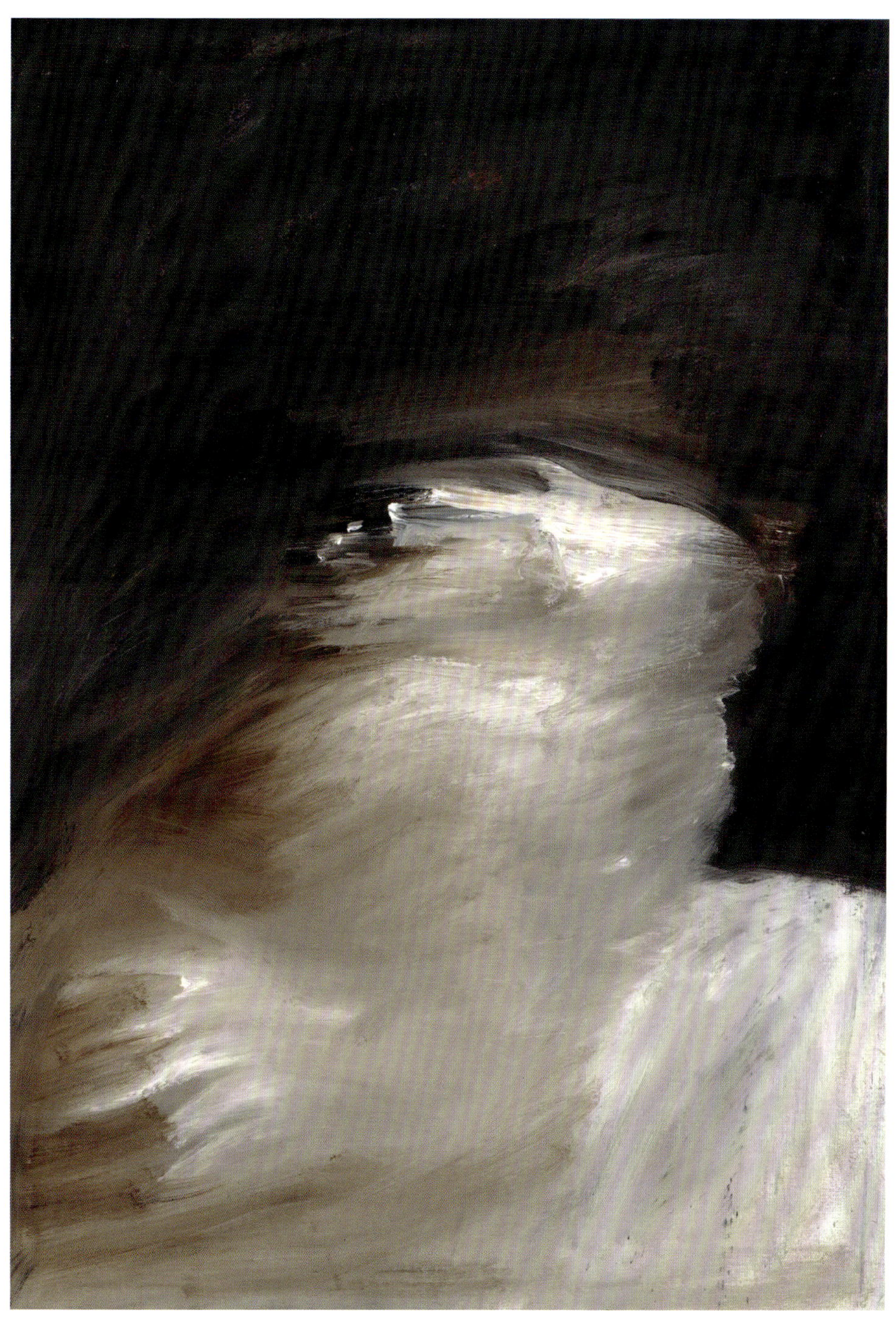

War Triptych, 1970
Oil on canvas
40 x 30 in. (101.6 x 76.2 cm)
Estate of the artist

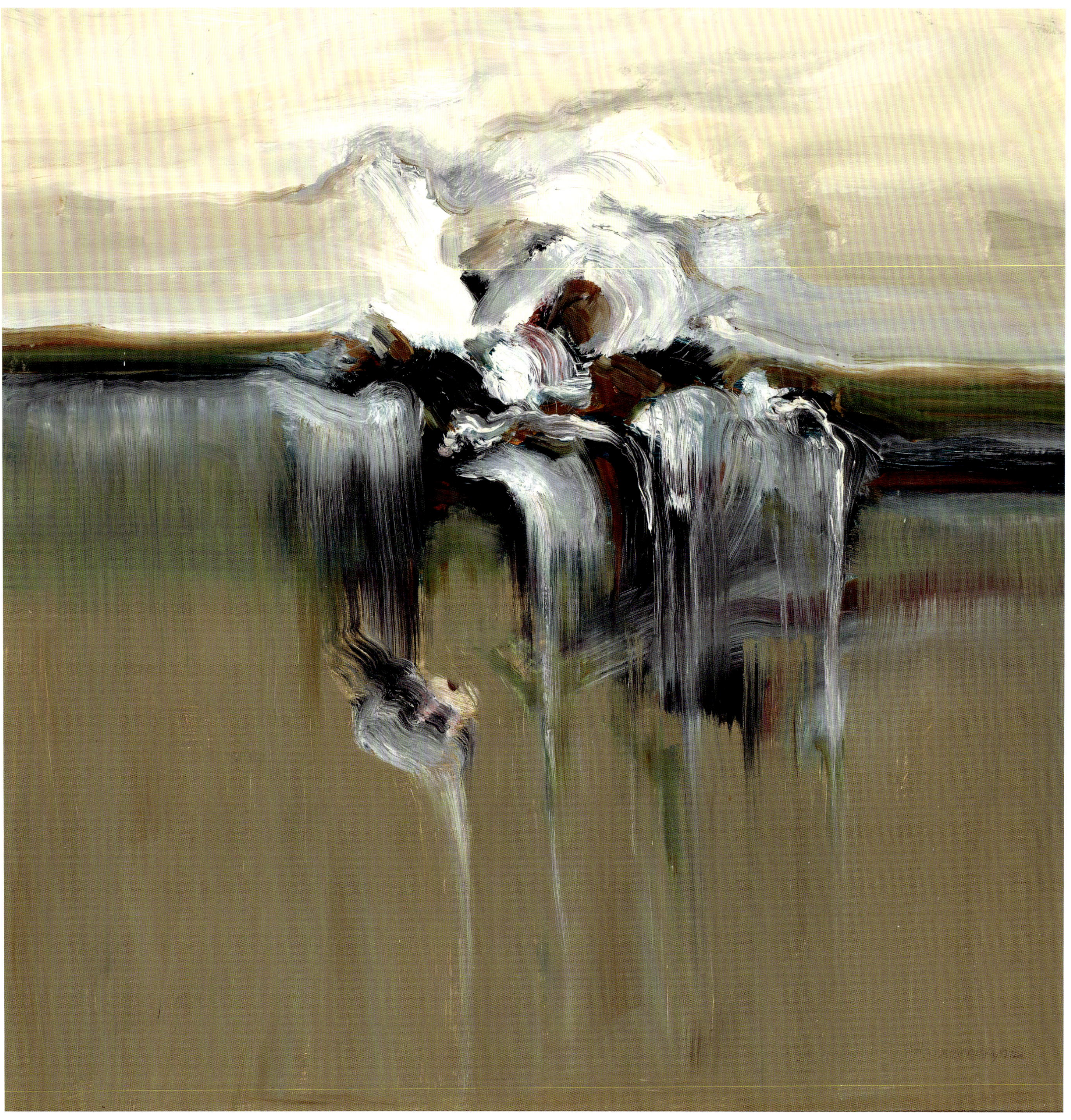

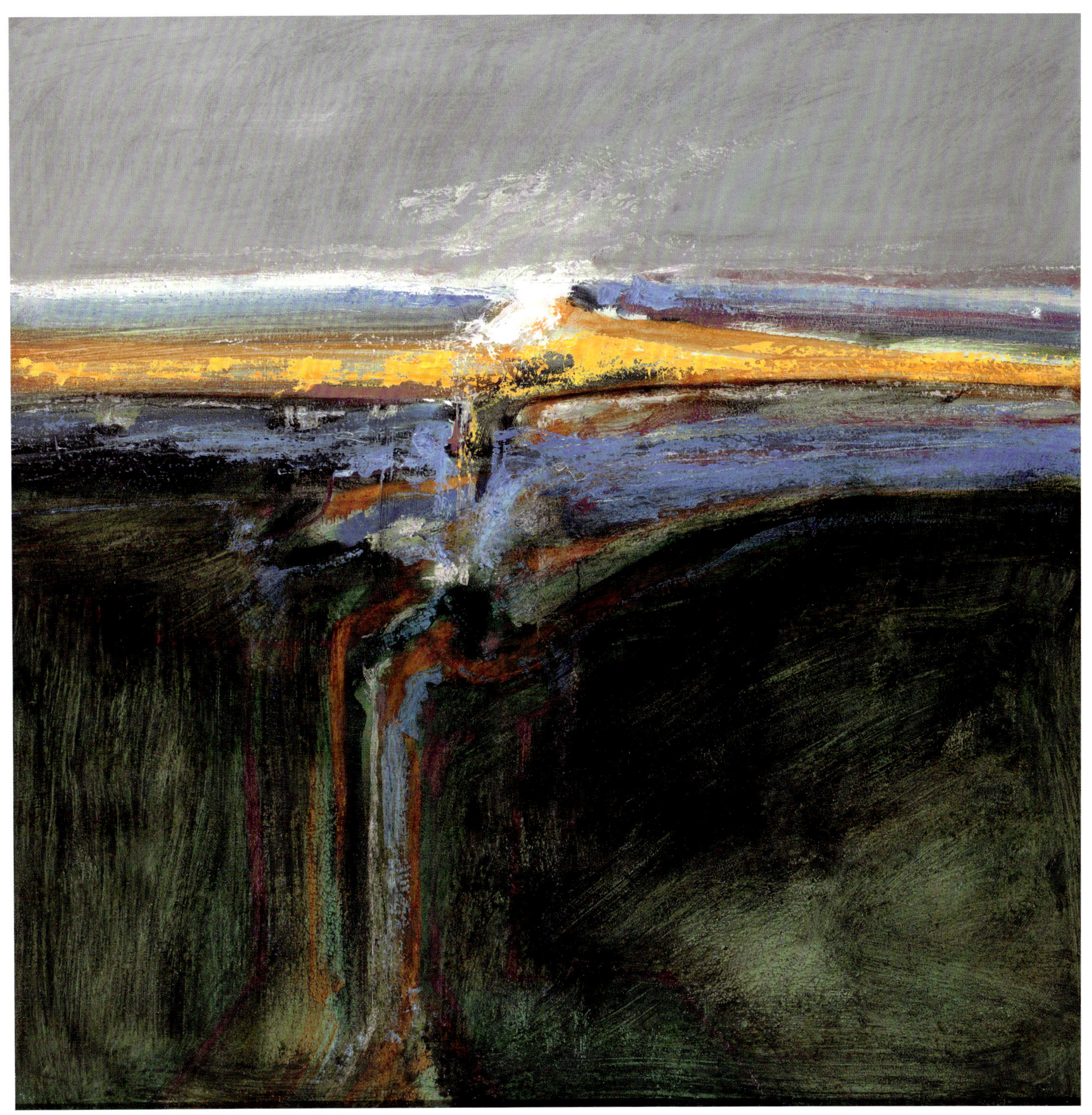

Earth, Sea, and Sky, 1972
Oil on Masonite
24 x 24 in. (61 x 61 cm)
Estate of the artist

Seascape at Sunset, Low Tide, Threatening Sky, 1972
Oil on Masonite
24 x 24 in. (61 x 61 cm)
Estate of the artist

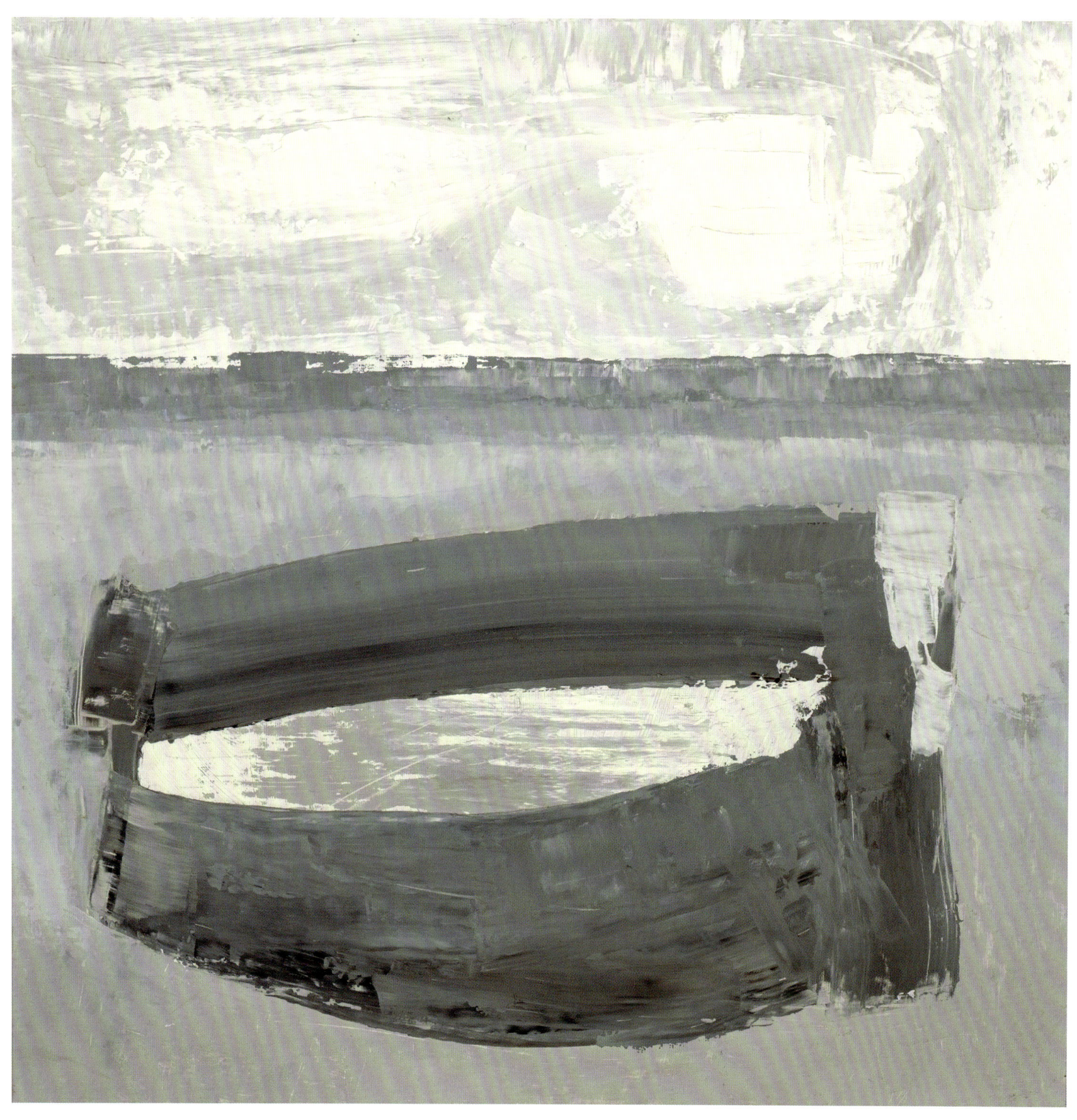

Leviathan, 1974

Oil on Masonite
24 x 24 in. (61 x 61 cm)
Collection of Elisabeth Hodermarsky and Sloan Wilson

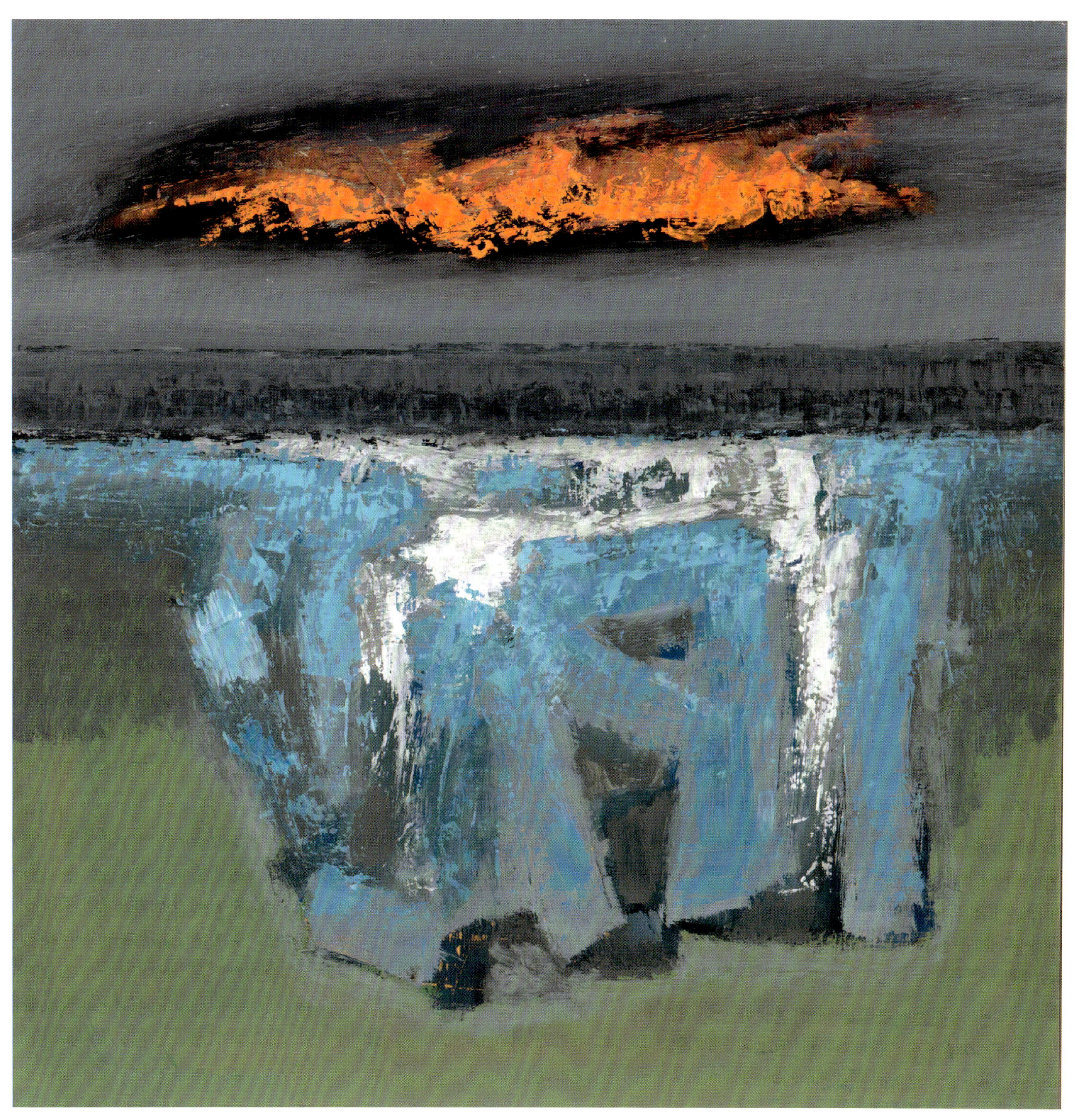

PLATE 25

Red Cloud, 1974
Oil on Masonite
24 x 24 in. (61 x 61 cm)
Estate of the artist

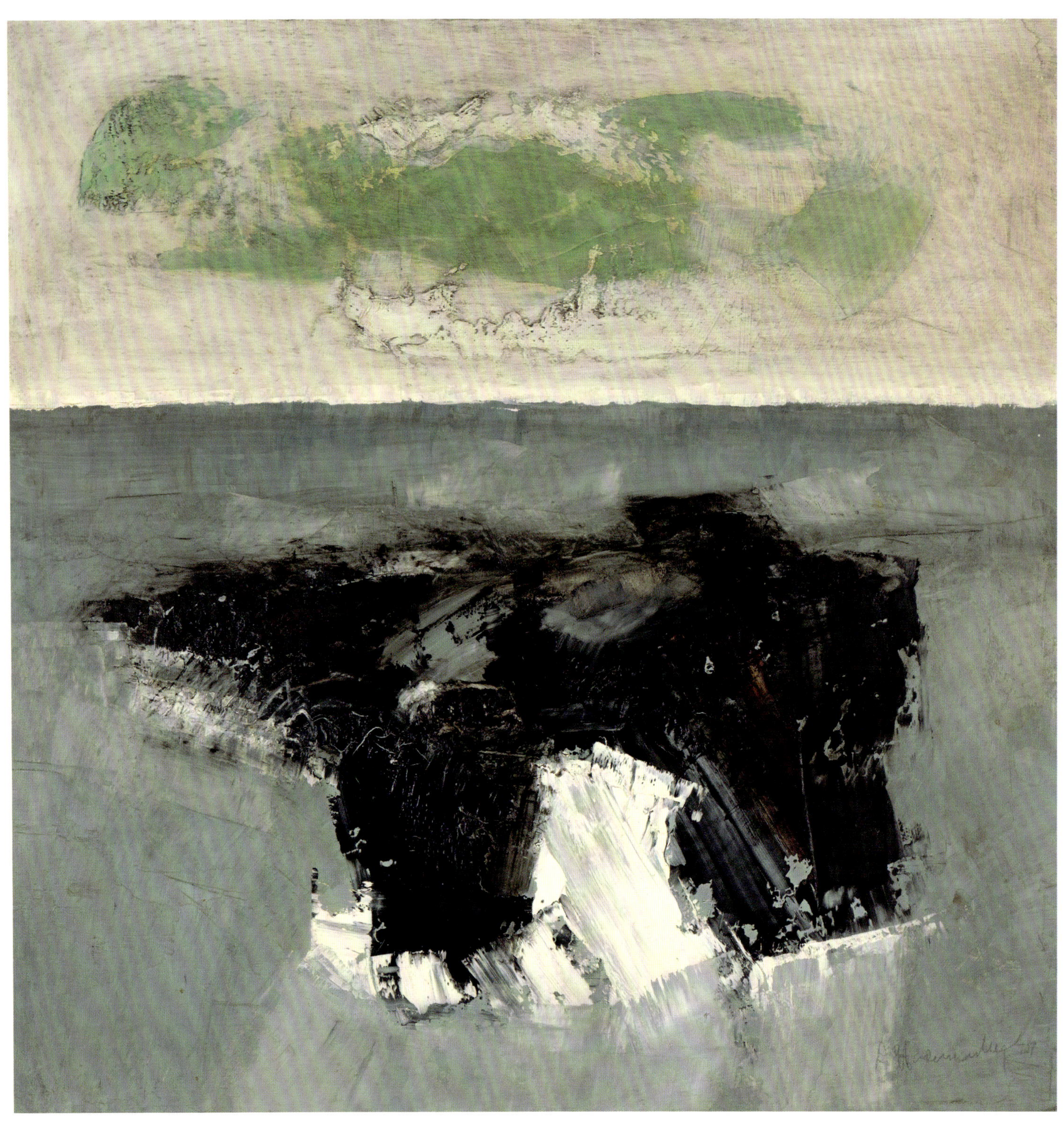

PLATE 26

Untitled, ca. 1974

Oil on Masonite
24 x 24 in. (61 x 61 cm)
Collection of Maria Hodermarska and Penn Rhodeen

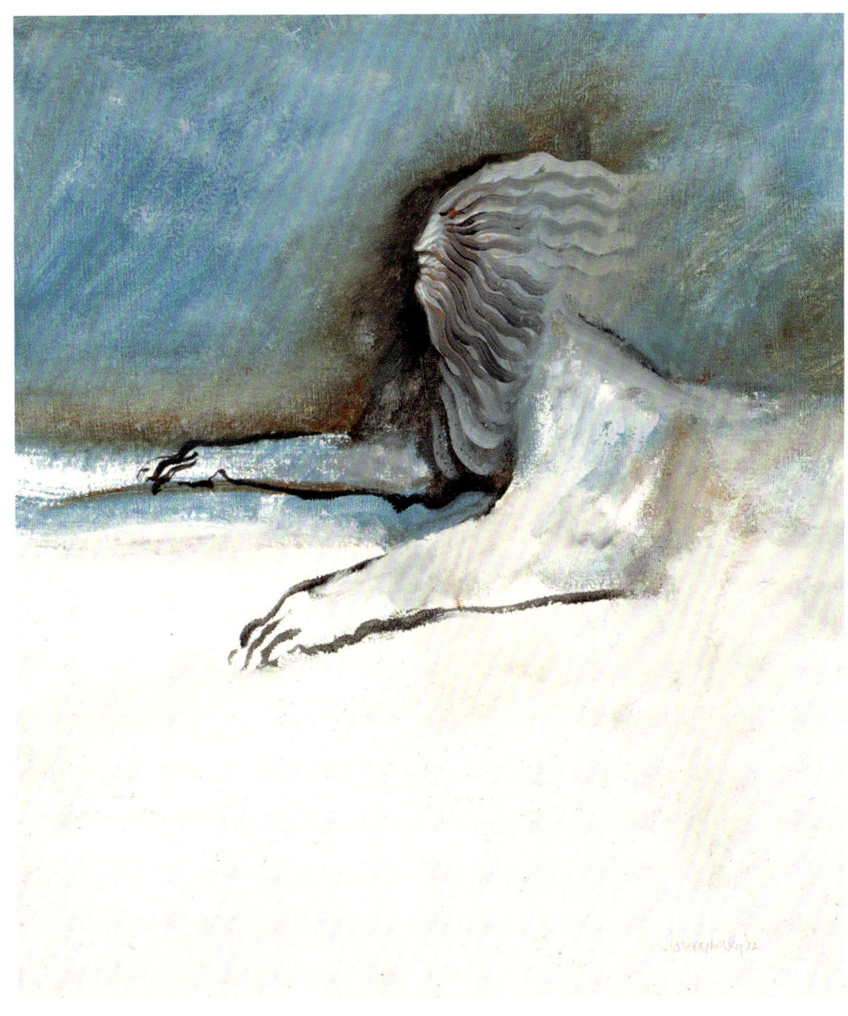

PLATE 27

Reclining Sphinx, 1972

Oil on wood
14 x 12 in. (35.6 x 30.5 cm)
Estate of the artist

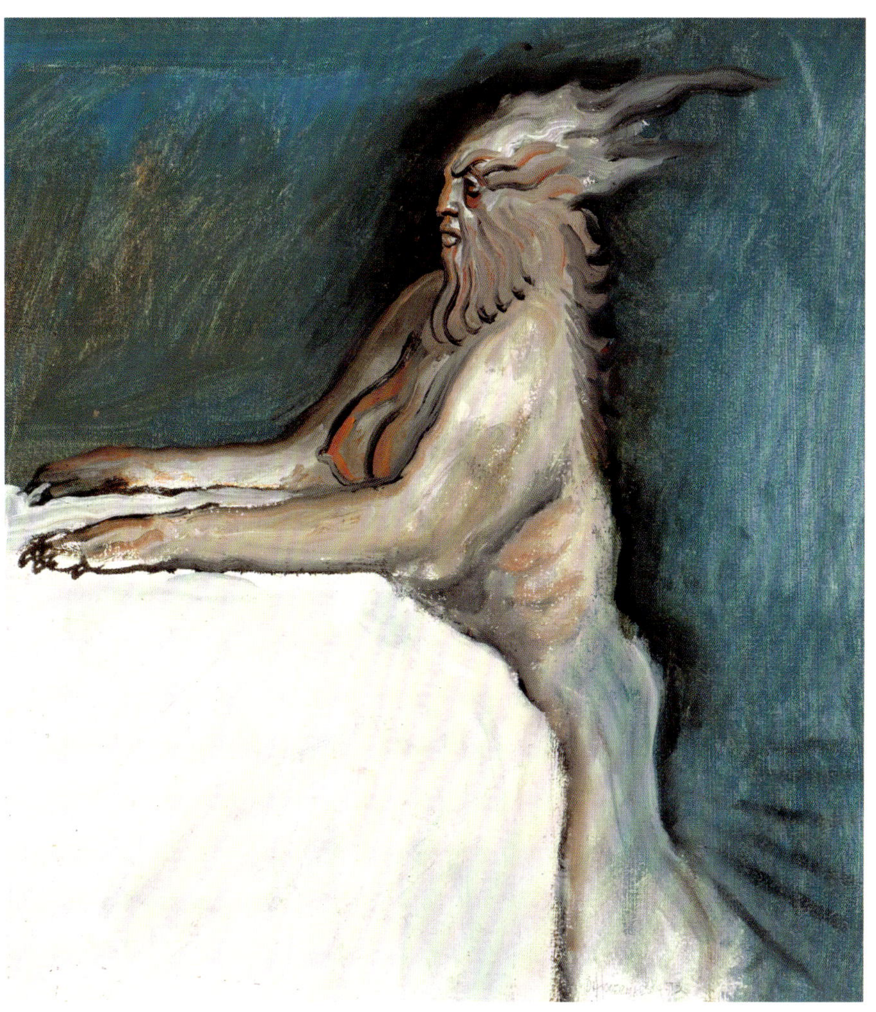

PLATE 28

The Sphinx, 1973

Oil on wood
14 x 12 in. (35.6 x 30.5 cm)
Estate of the artist

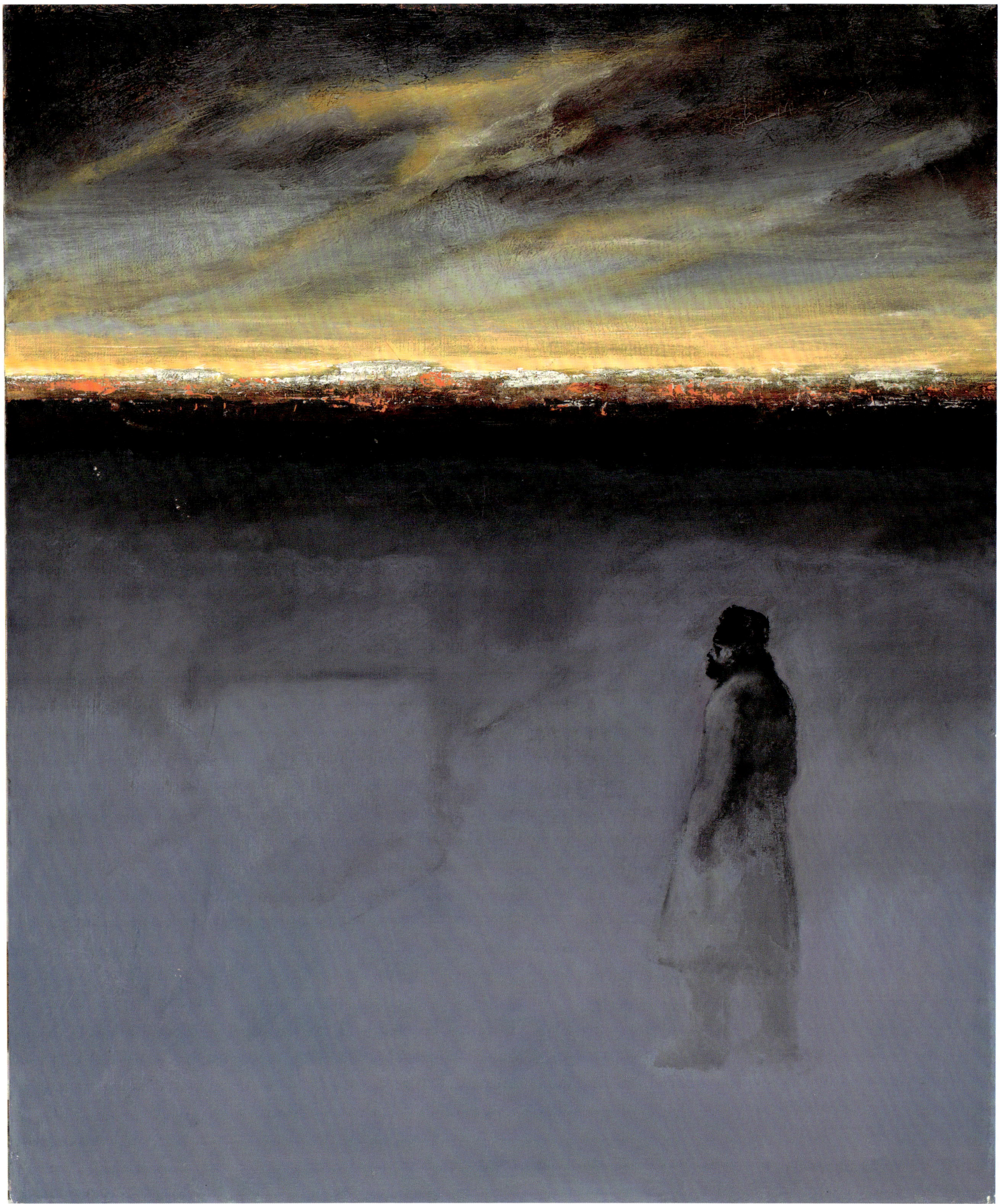

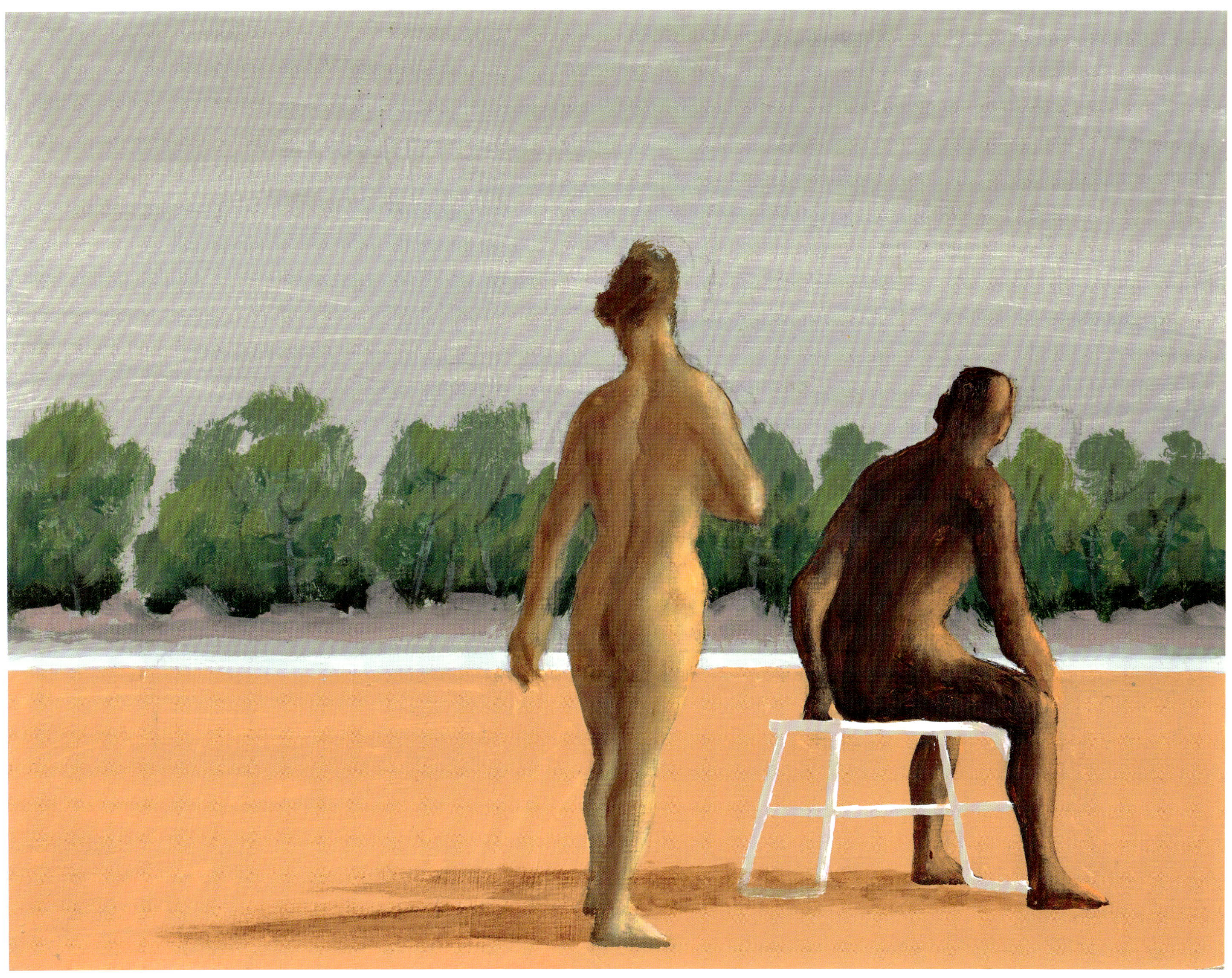

opposite: PLATE 29

Argy on the Gulag, 1987

Oil on canvas
24 x 20 in. (61.3 x 50.8 cm)
Estate of the artist

PLATE 30

Captiva, 1990

Oil on wood
10 x 13¼ in. (25.7 x 33.6 cm)
Estate of the artist

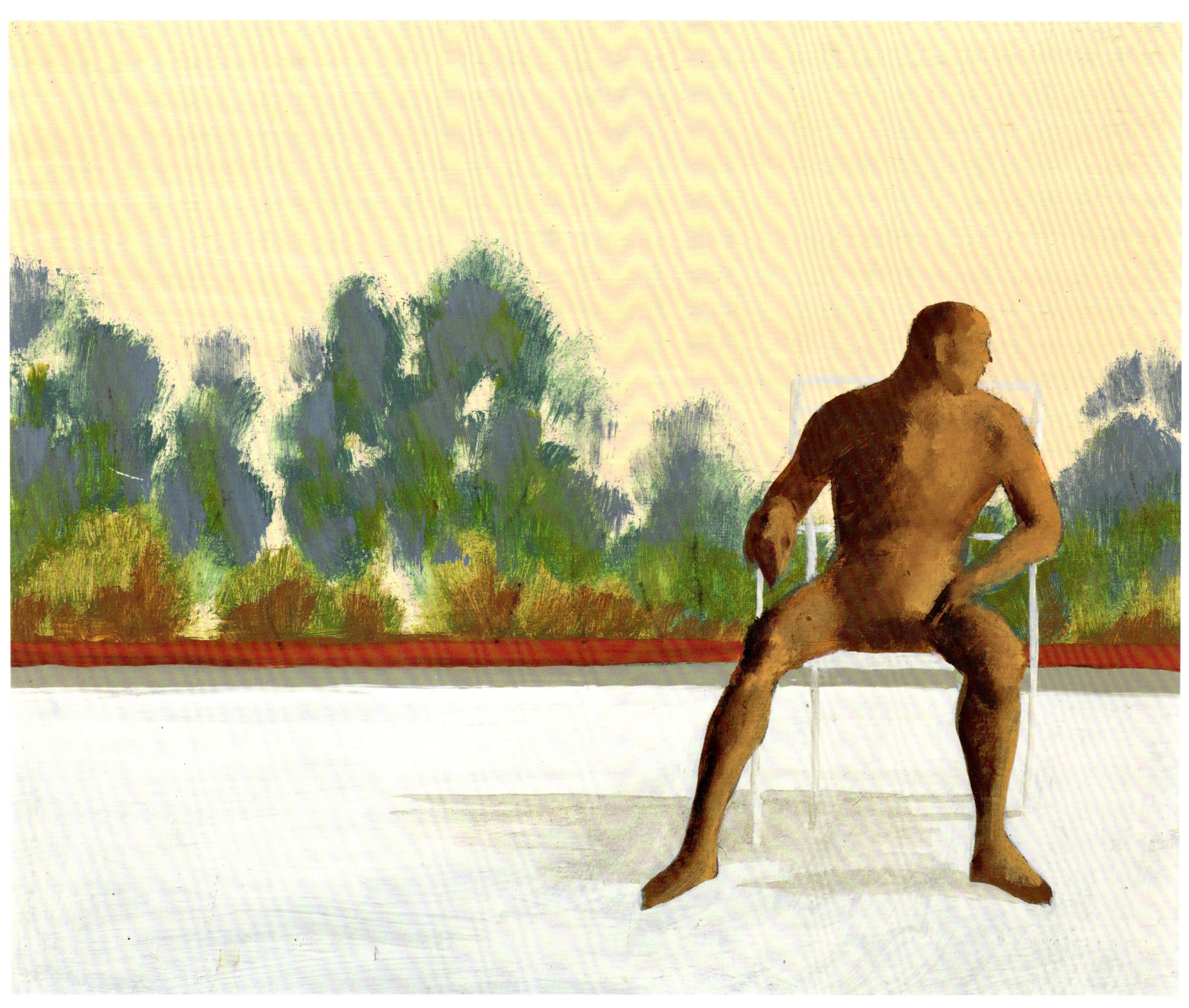

PLATE 31

Member of the Club, 1990

Oil on wood
10 x 12¾ in. (25.7 x 32.4 cm)
Estate of the artist

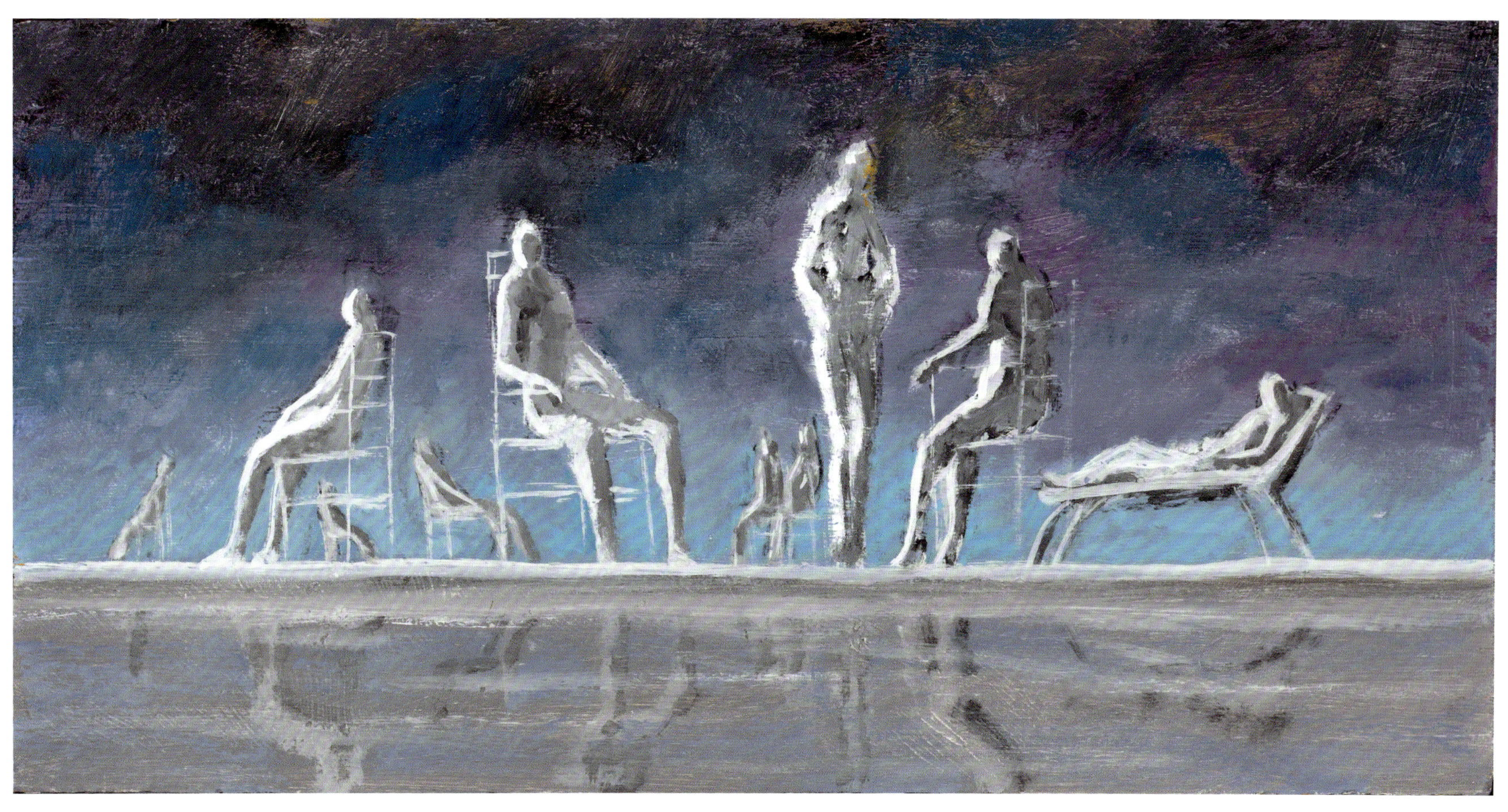

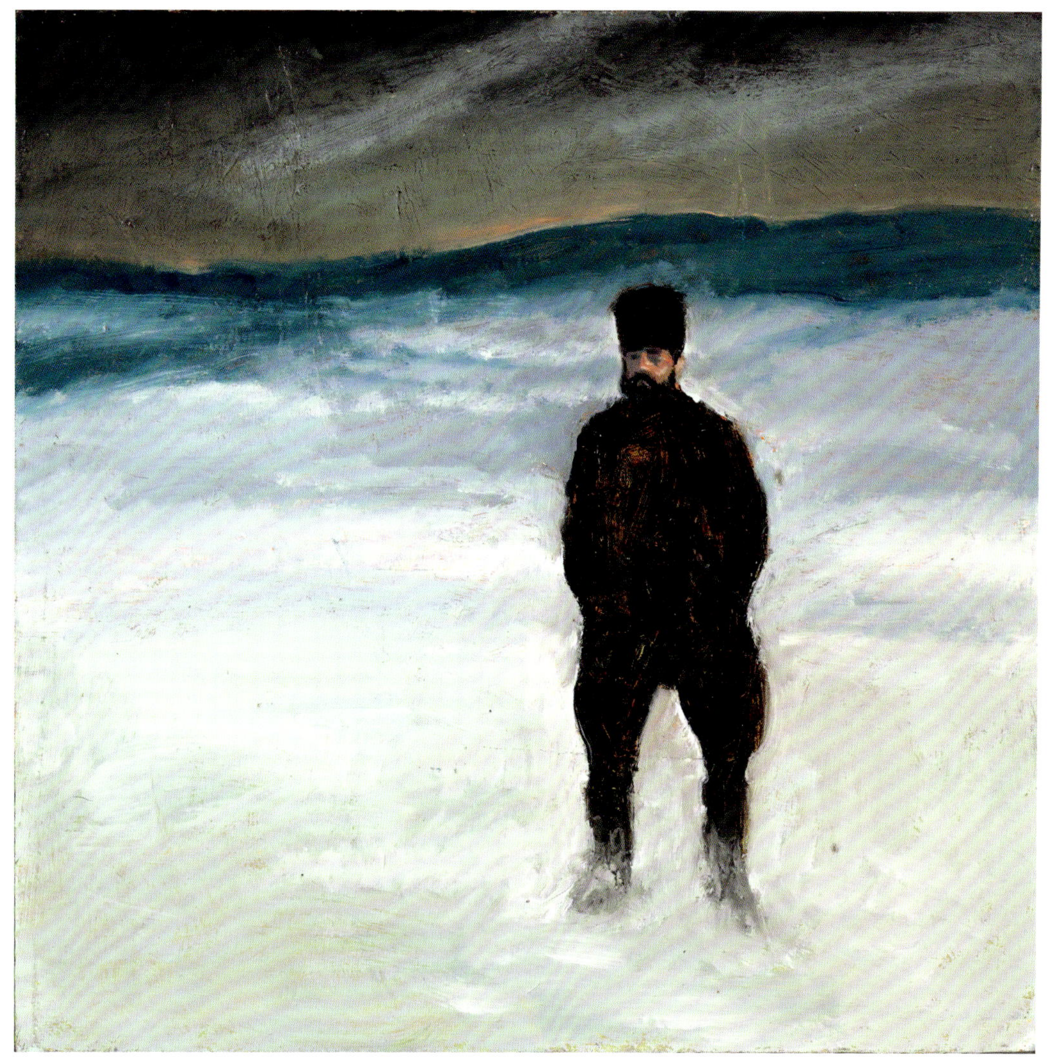

above: PLATE 32

Pale Men on the Beach, 1990

Oil on wood
11 x 23 in. (30.2 x 59.4 cm)
Estate of the artist

right: PLATE 33

Russian Man on Steppes, 1993

Oil on wood
11¾ x 12 in. (29.8 x 30.5 cm)
Estate of the artist

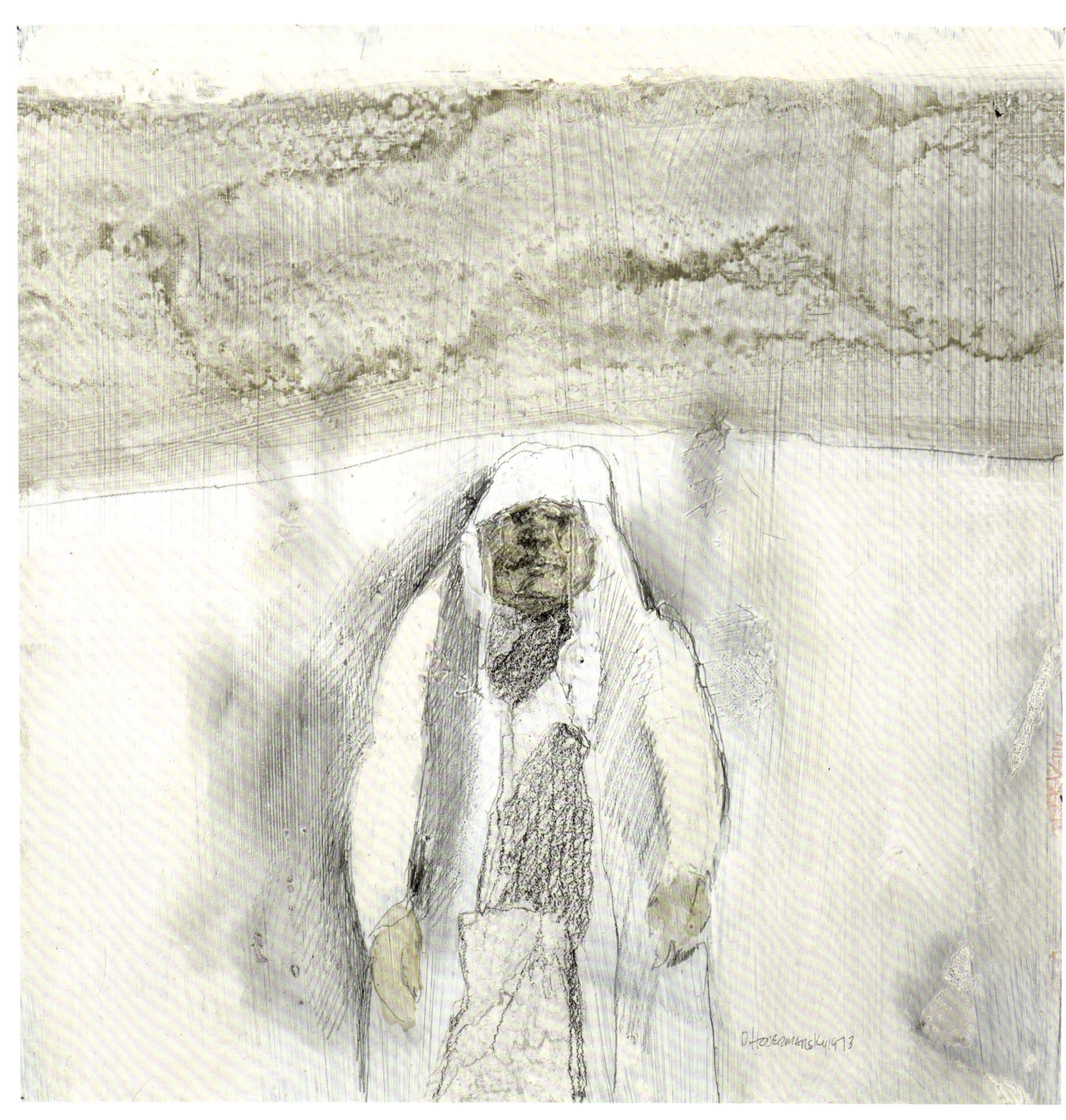

PLATE 34

Aunt Mary, "The Dirty," 1973

Oil on wood
11¾ x 11⅞ in. (29.8 x 30.2 cm)
Estate of the artist

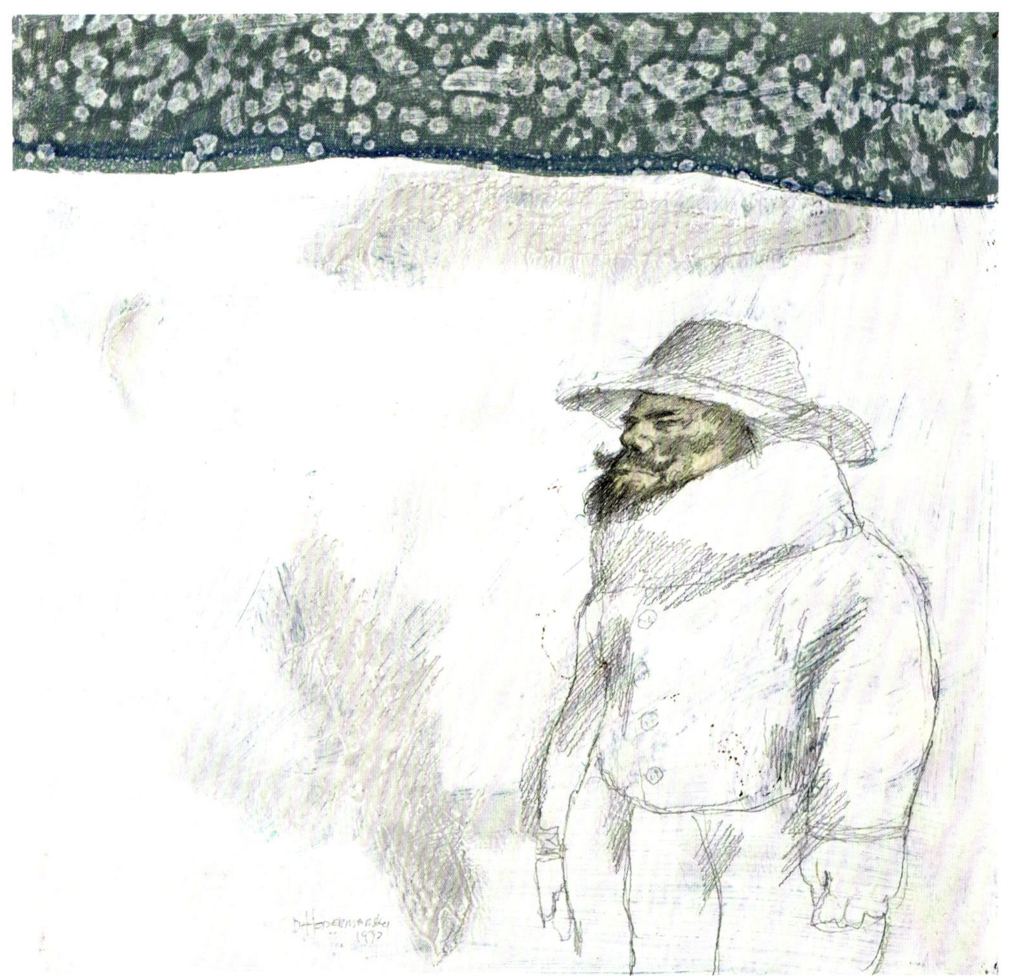

PLATE 35

The Landowner, 1972

Oil on wood
12 x 12 in. (30.5 x 30.5 cm)
Estate of the artist

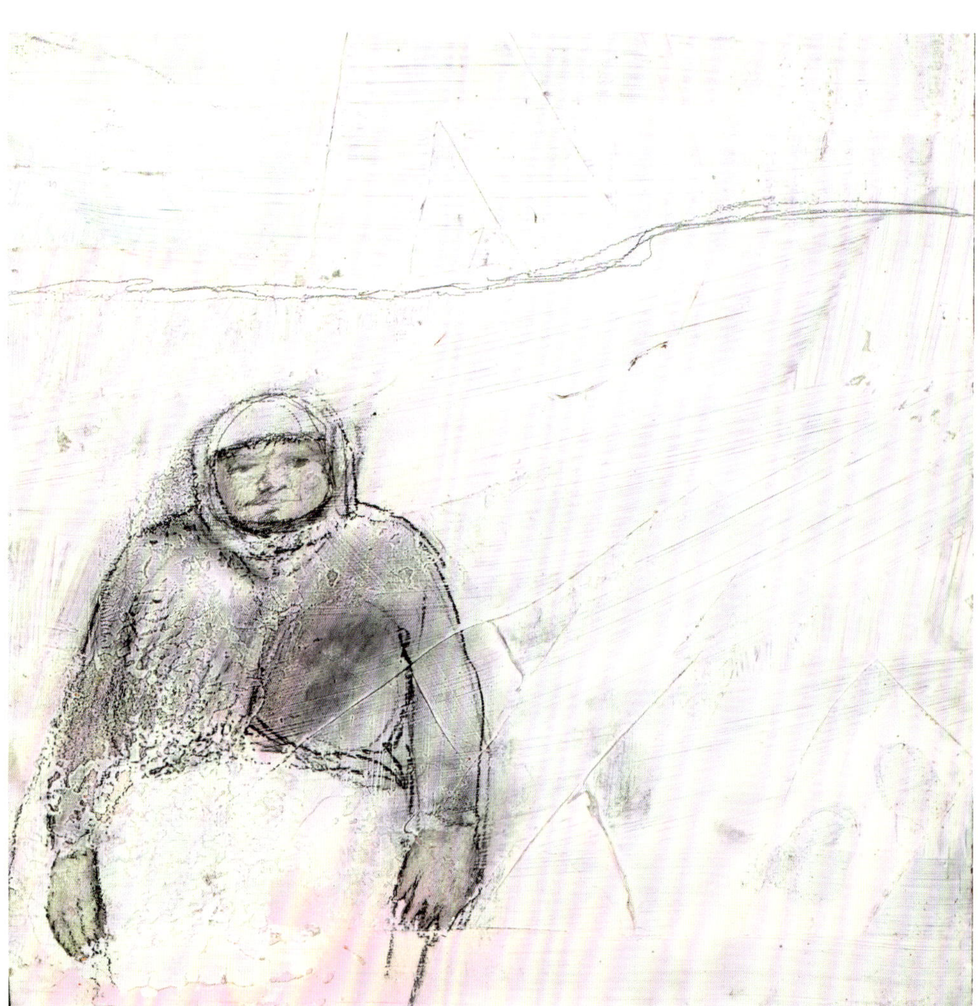

PLATE 36

Mama, 1973

Oil on wood
12 x 12 in. (30.5 x 30.5 cm)
Estate of the artist

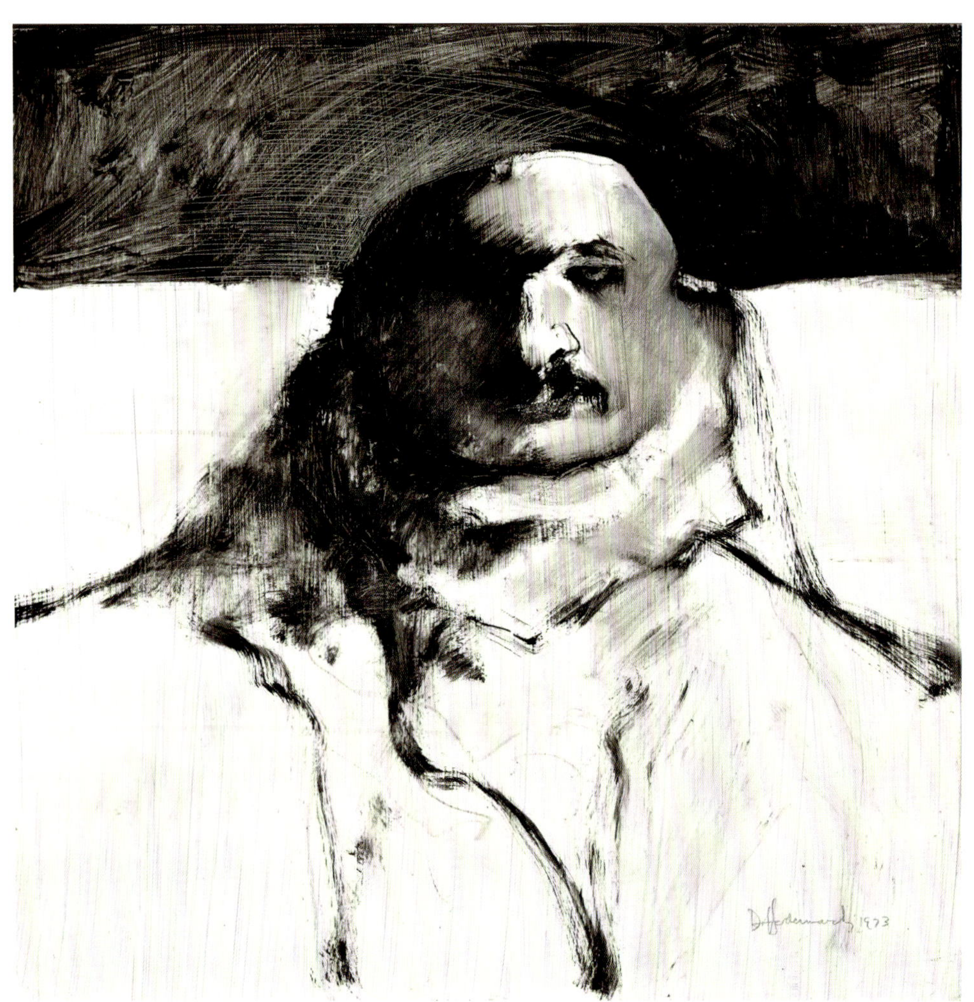

PLATE 37

The Mayor, 1973

Oil on wood
12 x 12 in. (30.5 x 30.5 cm)
Estate of the artist

PLATE 38

Up to His Neck in Winter, 1973

Oil on wood
12 x 12 in. (30.5 x 30.5 cm)
Estate of the artist

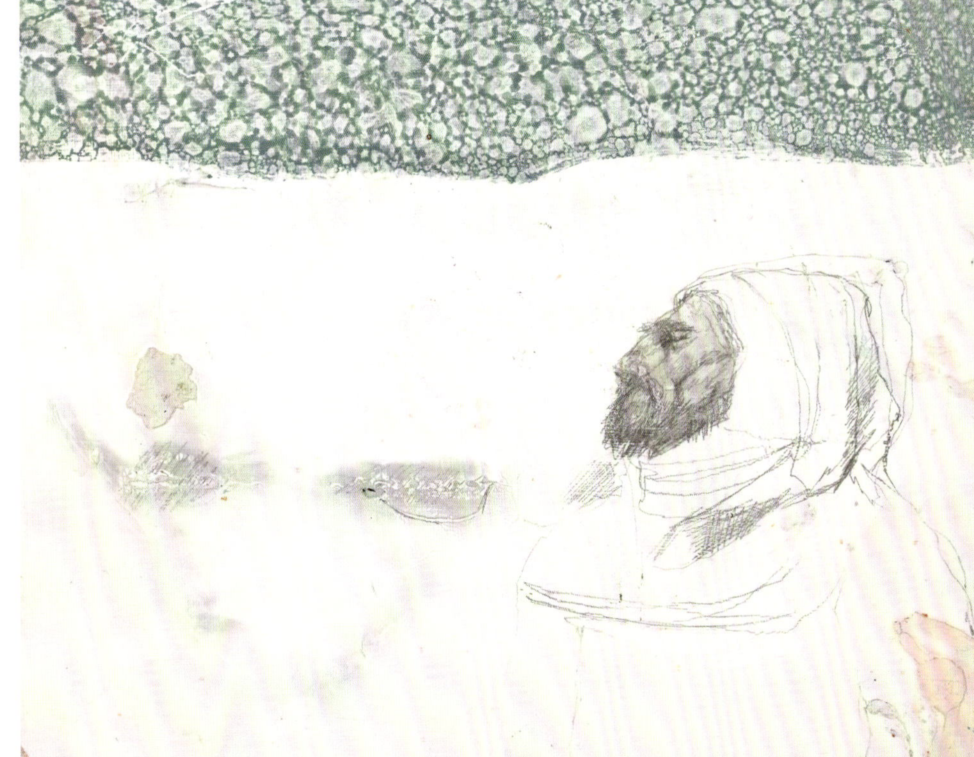

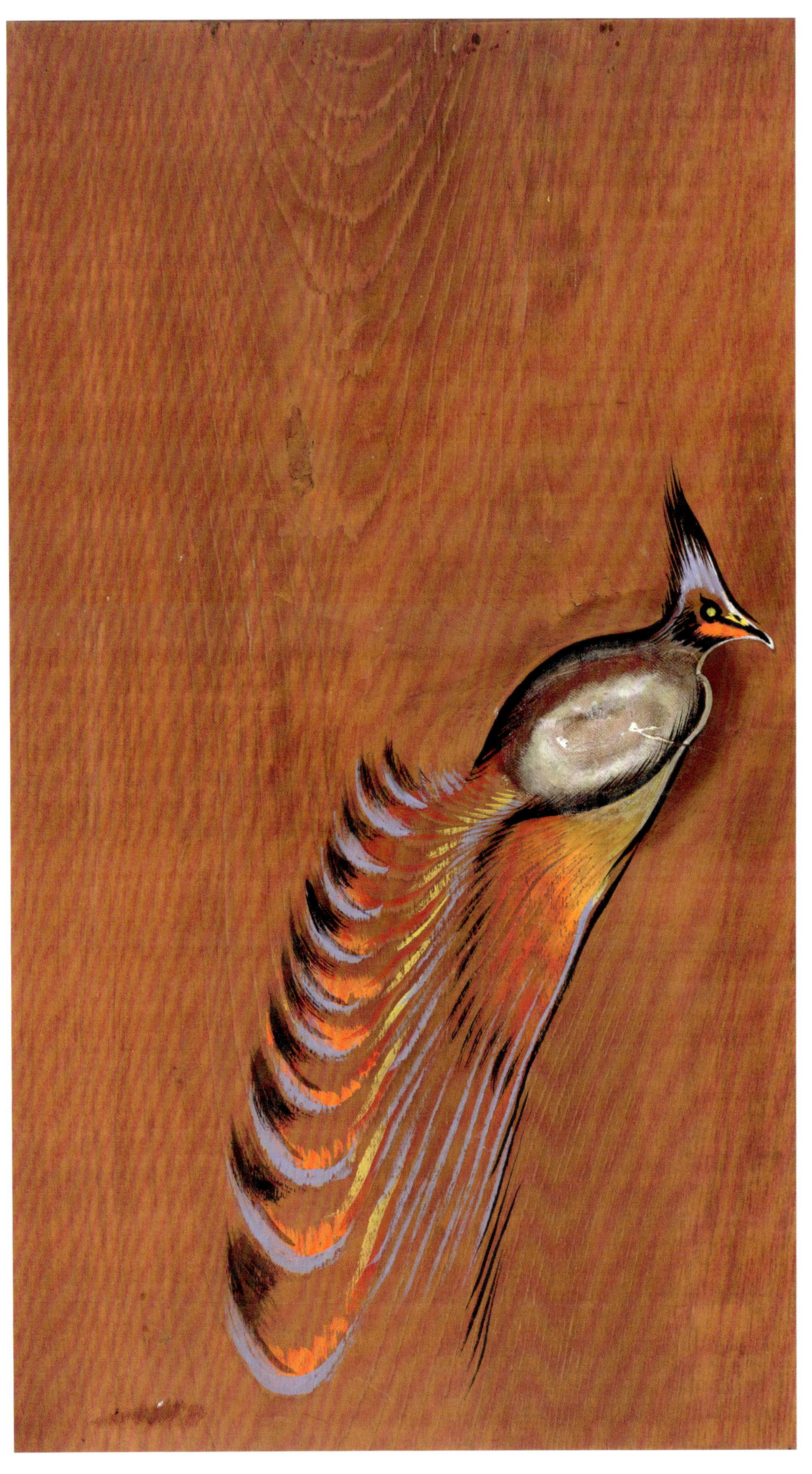

Blue Jay Rising from Fire, 1974

Oil on wood
11 x 6½ in. (27.9 x 16.5 cm)
Estate of the artist

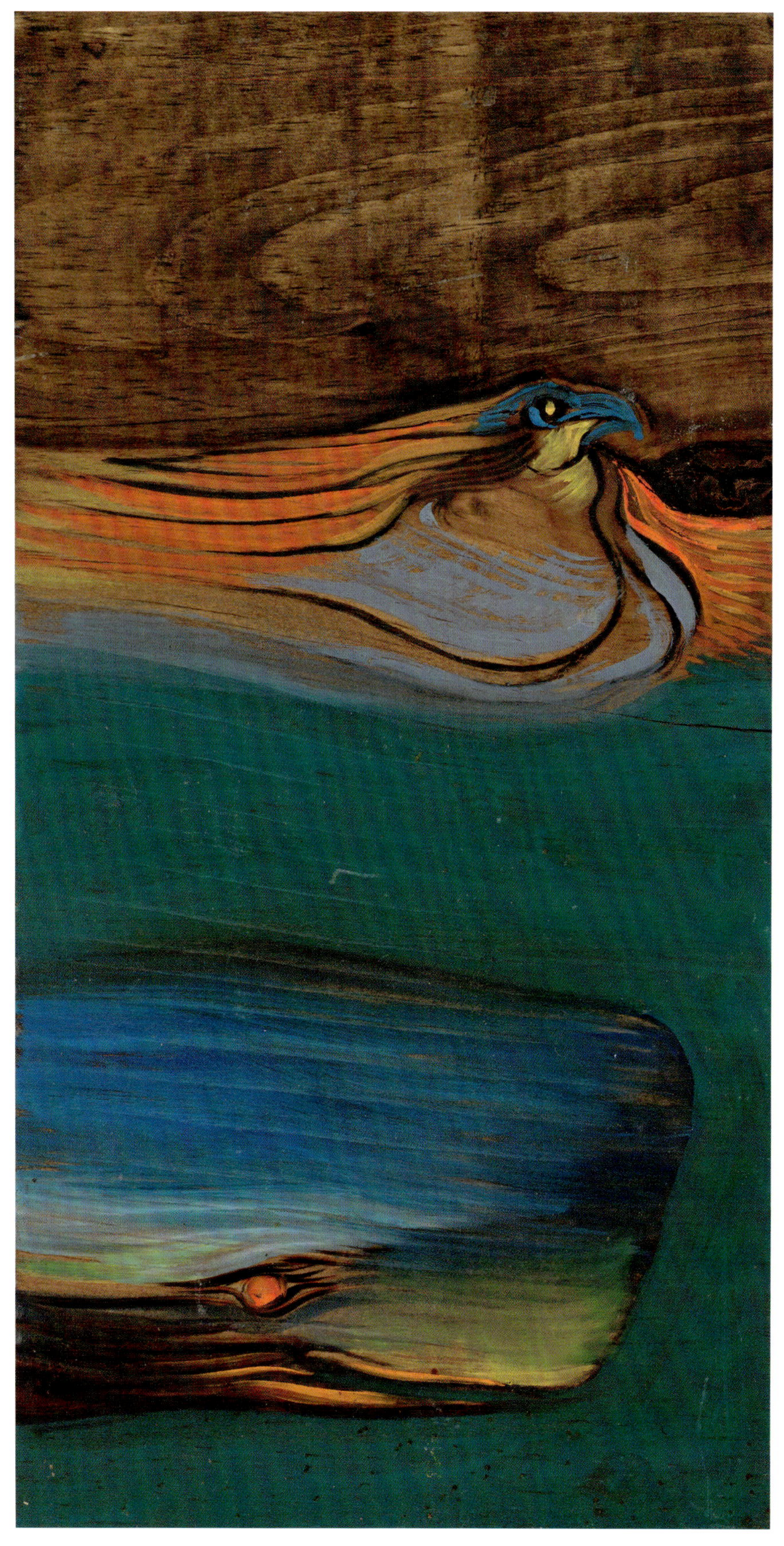

PLATE 40

Duck and Whale, 1974

Oil on wood
10⅞ x 5⅝ in. (27.6 x 14.3 cm)
Estate of the artist

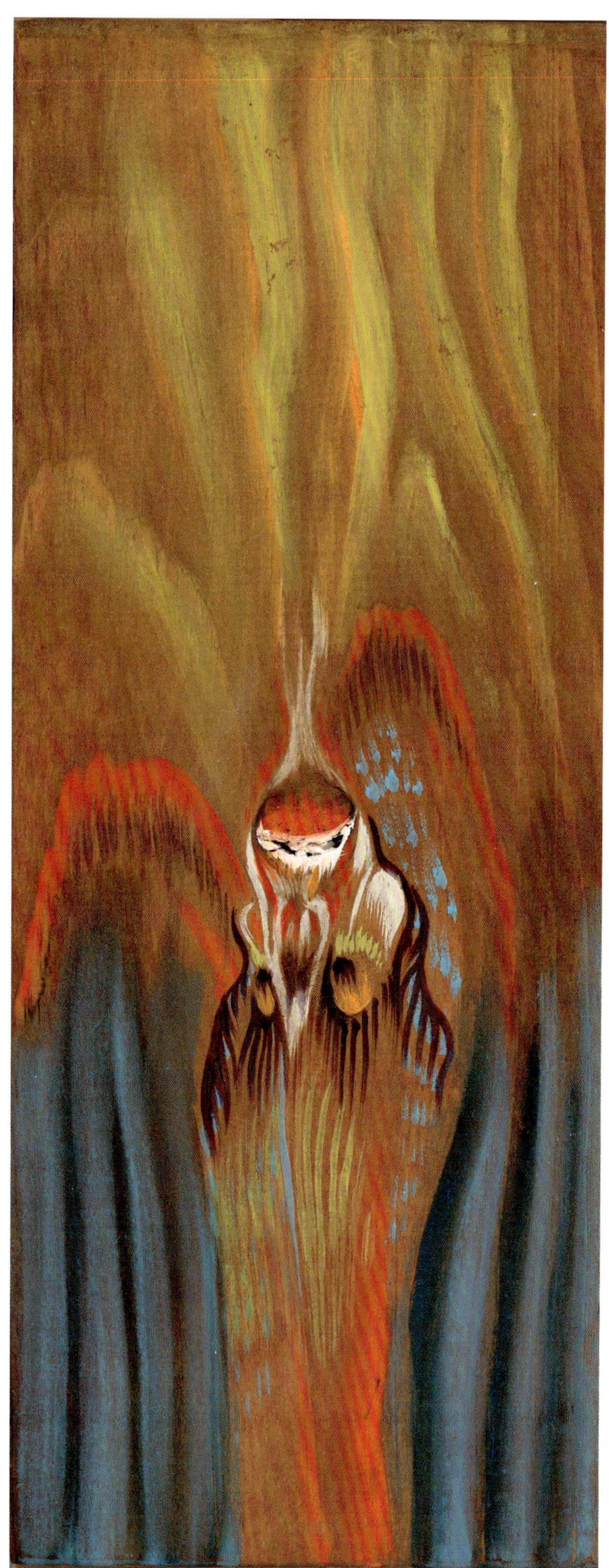

PLATE 41

Mighty Indian Bird, 1974

Oil on wood
11 x 4⅜ in. (27.9 x 11 cm)
Estate of the artist

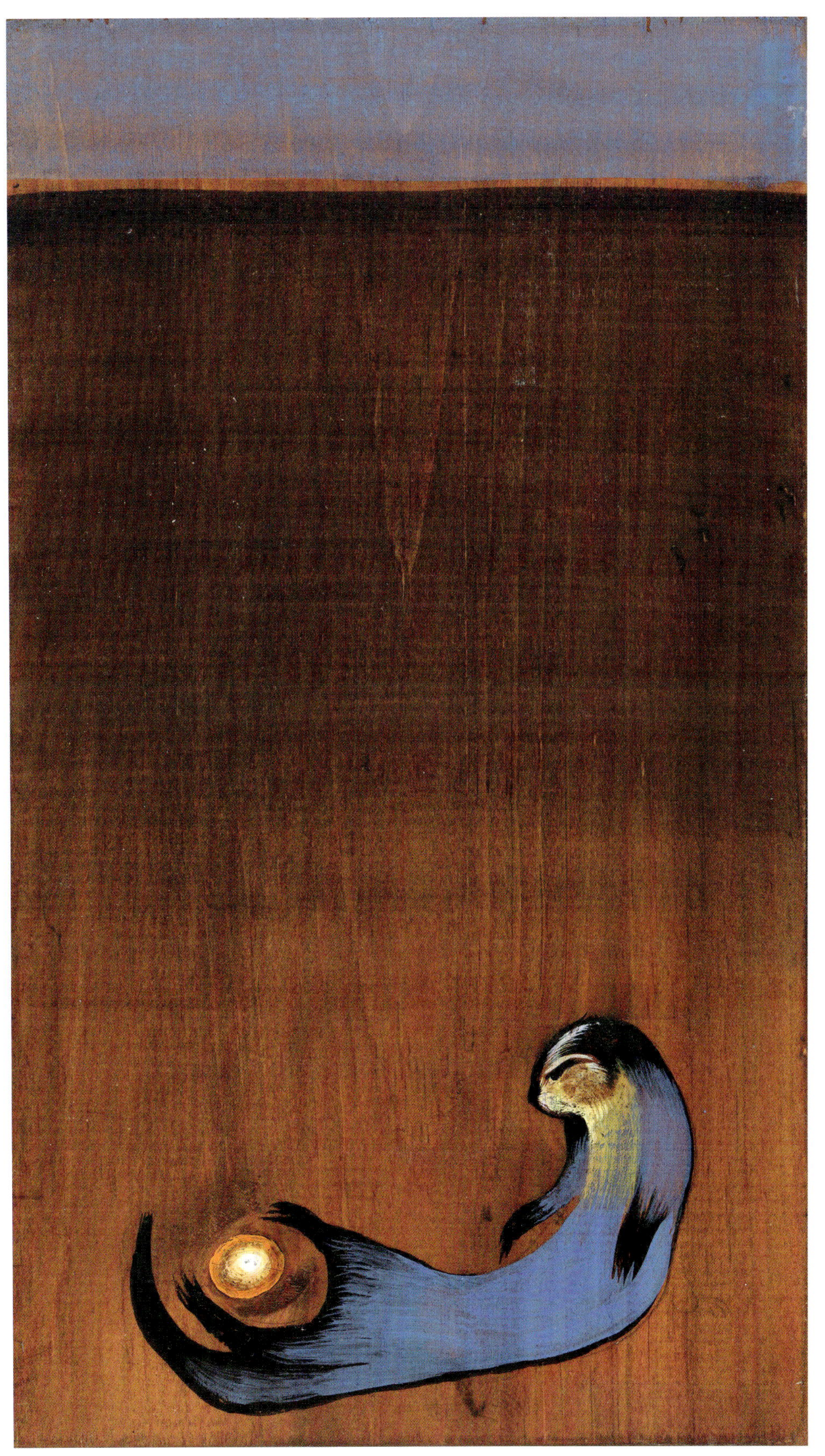

PLATE 42

Otter Holding the Moon, 1974

Oil on wood
12½ x 7⅛ in. (31.7 x 18.1 cm)
Estate of the artist

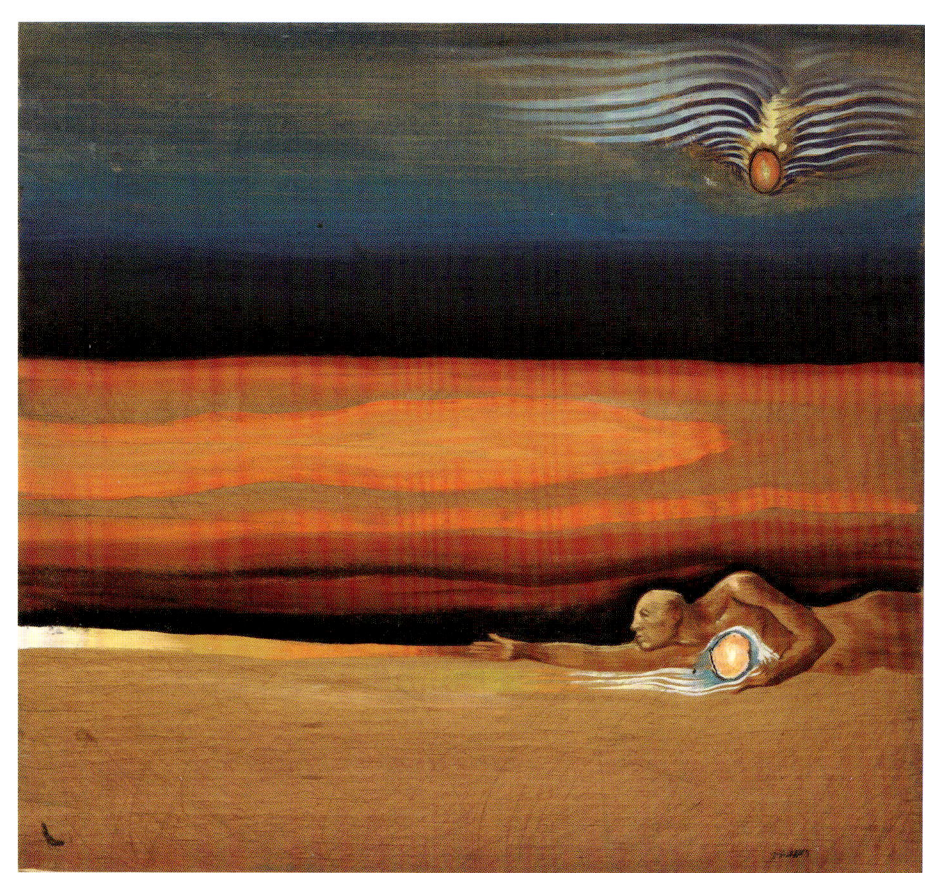

PLATE 43

Penobscot Spirit, Sunset Moonrise, 1974

Oil on wood
9 ¼ x 10 ⅛ in. (23.5 x 25.7 cm)
Estate of the artist

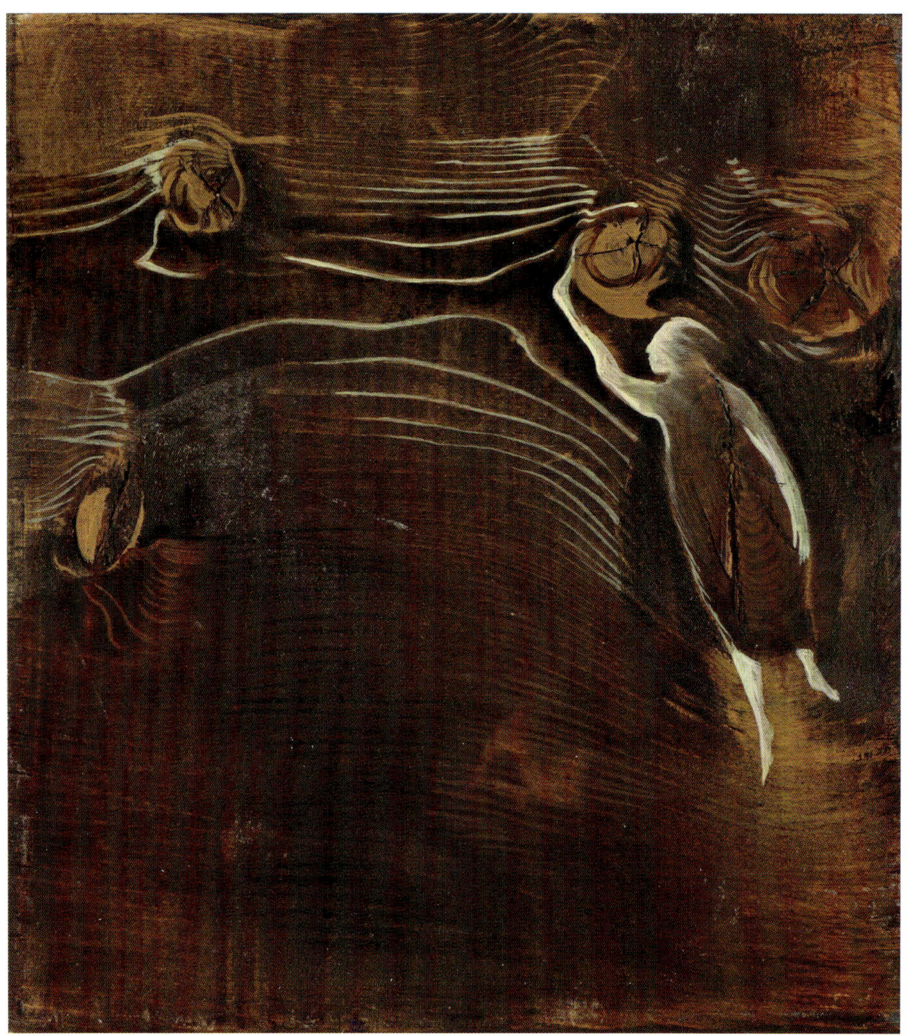

PLATE 44

Penobscot Woman Reaching for the Moon, 1974

Oil on wood
7⅜ x 6¾ in. (18.7 x 17.1 cm)
Estate of the artist

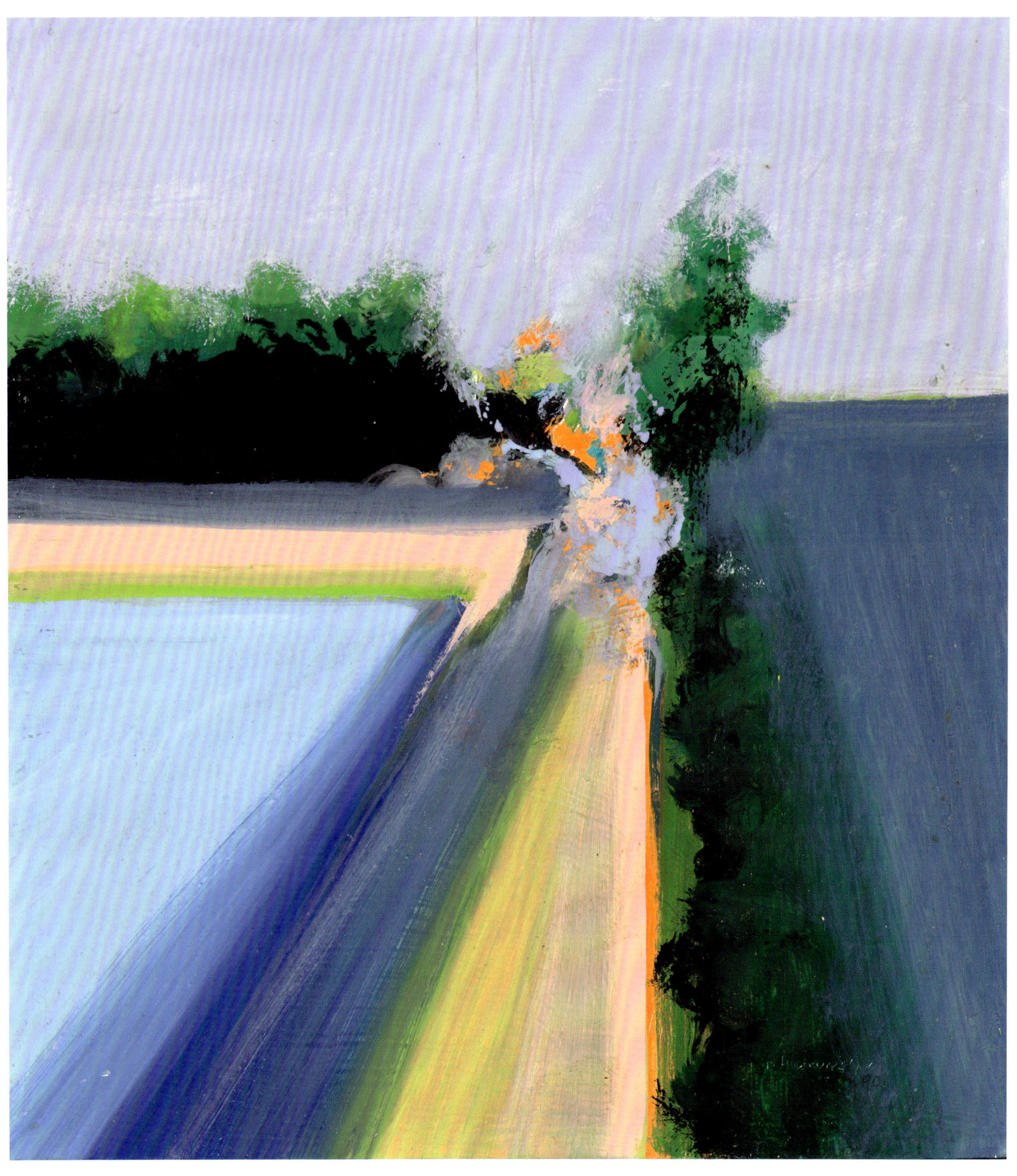

To the Edge of the Sea, 1990

Oil on wood
11¾ x 10⅝ in. (29.8 x 27 cm)
Estate of the artist

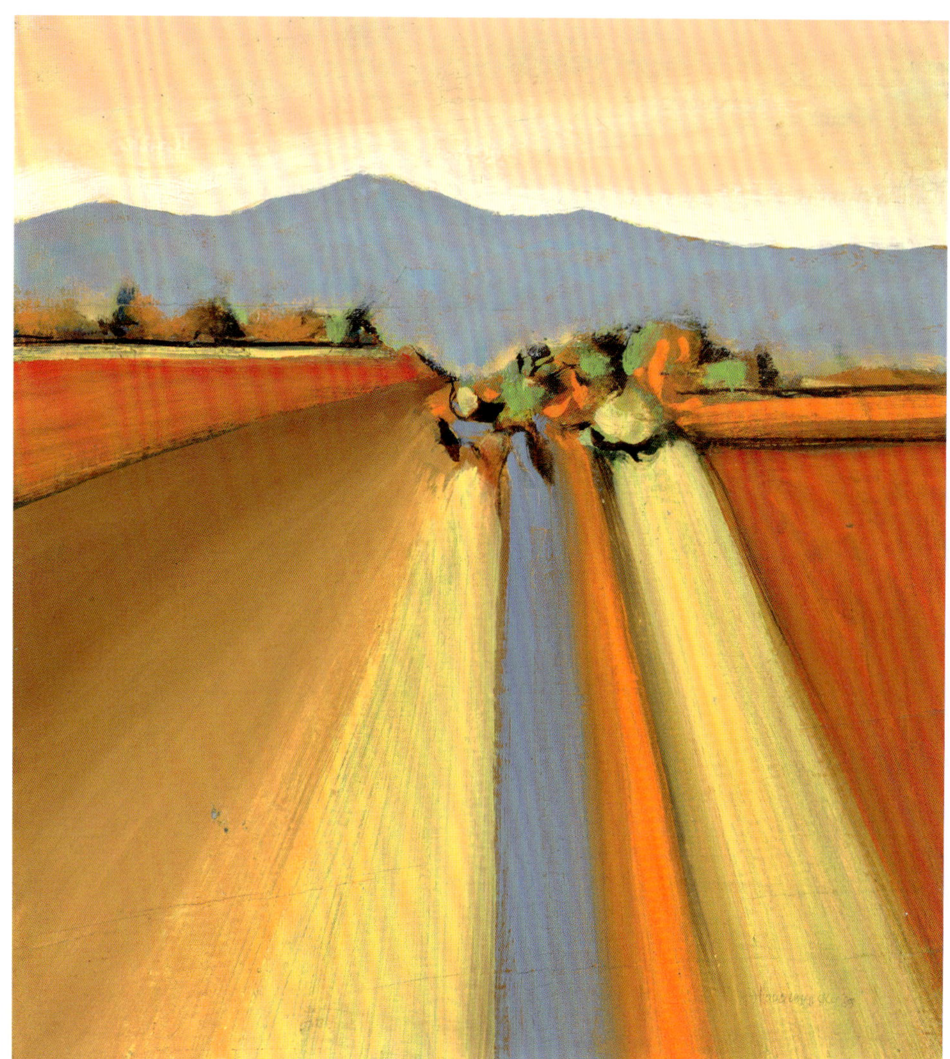

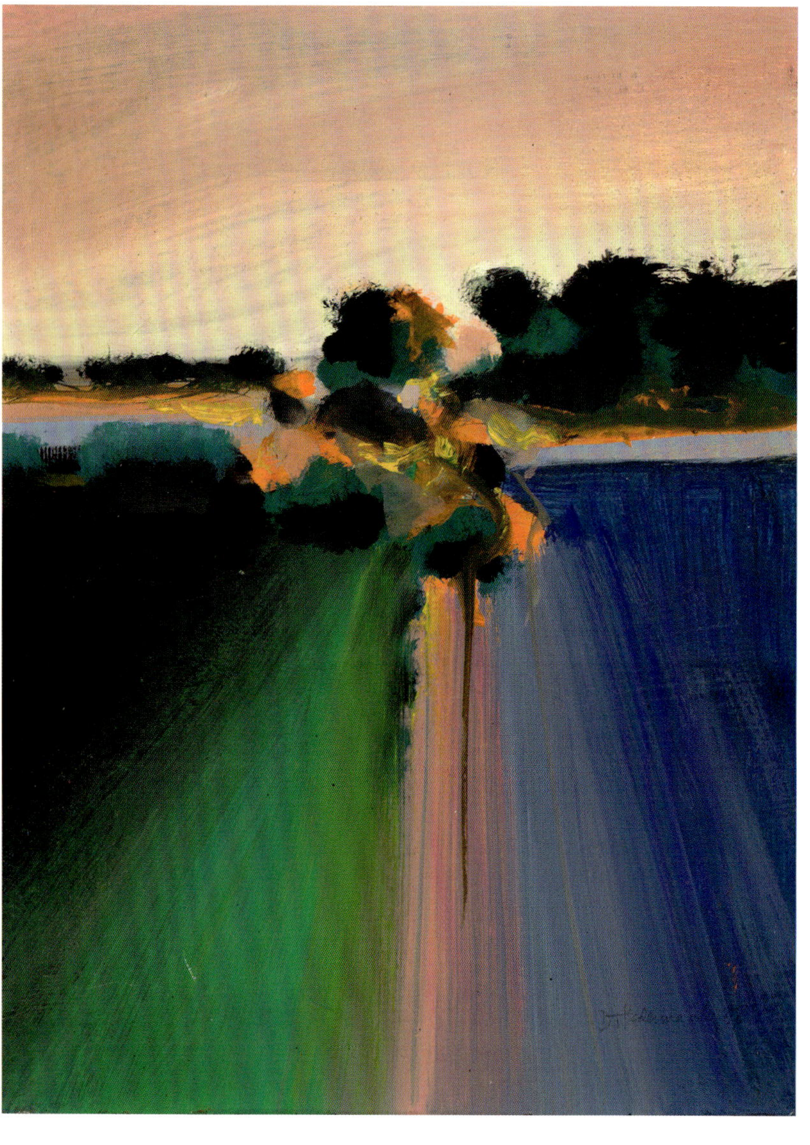

PLATE 47

Sunset, 1991

Oil on Masonite
11⅞ x 9 in. (30.2 x 22.9 cm)
Estate of the artist

opposite: PLATE 48

Paradise Tree (Early Gates of Paradise), 1974

Oil on Masonite
24 x 24 in. (61 x 61 cm)
Estate of the artist

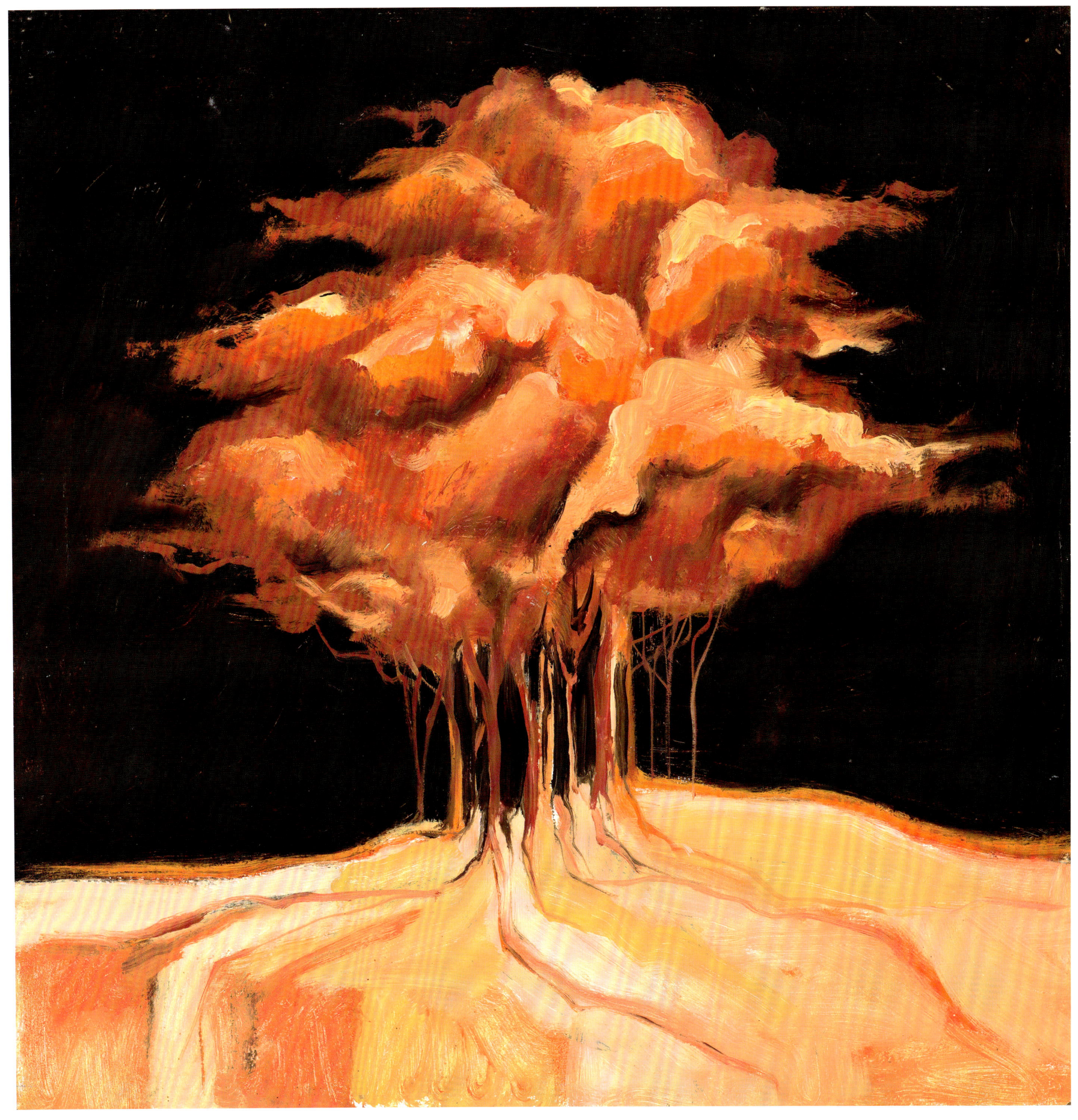

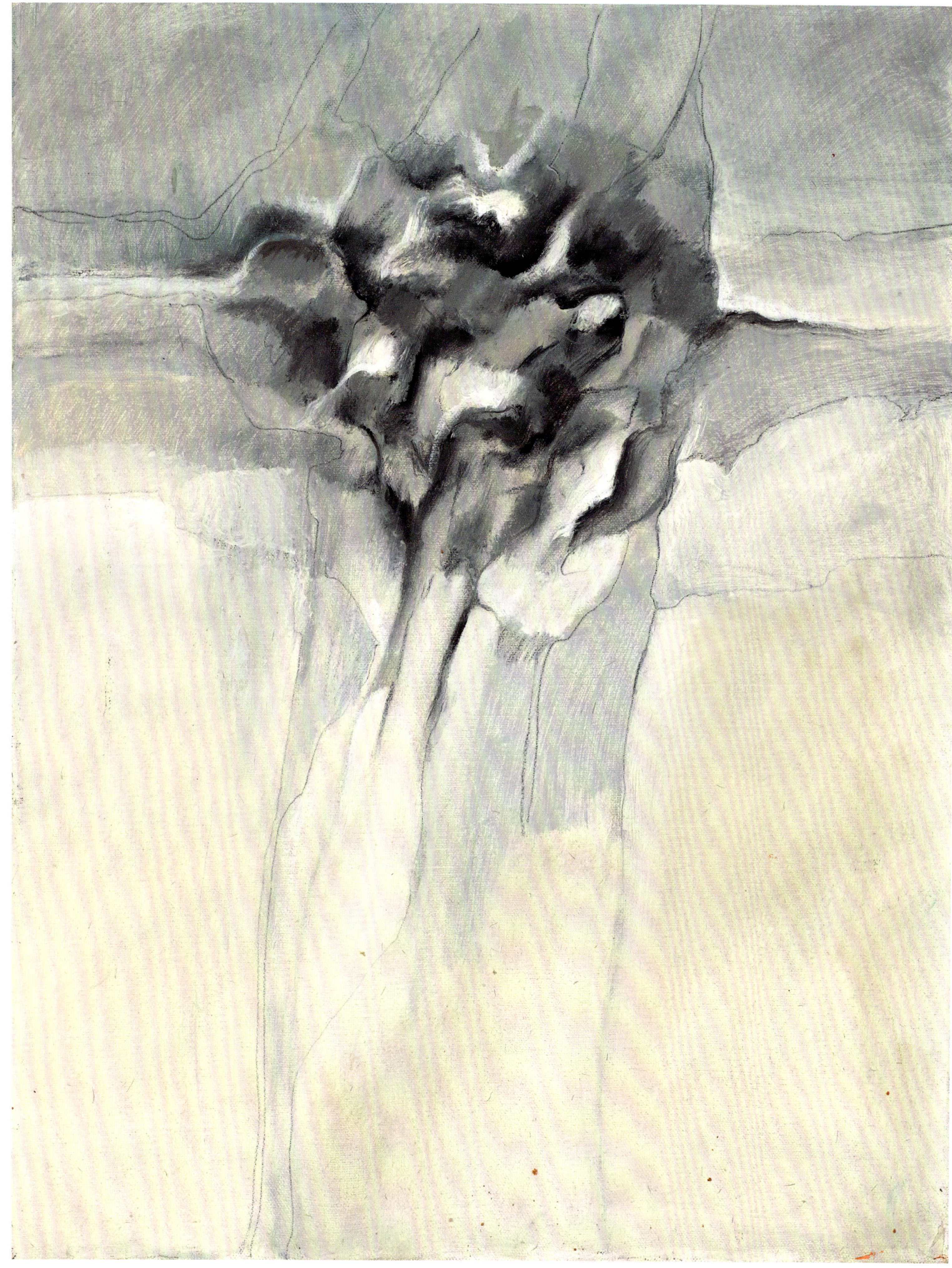

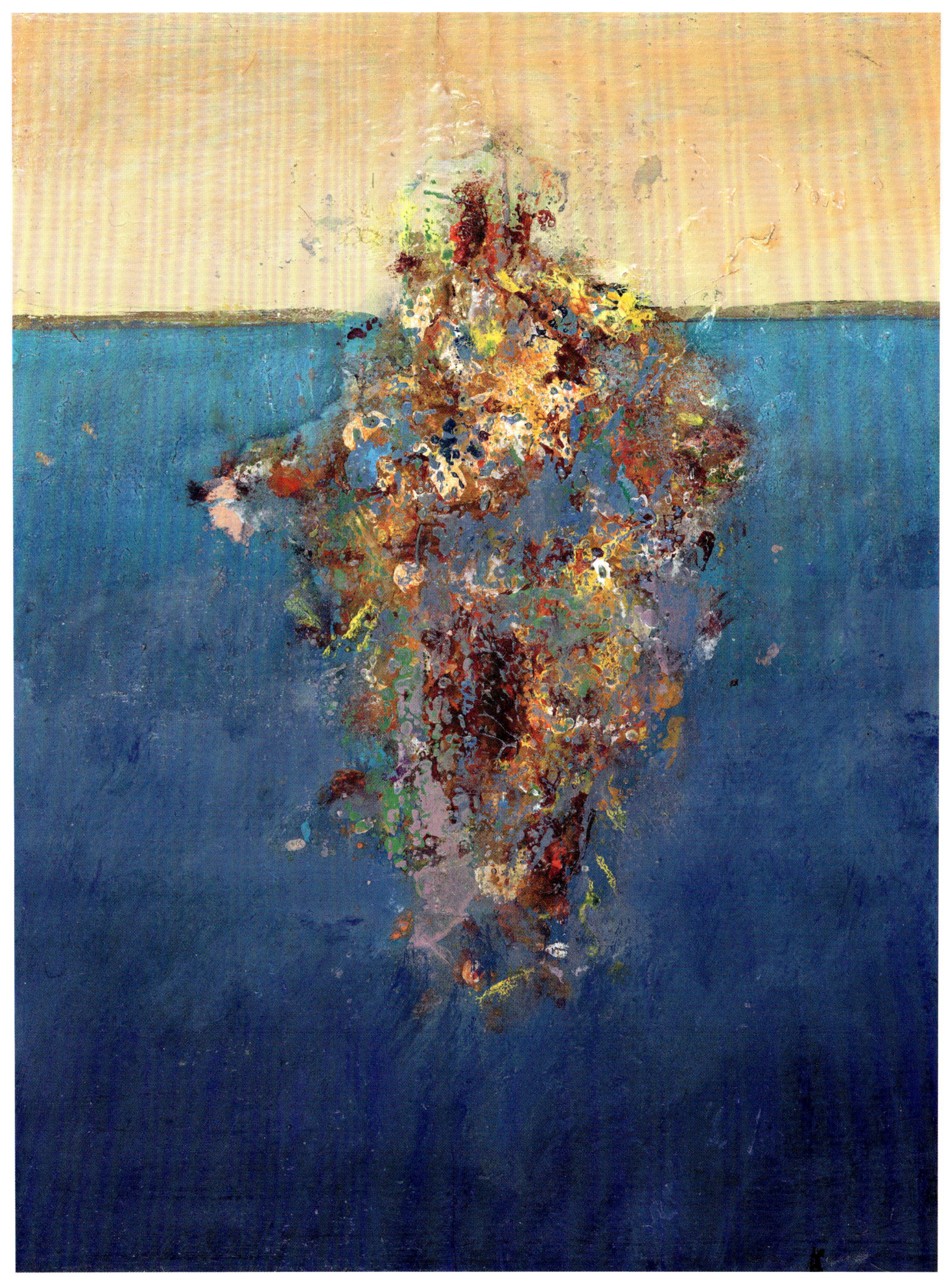

opposite: PLATE 49

Paradise Trees, 1978

Oil on canvas
18 x 14 in. (45.7 x 35.6 cm)
Estate of the artist

PLATE 50

Ambergris 16, 1991

Oil on wood
9⅛ x 7⅛ in. (23.2 x 18.1 cm)
Estate of the artist

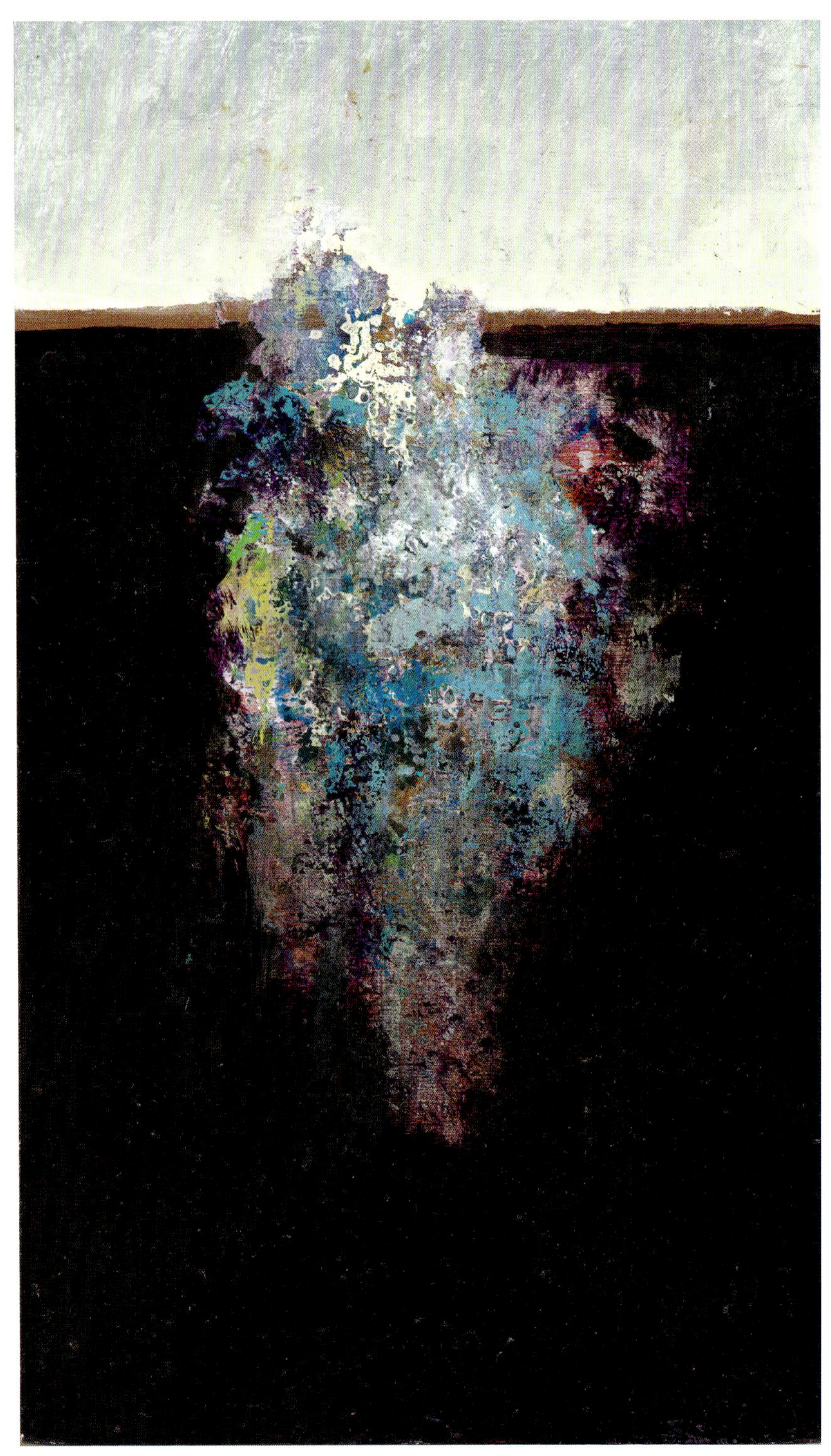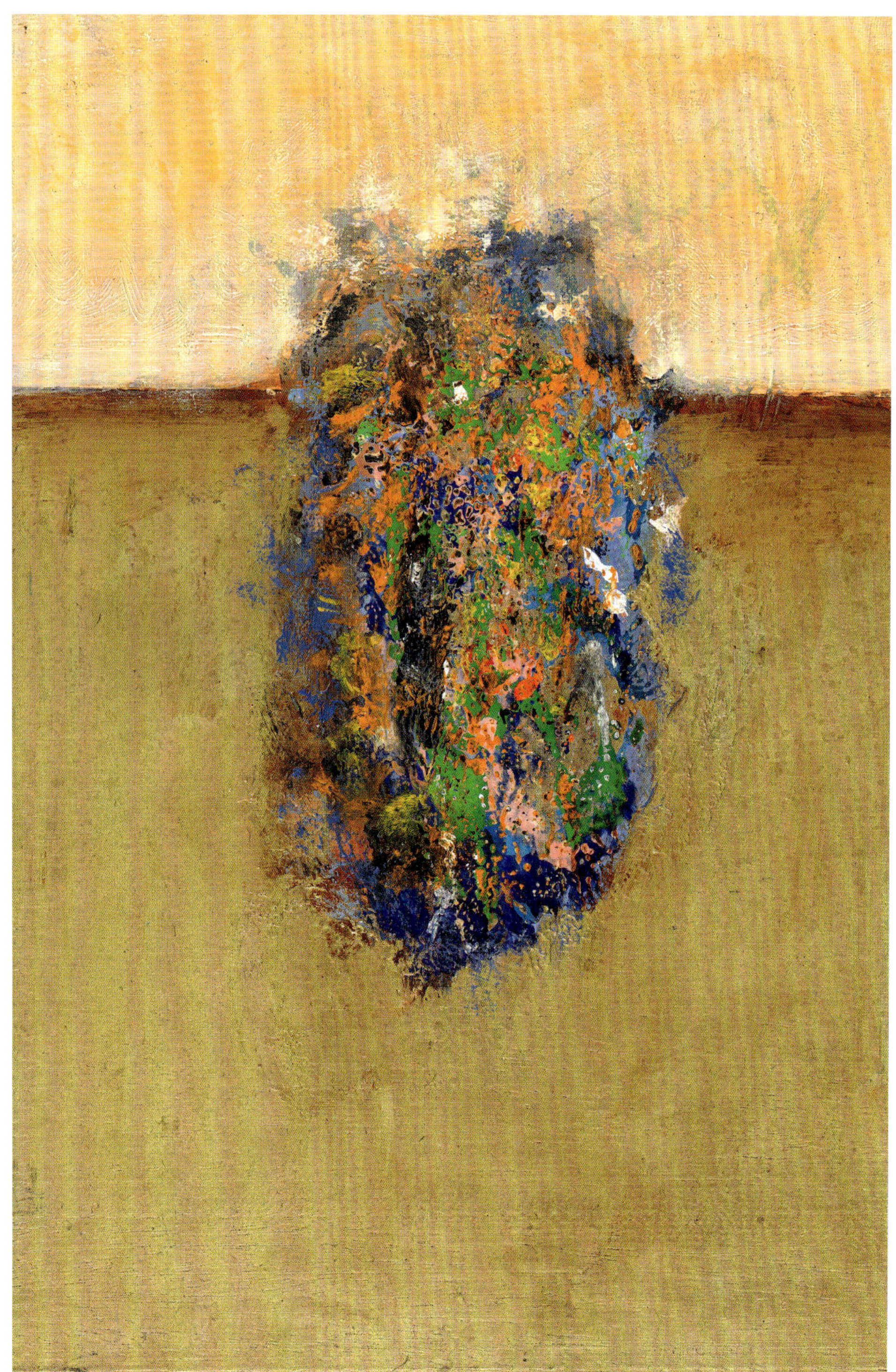

PLATE 51

Ambergris 19, 1991

Oil on wood
11¼ x 6⅝ in. (28.6 x 16.8 cm)
Estate of the artist

PLATE 52

Ambergris 25, 1991

Oil on wood
11¾ x 7¾ in. (29.8 x 19.7 cm)
Estate of the artist

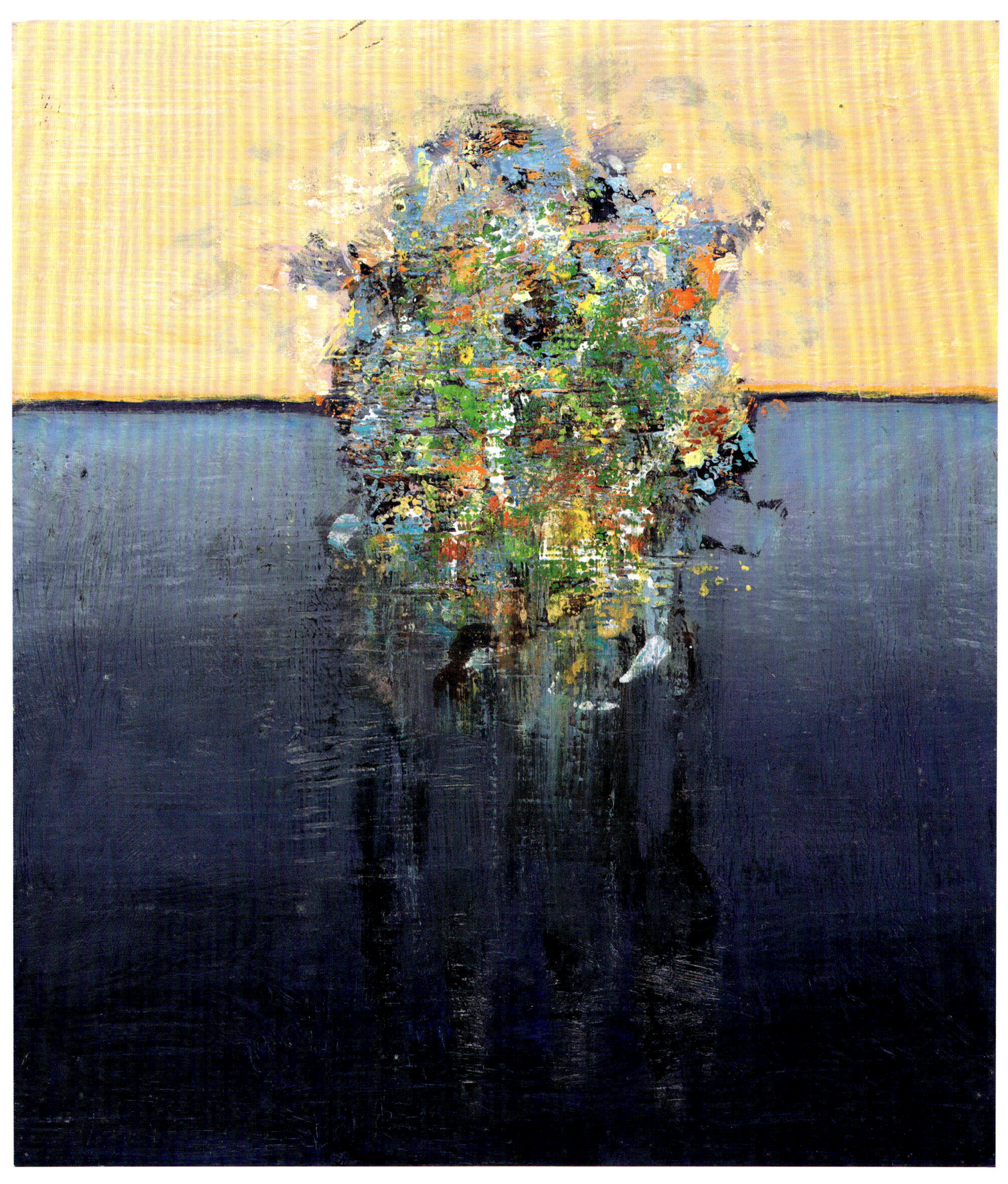

Ambergris, 1992

Oil on wood
14 x 13 in. (35.5 x 33 cm)
Estate of the artist

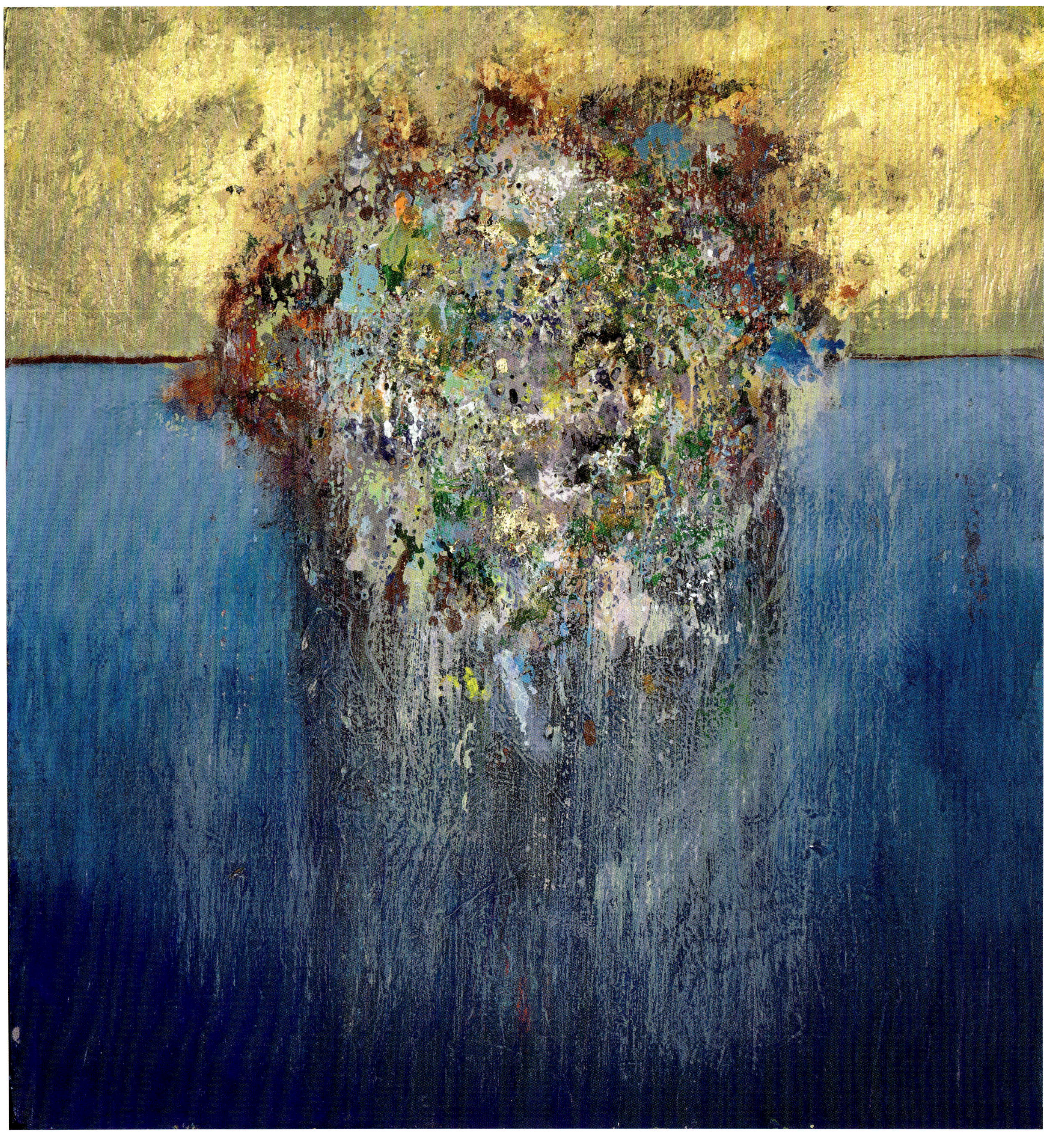

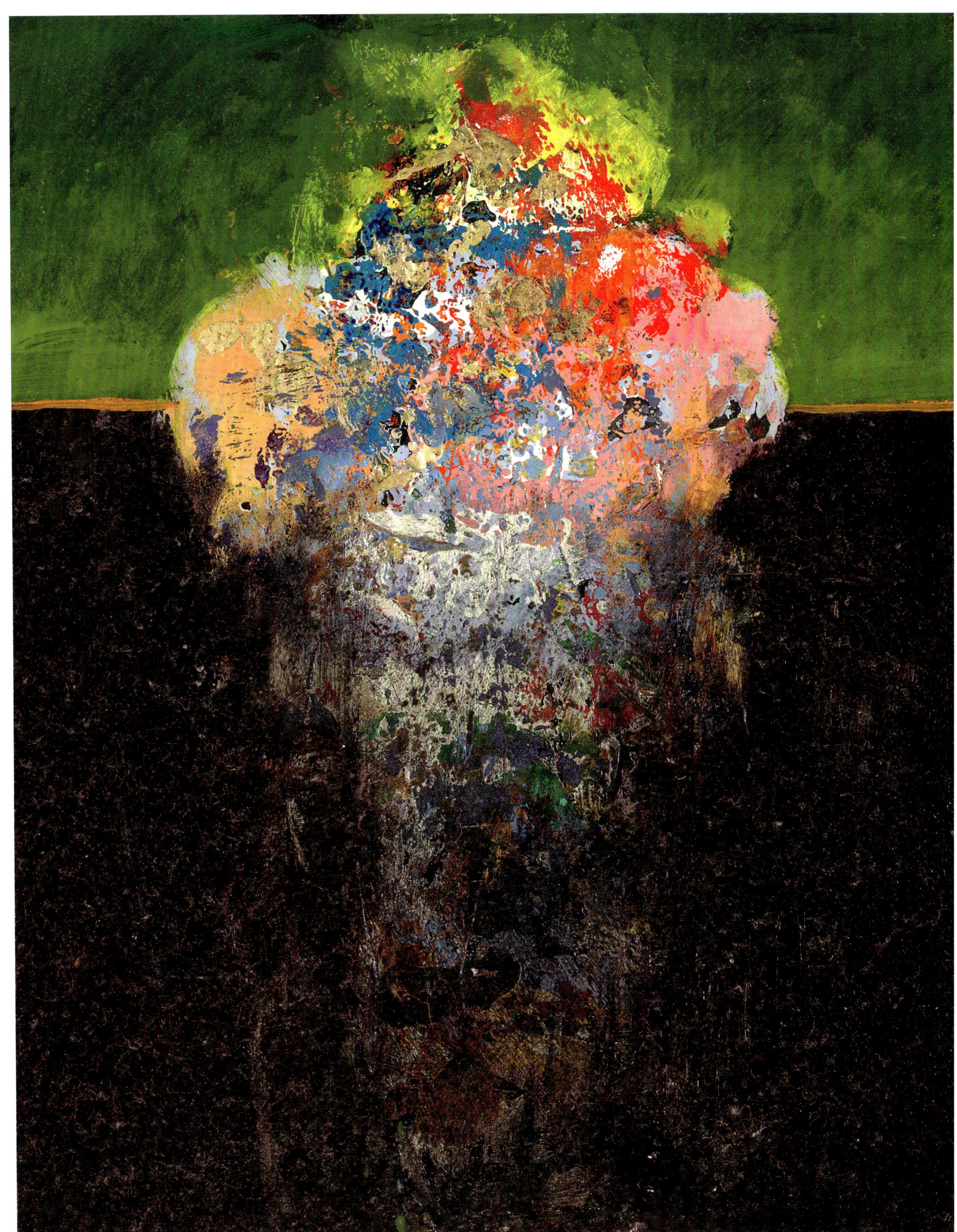

Orthodox Abstract, 1992

Oil on wood
13¼ x 12¼ in. (33.7 x 31.1 cm)
Collection of Nisha Sajnani

PLATE 55

Ambergris 24, 1996

Oil on wood
15 x 12 in. (38.1 x 30.5 cm)
Collection of Ethan Jones

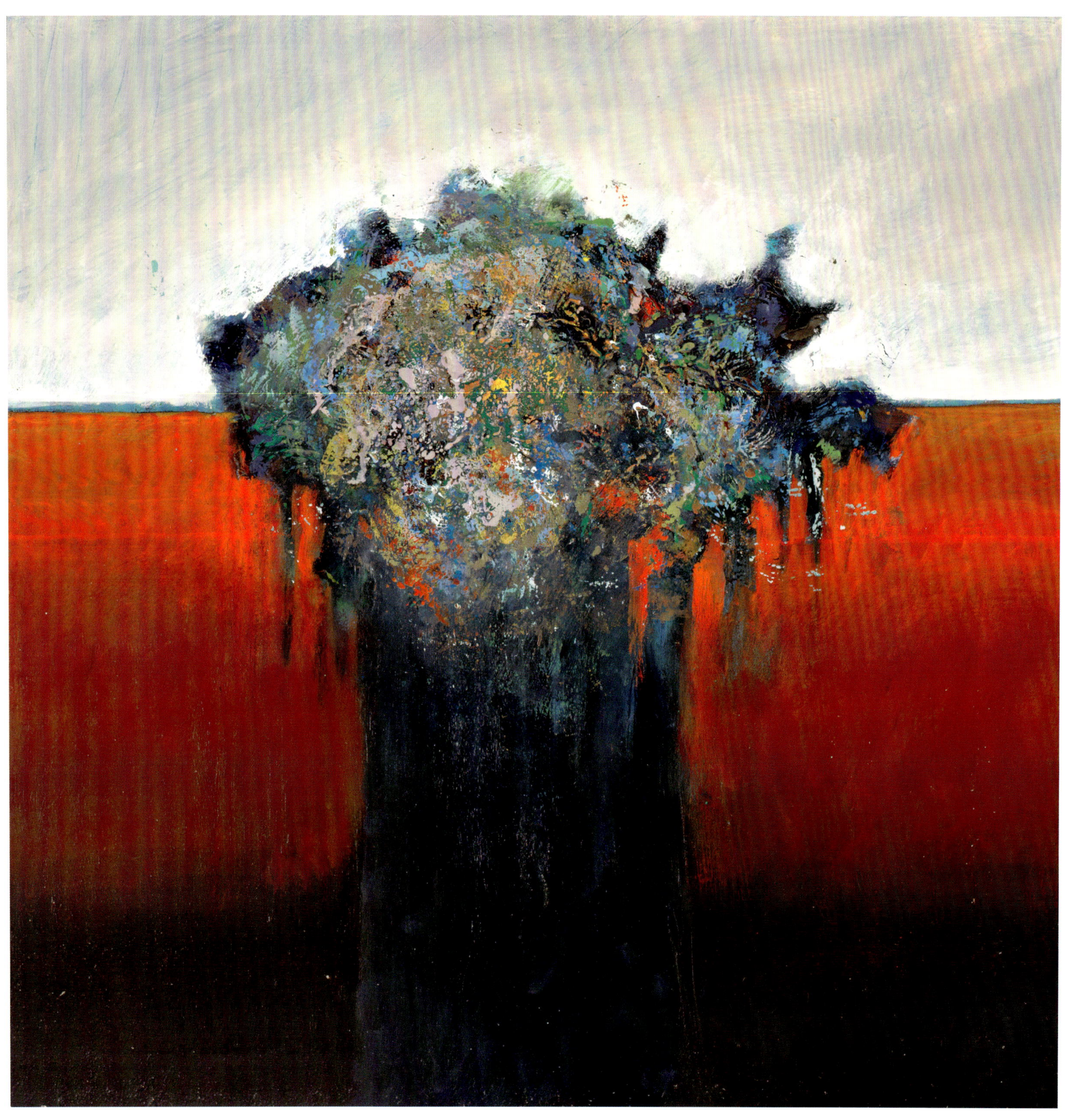

PLATE 56

De Profundis, 1991

Oil on Masonite
24 x 24 in. (61 x 61 cm)
Collection of Maria Hodermarska and Penn Rhodeen

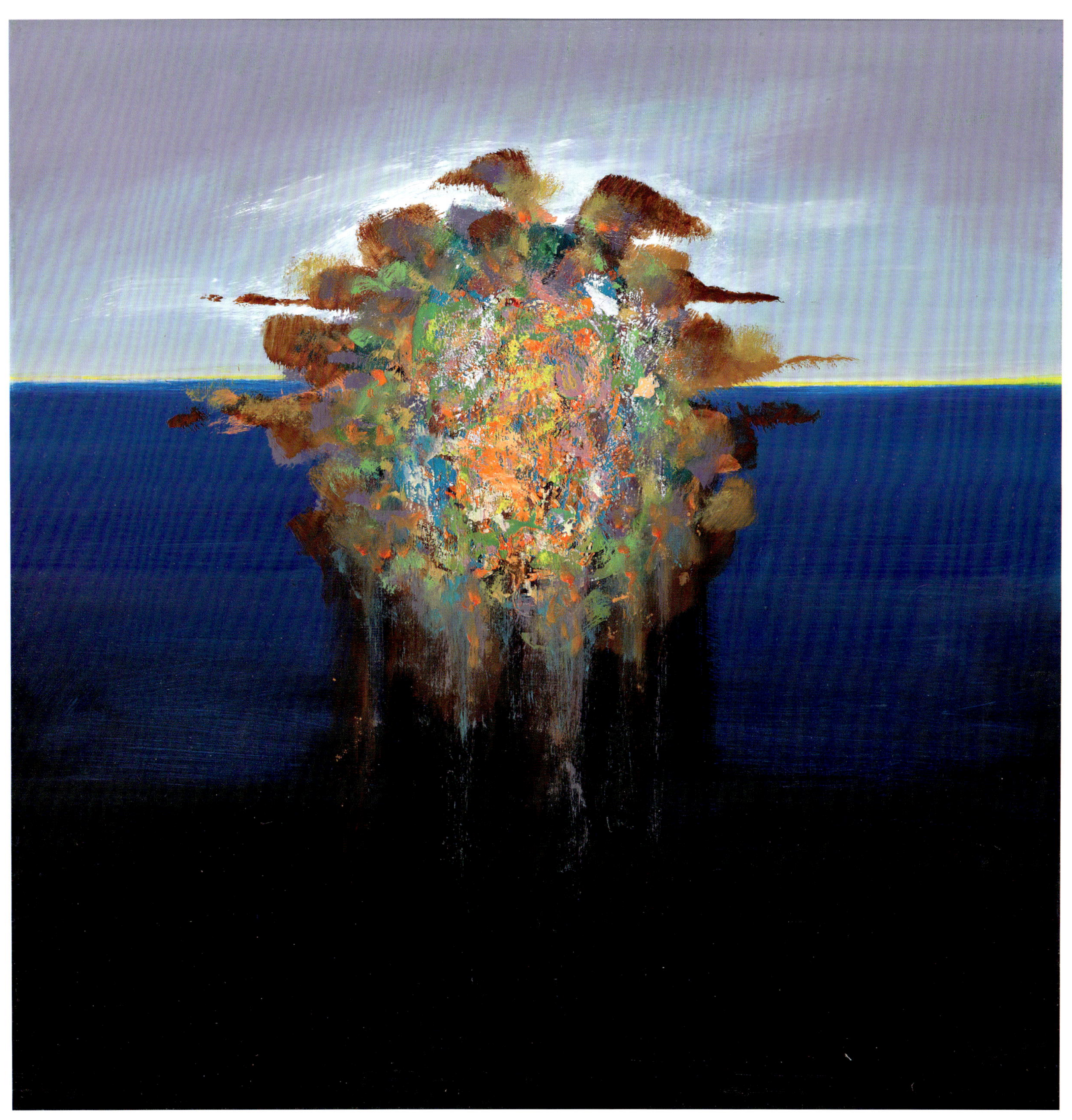

PLATE 57

De Profundis #4 1993

Oil on Masonite
24 x 24 in. (61 x 61 cm)
Estate of the artist

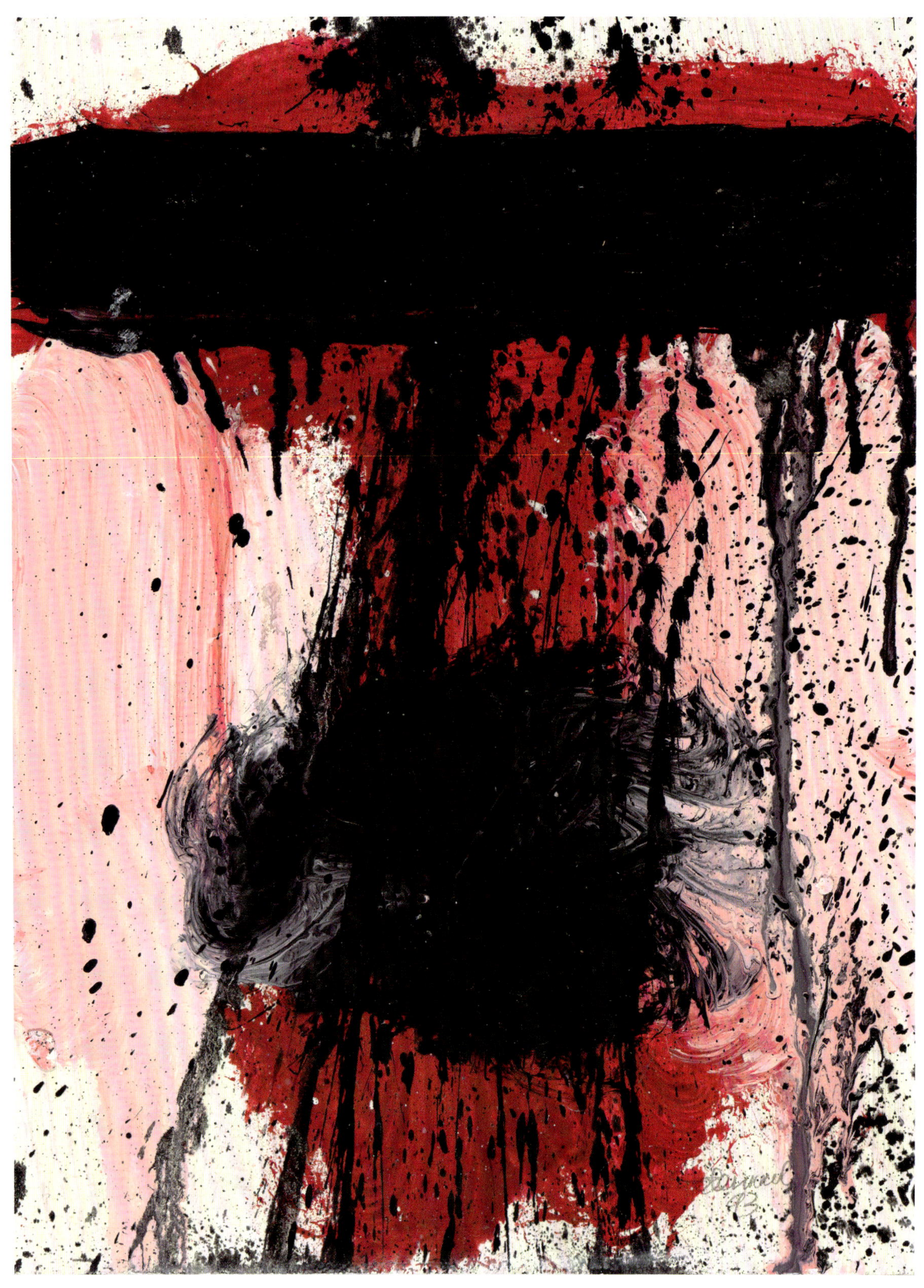

PLATE 58

Mexican Series #3, 1993

Oil on wood
10⅛ x 7½ in. (25.7 x 19 cm)
Estate of the artist

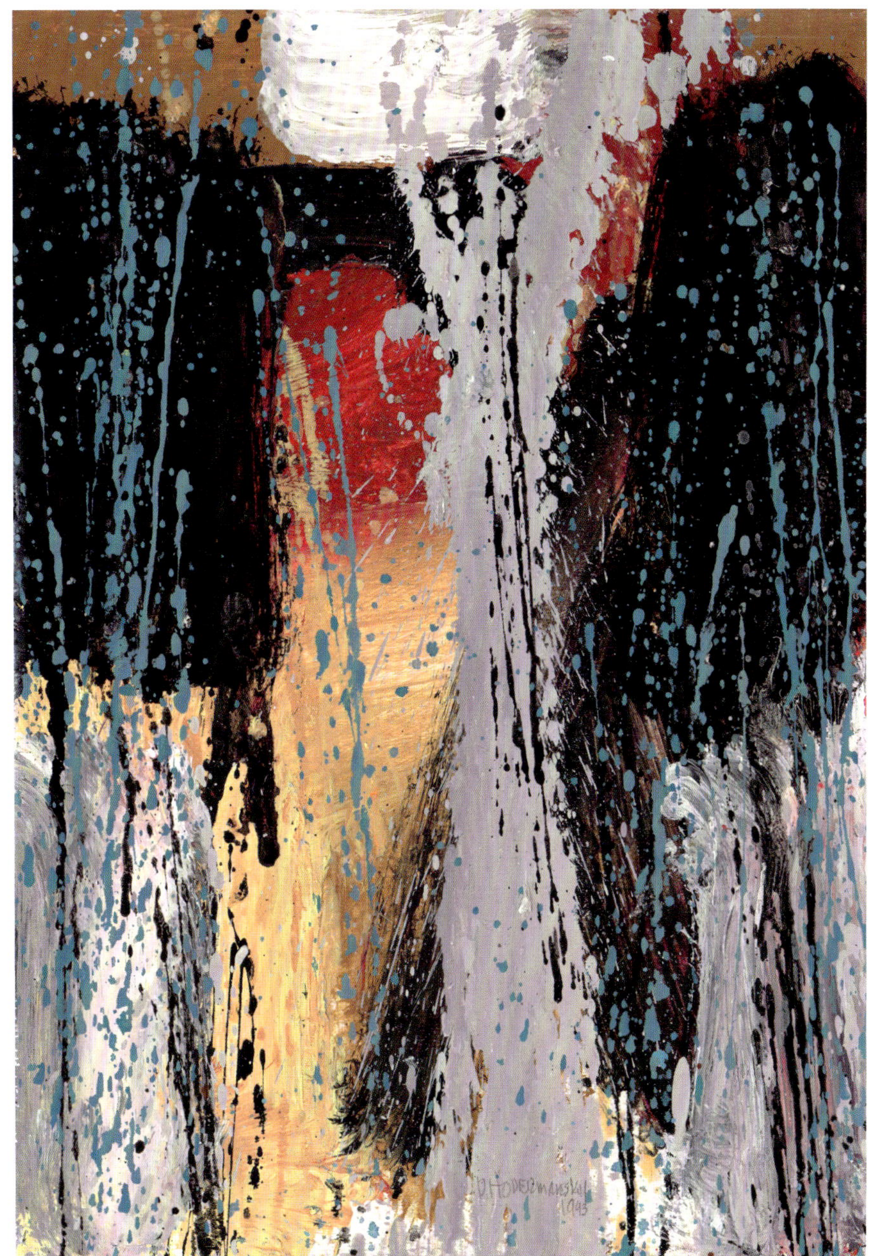

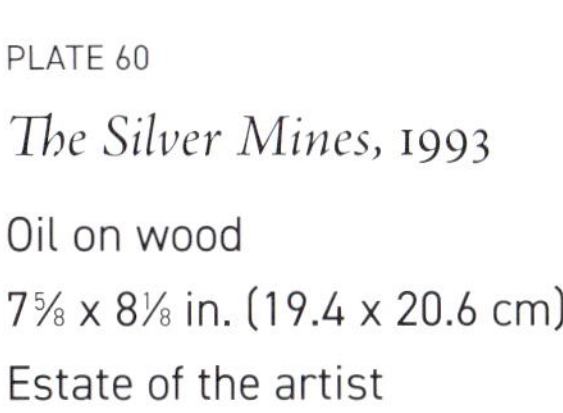

PLATE 59

Mexican Series #7, 1993

Oil on wood
11 x 7¾ in. (27.9 x 19.7 cm)
Estate of the artist

PLATE 60

The Silver Mines, 1993

Oil on wood
7⅝ x 8⅛ in. (19.4 x 20.6 cm)
Estate of the artist

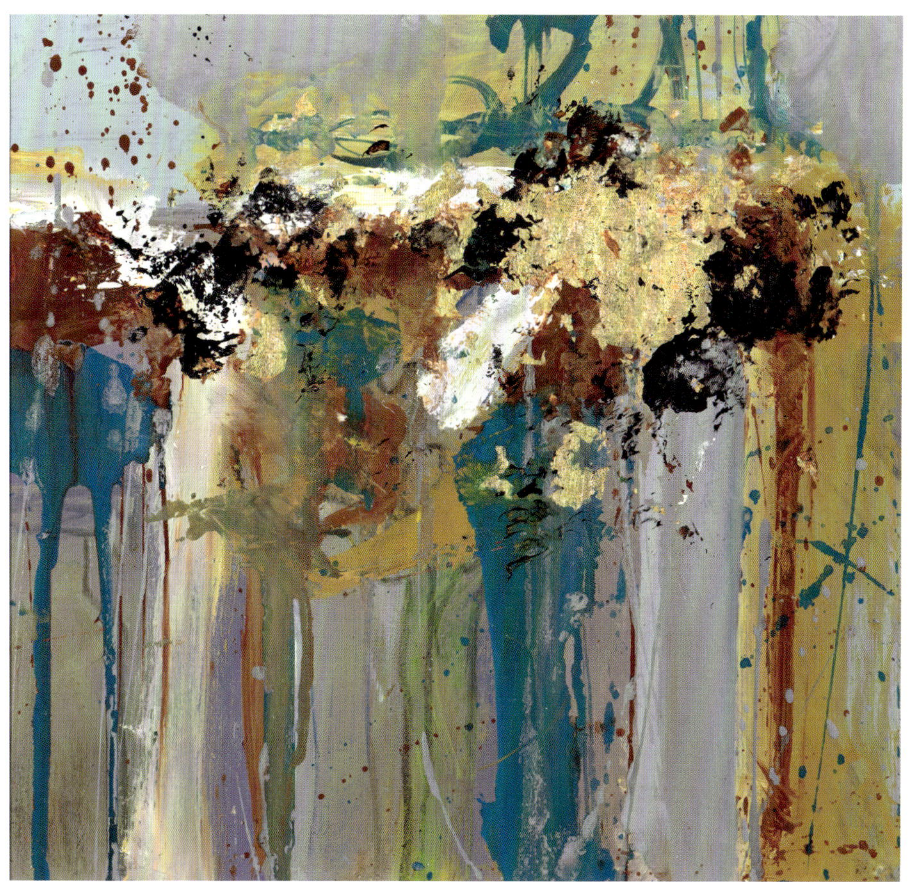

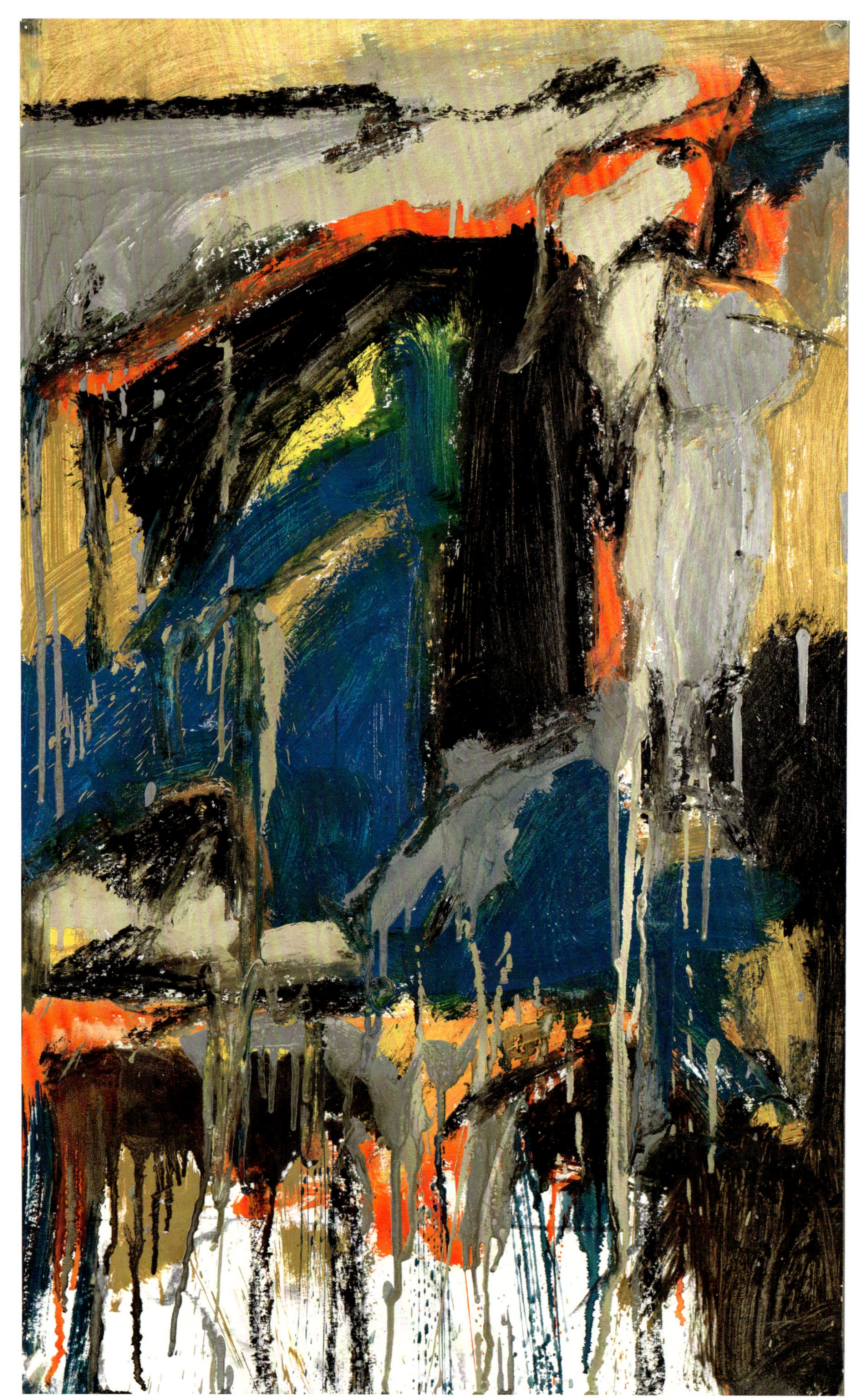

PLATE 61

Valenciano Abstract #10, 1993

Acrylic on paper (diptych)
32¼ x 20 in. (81.9 x 50.8 cm)
Estate of the artist

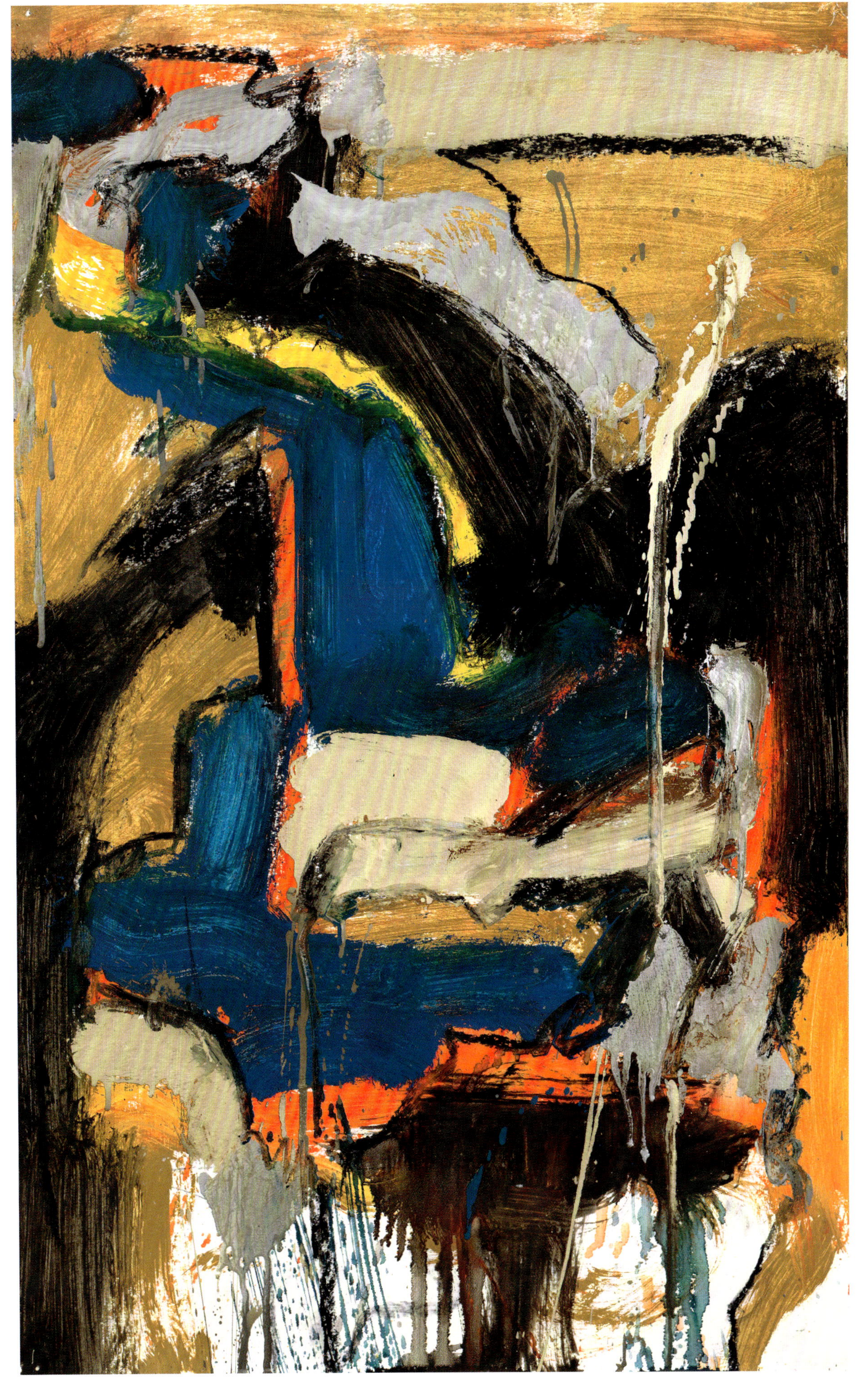

PLATE 62

Valenciano Abstract #11, 1993
Acrylic on paper (diptych)
32¼ x 20 in. (81.9 x 50.8 cm)
Estate of the artist

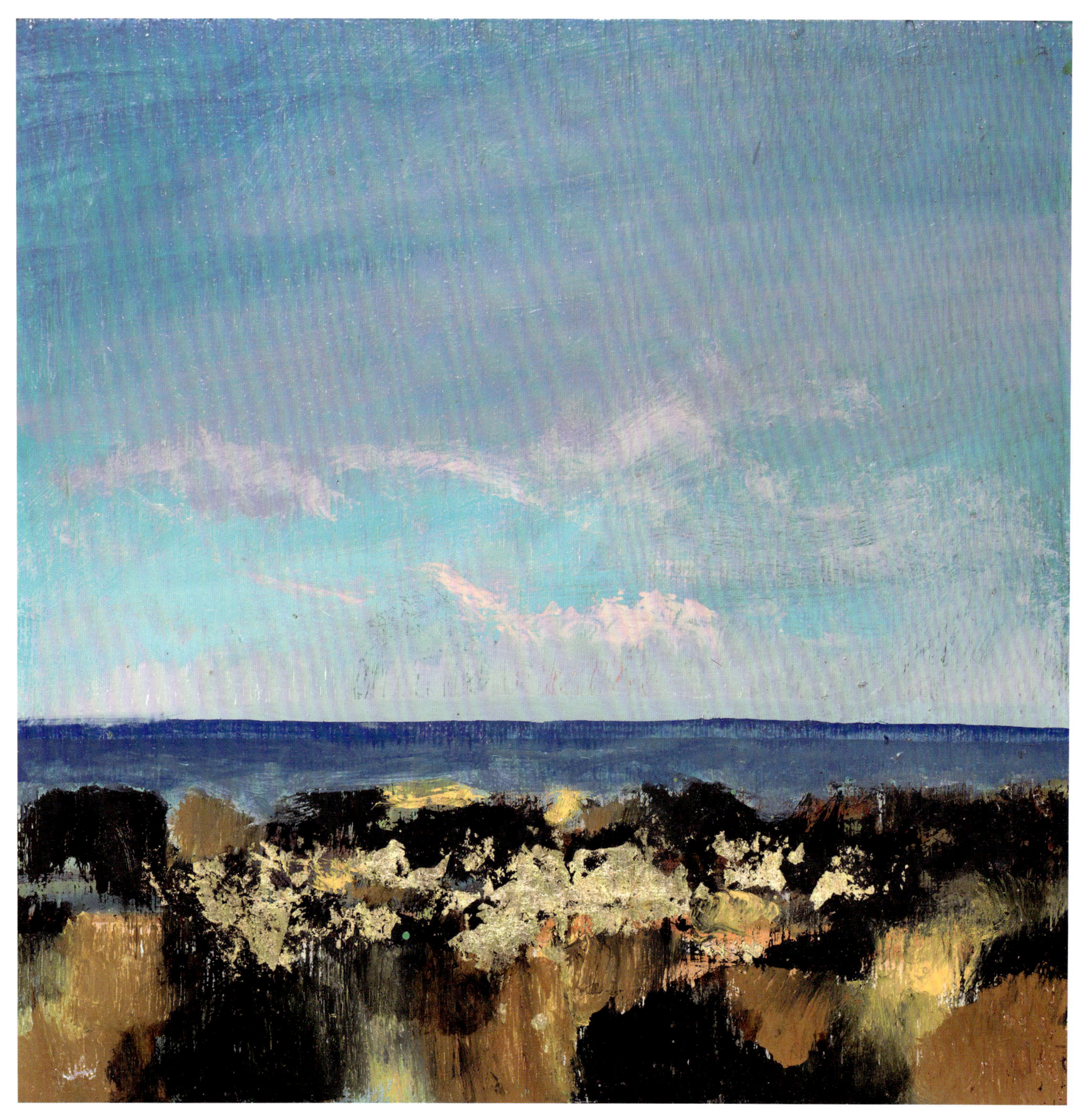

Gold at the Shore #2, 1991

Oil on wood
11¾ x 11¾ in. (29.8 x 29.8 cm)
Estate of the artist

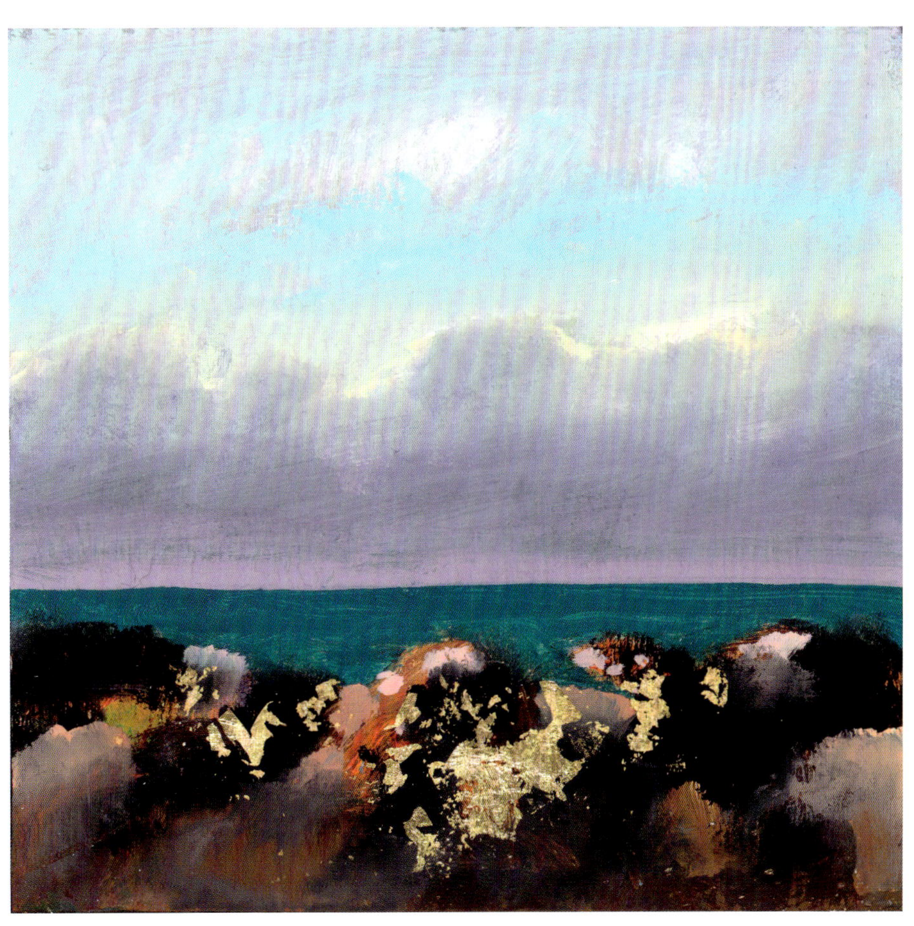

PLATE 64

Gold at the Shore #3, 1991

Oil on wood
11⅜ x 11⅞ in. (28.9 x 30.2 cm)
Estate of the artist

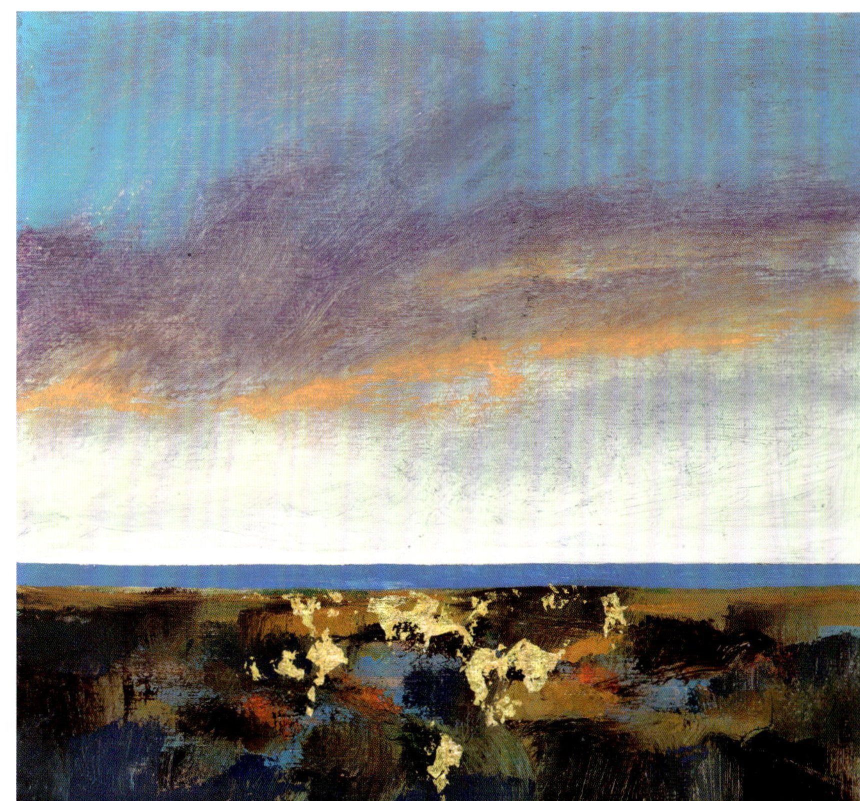

PLATE 65

Gold at the Shore #5, 1991

Oil on wood
12 x 12 in. (30.5 x 30.5 cm)
Estate of the artist

PLATE 66

Self-Portrait in Helmet, 1978

Brush and wash on paper
17¾ x 12 in. (45.1 x 30.5 cm)
Estate of the artist

Watercolors

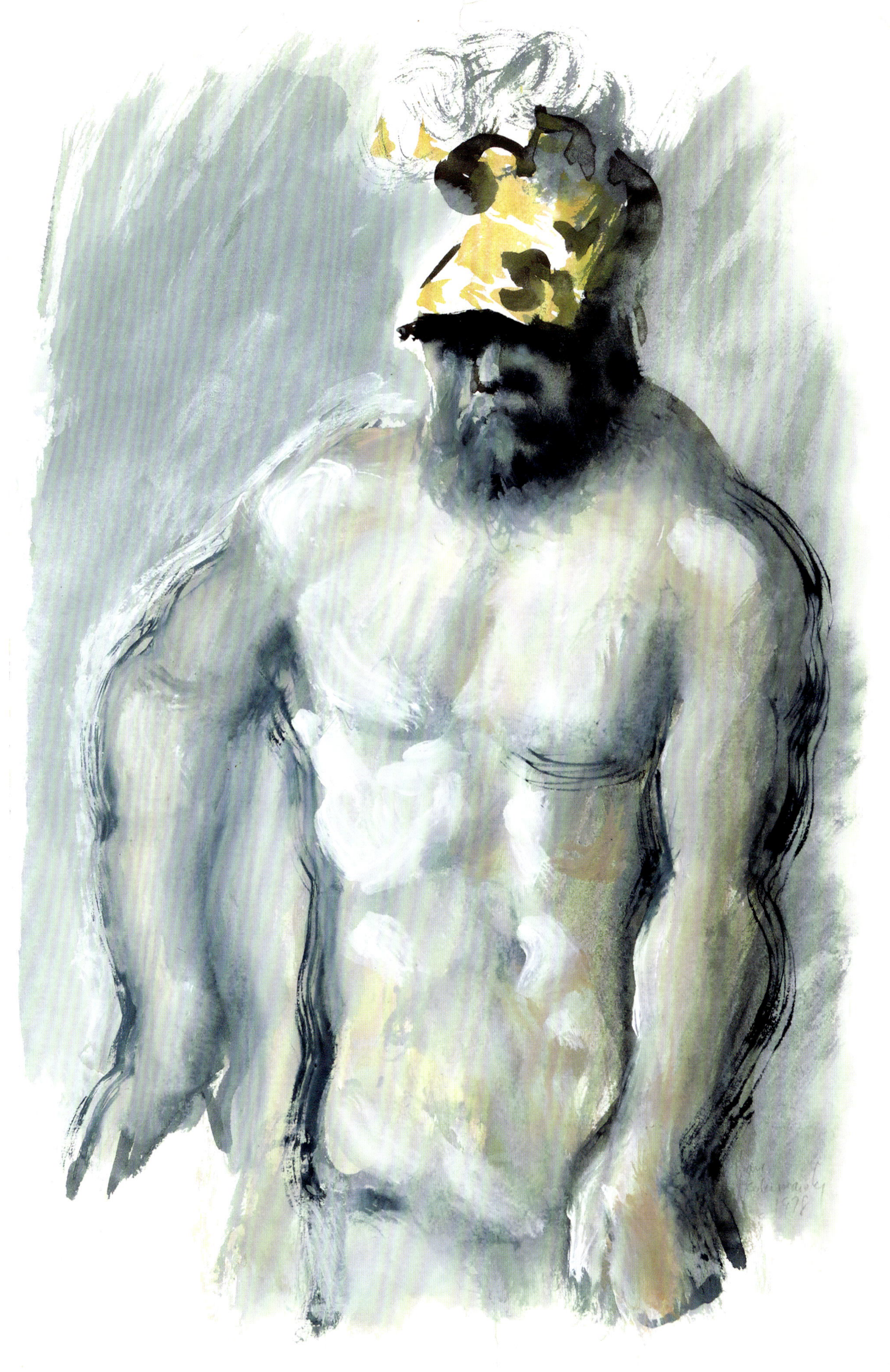

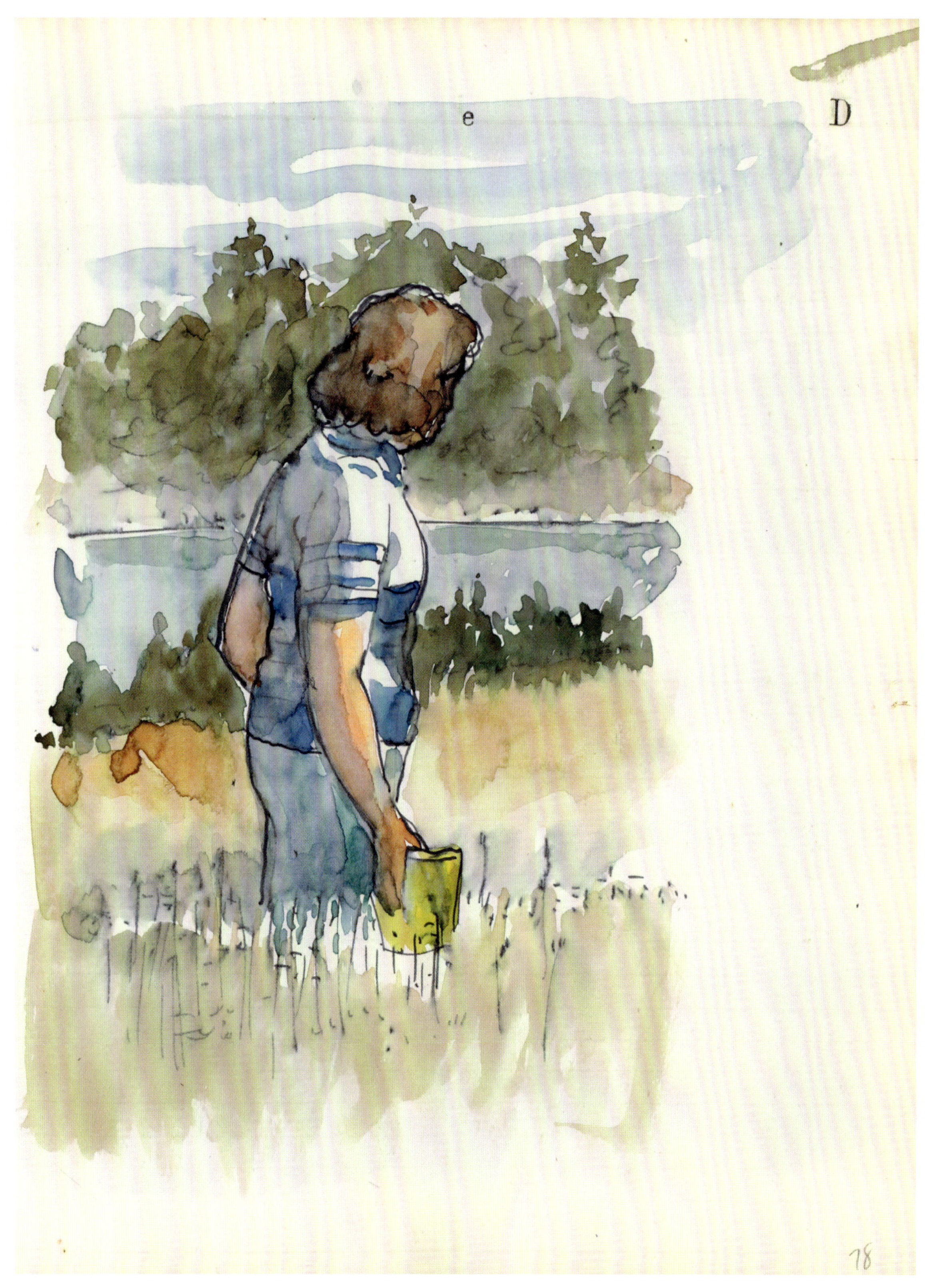

PLATE 67

Nancy Picking Blueberries in the Field, 1978

Pen, ink, and watercolor wash
10 x 7½ in. (25.4 x 19.1 cm)
Estate of the artist

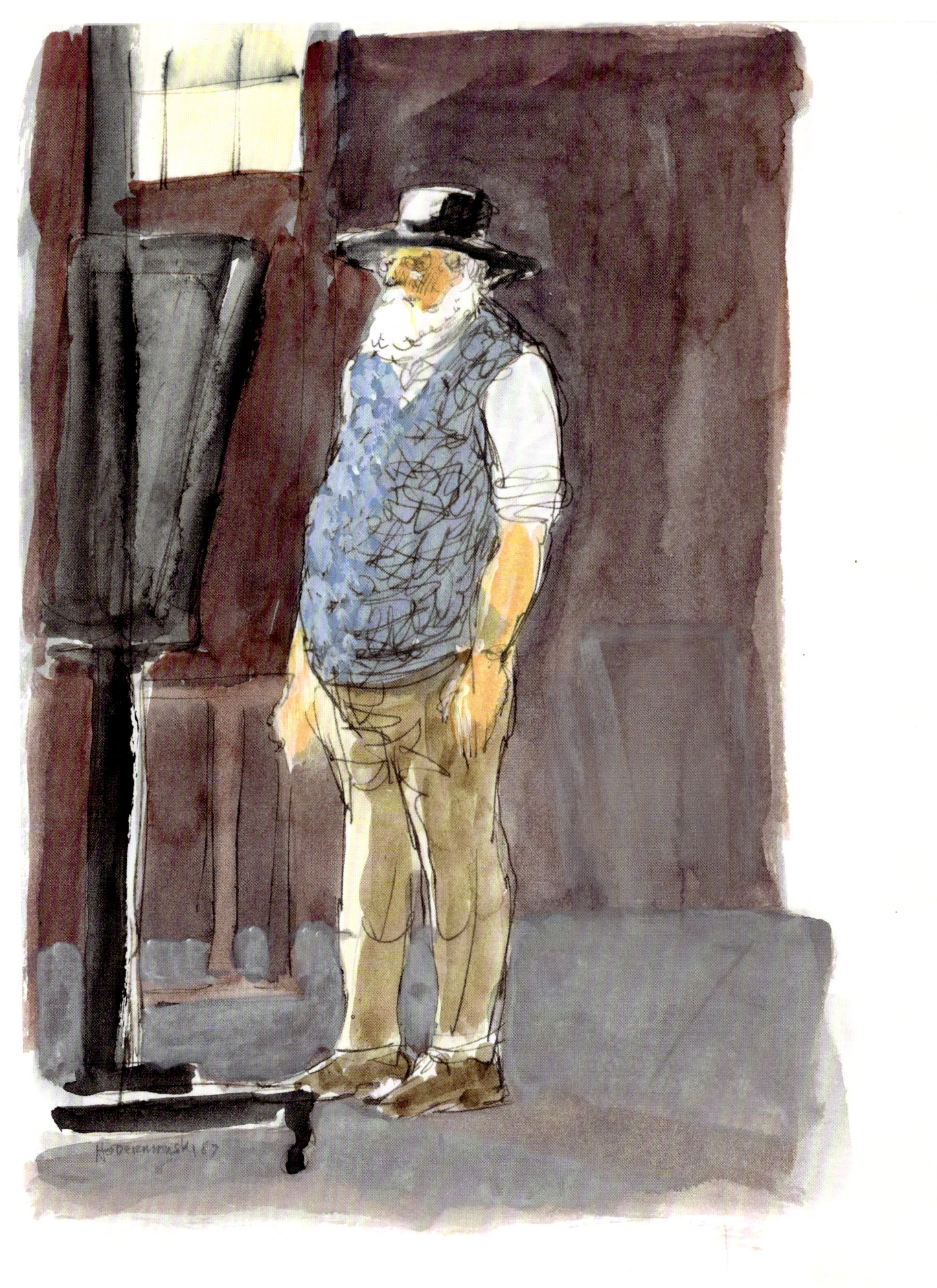

PLATE 68
Portrait of the Artist (Self-Portrait), 1989
Watercolor
9½ x 6½ in. (24.1 x 16.5 cm)
Estate of the artist

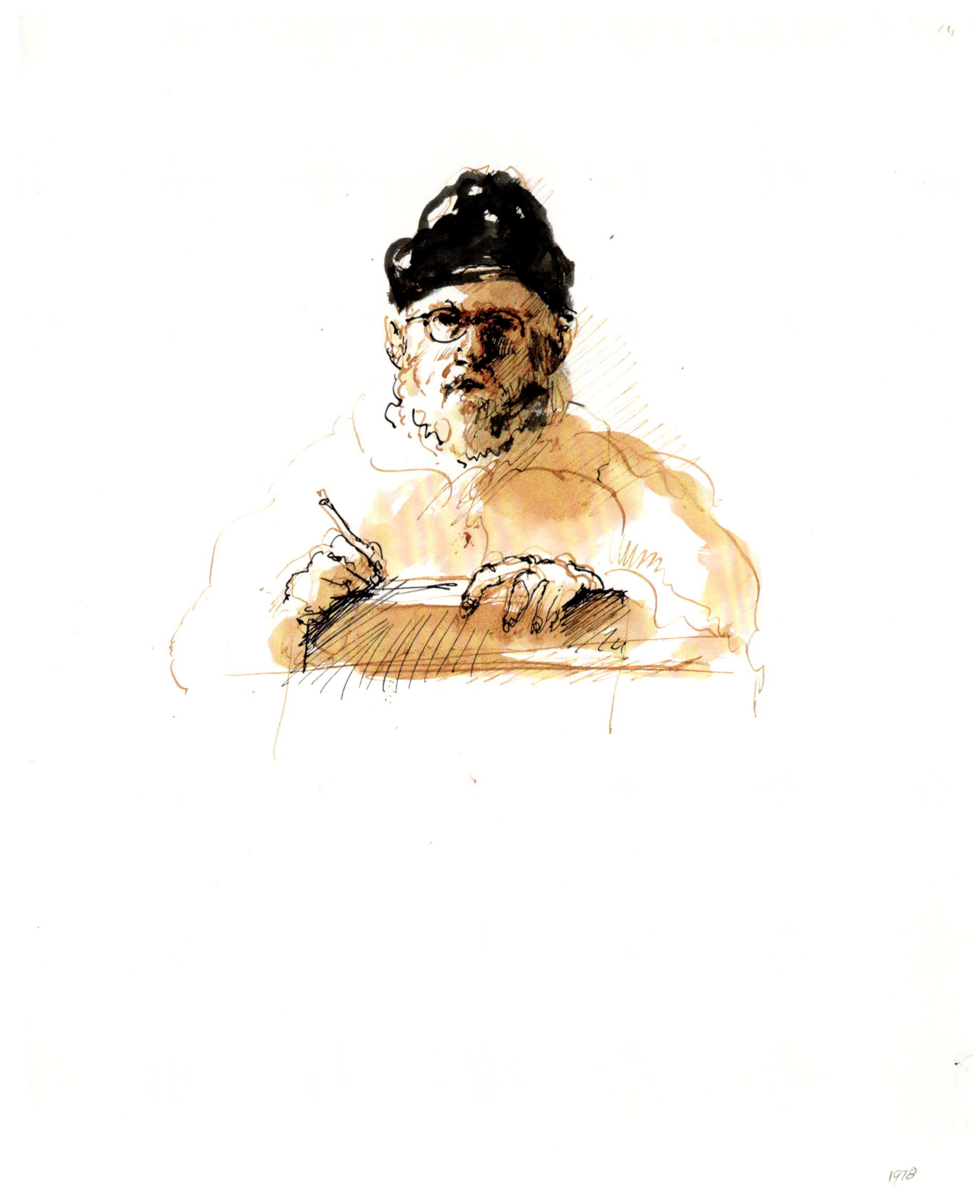

PLATE 69

Self-Portrait in Russian Hat, 1978

Pen, ink, and wash on paper
13¼ x 11 in. (33.7 x 27.9 cm)
Estate of the artist

opposite: PLATE 70

Self-Portrait Nude, 1978

Brush and wash on paper
24 x 18 in. (61 x 45.7 cm)
Estate of the artist

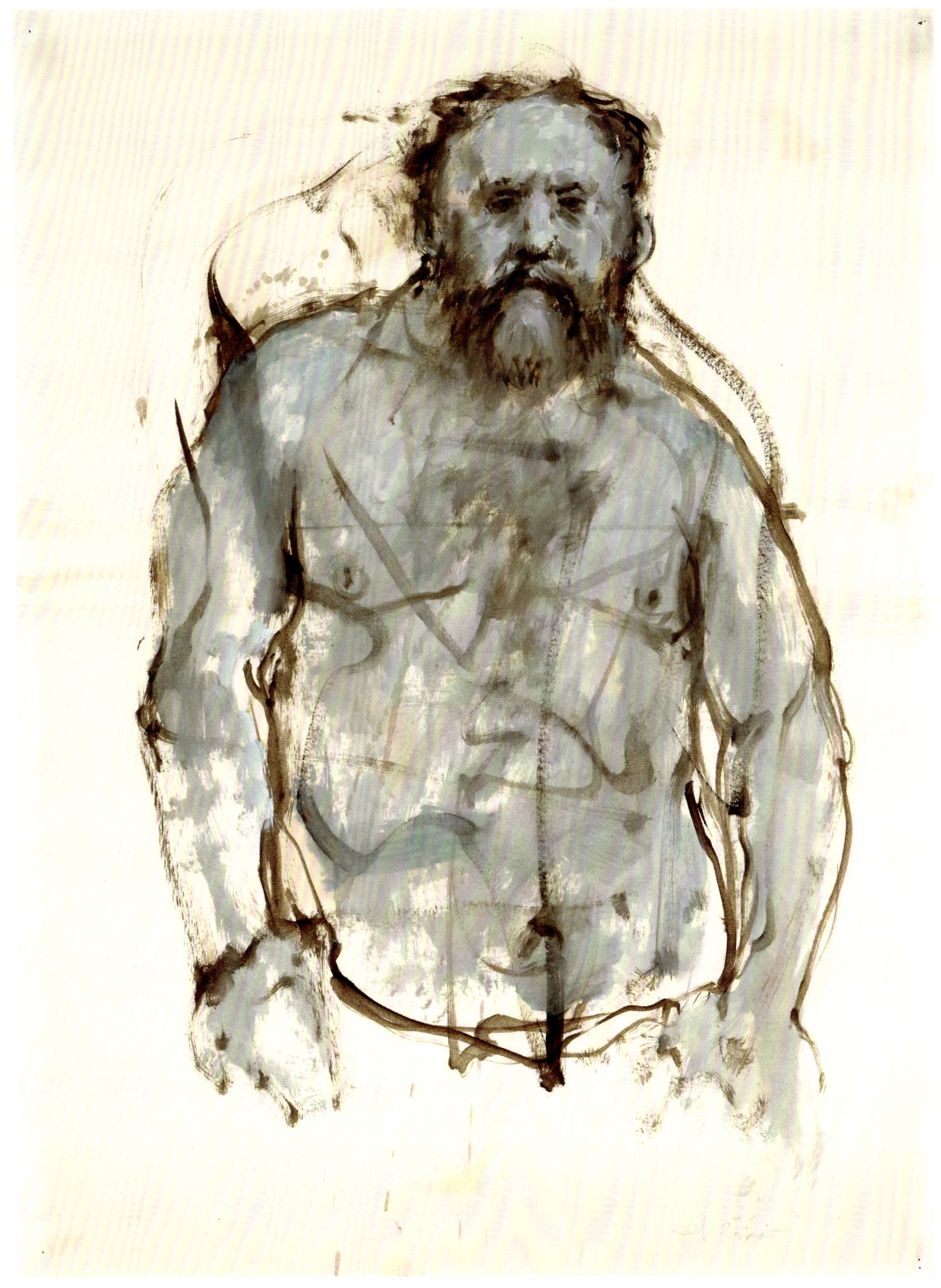

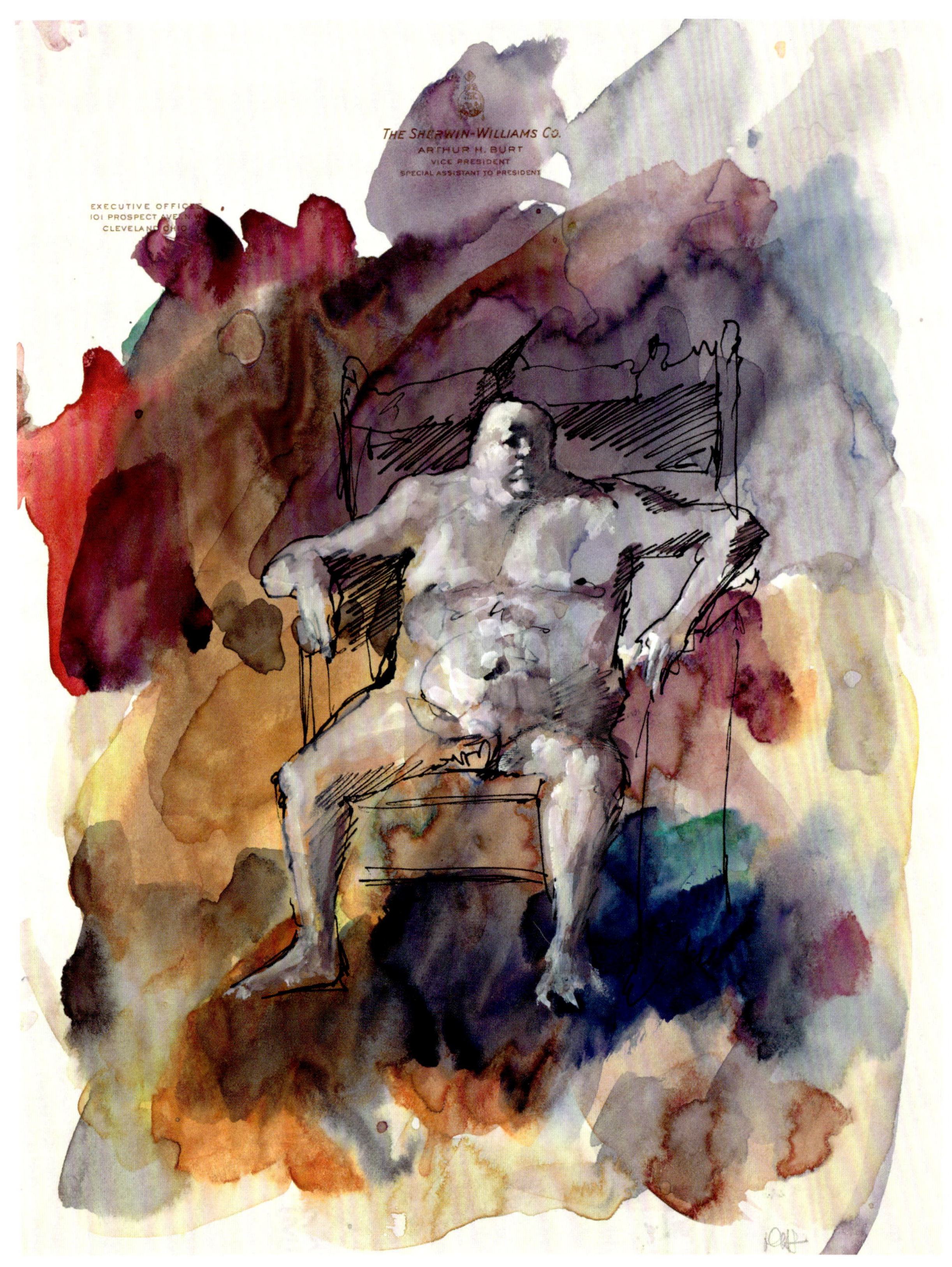

PLATE 71

Untitled (Figure Study), ca. 1970s

Pen, ink, and watercolor on Sherwin Williams Co. stationery
10⅞ x 8⅜ in. (27.6 x 21.3 cm)
Estate of the artist

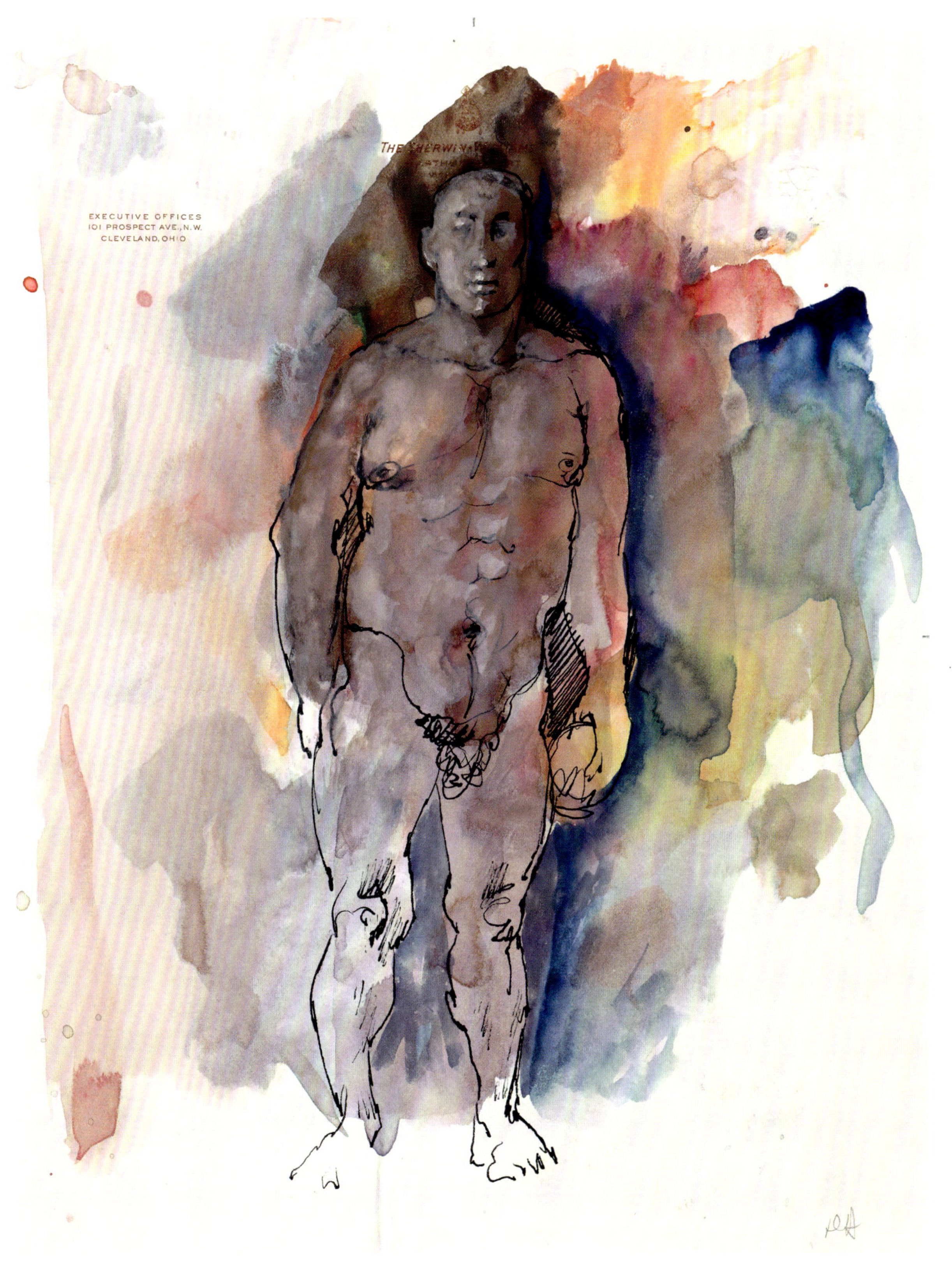

PLATE 72

Untitled (Figure Study), ca. 1970s

Pen, ink, and watercolor on Sherwin Williams Co. stationery
11 x 8 in. (27.9 x 20.3 cm)
Estate of the artist

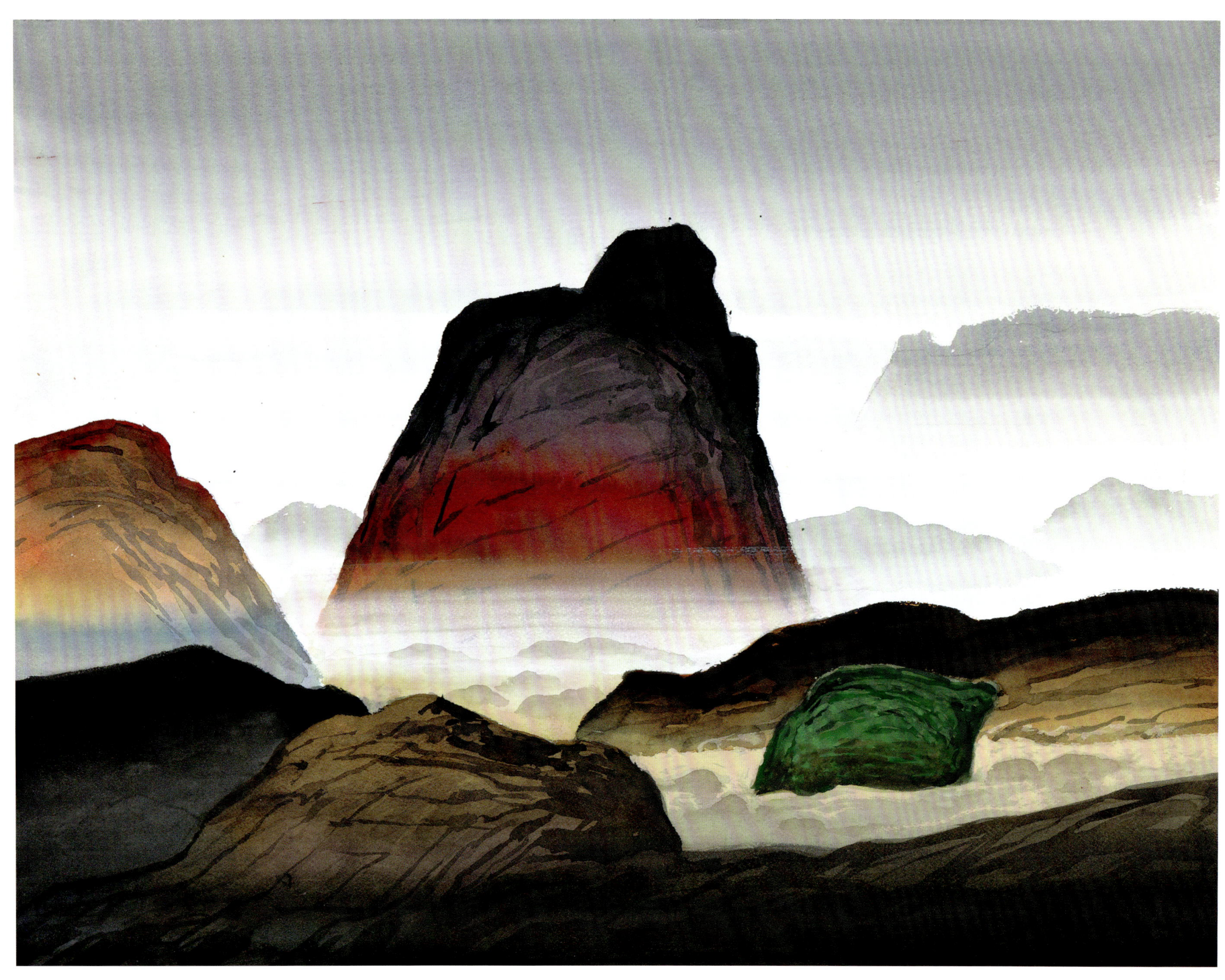

PLATE 73

Beauty at the Shore, 1979

Watercolor
18 x 24 in. (45.7 x 61 cm)
Estate of the artist

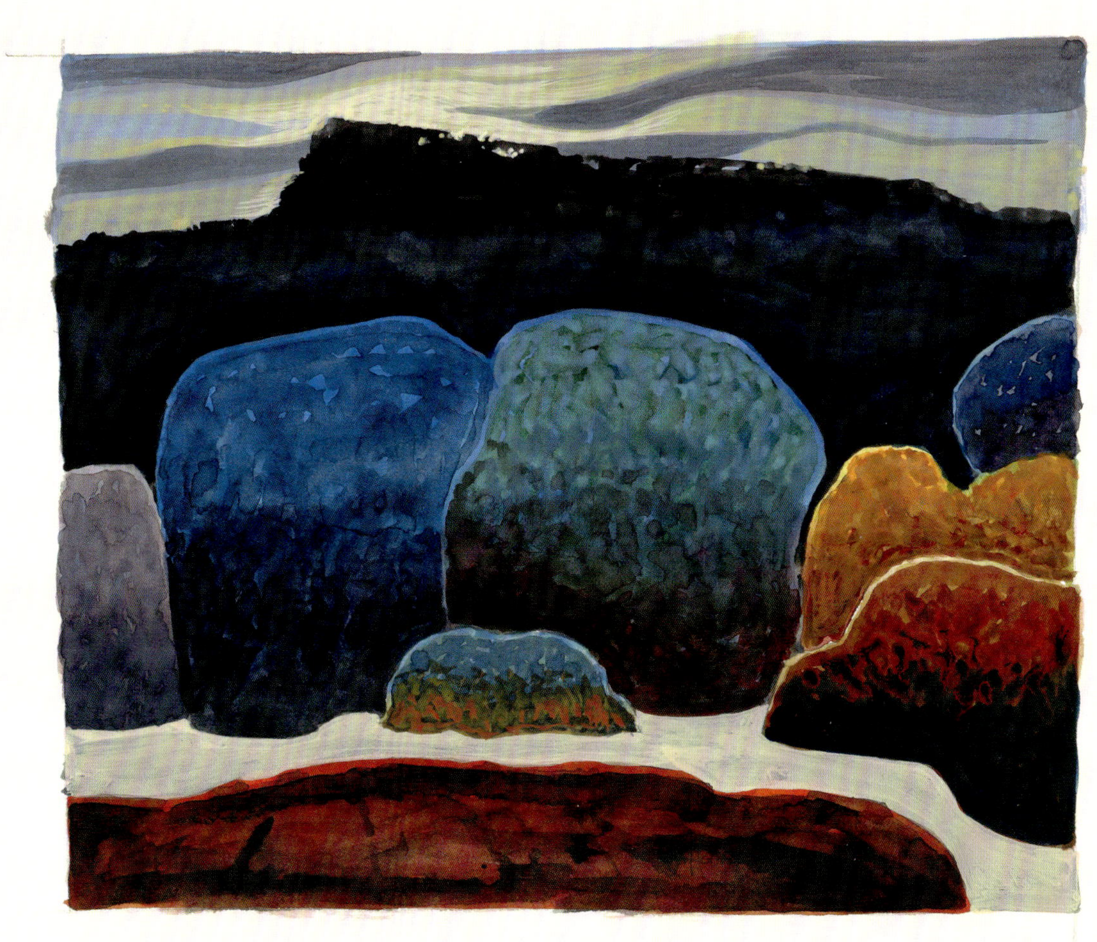

Blue Glow, 1979

Watercolor
Image: 6¾ x 8⅜ in. (17.1 x 21.3 cm);
sheet: 9 x 12 in. (22.9 x 30.5 cm)
Collection of Sloan Wilson

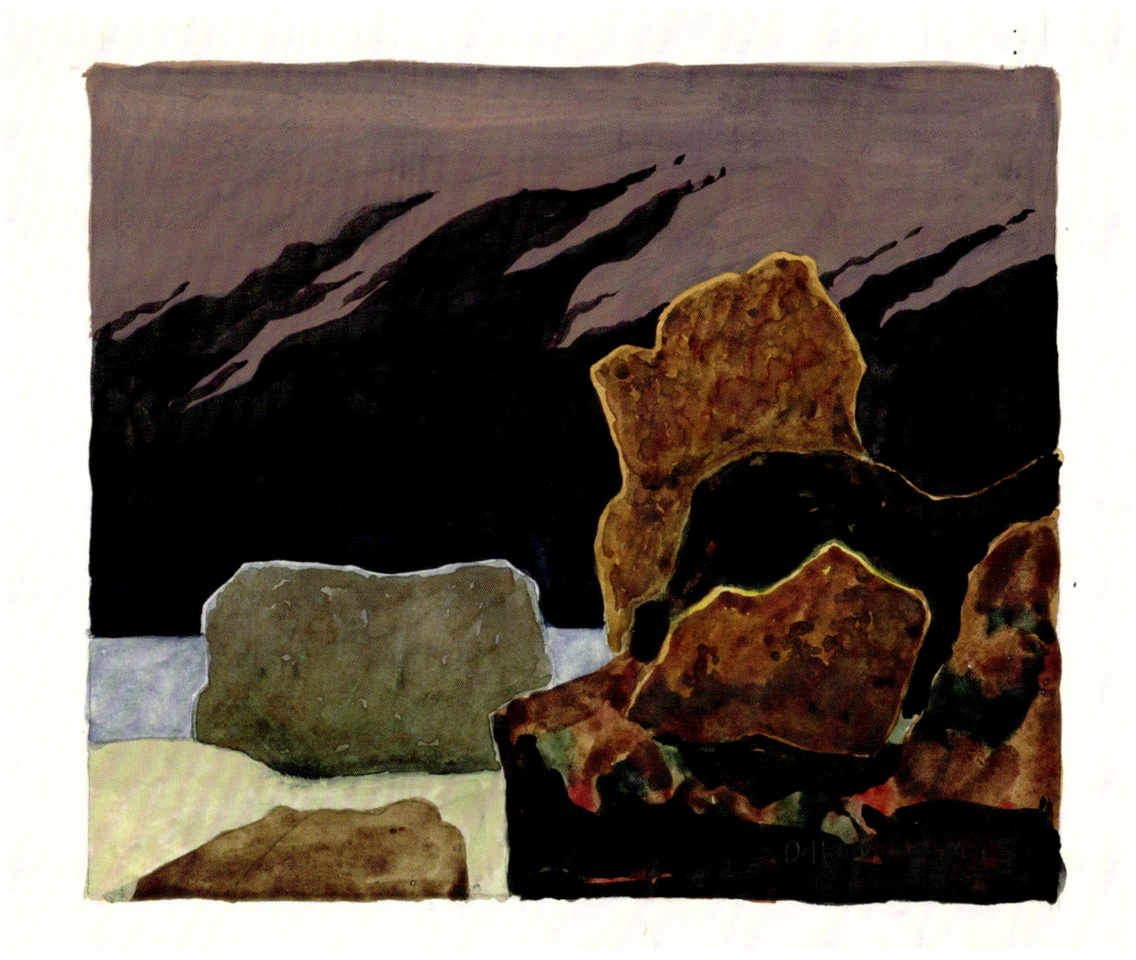

Night Shore, 1979

Watercolor
Image: 7½ x 8⅝ in. (19.1 x 21.9 cm);
sheet: 9 x 12 in. (22.9 x 30.5 cm)
Collection of Sloan Wilson

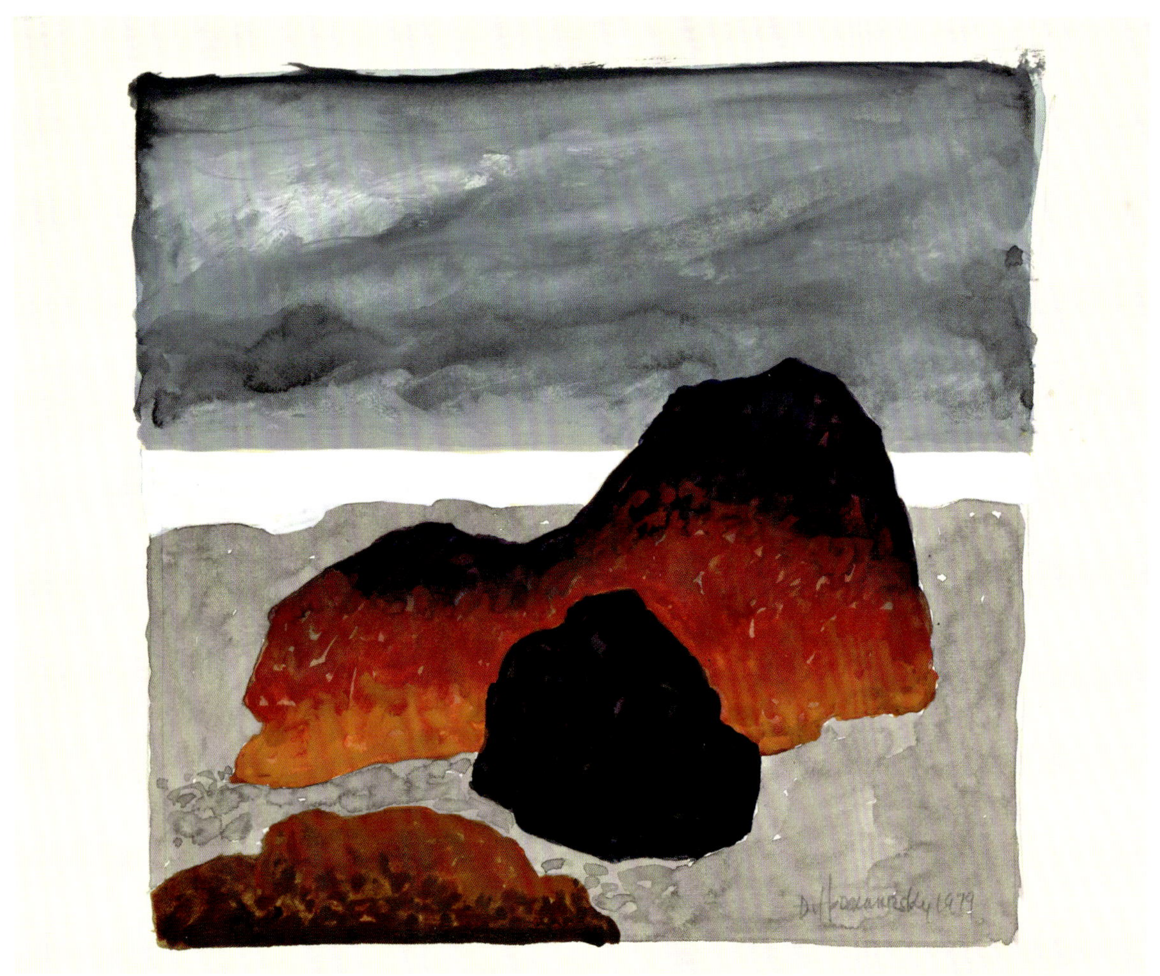

PLATE 76

The Red and the Black, 1979

Watercolor
Image: 7½ x 7⅝ in. (19.1 x 19.4 cm);
sheet: 9 x 12 in. (22.9 x 30.5 cm)
Collection of Sloan Wilson

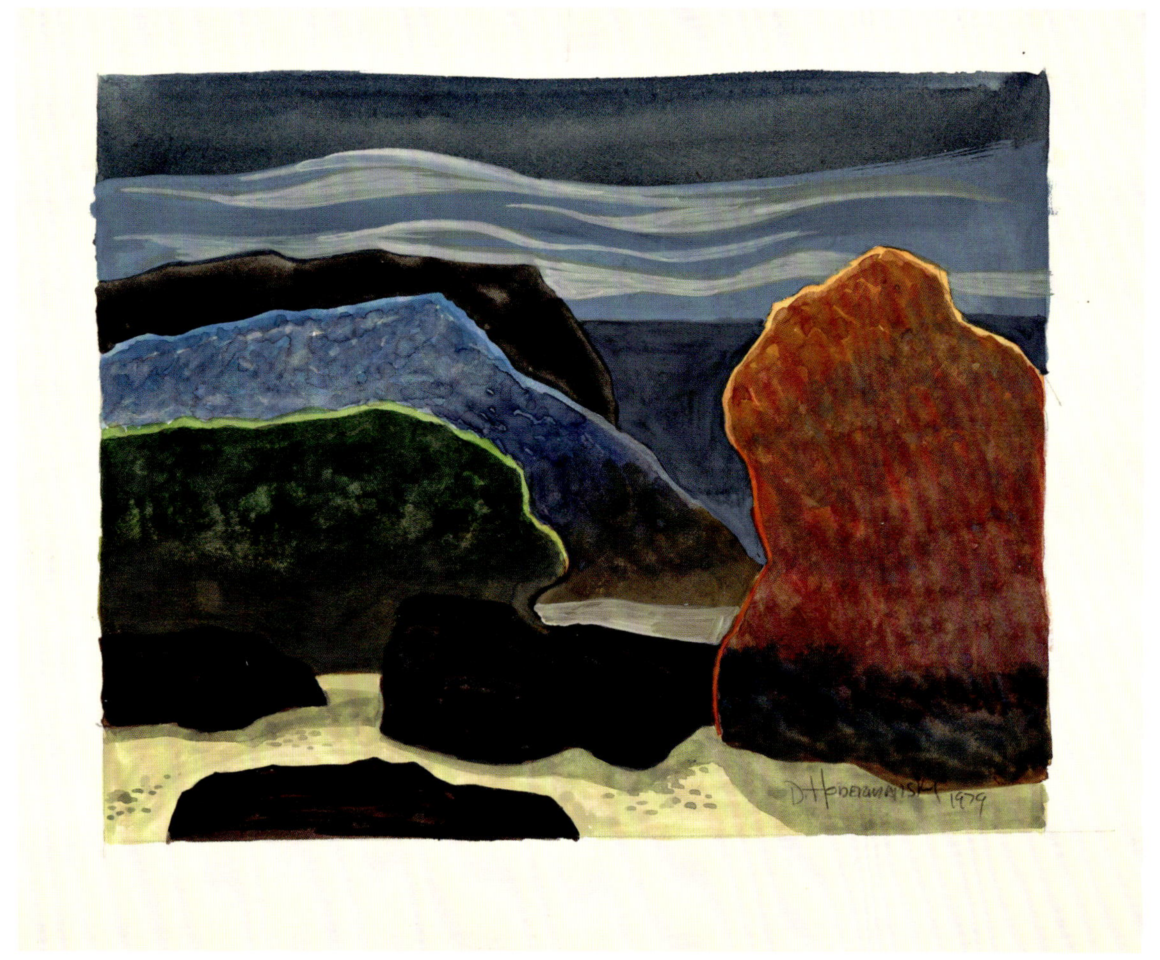

PLATE 77

Untitled, 1979

Watercolor
Image: 6¾ x 8⅝ in. (17.1 x 21.9 cm);
sheet: 9 x 12 in. (22.9 x 30.5 cm)
Collection of Sloan Wilson

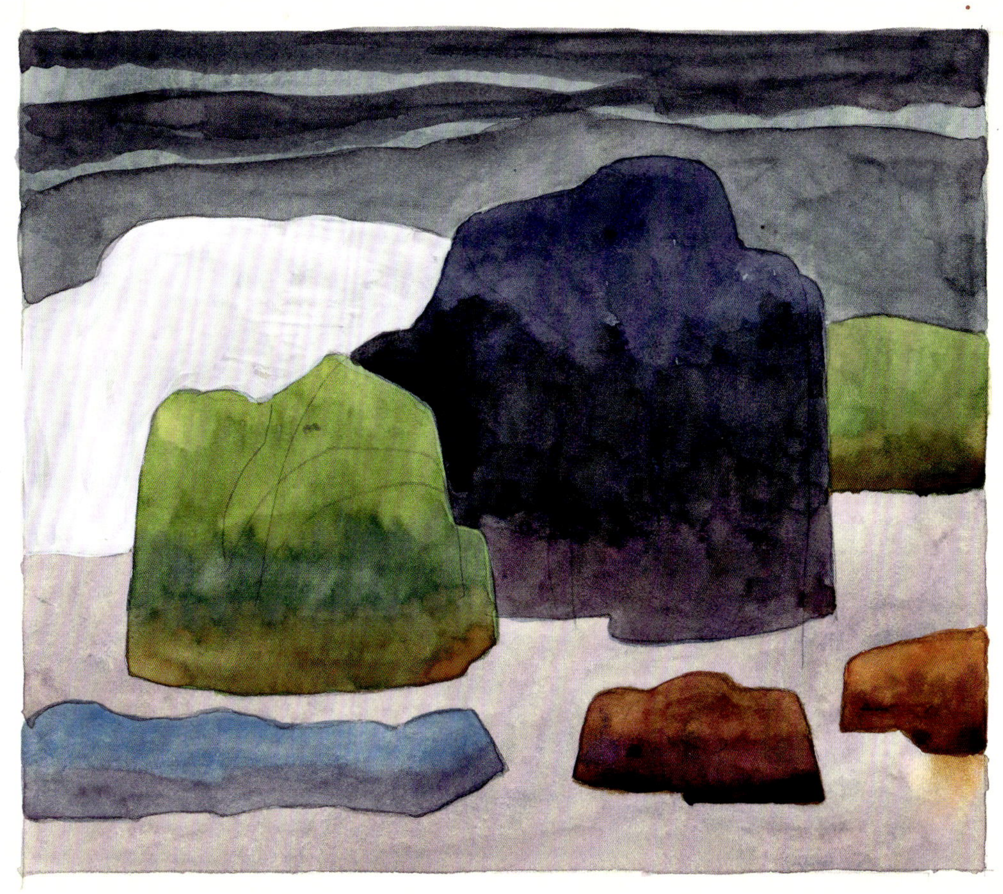

PLATE 78
Blue Rock, 1980
Watercolor
Image: 6⅛ x 7¼ in. (15.6 x 18.4 cm);
sheet: 9 x 12 in. (22.9 x 30.5 cm)
Collection of Sloan Wilson

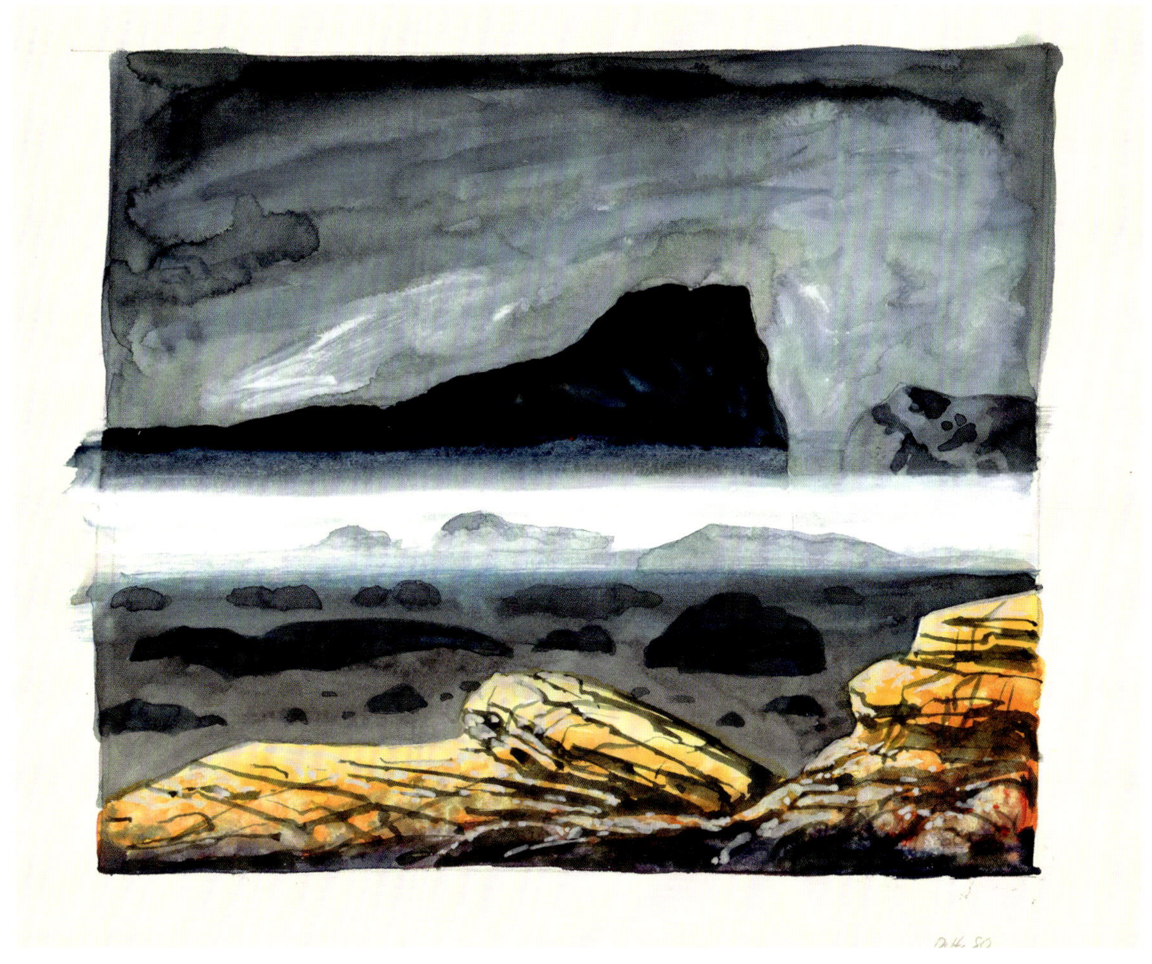

PLATE 79
Clouded Cold Shore, 1980
Watercolor
Image: 7¼ x 8½ in. (18.4 x 21.6 cm);
sheet: 9 x 12 in. (22.9 x 30.5 cm)
Collection of Sloan Wilson

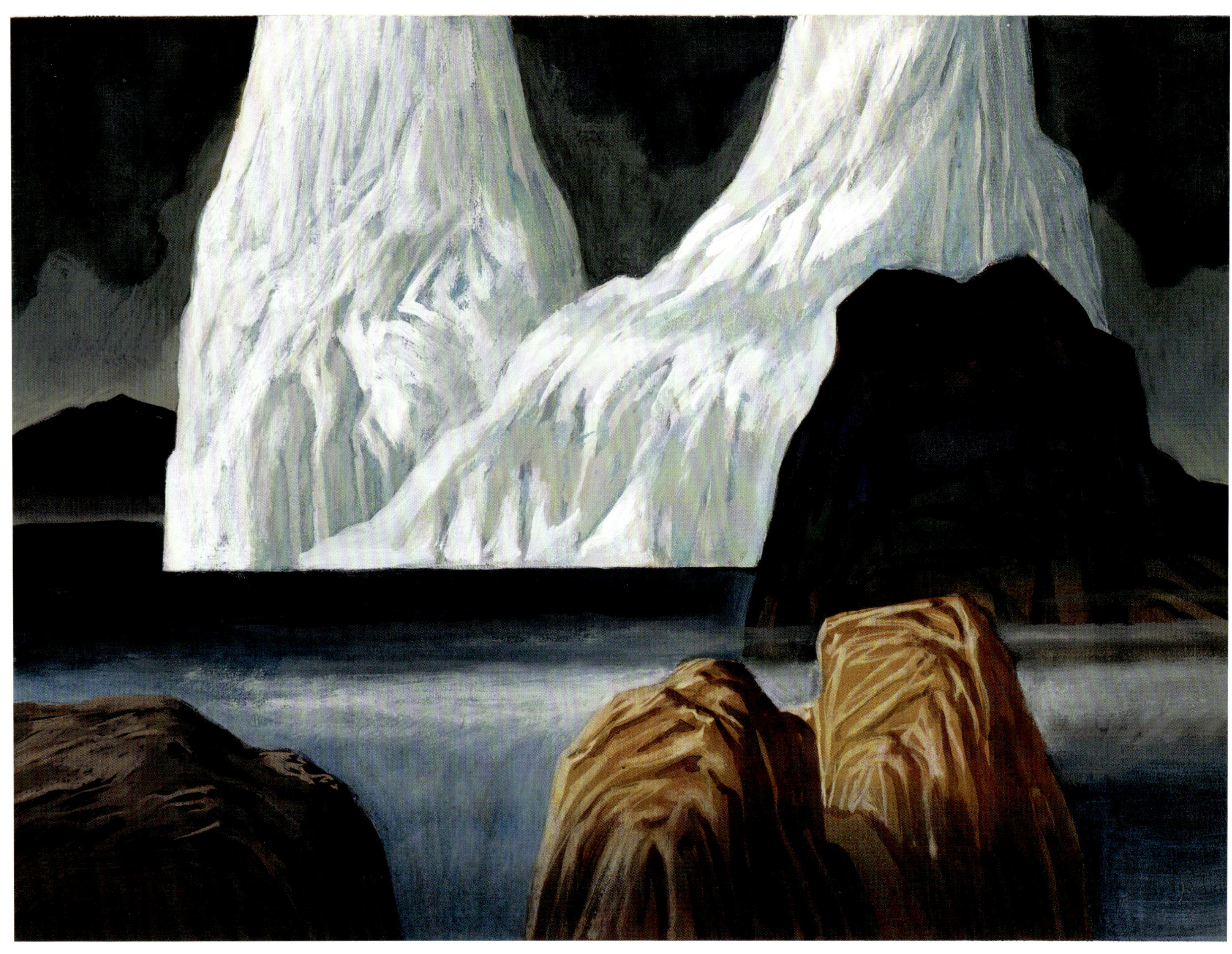

PLATE 80

Ice Dome, 1980

Watercolor
Image: 16⅜ x 22⅜ in. (41.6 x 56.8 cm);
sheet: 17 x 23 in. (43.2 x 58.4 cm)
Estate of the artist

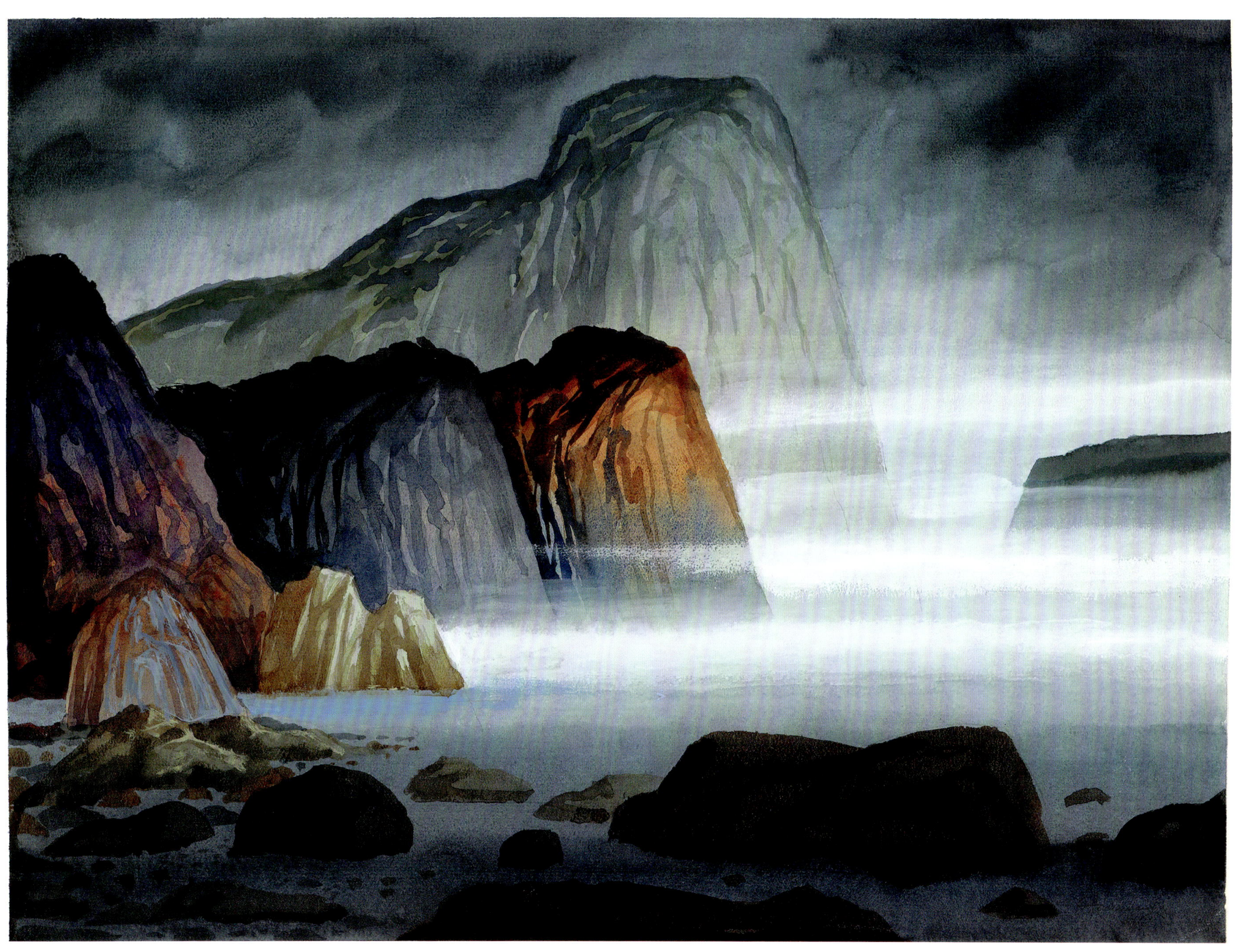

PLATE 81

Labrador Shore, 1980

Watercolor
Image: 16⅜ x 22½ in. (41.6 x 57.1 cm);
sheet: 17 x 23 in. (43.2 x 58.4 cm)
Estate of the artist

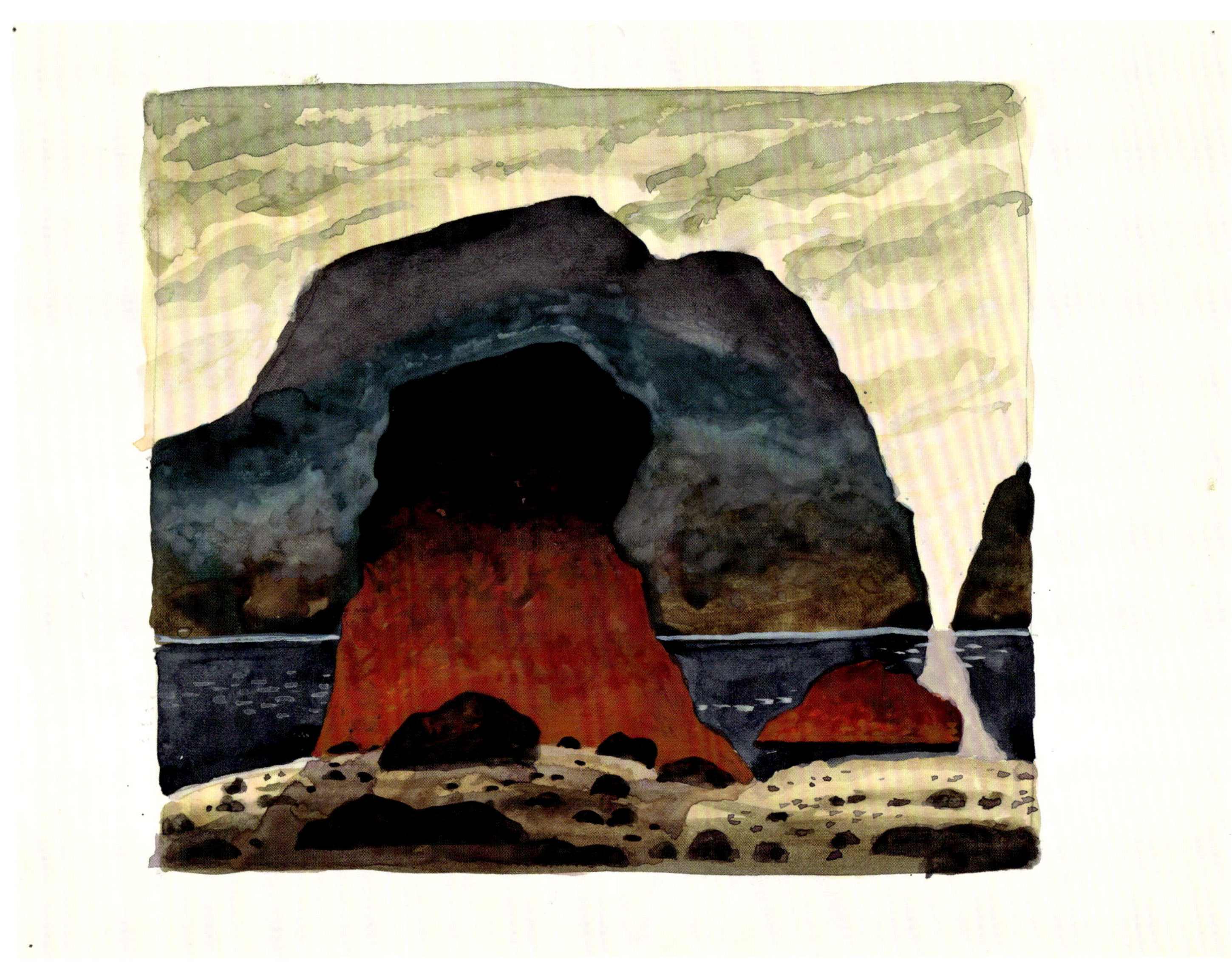

PLATE 82

Monhegan Barrier, 1980

Watercolor
7¼ x 8½ in. (18.4 x 21.6 cm)
Collection of Sloan Wilson

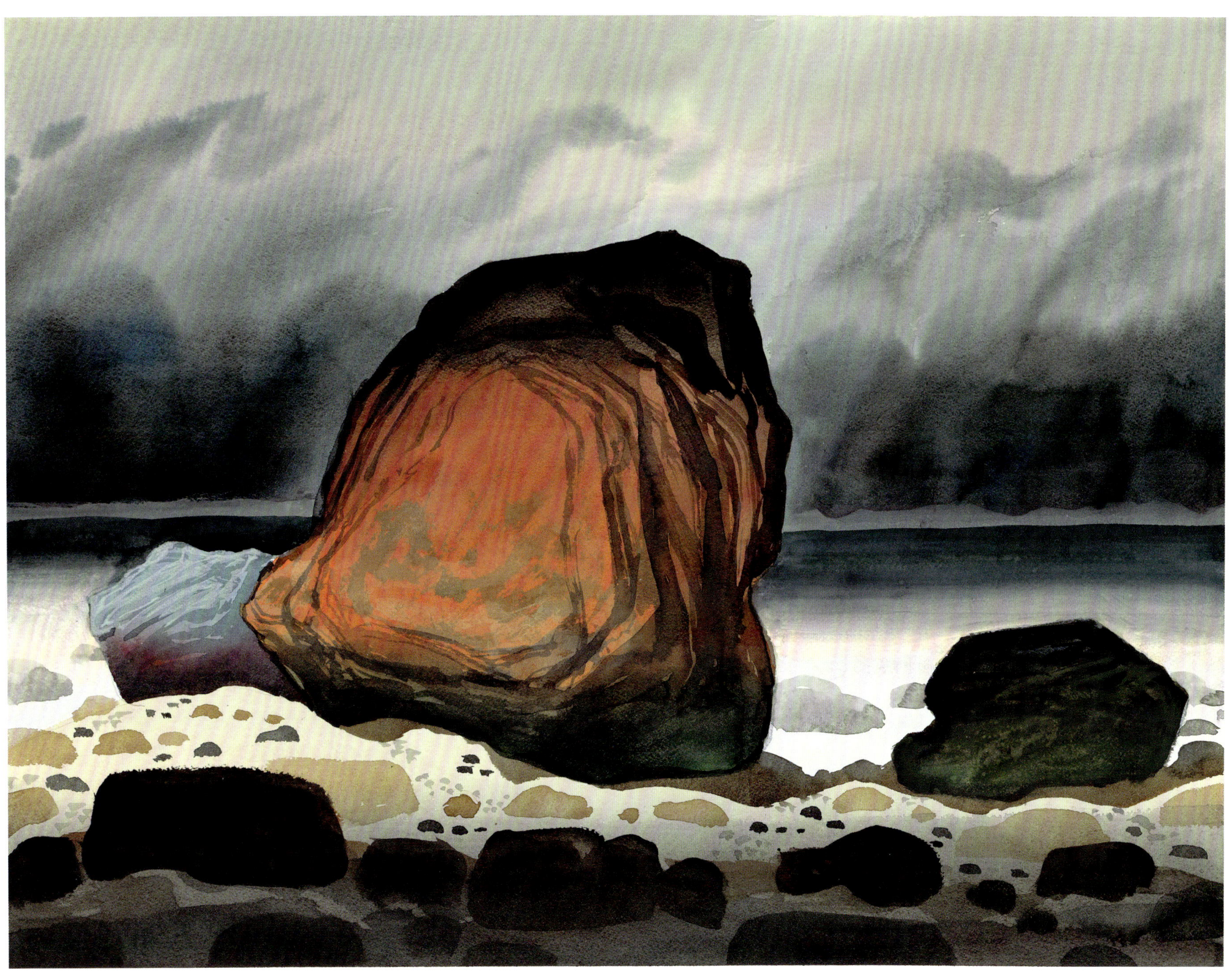

PLATE 83
Red Rock, 1980

Watercolor
Image: 17⅜ x 23¼ in. (44.1 x 59.1 cm);
sheet: 18 x 24 in. (45.7 x 61 cm)
Estate of the artist

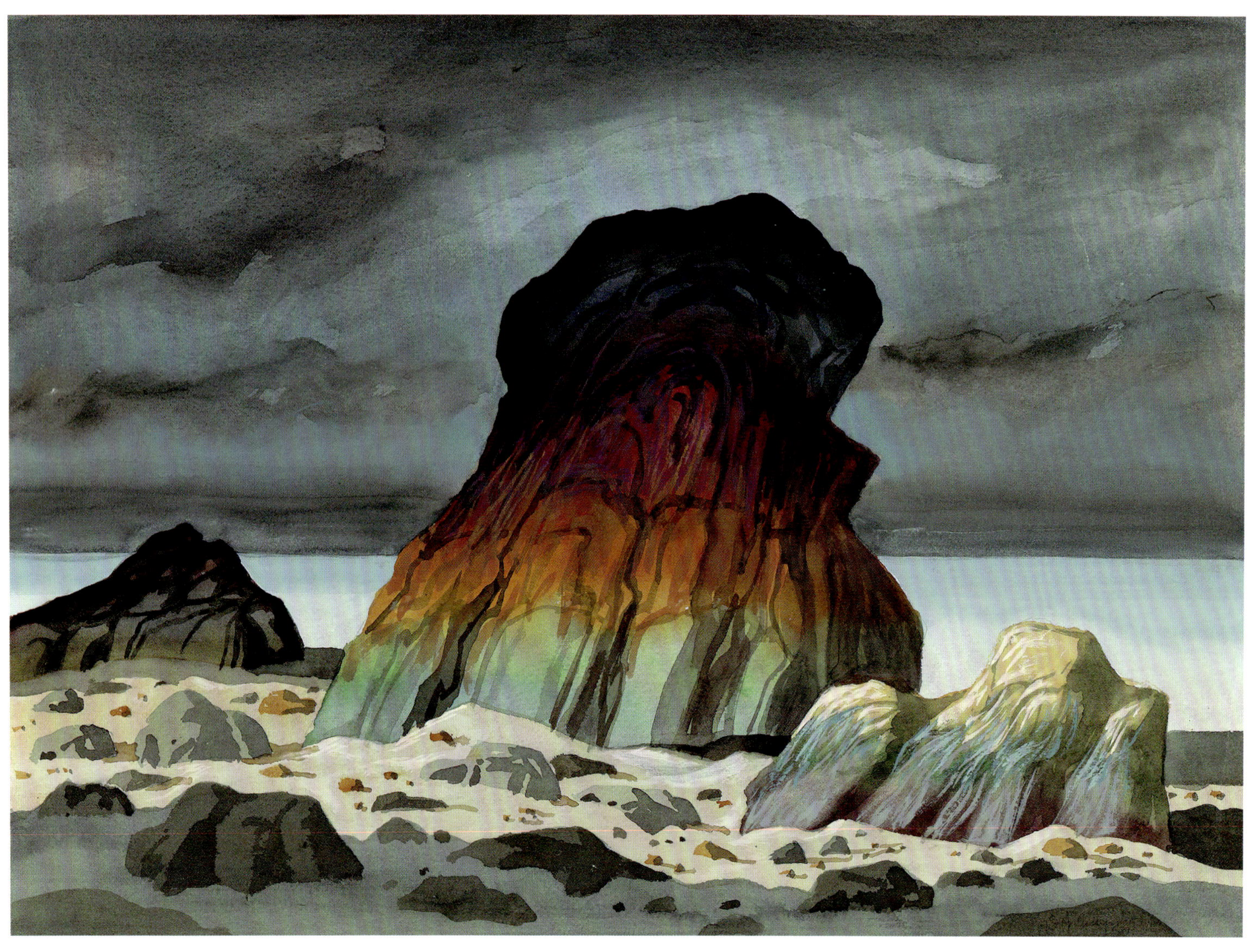

Early Morning at the Shore, 1981

Watercolor
Image: 17⅜ x 23⅞ in. (44.1 x 60.6 cm);
sheet: 18 x 24 in. (45.7 x 61 cm)
Estate of the artist

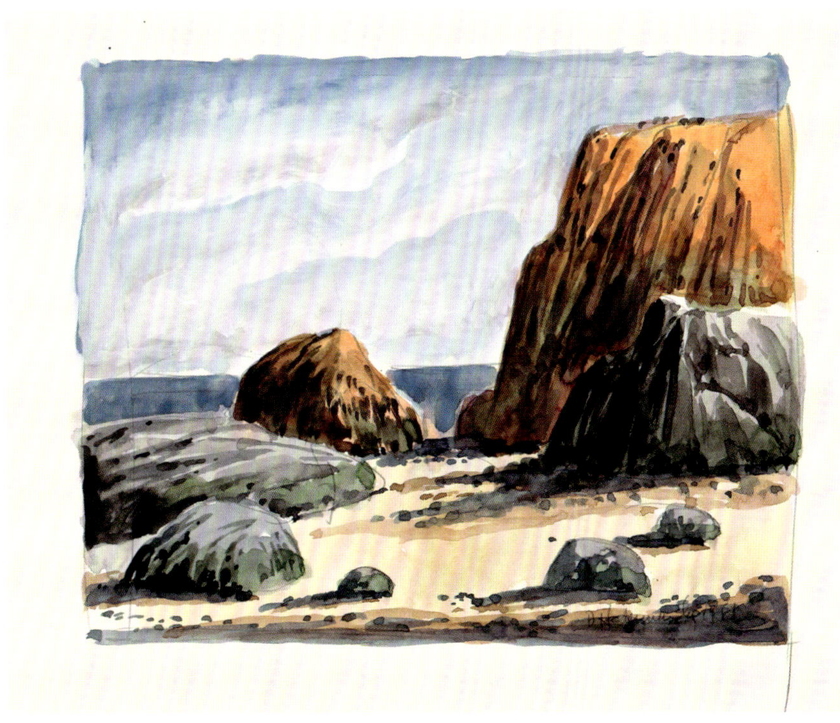

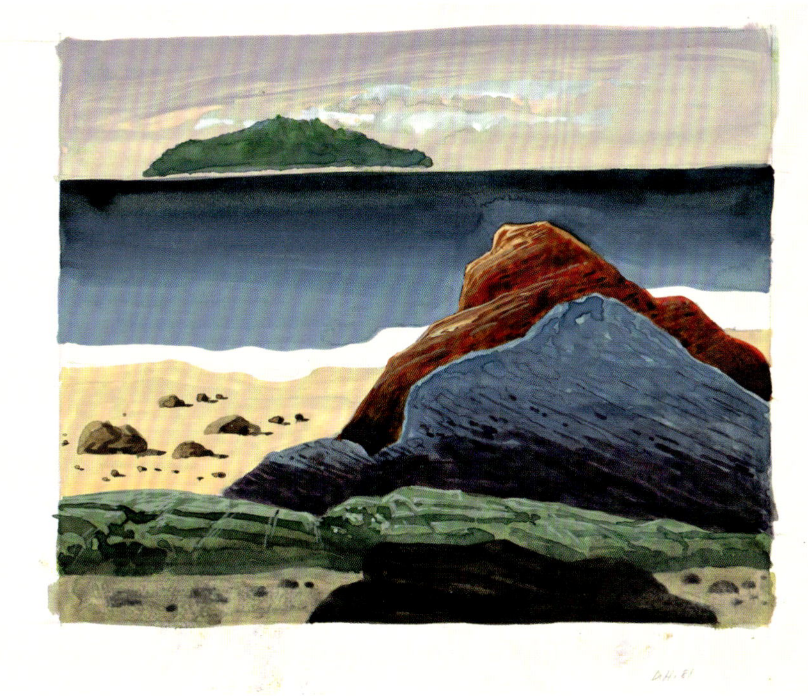

Rocks on an Outer Island, 1981

Watercolor
Image: 6⅛ x 7⅝ in. (15.5 x 19.4);
sheet: 8 x 11 in. (20.3 x 27.9 cm)
Collection of Sloan Wilson

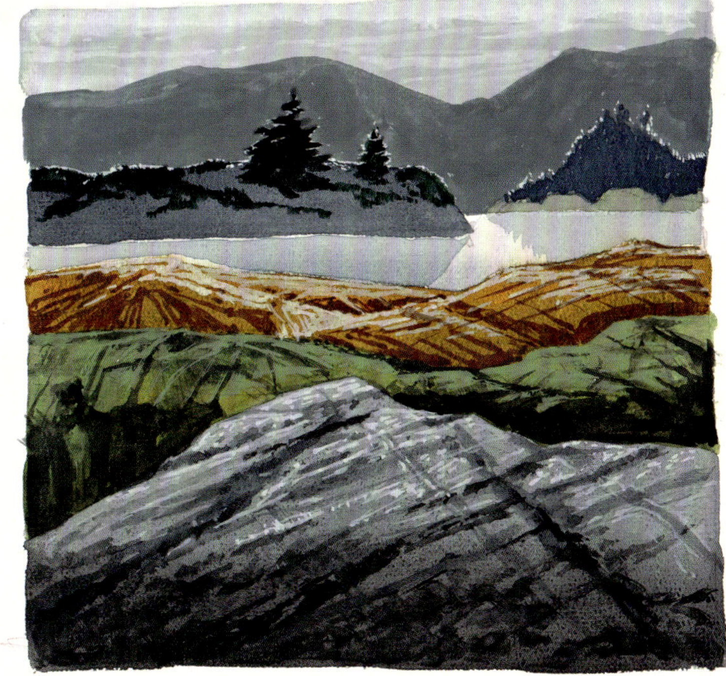

PLATE 87
High Noon, 1983

Watercolor
Image: 7¼ x 7¾ in. (18.4 x 19.7 cm);
sheet: 8¾ x 11½ in. (22.2 x 29.2 cm)
Collection of Sloan Wilson

PLATE 86
Still Water, 1981

Watercolor
Image: 7 x 8¾ in. (17.8 x 22.2 cm);
sheet: 9 x 12 in. (22.9 x 30.5 cm)
Collection of Sloan Wilson

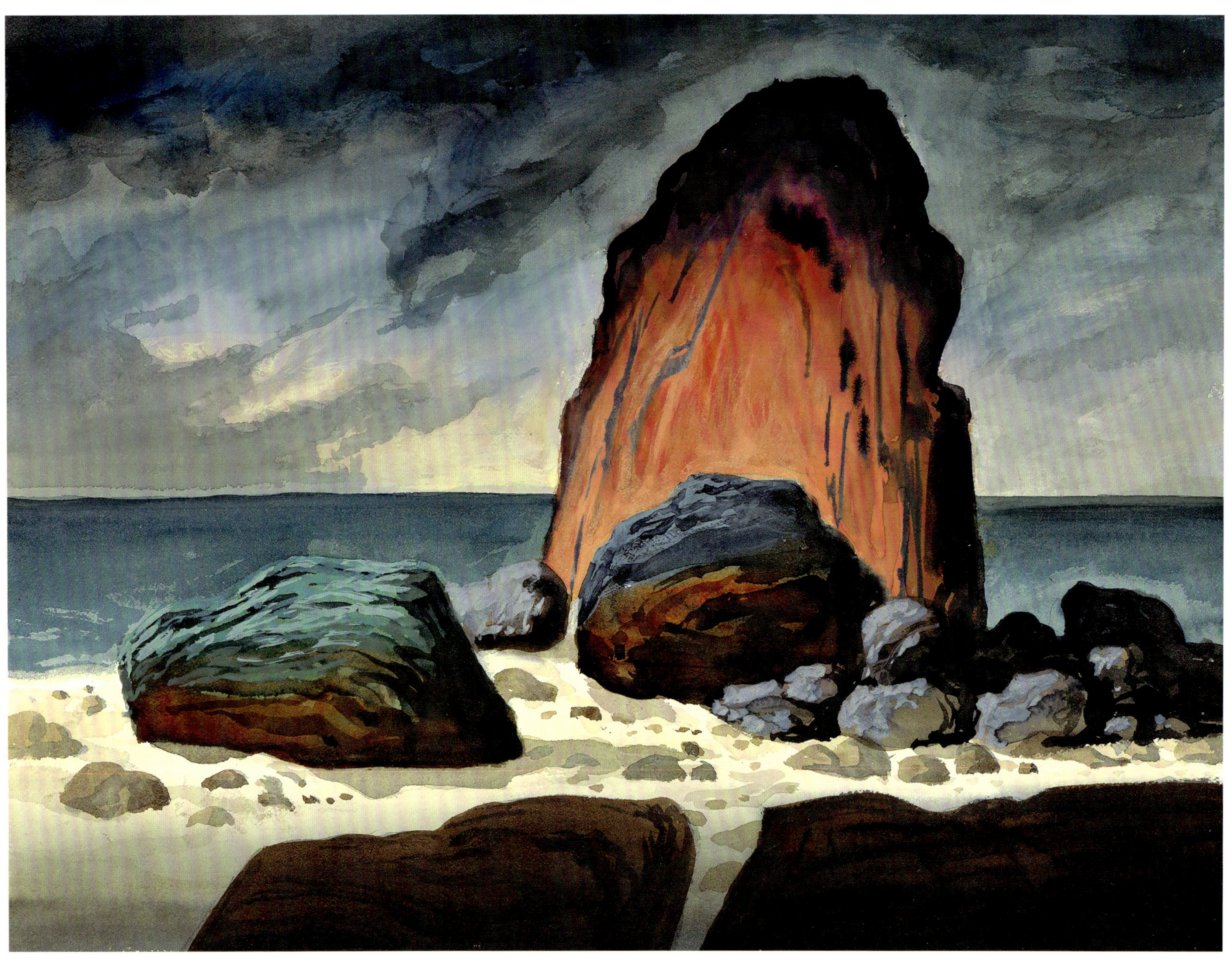

PLATE 88

Great Presence at the Shore, 1983

Watercolor
18 x 24 in. (45.7 x 61 cm)
Estate of the artist

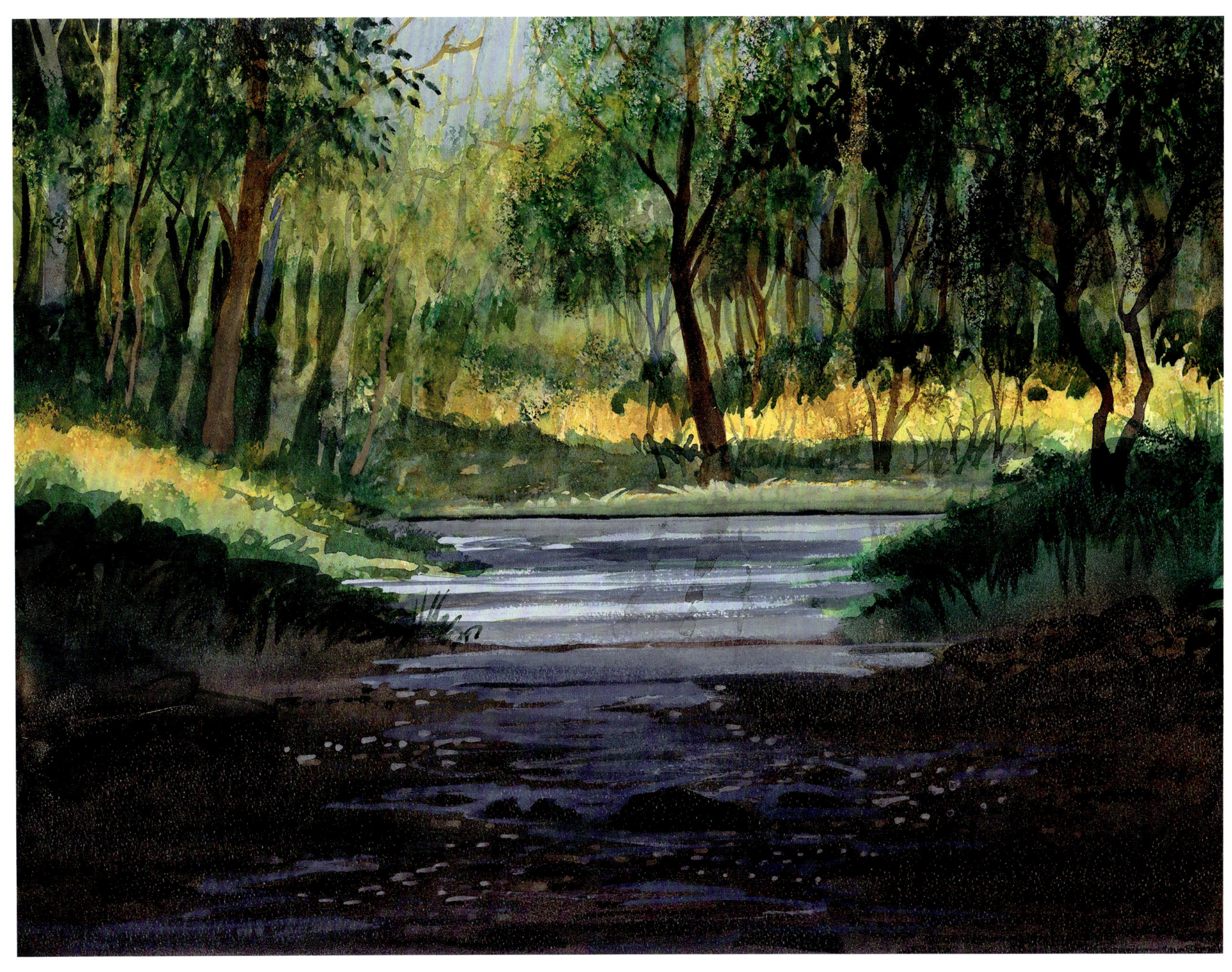

Deerfield River Shallows, High Summer, 1983

Watercolor
Image: 16¾ x 22½ in. (42.5 x 57.2 cm);
sheet: 17½ x 23 in. (44.5 x 58.4 cm)
Estate of the artist

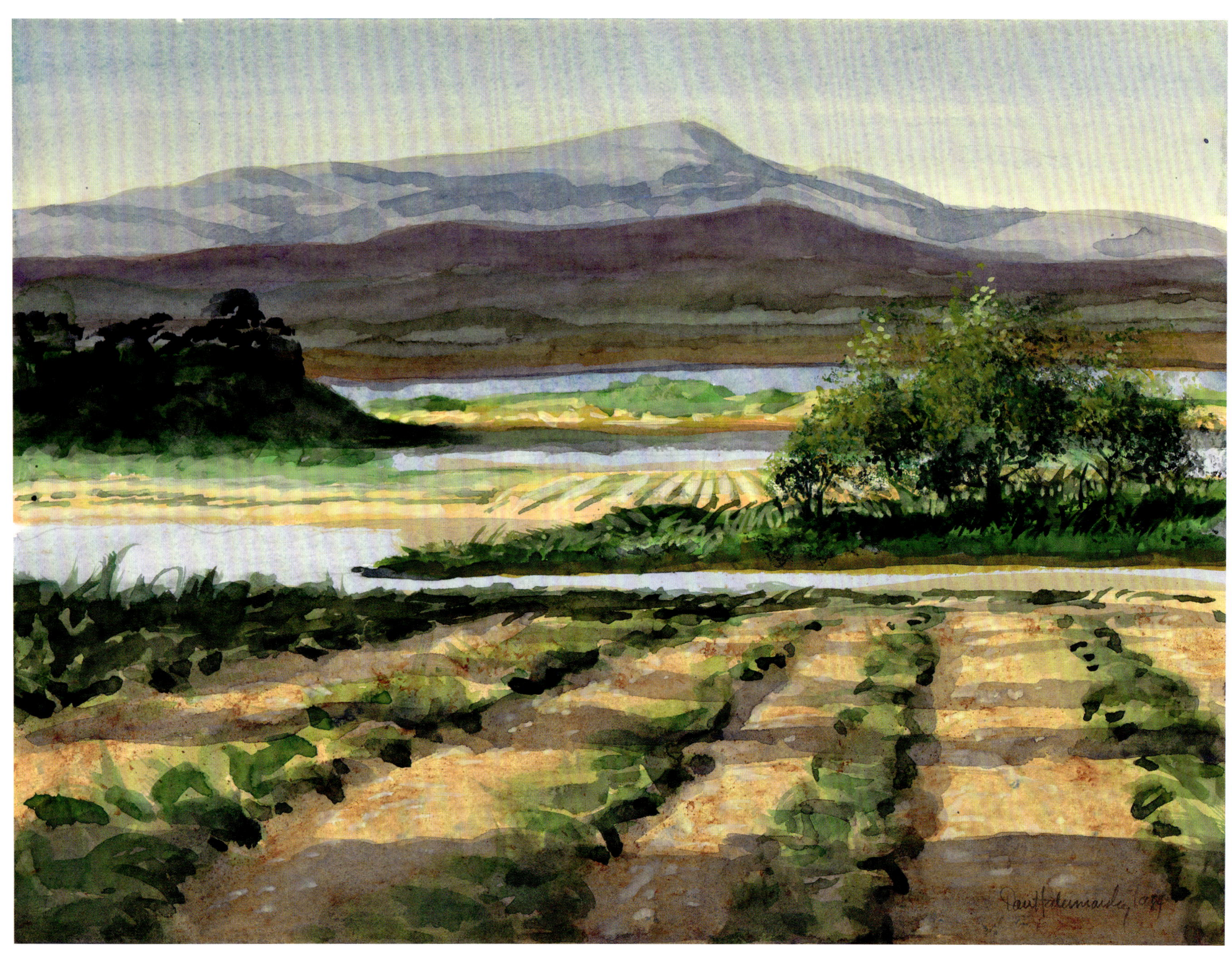

PLATE 90

Valley Farm, Spring, 1984

Watercolor
Image: 14 x 19⅛ in. (35.6 x 48.6 cm);
sheet: 14¾ x 19⅞ in. (37.5 x 50.5 cm)
Estate of the artist

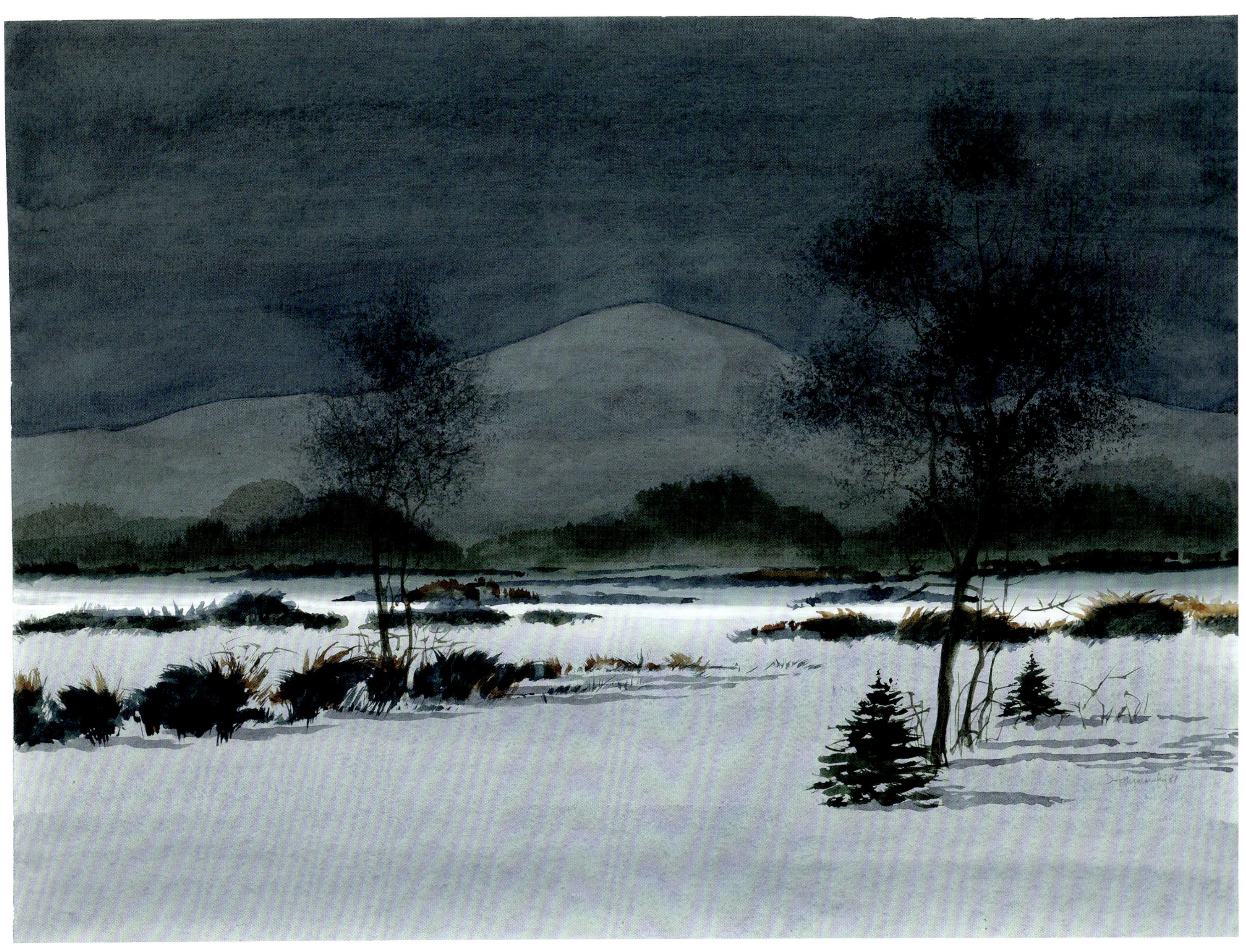

PLATE 91

Belknap Night, 1987

Watercolor
Image: 21¼ x 28⅞ in. (54 x 73.3 cm);
sheet: 22¼ x 29⅞ in. (56.5 x 75.9 cm)
Collection of Elisabeth Hodermarsky and Sloan Wilson

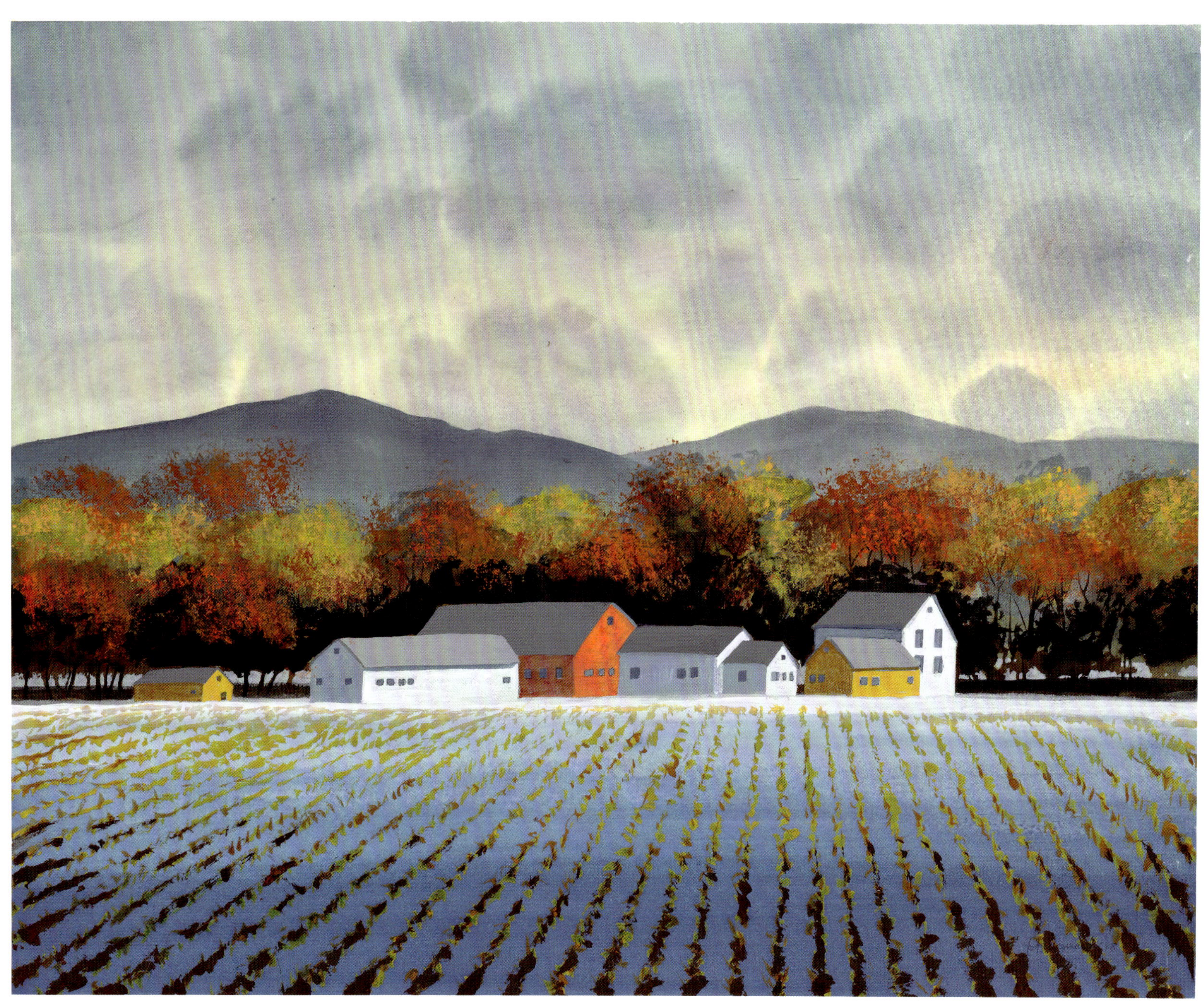

PLATE 92
Valley Fields, Winter, 1988
Watercolor
Image: 21⅝ x 27⅜ in. (54.9 x 69.5 cm);
sheet: 23 x 28⅝ in. (58.4 x 72.7 cm)
Estate of the artist

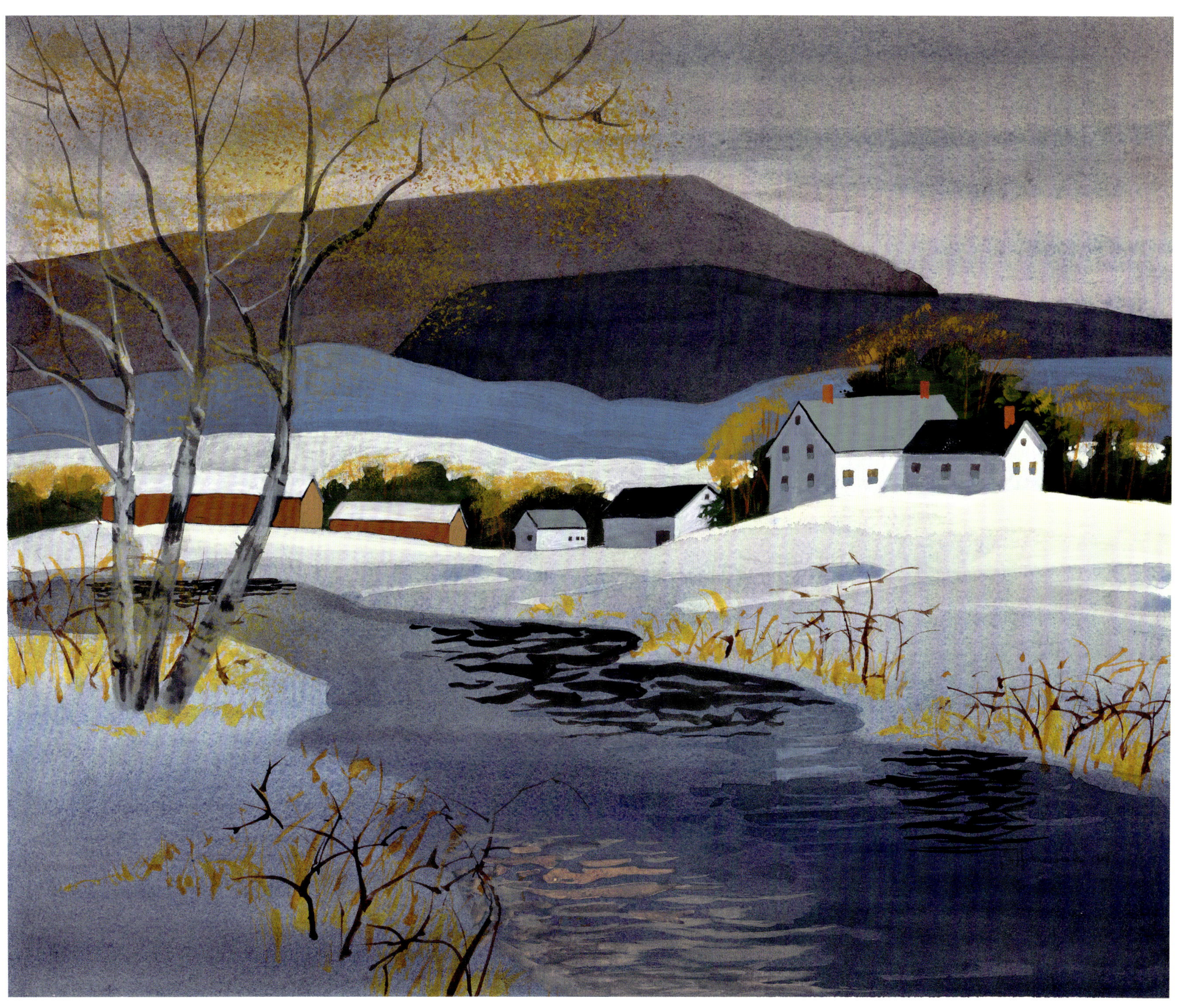

PLATE 93
Winter at the Farm, 1988

Watercolor
Image: 18⅝ x 22⅞ in. (47.3 x 58.1 cm);
sheet: 19½ x 23⅝ in. (49.5 x 60 cm)
Estate of the artist

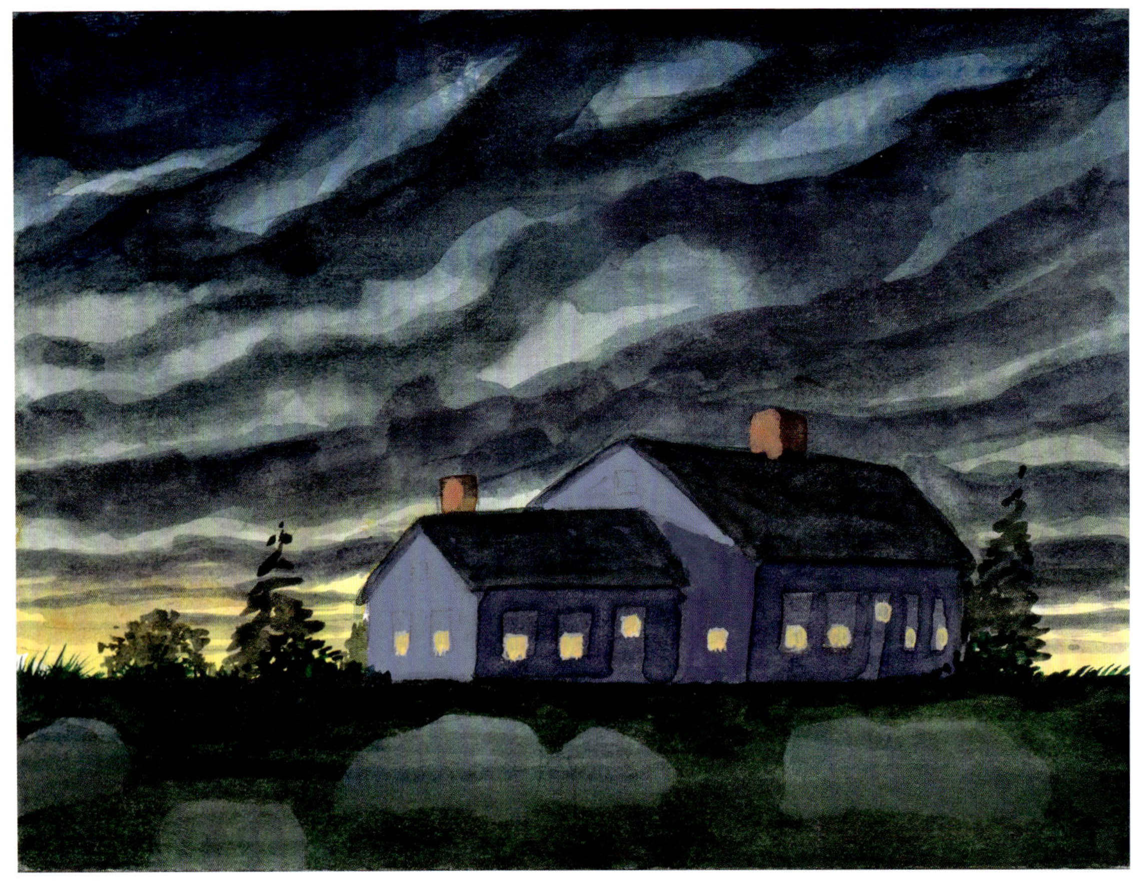

PLATE 94
Home at Dusk, 1988
Watercolor
4 x 6 in. (10.2 x 15.2 cm)
Estate of the artist

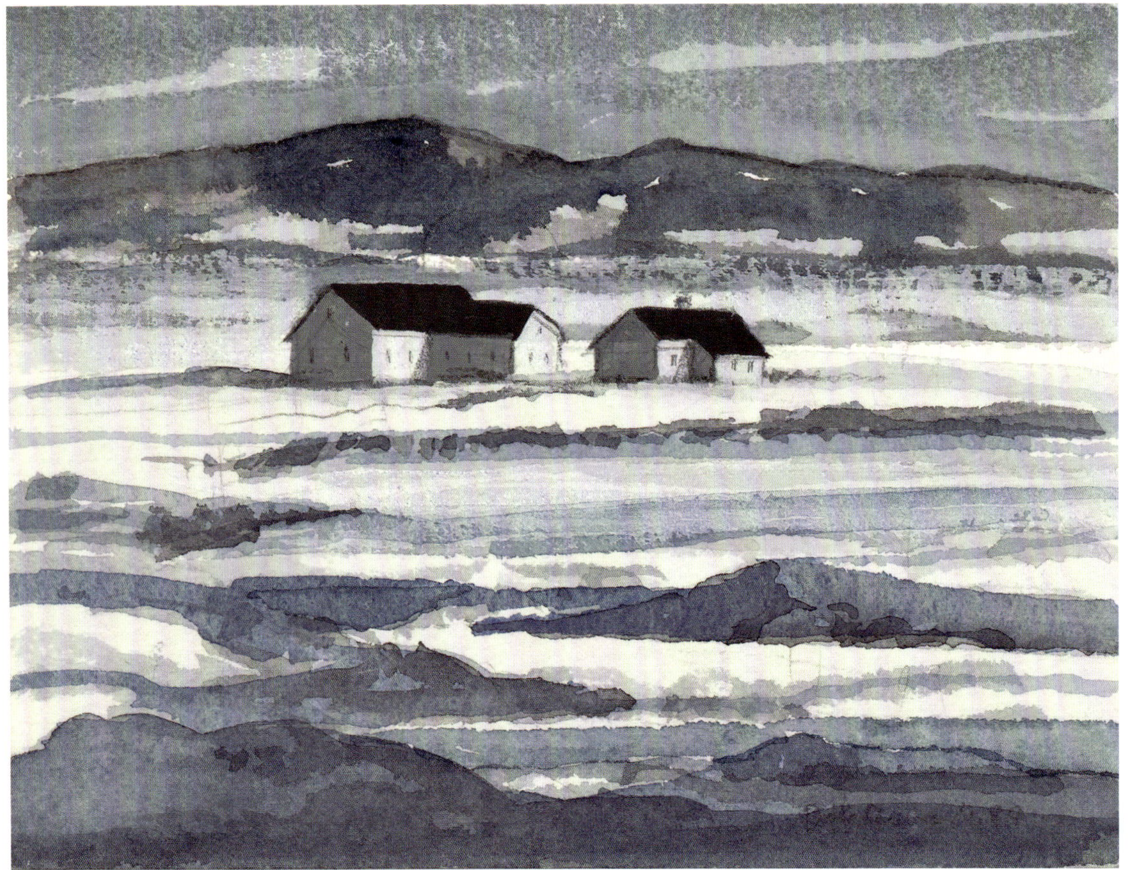

PLATE 95
Winter Blues (Deerfield Meadows), 1989
Watercolor
5 x 6½ in. (12.7 x 16.5 cm)
Estate of the artist

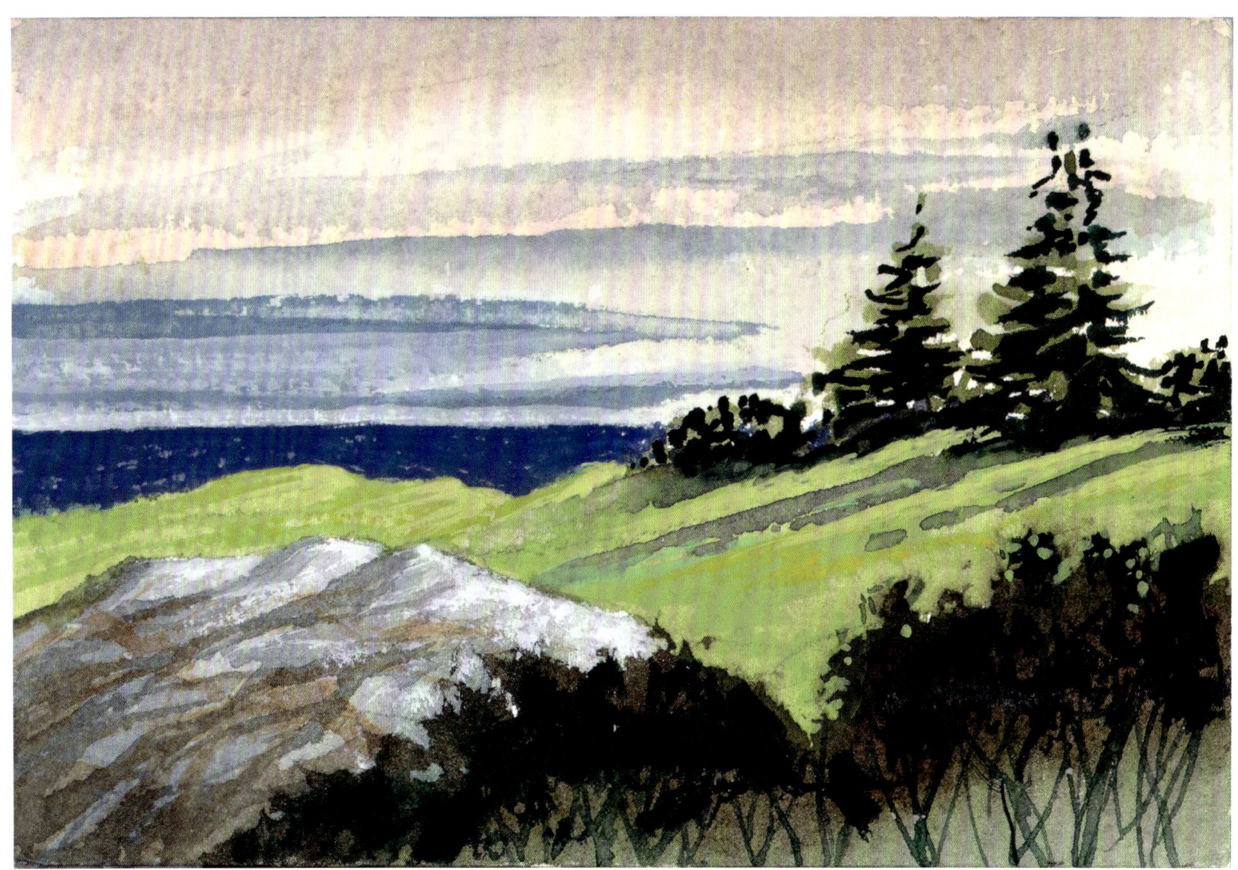

PLATE 96
To the Open Sea, 1991

Watercolor
3⅞ x 5¾ in. (9.8 x 14.6 cm)
Estate of the artist

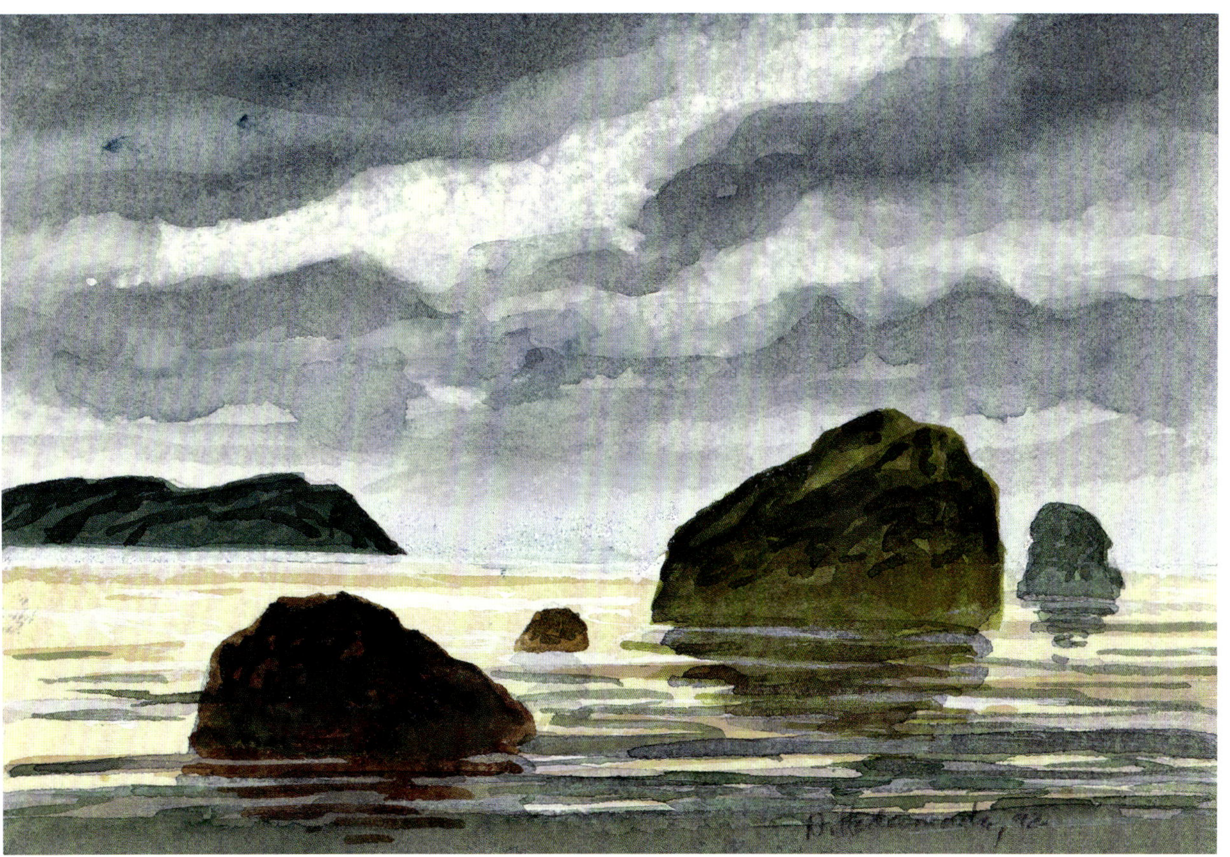

PLATE 97
One, Two, Three, Four, 1992

Watercolor
4 x 6 in. (10.2 x 15.2 cm)
Estate of the artist

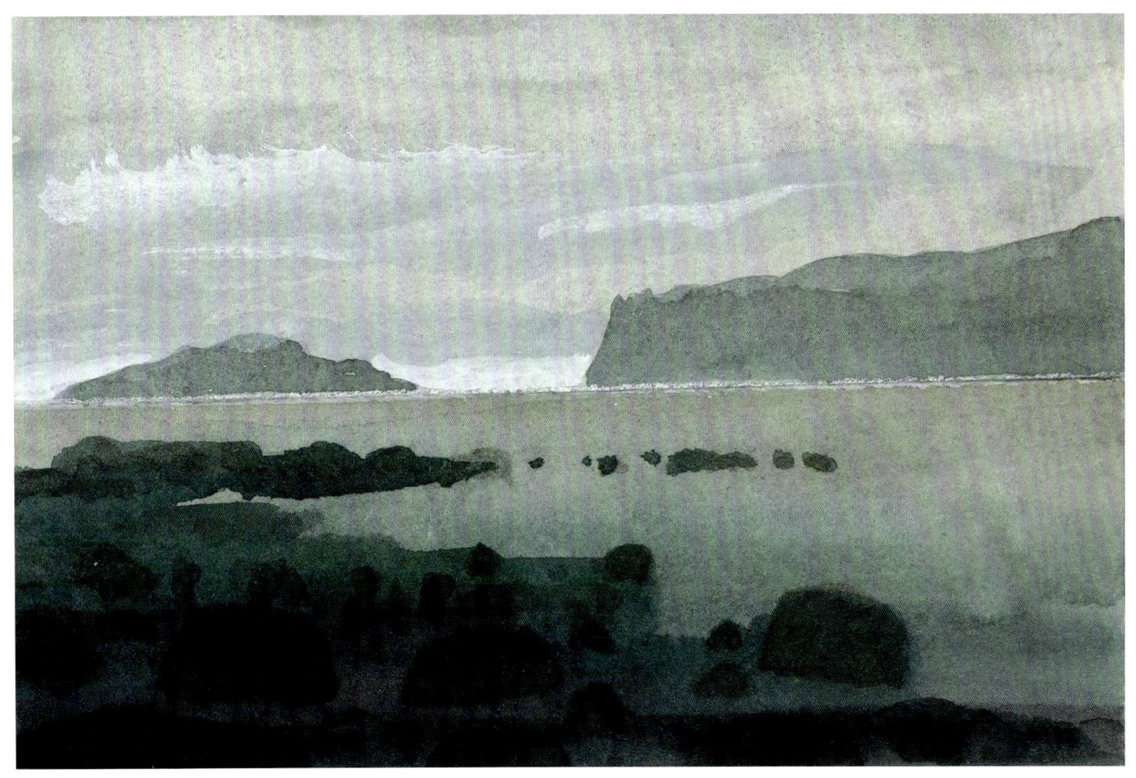

PLATE 98
Thoughts on the Quiet of Islands, 1993
Watercolor
4 x 6 in. (10.2 x 15.2 cm)
Estate of the artist

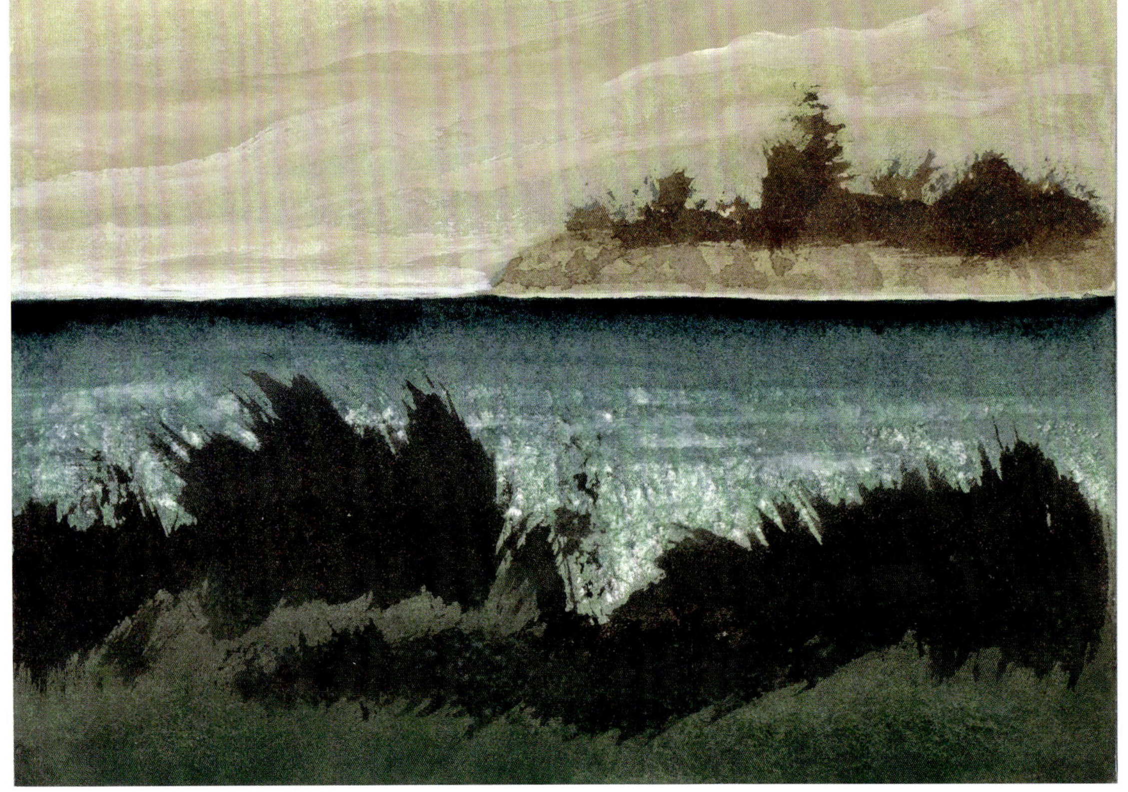

PLATE 99
Winter Study, 1993
Watercolor
5 x 7 in. (12.7 x 17.8 cm)
Estate of the artist

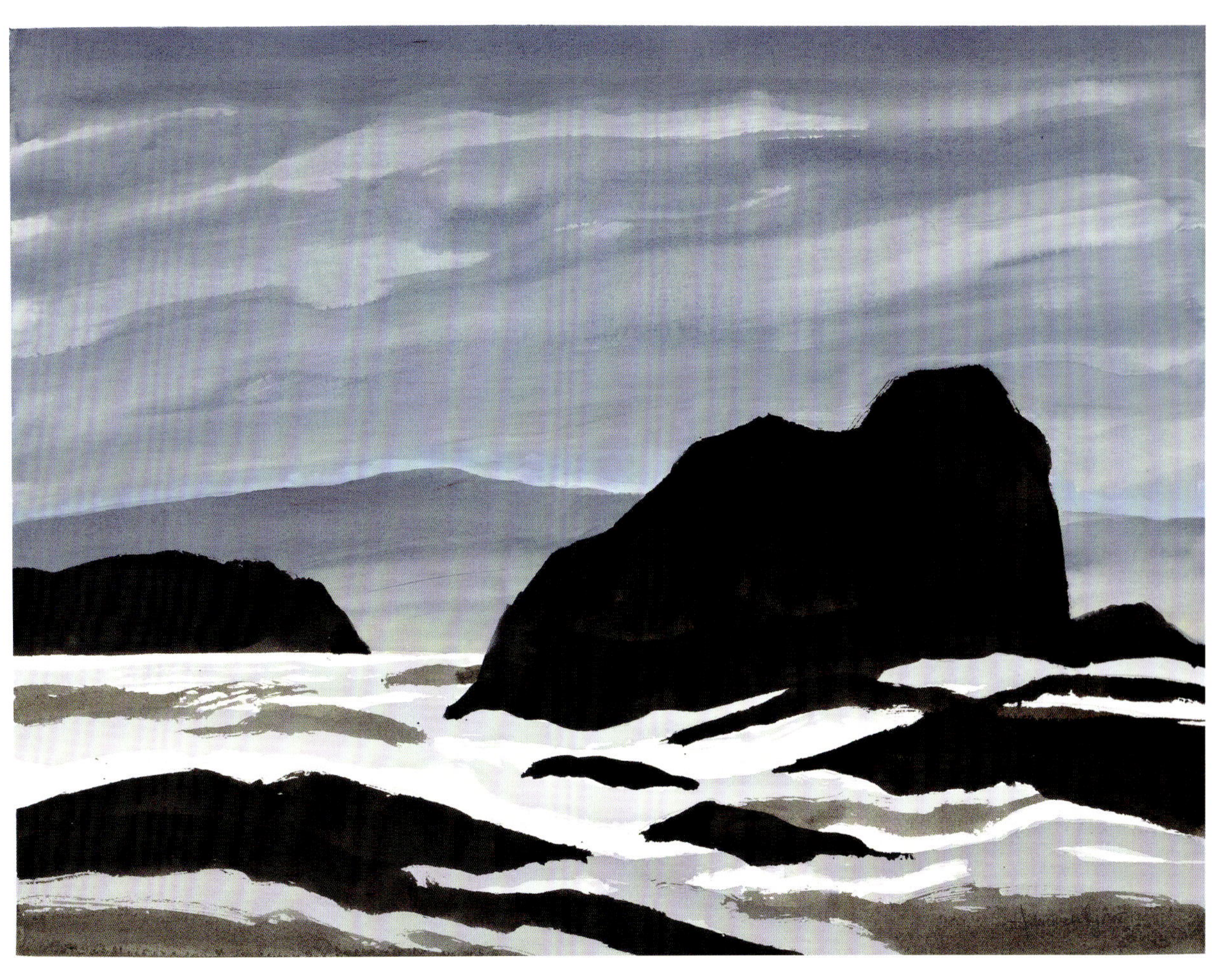

Black Rocks on the Winter Shore, 1995

Watercolor with India ink
Image: 21⅜ x 29 in. (54.9 x 73.7 cm);
sheet: 22¾ x 30⅛ in. (57.8 x 76.50 cm)
Estate of the artist

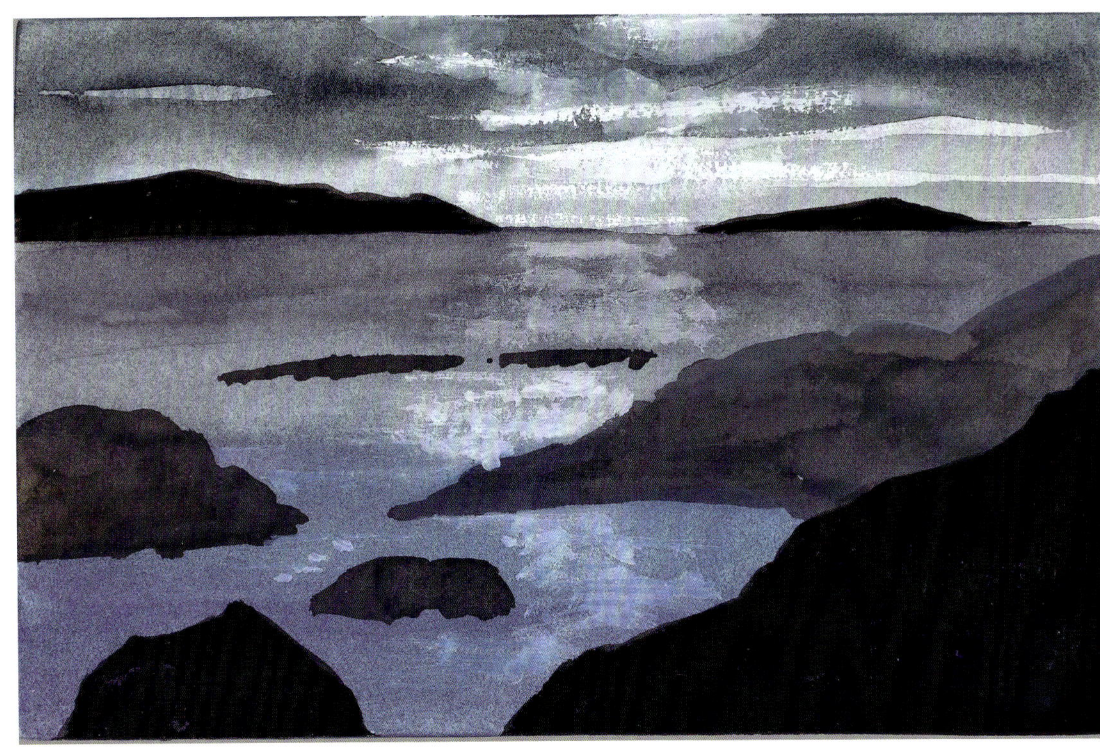

PLATE 101

Full Moon, 1995

Watercolor
3¾ x 6 in. (9.5 x 15.2 cm)
Estate of the artist

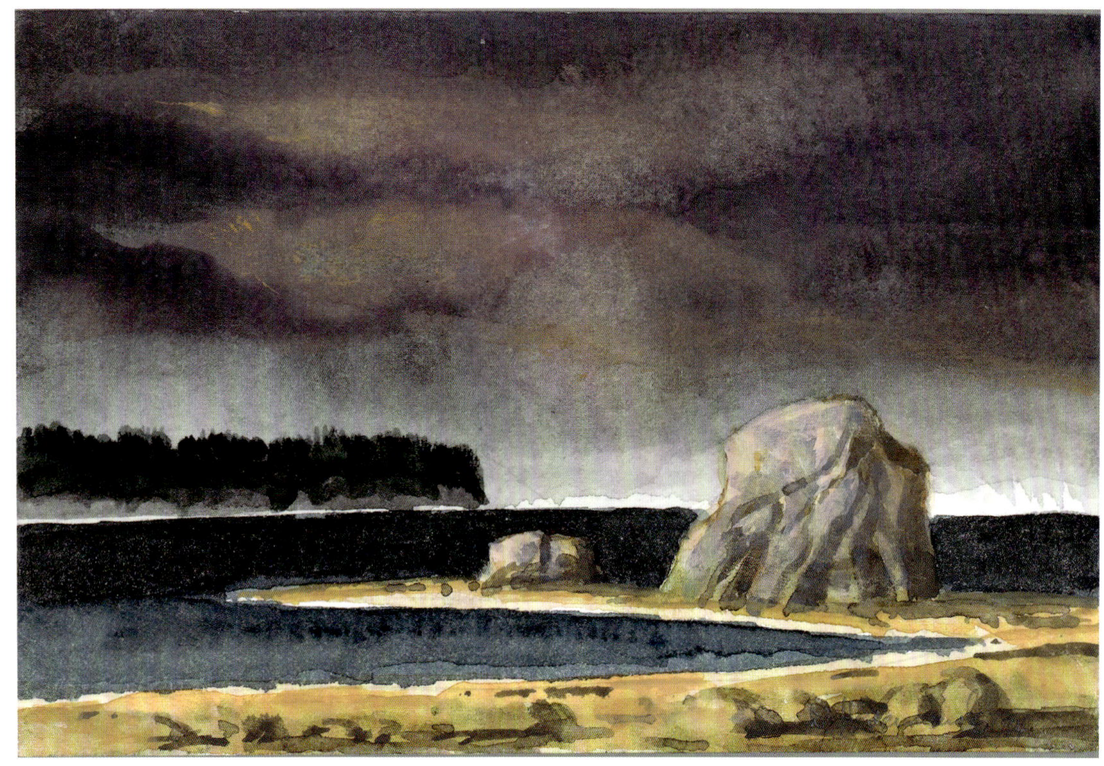

Storm over the Harbor, 1995
Watercolor
4 x 6 in. (10.2 x 15.2 cm)
Estate of the artist

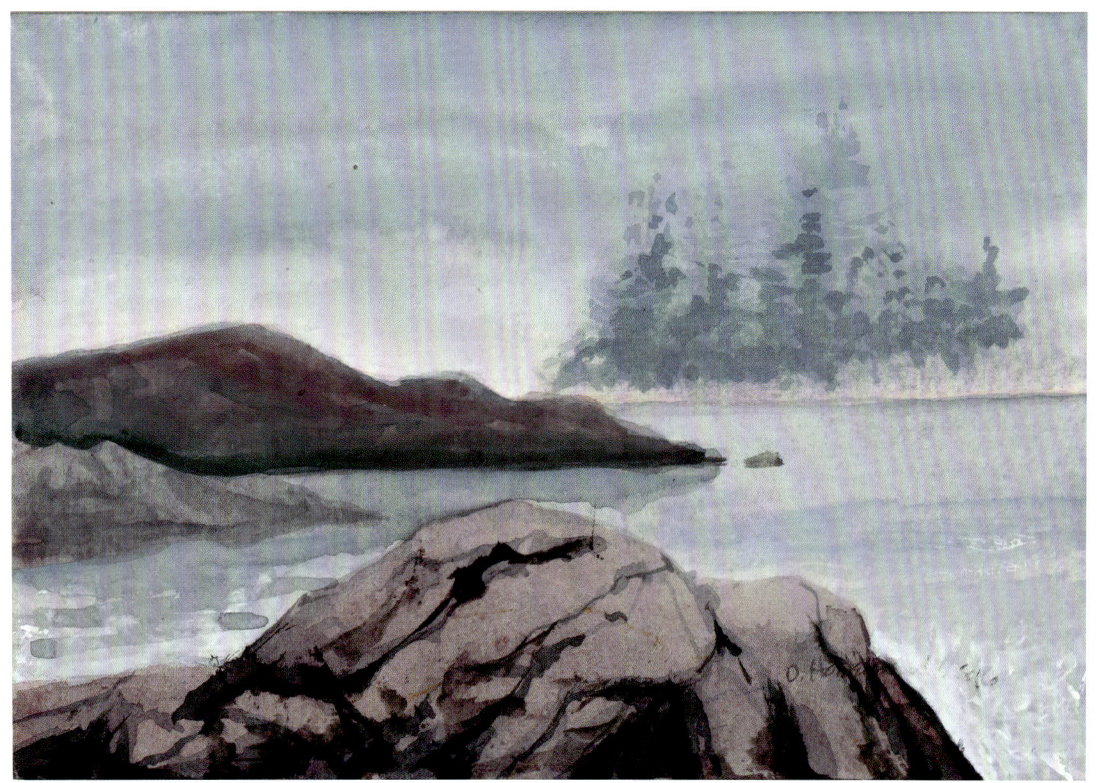

Fog Lifting, 1996
Watercolor
4 x 6 in. (10.2 x 15.2 cm)
Estate of the artist

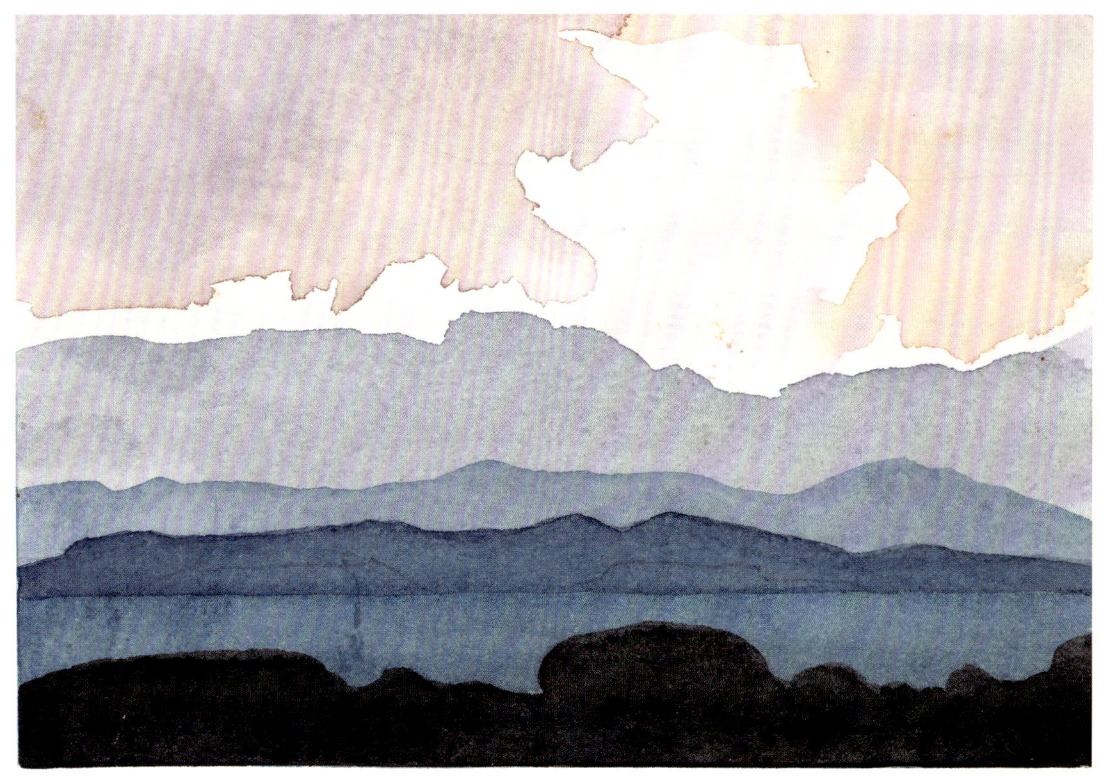

PLATE 104
New Light, 1993

Watercolor on paper
4 x 6 in. (10.2 x 15.2 cm)
Private collection

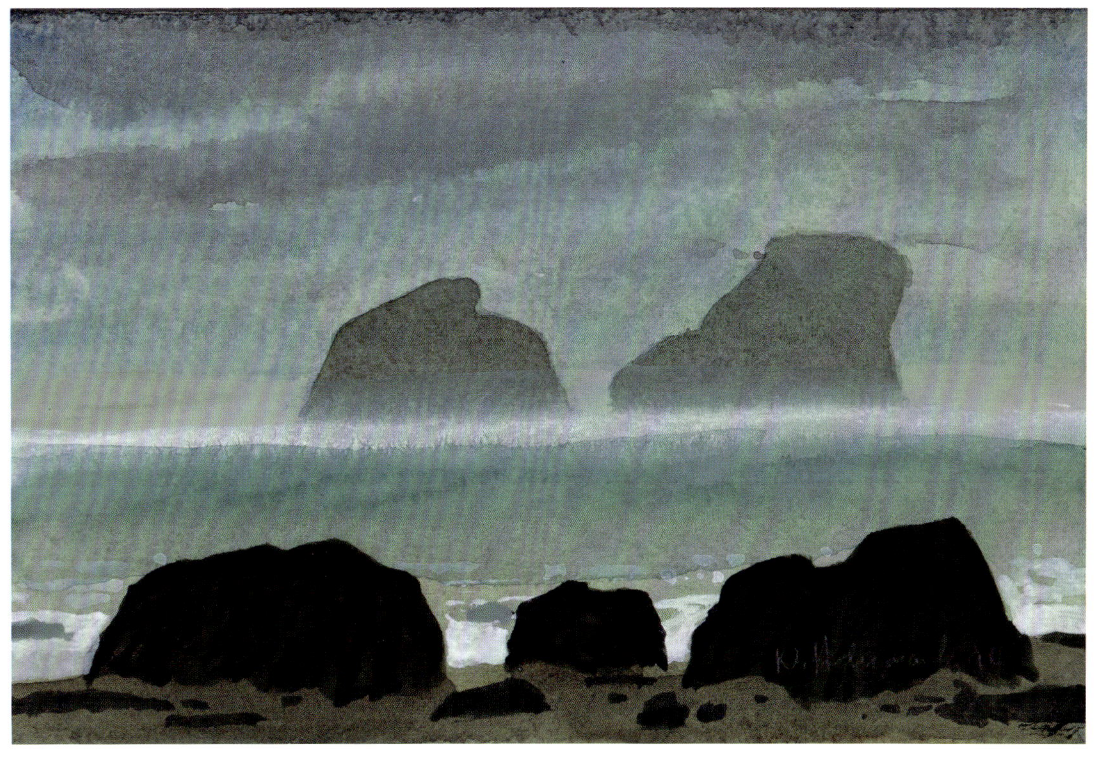

PLATE 105
Night Watch, 1995

Watercolor on paper
4 x 6 in. (10.2 x 15.2 cm)
Private collection

Drawings

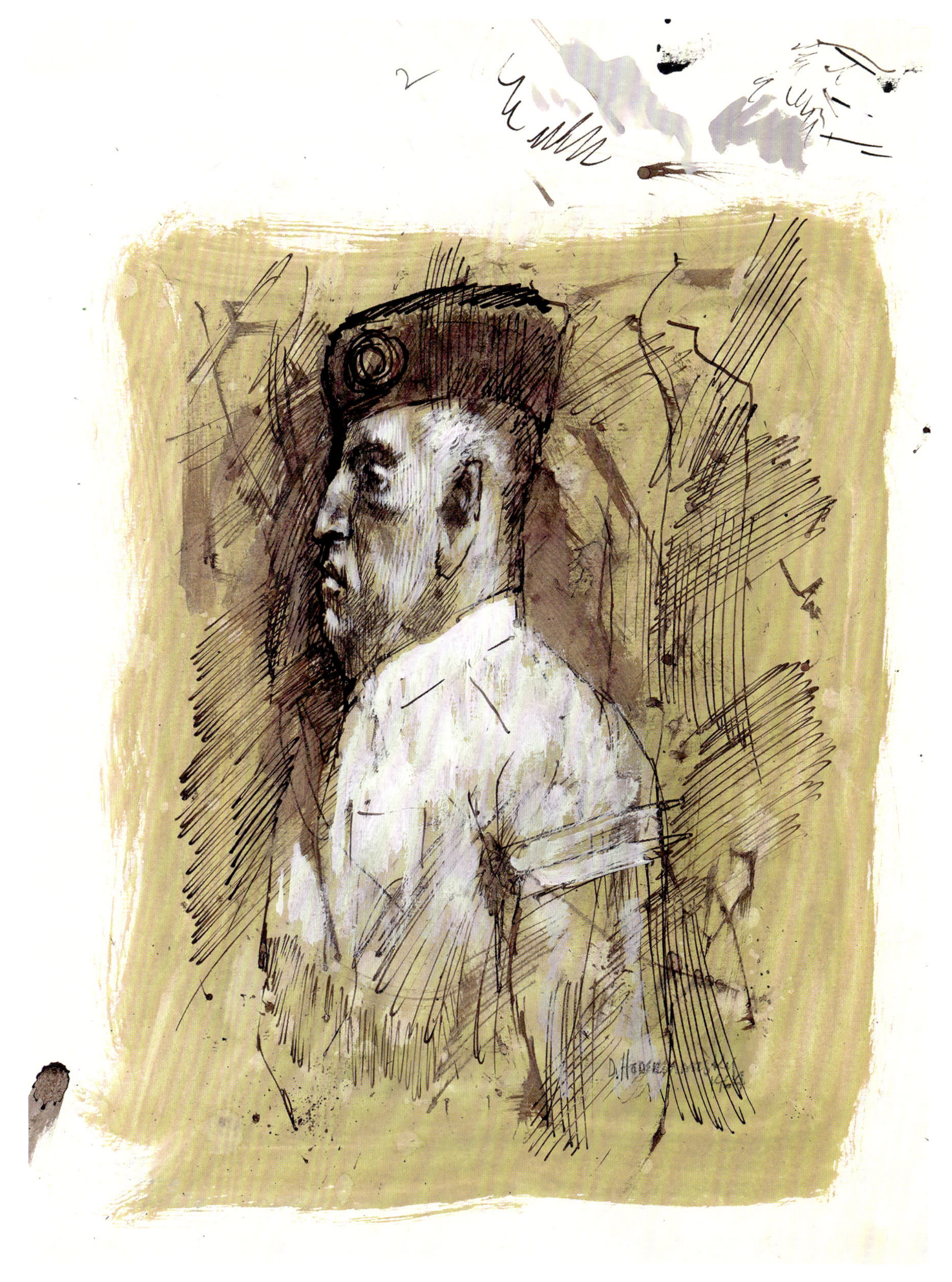

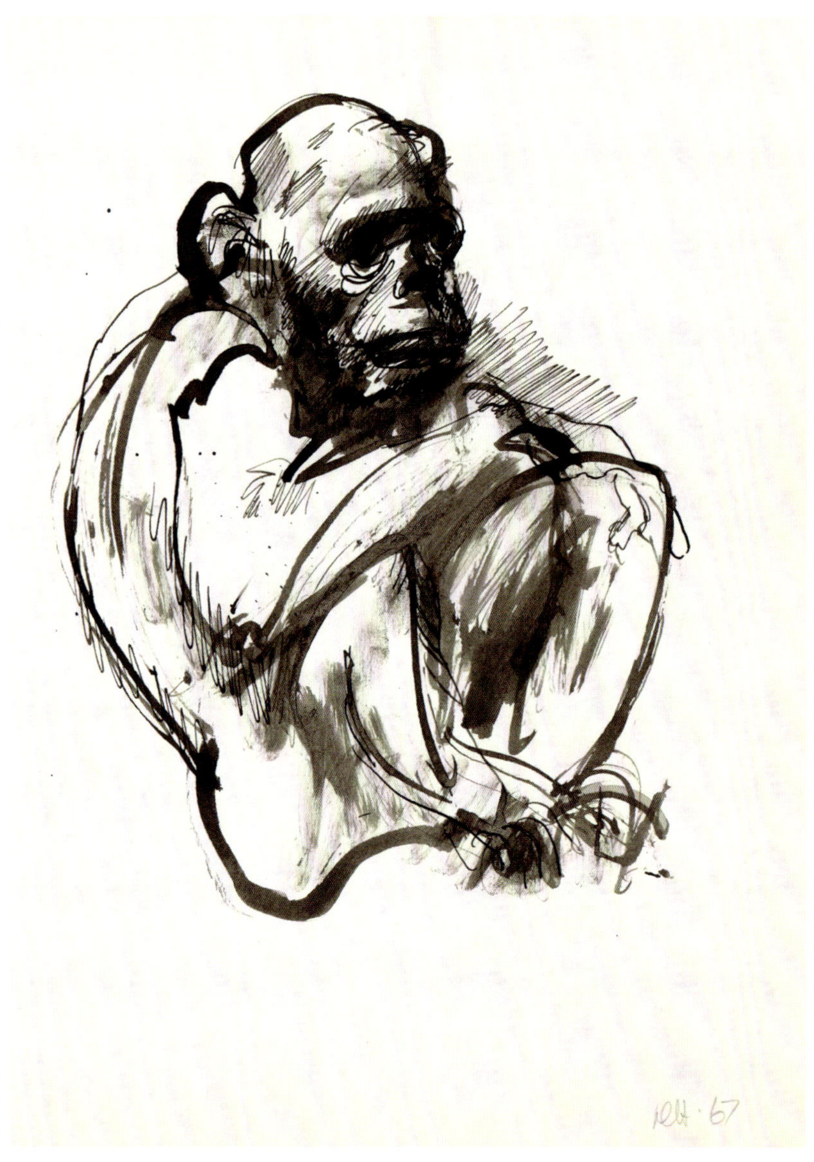

PLATE 107

Untitled (Animal Study), 1967

Pen and ink
10¾ x 8⅛ in. (27.3 x 20.6 cm) (irregular)
Estate of the artist

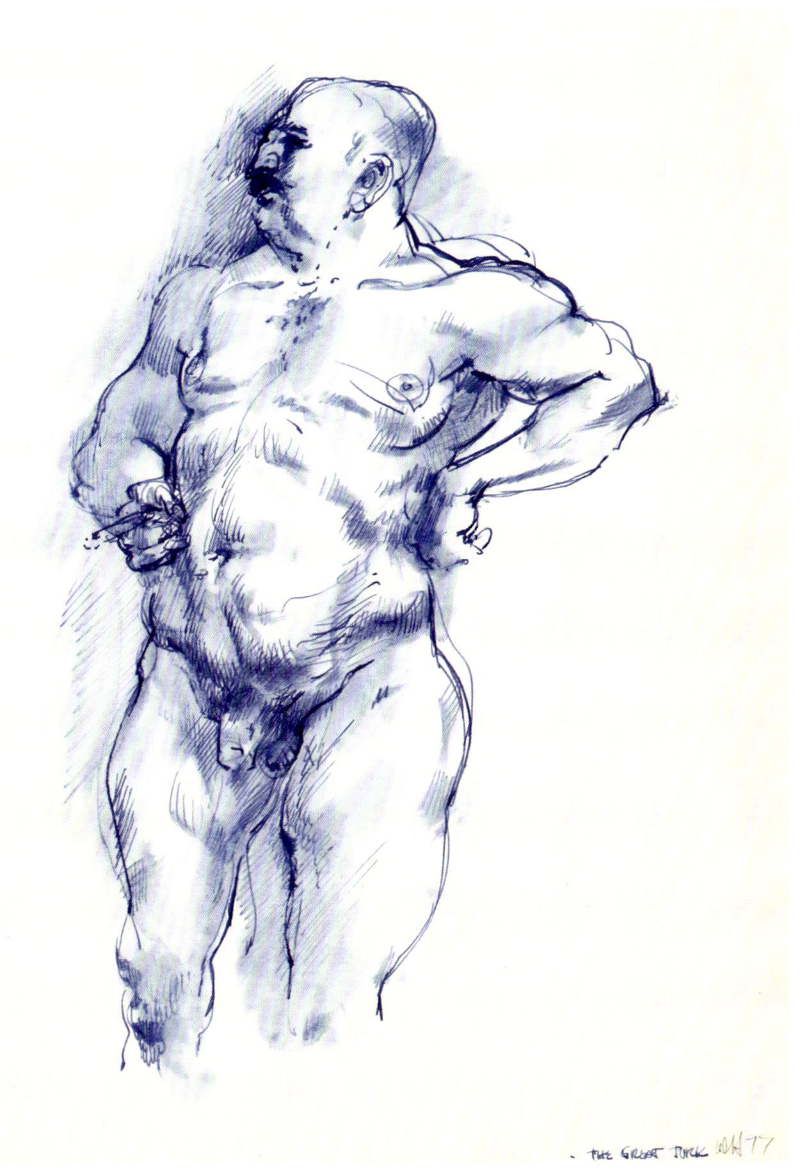

PLATE 108

The Great Turk, 1977

Pen, blue ink, and wash
11 x 8¼ in. (27.9 x 21 cm) (irregular)
Estate of the artist

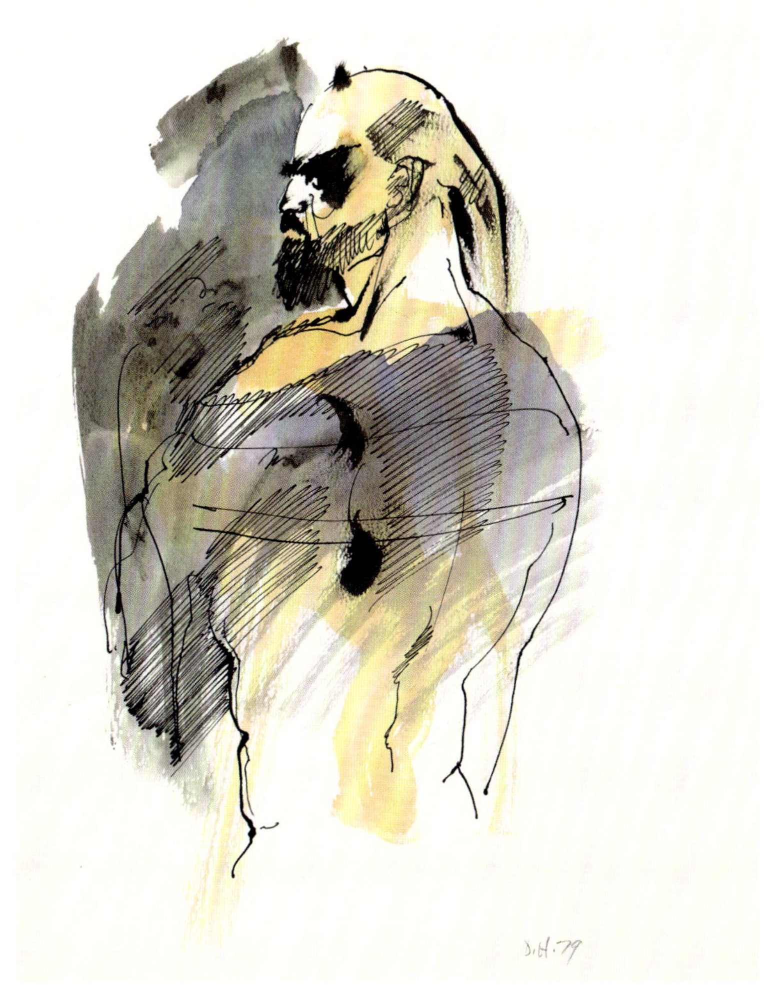

PLATE 109

Untitled (Figure Study), 1979

Pen, ink, and watercolor wash
12 x 9⅛ in. (30.5 x 23.2 cm)
Estate of the artist

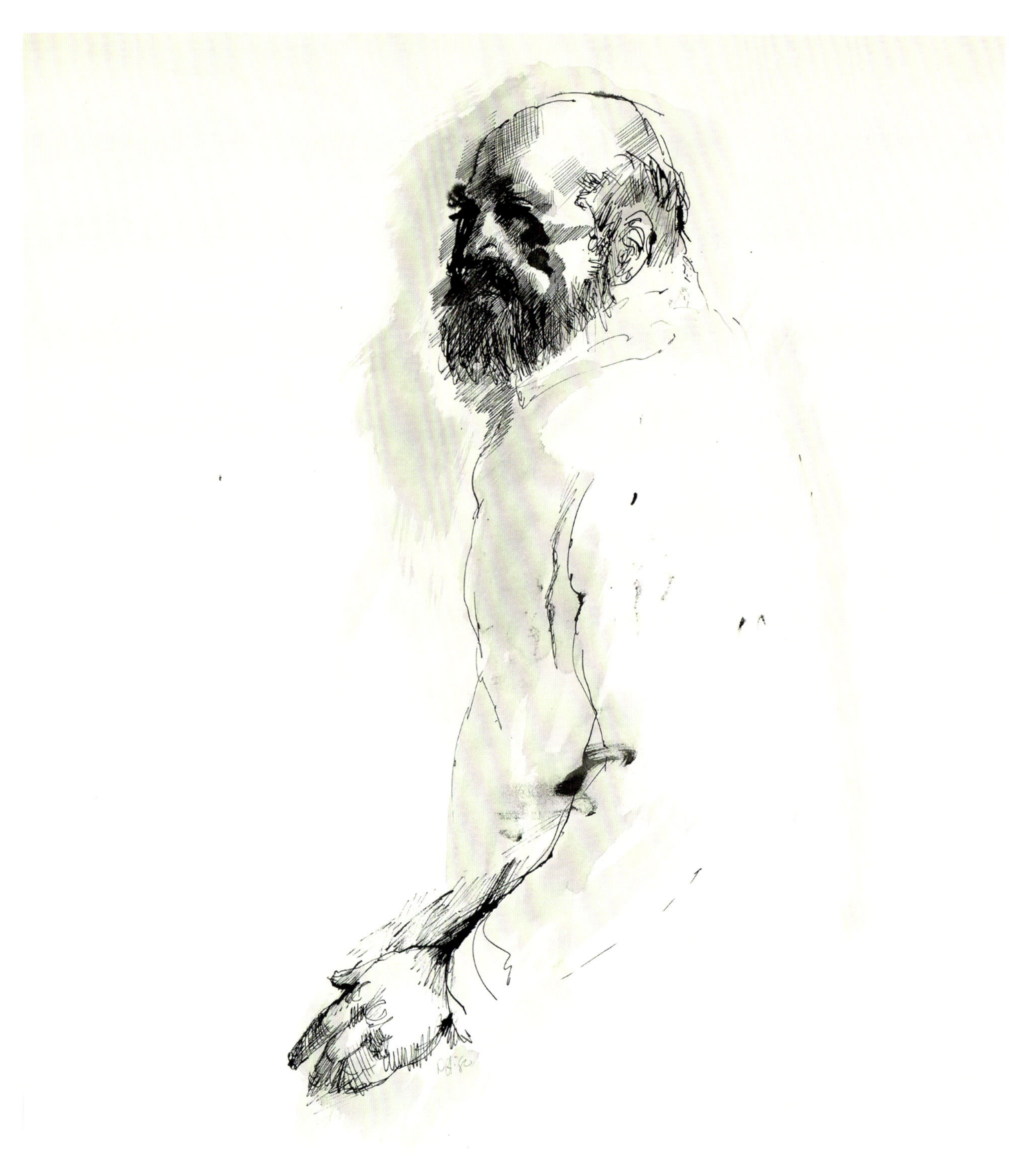

Bearded Man in Three-Quarter Profile, 1980

Pen and ink
24 x 18 in. (61 x 45.7 cm)
Estate of the artist

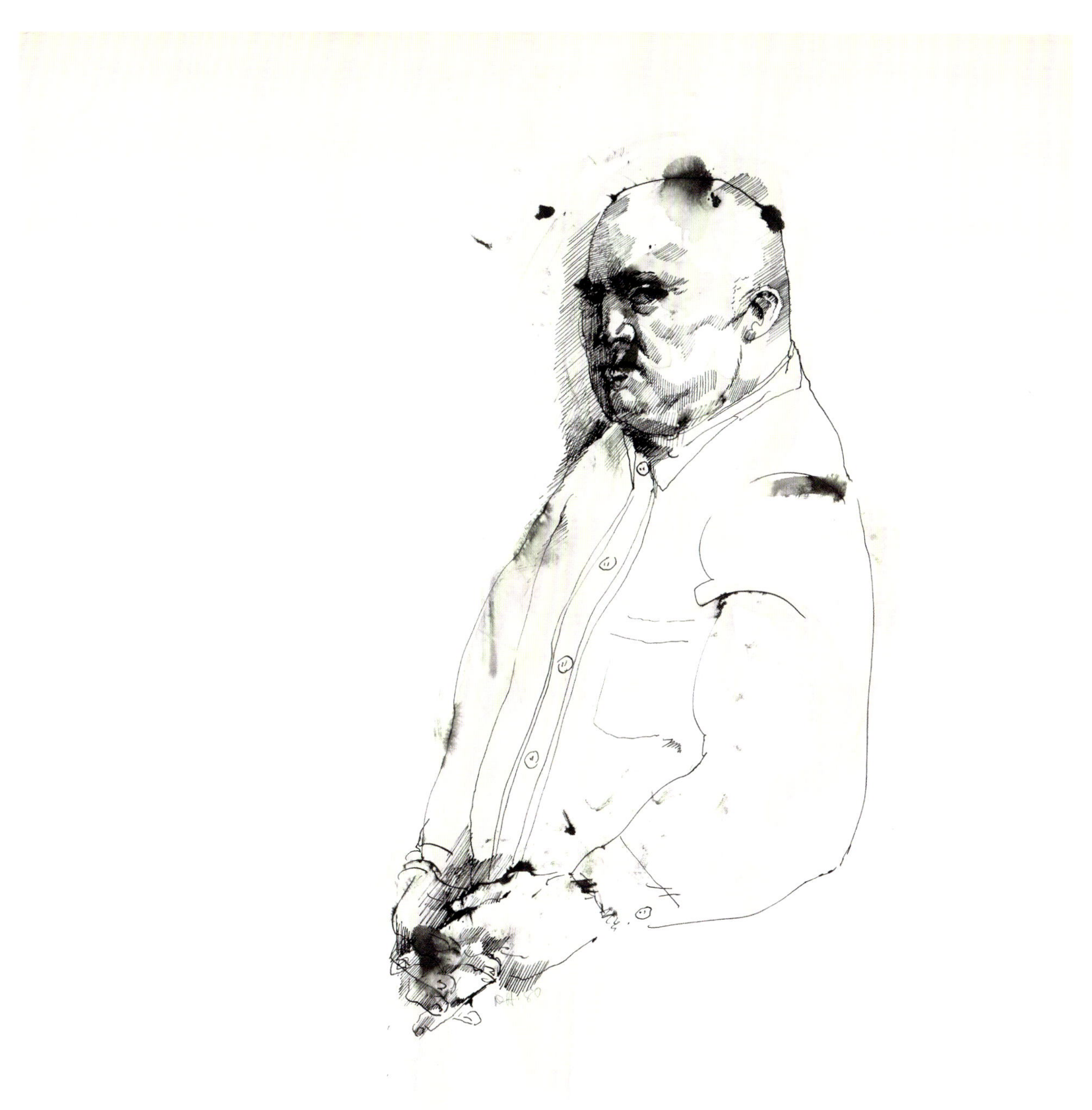

PLATE 111

Sinister Man in Three-Quarter Profile, 1980

Pen and ink on paper
24 x 18 in. (61 x 45.7 cm)
Estate of the artist

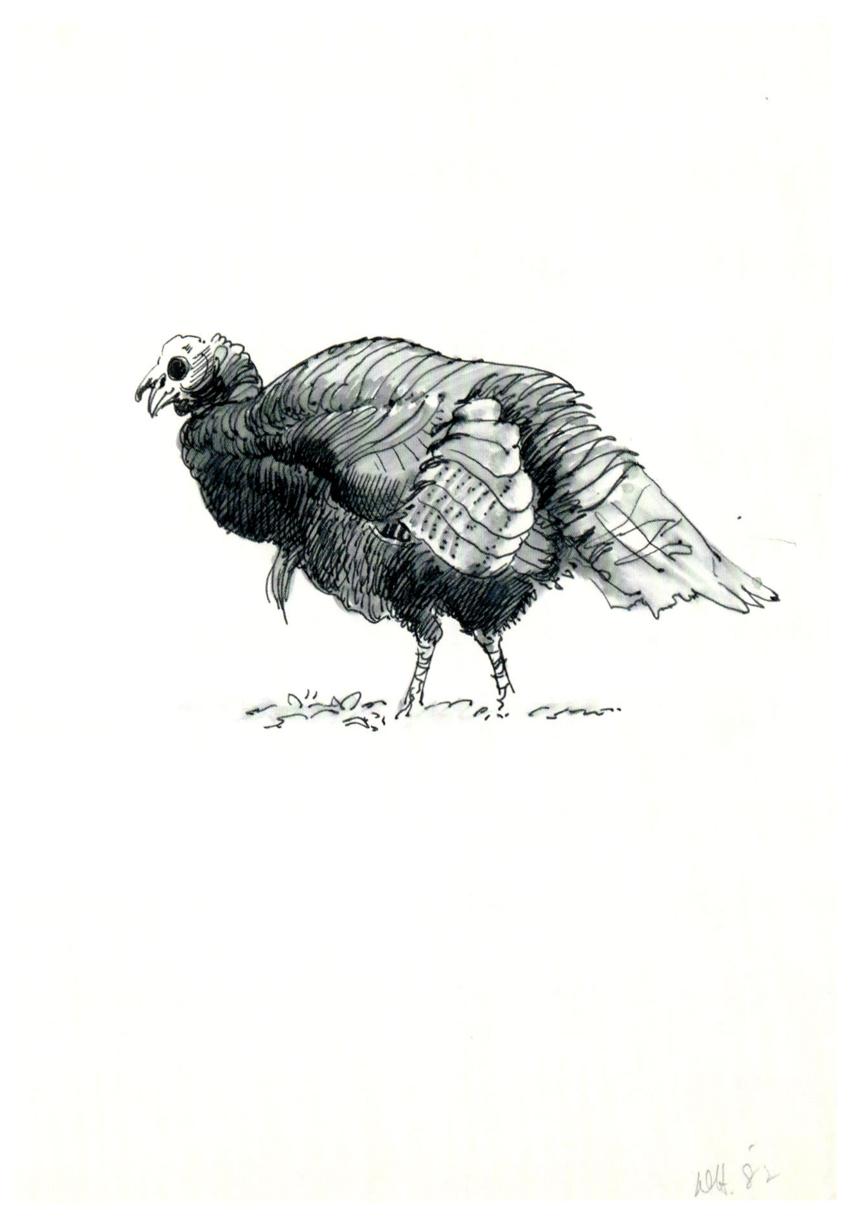

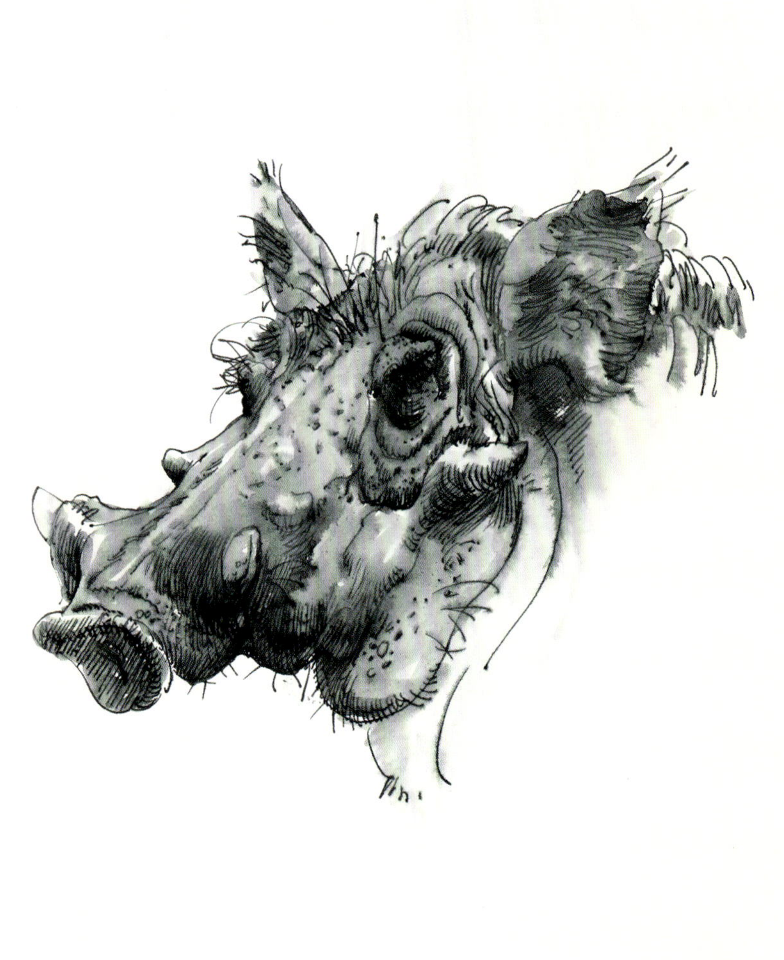

PLATE 112
Turkey, 1982

Pen and ink
11 x 8 in. (27.9 x 20.3 cm) (irregular)
Estate of the artist

PLATE 113
Boar, 1982

Pen and ink
11 x 8¼ in. (27.9 x 21 cm) (irregular)
Estate of the artist

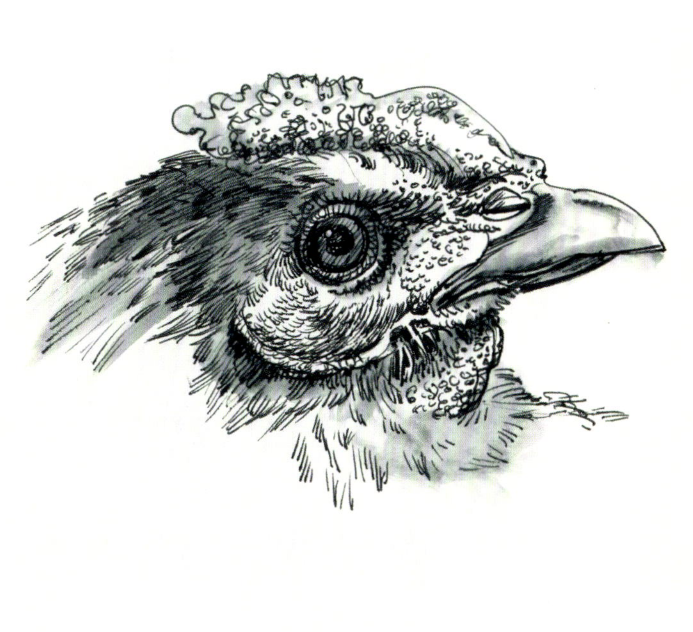

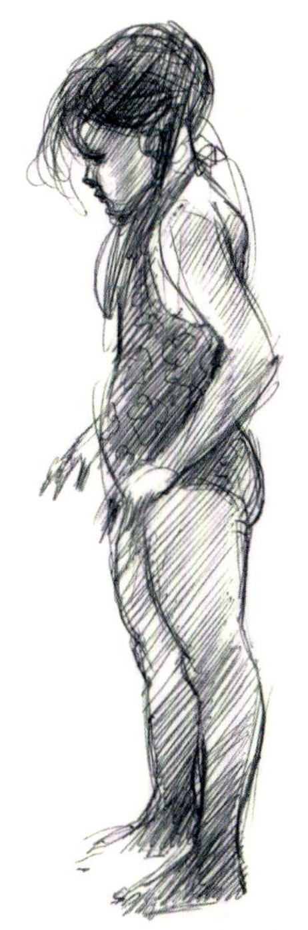

PLATE 114
Bird, 1982
Pen and ink
11 x 8 in. (27.9 x 20.3 cm) (irregular)
Estate of the artist

PLATE 115
Lisa at the Lily Pond, ca. 1971
Pen and ink
10½ x 8¼ in. (26.7 x 21 cm)
Estate of the artist

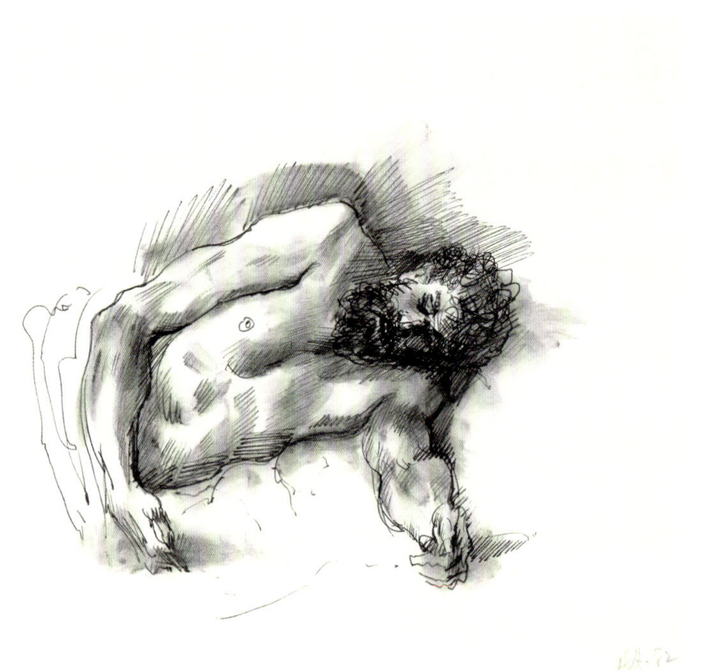

PLATE 116
Reclining Man, 1982

Pen, ink, and charcoal
8 ⅛ x 10 ⅞ in. (20.6 x 27.6 cm)
Estate of the artist

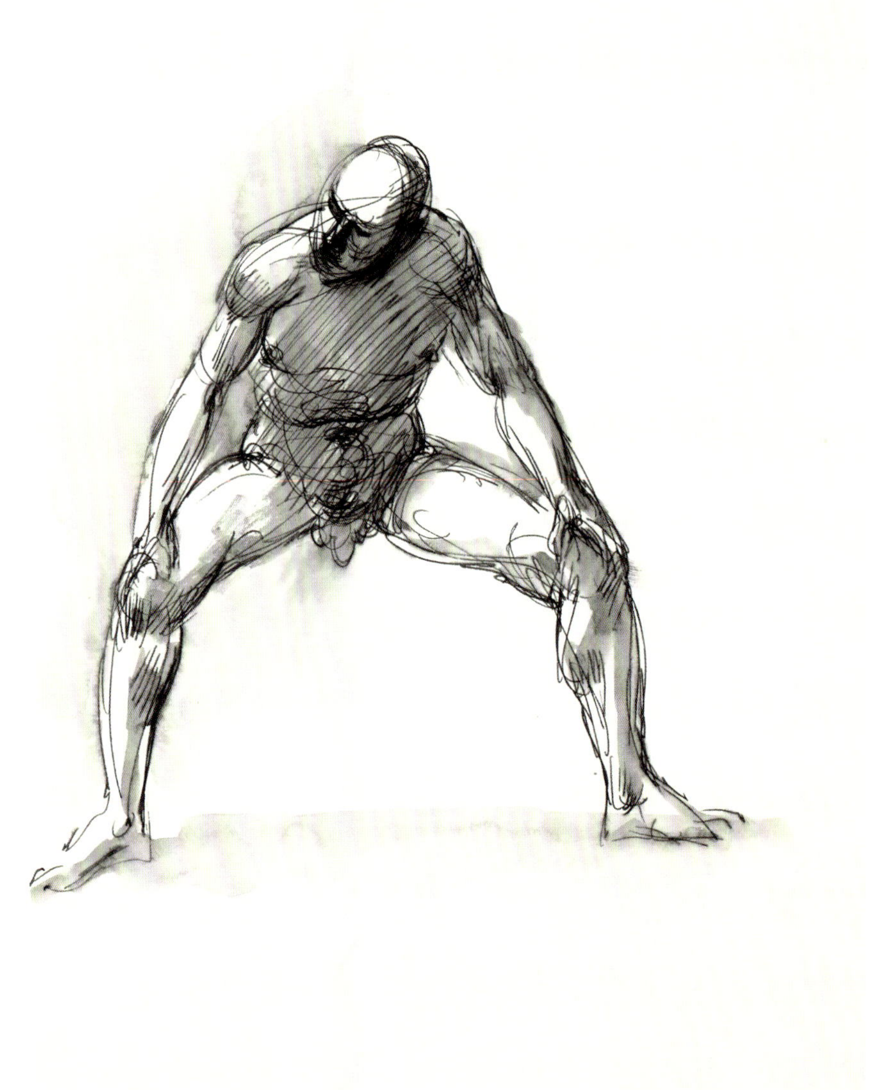

PLATE 117
Untitled (Figure Study), 1985

Pen, ink, and ink wash on paper
11 x 8 in. (27.9 x 20.3 cm)
Estate of the artist

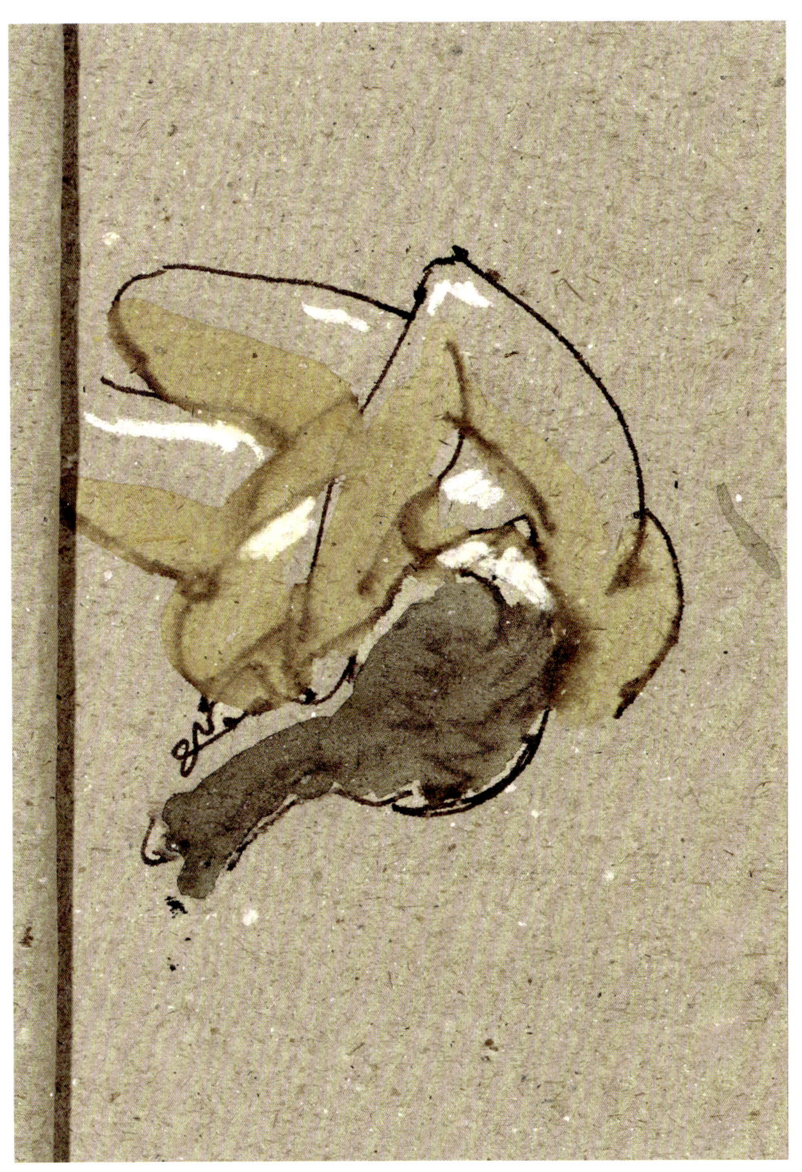

PLATE 118

Untitled (Figure Study), ca. 1989

Pen, ink, and watercolor wash with gouache

5 x 3 in. (12.7 x 7.6 cm)

Estate of the artist

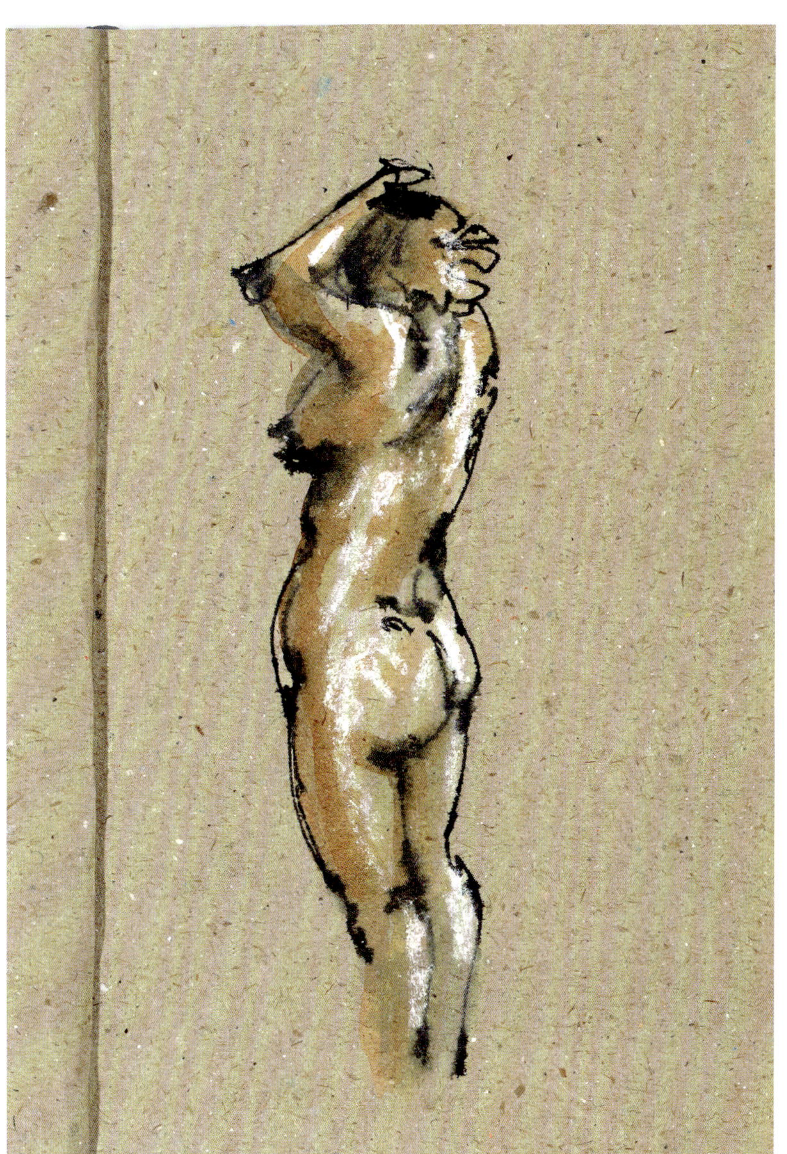

PLATE 119

Untitled (Figure Study), ca. 1989

Pen, ink, and watercolor wash with gouache

5 x 3 in. (12.7 x 7.6 cm)

Estate of the artist

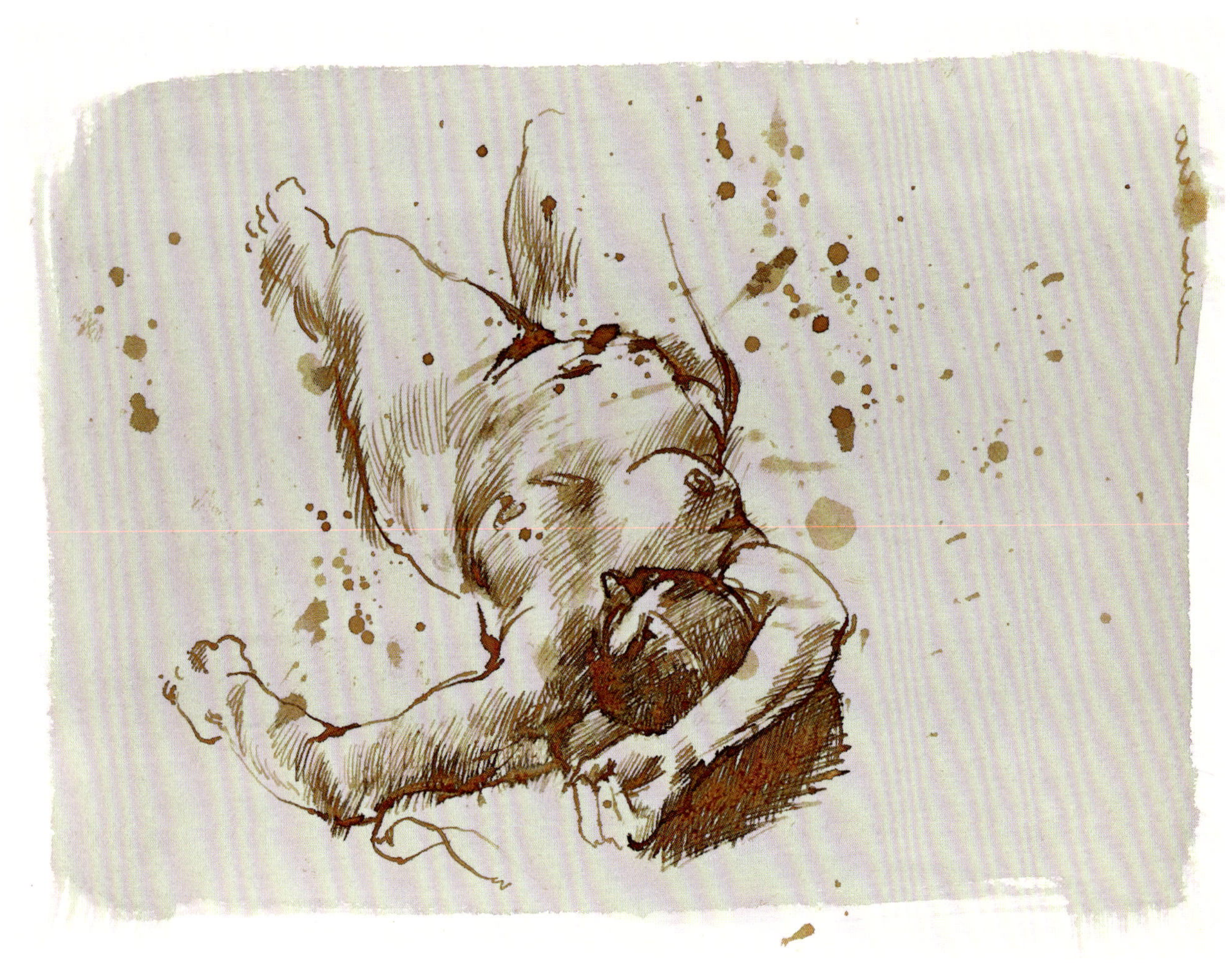

PLATE 120

Untitled (Figure Study), ca. 1980s

Pen and ink
Image: 7½ x 10½ (19.1 x 26.7 cm);
sheet: 9 x 12 in. (22.9 x 30.5 cm)
Estate of the artist

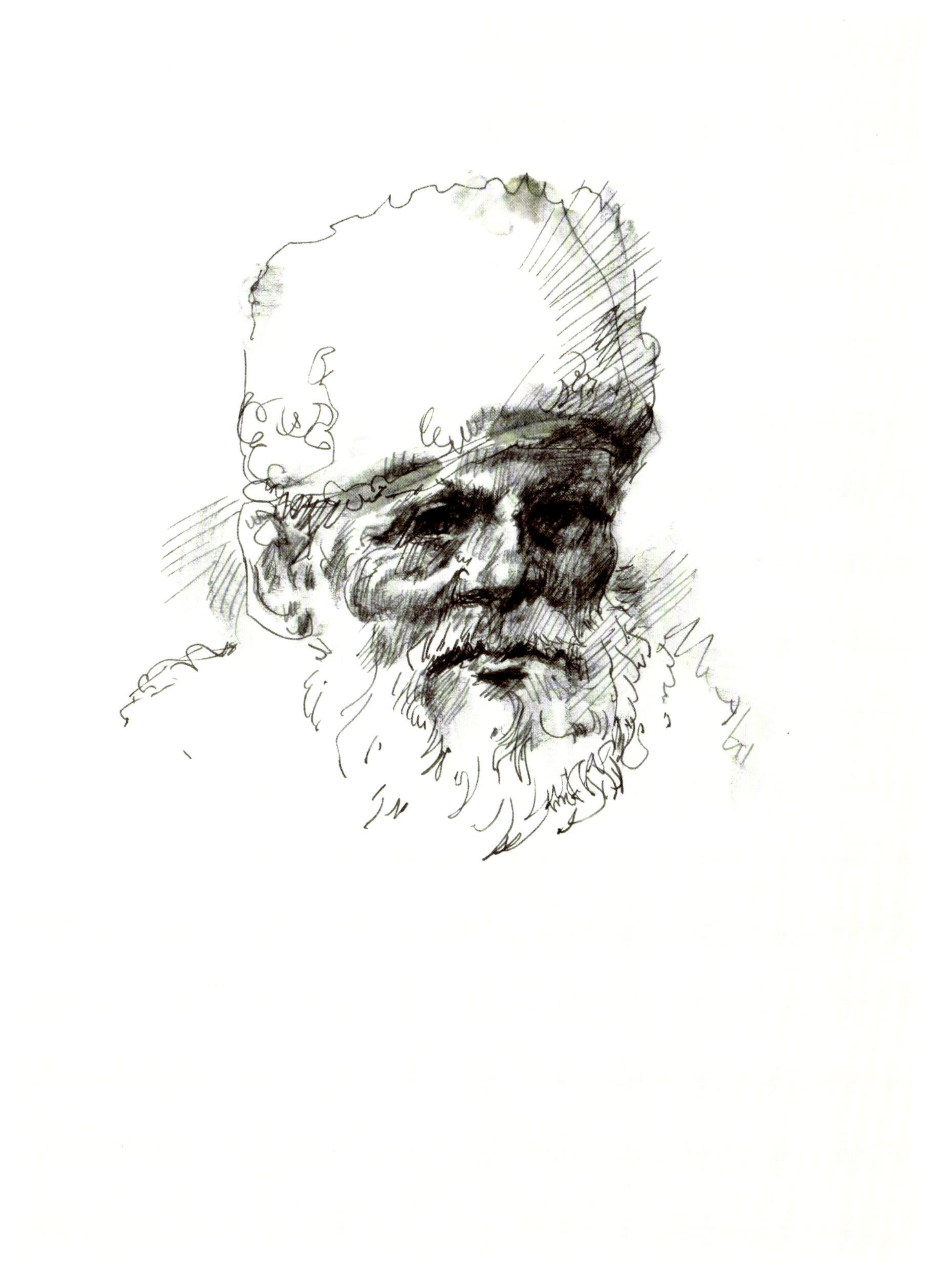

PLATE 121

Untitled, ca. 1980s

Pen, ink, and charcoal
12 x 9 in. (30.5 x 22.9 cm)
Estate of the artist

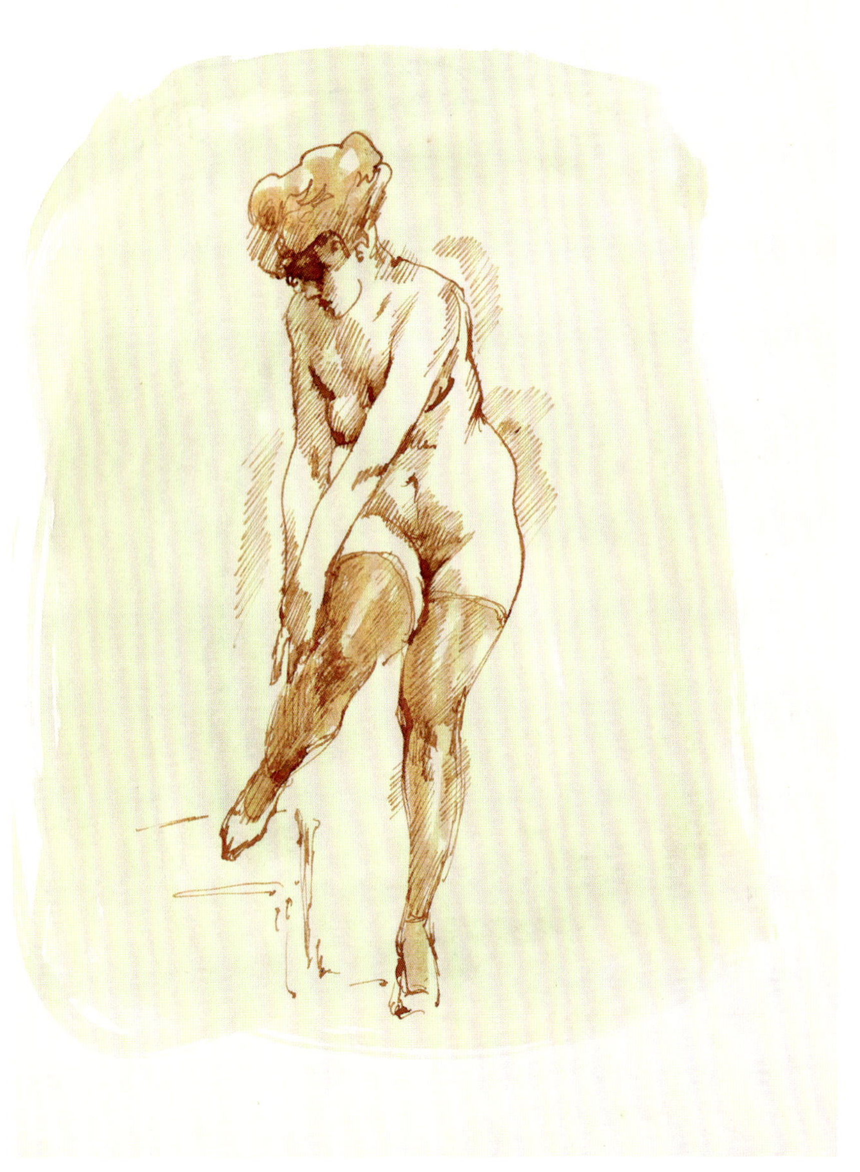

PLATE 122

Untitled (Figure Study), ca. 1980s

Pen, ink, and watercolor wash
12 x 9 in. (30.5 x 22.9 cm)
Estate of the artist

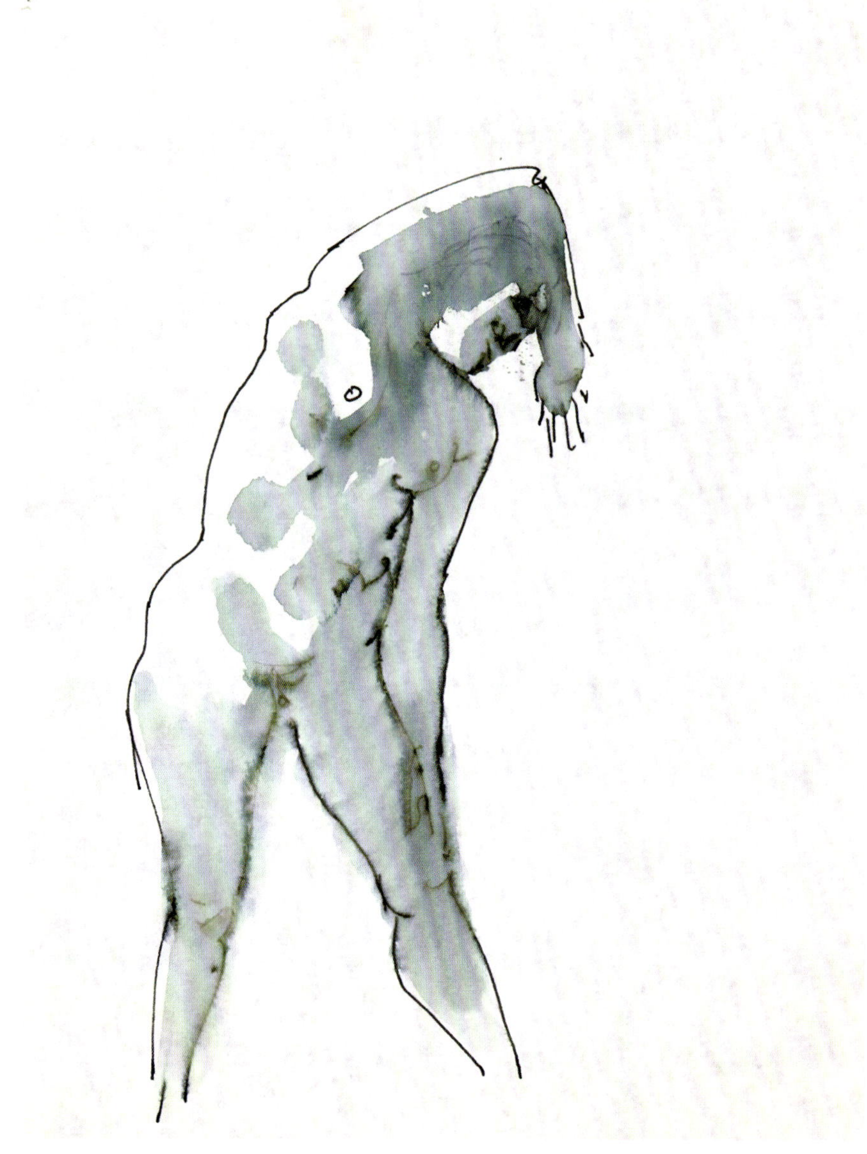

PLATE 123

Untitled (Figure Study), ca. 1980s

Pen, ink, and watercolor wash
11 x 8½ in. (27.9 x 21.6 cm)
Estate of the artist

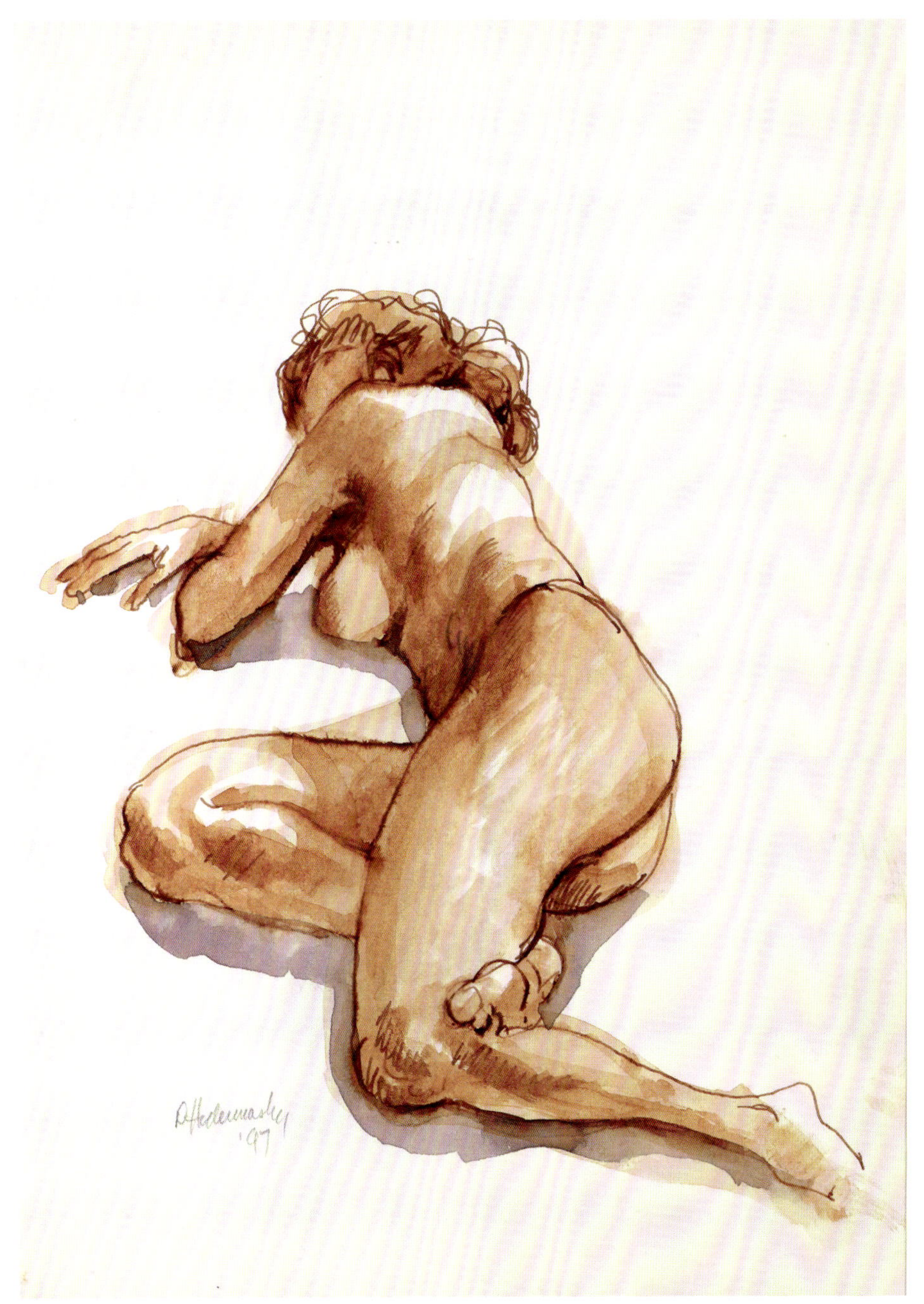

PLATE 124
Untitled (Figure Study), 1997

Pen, ink, and watercolor wash
10⅝ x 7⅝ in. (27 x 19.4 cm)
Estate of the artist

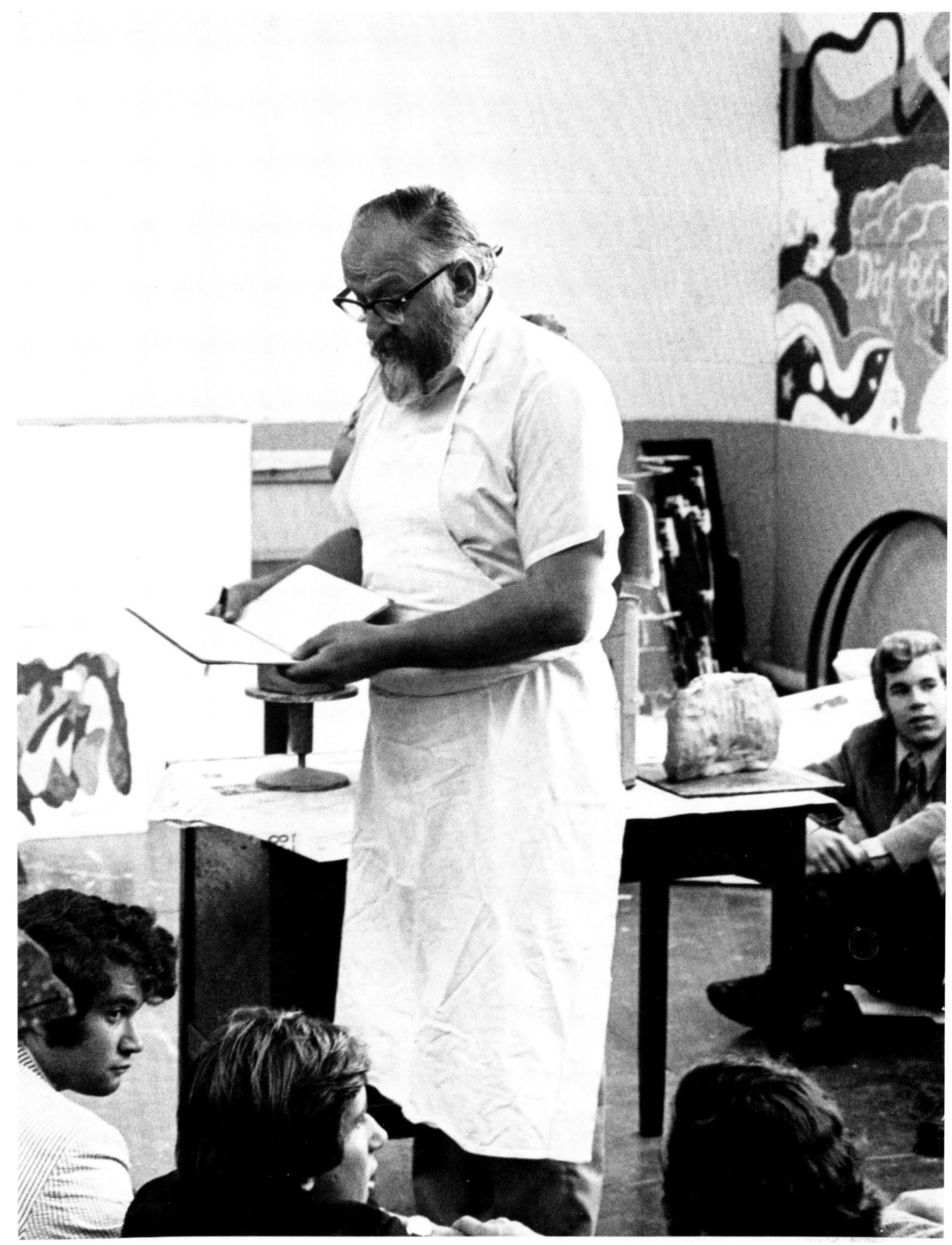

Giving Lead:
Interviews with Michael Tracy and Stephen Hannock

ANNA HAMMOND

Teaching was at the heart of daniel hodermarsky; Dan's heart was in teaching. While for some artists it's a necessary evil—a way to pay the bills—for Dan it was a way to connect to the team while inspiring the individual to realize his own potential, whatever that potential might be. Connecting body to mind, finding peace or passion, exploring essence or just plain appreciating the world through the act of close observation, opening up the human spirit through artistic expression was a calling.

In 1955, Dan began as an instructor at Lakewood High School in Lakewood, Ohio, went on to teach at the Cleveland Institute of Art, Shaker Heights High School, the Bussed-in Arts Program for the Cleveland Supplementary Educational Center and eventually, to found the art department at Deerfield Academy. After retirement, he tutored students one on one, leaving indelible impressions on young people in Deer Isle, Maine. He was a rigorous instructor who was deeply interested in young people and in helping them express their own unique reactions to the world.

Two of Dan's students in particular, Michael Tracy and Stephen Hannock, went on to have illustrious careers as artists. They remained close friends with Dan over many decades.

Dan teaching at Deerfield, ca. 1973
Deerfield Academy Archives,
Deerfield, MA

Interview with Michael Tracy

Michael Tracy was born in 1943 in Bellevue, Ohio. His work can be found in numerous museum collections including The Metropolitan Museum of Art, New York City; the San Francisco Museum of Modern Art, California; the Dallas Museum of Art and the Museum of Fine Art, Houston, both in Texas; the Museum of Contemporary Religious Art, St. Louis, Missouri; and The Menil Collection, Houston, Texas. He also exhibited in the 1982 Venice Biennale. Tracy lives and works in San Ygnacio, Texas, where, in 1990, he established the River Pierce Foundation to restore the Treviño-Uribe Rancho, one of six National Historic Landmarks on the Texas–Mexico border, and to share the town's quiet isolation with other artists while preserving its historic character. This interview with the artist took place in his studio in San Ygnacio in June 2022.

When did you meet Dan, and under what circumstances?

In 1959. I was 15. There was an outdoor municipal-sponsored art show in early summer in Westlake [Ohio]. And I had a painting called *Autumn* that was about 12 inches wide and three feet high, or maybe taller, and I had hung that on the fence. Dan came as a Lakewood High School art teacher to see what was happening. He might have been the judge. Somehow, we got to talking.

I think he acknowledged that my painting, as simple as it was, was abstract and colorful, and did not seem to embody, for lack of a better word, bourgeois living-room-painting values. In any regard, he proceeded to offer, if I could do it, to go to Lakewood High School for art classes. He let me know how to get in touch with him. And my parents gave me permission to walk the six-block-long walk from St. Edward High School in Lakewood weather—raining or snowing. Anyway, that's what happened.

I got out of high school in 1961. And I asked Dan to go to see my parents, to tell them that he would like to see me go to the Cleveland Institute of Art. I remember him going up the front steps of my house and having a long meeting with them and explaining how this would work. But my parents said no, because I had gotten a full scholarship to St. Edward's University in Austin, Texas.

Three years later, I graduated, and I relied on Dan's help to get me into the Cleveland Institute of Art. I went from an undergraduate BA in English and philosophy to an undergraduate art school. I was three or four years older than all those other kids. So that was another thing that was in my favor because they knew I was very serious.

You and Dan developed a relationship, but you said he wasn't your teacher. What was it about your relationship that was compelling and how did that develop?

Before I returned to Texas for graduate school in 1967, I was in my early twenties, in school, painting—I babysat his children and painted walls, etc., in their house and was the waiter at their parties. Dan was teaching full time at Shaker Heights High School in the art department, and part-time at the institute. And so whatever time we had together was really in his house, in his studio, or having odd-job tasks. So I was making paintings in and around those little jobs while interacting a lot of the time with Dan.

Portrait of Michael Tracy, 1976
Oil on canvas
50 x 40 in. (127 x 101.6 cm)
Estate of the artist

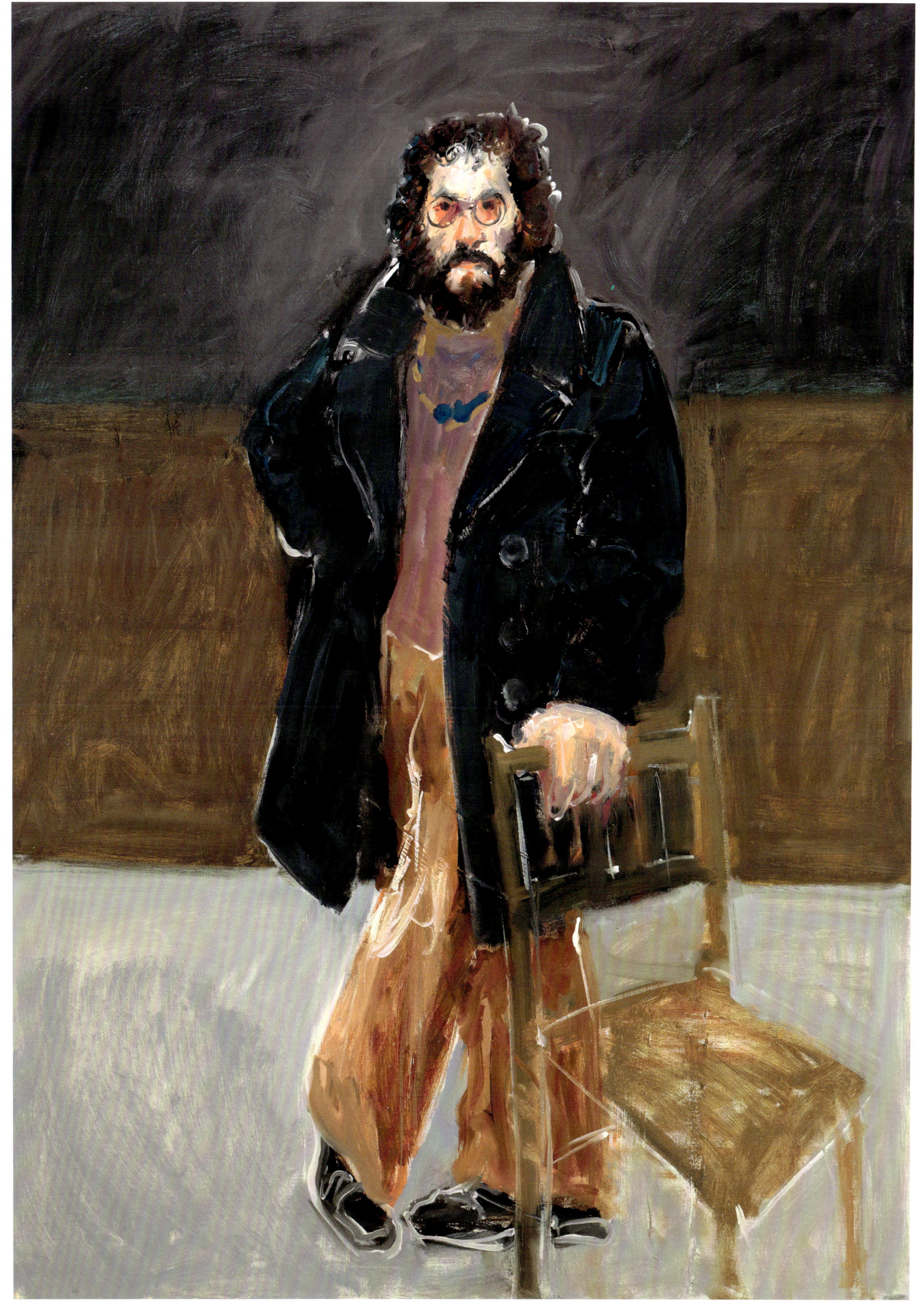

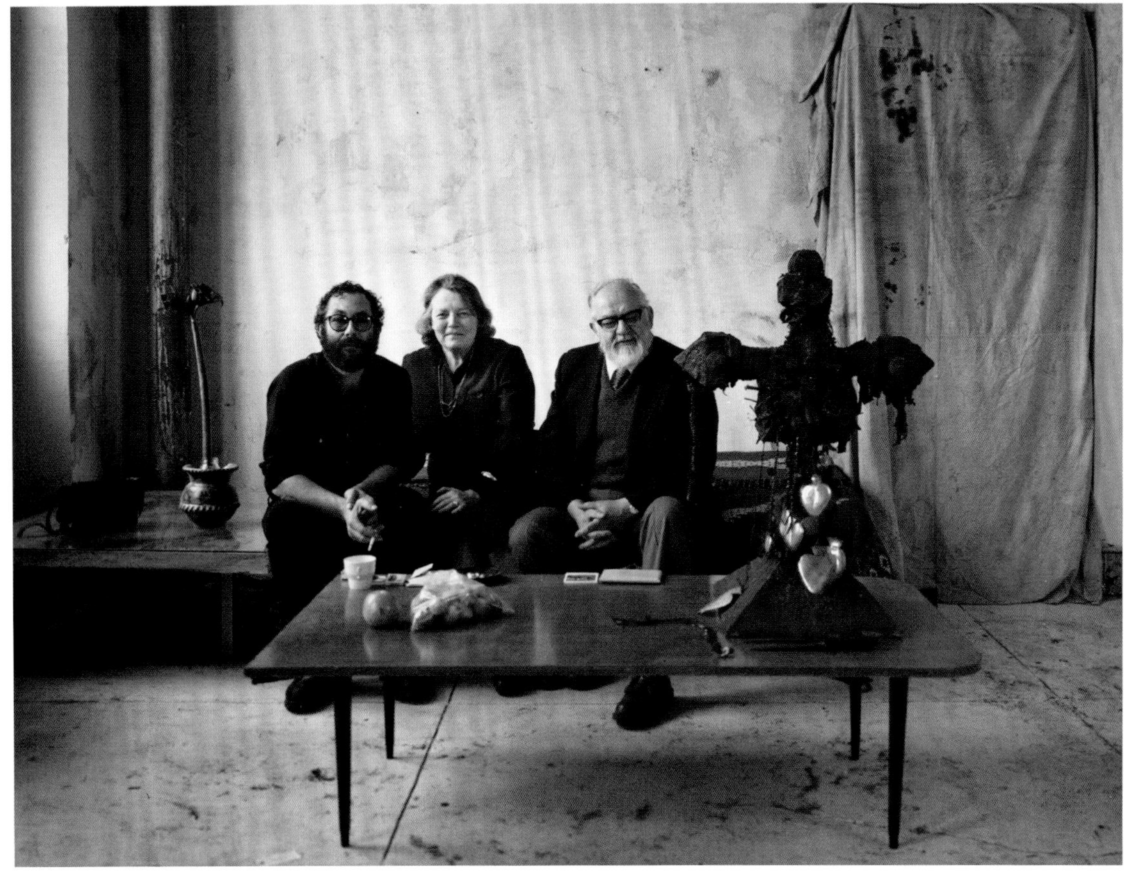

Michael Tracy with Dan
and Nancy, 1982
Gelatin silver print
10⅞ x 13⅞ in. (27.6 x 35.2 cm)
Estate of the artist

Dan was giving you jobs as a way of helping you financially?

Yes. But also we wanted to hang out together.

Can you talk more about that closeness and, if you can remember, the nature of the conversations.

Oh no, that's much too personal and detailed. It was about everything.

While respecting the privacy of your friendship with him, may I ask, did he talk to you about his experiences in the war?

Oh, well I suppose, yes. Yes, definitely.

   While I was in Cleveland, there was a lot of helping each other and moving paintings and I don't know what all. So we would end up in these places in Cleveland on Saturdays. It'd be freezing and we'd have a drink someplace.

   He carried this pill, said he had it in his pocket all the time. That was he was going to take if he had unmanageable anxiety. And I realized he wasn't just straight old, reliable, loveable Dan.

So Dan became a friend, more than a mentor?

Well, it evolved that he kind of became an older-brother type almost.

I had an apartment on Random Road in Little Italy [in Cleveland]. And that was where I had a studio. It was a very tiny apartment. There was a lot of exchange and we were more like friends than we were teacher–student, it seemed. I was very encouraging to him and he to me.

There was a lot of emotional support that was kind of unconditional. That charged my batteries, switched me on—being around him for some reason.

After I got out of the University of Texas with a master's degree and so on, I was living in Austin on East 6th Street, in a huge loft, and in 1971 I had big exhibition at the McNay Museum in San Antonio. Dan came. And to my shows at Mary Boone [Gallery in New York] in the early 1980s And when I had my first big solo exhibition at MoMA PS1 in 1987 [in Queens, New York]. And I visited them [the Hodermarskys] in Deerfield. And they came to my show at the Mattress Factory in Pittsburgh. That was a major installation—like a church, a chapel, underground. And of course they were here for the River Pierce in 1990. There's a great photograph by Graciela Iturbide of Dan under an umbrella during the event.

Dan and Nancy also spent some time in your place in Mexico, in Valenciana.

Yes, they were there for a while. He worked in my studio with my stuff, and got into the wax with his fingers. And that was really a great joy for me, because I thought if he could change mediums, he might let more out. I felt he was constantly under this pressure of not having the room emotionally, perhaps more than anything, to do what he seemed to aspire to do.

You've talked about a really strong connection that felt alive over time.

I think Dan could identify with me because I was still working class. I didn't know that he was in that kind of post-traumatic-stress jeopardy. He must've had some help, because he seemed stable and empathetic and was such a beloved teacher. Do you know where Dan was during the war?

Yes. He was in the 400th Armored Artillery Battalion which was called, colloquially, the "Bastard Battalion" because they were sent wherever they were needed and not attached to a particular division. So they were in almost every major battle in the European theater. They saw combat 95% of the time they were in Europe.

So Dan maybe just wanted to teach. Maybe that was one of the things that calmed him down. Right?

Yes, being with people. Being with young people.

Well, Dan was having his life and it was interesting and exciting and he loved his woman and these children. He was crazy about them and they always were included in everything. I mean he dragged them everywhere.

It was fun to be around them. And then he wasn't so alone.

But those conflicted paintings, men in chairs [pp. 14, 34], these chairs all came out of his war experiences basically. I liked all those simple landscape paintings, with chairs and men in chairs. It went on for some time. Then they became generals and CEOs, and then naked women. Some of it is old-fashioned figure painting, but it was personal and I liked that.

Dan was very inclusive. Dan was broad-minded. You see, the art market in New York is not inclusive. It doesn't include what they consider religious art or Christian. It's been drained of any spirituality.

I remember going together to the Cleveland Museum of Art in the early sixties and there was a [Francis] Bacon in a show. And man, he just was wild about that painting. And I was, too. And it was just really like [Bacon saying] fuck you, every single one of you people, especially you people in Shaker Heights, because this is what we do in London. We butcher people and eat them and then we walk around with our umbrella to keep the blood from falling on our head. Something like that. And it was very powerful.

We talked about things, serious things. We were a generation apart, but it seemed that the problems that he was talking about, in terms of art, were things that I was dealing with. I loved that. And that gave me some lead in my pencil, so to speak.

And I think he was able to do that. That was part of his gift. It was to put lead in people's pencils. They had to figure out what to do with their pencil. But they had lead in it. And they could write, or they could break their pencil, or they could throw their pencil away, or they could buy the pencil company, or buy the lead company, or make a new pencil. But they had something to work with that was real.

Interview with Stephen Hannock

Stephen Hannock was born in 1951 in Albany, New York, and lives and works in Williamstown, Massachusetts. Hannock's work can be found in numerous public collections throughout the United States, including The Metropolitan Museum of Art and the Whitney Museum of American Art, both in New York City; the National Gallery of Art, Washington, DC; the Museum of Fine Arts, Boston, Massachusetts; the Museum of Contemporary Art San Diego, California; the Museum of Fine Arts, Houston, Texas; and Yale University Art Gallery, New Haven, Connecticut. This interview was conducted via Zoom in May 2022.

What year did you came to Deerfield?

The fall of 1969.

I was sent to Deerfield by the coach at Brown University, who I met at summer camp in northern Ontario. He wanted me to get my academic act together and keep playing hockey in a serious program so that I could go to Brown, skate, and keep up with the books.

And then you met Dan. How come you signed up for his class in the first place?

Well, I hadn't taken an art course since grade school. But drawing always came easily to me. I went to

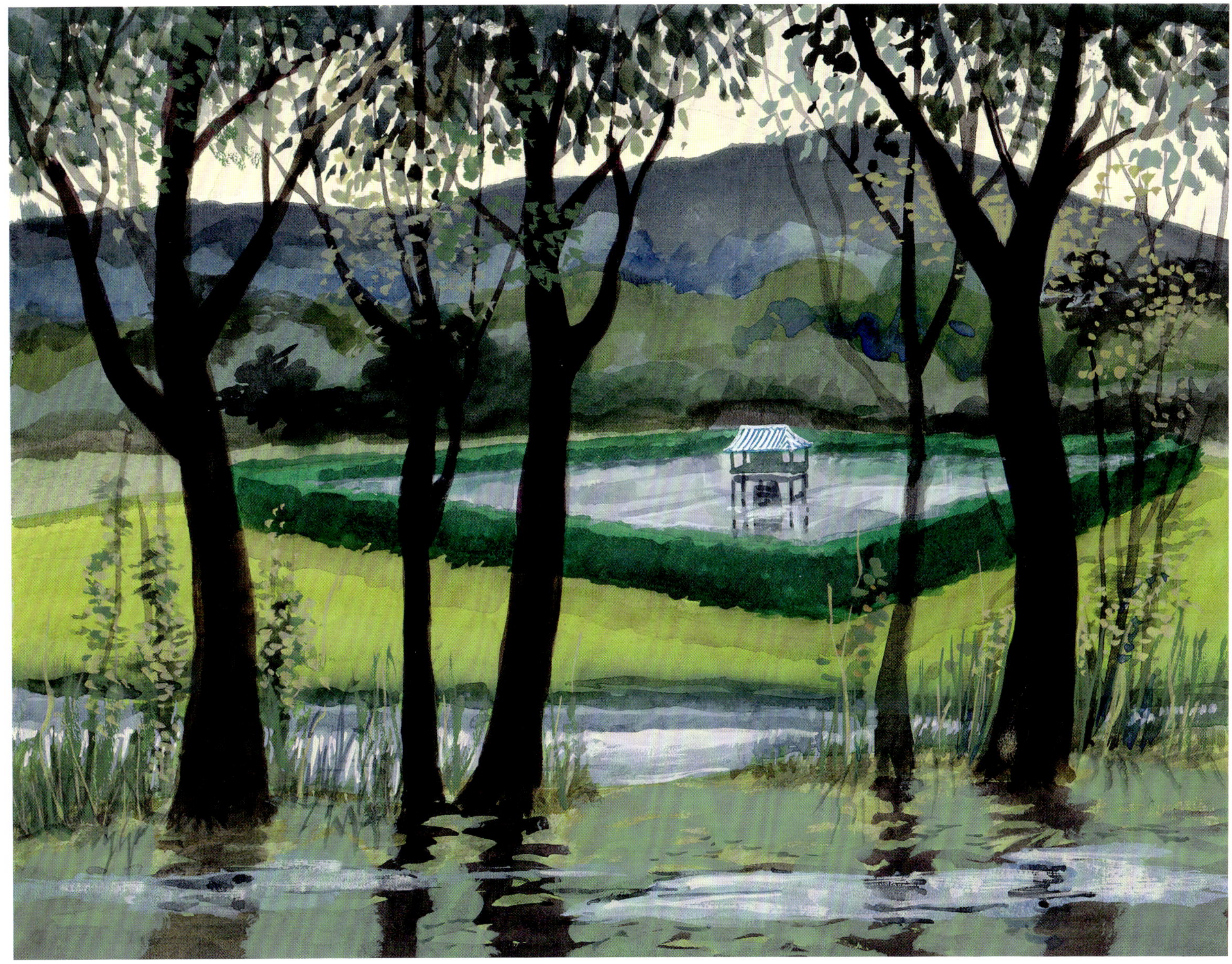

Flood on the Lower Level,
Deerfield Academy, 1983
Watercolor
Image: 16⅞ x 22¼ in.
(42.9 x 56.5 cm);
sheet: 17½ x 23 in.
(44.5 x 58.4 cm)
Estate of the artist

Dan and said I wanted to take art, but I had been told not to take any arts or culture courses at my previous high schools. Essentially, when you get into these athletic programs the coaches don't want you padding your curriculum with "gut courses" [non-academic]. And Dan's remark was, "Are you kidding me? This place is so tough, nobody is going to accuse you of taking the easy way out." That gave me a certain license right off the bat. So I signed up for art class, and then he kinda kicked me out! [laughs]

What?!

Not really. But I mean, I was there in artist Jim Gidding's class when Dan came in and saw my drawings. He took me aside and said, "Go. . . !"

And I'm looking around, wondering, "Did I screw up?"

And Dan said, "Just go out and draw. Draw anything you want. Then bring the work to me every week or two."

I couldn't believe it. I knew that these boarding schools with great hockey programs kept track of your every minute throughout the day. So to be given the freedom of two hours a week to just go out and draw on my own was a currency I recognized was very rare.

Dan would say, "The first thing you do as a young artist is to observe where you are. See what is going on around you." So I went out and did pen-and-ink drawings with watercolor washes of the campus. I just painted what I saw.

What really struck me about this time was that Hodermarsky helped illuminate how similar the thought process in athletics was to that of making art. It's all a matter of creativity. But at the foundation is non-stop, relentless practice. And then, at that moment of execution, at that moment of bringing the idea to life, you just react. You do not have time to think.

And then there was the other factor: Dan never approached me as an artist. He never approached anyone as an artist. He related to everybody in his classes as young men trying to figure it all out. And it was during this time that art just happened for me. From that time until now, I have never met another artist who related to other artists that way: that if you embraced your complete life, art would happen on its own.

Dan was such a great advocate of the value of an art education, no matter what it is you would do in life. Can you talk a little bit more about what it was about him when you first met that drew you to him?

First and foremost, the fine art arena tends to celebrate exclusivity. Practitioners and art historians tend to circle the wagons. But Dan was about inclusivity. Dan included everybody in every conversation. And, again, the conversations were about living. They were about life. "You kids are here; you have an amazing opportunity."

That's right where he went and the art came along as a part of the inclusion.

Occasionally—and this would blow our minds—he would come into class, sit a kid on a chair that was up on a desk, and bang out a remarkable drawing before our very eyes. He would often make a drawing where he would put the point of the pen on paper and never lift it off of that paper until the drawing was completed, with remarkable likeness.

He would then turn to us: "This is only how *I* make a drawing. Now, let's see how *you* make a drawing."

There was never any right or wrong. And of course, every other thing we were doing at this high-pressure school seemed to have a *right* or *wrong* way to do things. In 1970, Hodermarsky's rooms were such non-judgmental havens that everybody flocked to them. Whether they were taking an art class or not. And the back part was what Dan took over for his studio and while he was working on his own paintings, Dan would tell stories to whomever was there in his small working area and other people would tell stories. Dan listened better than any than any teacher I can remember. Dan was just glued to listen.

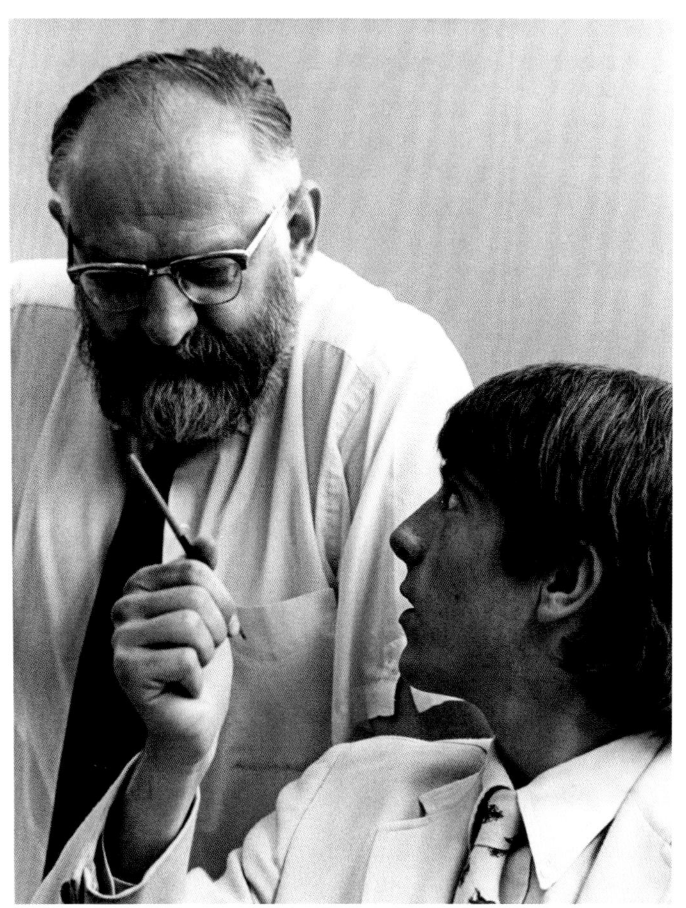

Dan and Stephen Hannock,
Deerfield Academy
Archives, Deerfield, MA,
ca. 1970

You did one school year at Deerfield. You were seeing Dan, you were working with him a couple times a week, he's encouraging you, then you leave, but you continue to have a relationship. Tell me about that.

Particularly after Deerfield, the overwhelming thing about Hodermarsky was the consistency of his concern for how my life was going. Once again, things were never compartmentalized into ART, and then the rest of living. It was all one phalanx. We would talk about family, friends with whom I was working, did I miss hockey, and then how a given lady friend was doing.

A critical part of Dan's concern was how I would fare on the front lines of the "Art Wars" as we affectionately referred to biting the bullet, when I was thinking about moving to New York City, and diving into the contemporary art arena. In spite of the 12 exhibitions at museums and art centers under my belt, we all knew I'd be starting over from scratch. Dan had coached a lot of kids about the relentless criticism that was a part of the gallery scene, how to thicken their skins in preparation for the inevitable bumps. Confidence in the arts is difficult to maintain even under the kindest of circumstances. In the hyper-competitive arena of the New York gallery scene, this confidence is all the more fragile.

Art had to be the foundation. And the relentless focus had to be central.

Embracing this understanding turned out to be critical as I entered the contemporary art scene in lower Manhattan. The night clubs, where much contemporary art was exhibited, were full of men and women who wanted to be art stars. But the real working artists were much fewer. The working artists were *working*. I was working. I'd be in bed by 11 PM. And the clubs where I was showing my paintings wouldn't even open until midnight. But that was okay. Because it was "the next piece" that held the magic. It was the next piece that held the mystery. And the "next piece" never happened unless I worked every day.

But Dan's initial advice came in the form of a roaring wave of laughter. He said, "Hannock, they're never going to see you coming." He was referring to the fact that I'd been a goalie who was already used to getting beat up.

And he was right.

He thought it was hilarious, but was also utterly confident in me. So when The Metropolitan Museum made their first acquisition, we really celebrated.

You remained friends until Dan died. Close friends, even colleagues. Could you tell me at what point did your relationship shift from being student to teacher to artist to artist?

What evolved during those early years was me, my growing up. Art was the primary anchor. It just was. We didn't talk about his past. Ever. And this is why Nancy's stories about Dan's struggle with PTSD came as such a shock to me. I never knew that those paintings he made—the images of war—were from his own experiences. We always assumed they were remarkable images of our all-consuming war in Southeast Asia.

He just was always so enthusiastic about whatever I was doing, and whatever was going on in my life.

So lastly, it's particularly invigorating to know that my fluorescent murals, paintings that glow under black light that Dan was so enthusiastic about, are once again being brought to the contemporary art arena, *40 years later!* Now that exhibition spaces are set up for "installations," we are reintroducing the musically accompanied exhibition of luminous murals. Anthony Davis, with whom I even did a presentation at Deerfield in the late '70s, will once again be performing piano improvisations within our updated environment: paintings from the 1970s as well as new works from the 2020s. Dan would be thrilled.

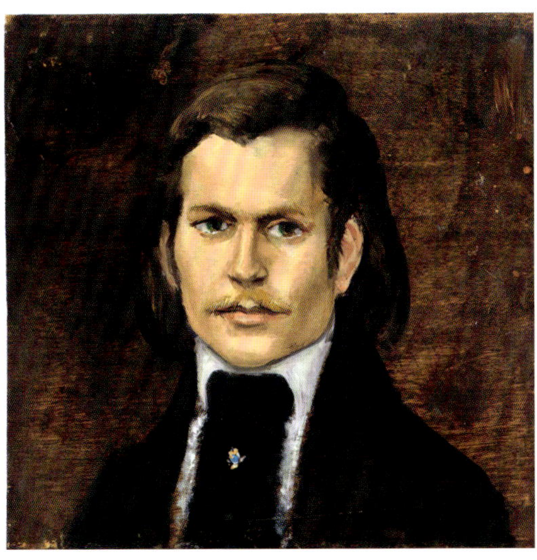

Portrait of Stewart W. Read, Deerfield Academy
Class of 1973, whose steadfast support brought
this book from dream to reality

1973
Oil on board
10 x 10 in. (25.4 x 25.4 cm)
Private collection

RR #1 Box 25 Dow Road
Deer Isle, Maine 04627
March 22, 1998

Stewart W. Read

Dear Stewart:

Yes, it is difficult to believe a quarter of a century has passed since we were together on the Deerfield campus, that all of you in the Class of '73 have almost attained the age I enjoyed when you first met me.

This is a good time for many of you, I am sure, to reflect upon those hours and days that marked your steps into adulthood. For some of you leaving Deerfield may have been an escape from tyranny. For others a soft, warm sentimentality for the school lingers on even to this day.

So it is with this old teacher. Without mentioning specific names here, I remember a remarkable group of young men, young men of great humor, wit, intellect, exuberance, energy, young men who were dedicated to learning and to friendships.

What has given me the most pleasure over the years has been my continued friendship with many members of the Class of '73. Our encounters through cards and letters, at Deerfield reunions, at lunches, dinners and visits throughout the East, have always made me feel proud to know you. For those with whom I have not had the opportunity to be in contact, I hope that each one of you has continued to be that unusual, exciting and singular individual I knew at Deerfield.

Certainly my most sincere wish for all of you in the years ahead is that you will be able to be thoughtful, humane and wise in all things, relishing the pleasure of life itself.

Thank you, Stewart, for your loyalty over the years and particularly for your many thoughtful kindnesses to me when you were a student at Deerfield. I have never forgotten them. My warmest good wishes to you, your wife and your family,

Daniel Hodermarsky

Letter from Daniel Hodermarsky to Stewart Read, 1998, upon the twenty-fifth reunion
of Deerfield Academy's Class of 1973

ACKNOWLEDGMENTS

Among the most vivid of childhood memories we have of our father, Daniel Hodermarsky, was his welcoming of a steady stream of high school students to our home on Deer Isle, Maine. Summer after summer, between June and August, students would pilgrimage to our farmhouse by car, bus, bicycle, or by hitching rides, to crash on our living room floor. Our father never formally invited them, and it was unclear to us all at the time why they came, but in retrospect it is certain that they were compelled to be near Dan. Ever the nurturer, our mother Nancy was equally welcoming to all—and, no doubt, did the lion's share of the care giving. When we, their daughters, complained about the lack of privacy and family time, Dad urged us to be accepting—explaining that so-and-so were "finding themselves" and needed to be in that place at that time. As this book reveals, over the course of Dan's own young adult life he himself had experienced a similar sense of feeling unmoored. In opening his home to these restless youths throughout the 1970s and 1980s, he was clearly paying it forward.

Unbeknownst to his family until relatively recently, this book had been brewing for some time amidst an ever-growing core of Dan's former students—many of whom were among those who had parked themselves on our floors during those early years. These students—now our dear friends—remained close to Dan throughout his life. Each in their own way has expressed how Dan's sudden death in early 1999 provided them no closure, and that a commemoration of his formidable oeuvre was important. By the spring of 2020, a critical mass of supporters had coalesced—a group spearheaded by the remarkable Stephen Hannock (a Deerfield Academy Class of 1970 postgraduate senior), along with Duncan Christy (Deerfield Academy Class of 1970 President)—whose words grace this book—as well as the unwaveringly generous Stewart Read (Deerfield Academy Class of 1973). We thank in earnest the river of other generous supporters, in alphabetical order, for their love and embrace of this project: Michael Bartlett, Michael Berman, Jeffery Bewkes, James Edwards, Scott Halsted, Arthur Hardigg, David Koeppel, Olav and Judith Kollevoll, Gill Lamphere, James Madden, Jim Lindsay, Jonathan Masters, Scott McCallister, Tom Montgomery, Elizabeth Moore, Rebecca Moore, Charles and Nancy Trautmann, Benjamin Van Dusen, Alfred Van Ranst, Robert Dell Vuyosevich, David Weller, Stephen Wheeler, Tuck Whitehurst, and Paul Wolf.

Our sincerest gratitude is due the A-team of authors whose words provide varied and deep insight into Dan's work. First, to the unstoppable Anna Hammond who served as content editor as well as conductor of the artist interviews. Anna is one of our family's oldest and dearest of friends who knew Dan well from our childhoods together on Deer Isle and authored previous extraordinary essays on his work. Her support throughout the production of this book has been invaluable. We genuinely thank lead author Allison Rudnick for her evocative essay that places Dan's art staunchly within the canon of his time and draws out its beauties and intricacies. Kat Lee focused her investigation on the interplay between Dan's art and his PTSD in a heart-wrenchingly bold and inspiring tribute. Having never met Dan, it is astonishing how well both essayists intuited so intimately his art and his humanity in their richly layered prose.

Duncan Christy, one of the generous principal instigators of this book, authored the gorgeous foreword that speaks to Dan's remarkable artistic skill as well as his ability to both connect with and inspire teenage students in their vulnerable years. We thank lifelong friend Michael Tracy for his willingness to add a deep and resonant voice with his revealing interview that paints a concentrated portrait of a side of Dan about which we knew little.

And then, there is the indomitable Stephen Hannock. This book was his vision, a vision that he developed, championed, and ferried to publication. His belief, reflected in his own artwork, that everyone—passed and present—is part of the canvas, is astounding. The artist interviews with both Stephen and Michael herein articulate so richly the spirit of Dan, his under-recognized work, his dynamic life force, and his deep capacity to love.

Enormous thanks are due Stephen Petegorsky who worked tirelessly to photograph all of Dan's artwork, both in Stephen's Massachusetts studio and by traveling to Deer Isle, Maine, in July of 2022. His master images beautifully capture not only Dan's palette but also the extraordinary, layered depth and brushwork of the paintings. We are grateful to Stephen, as well as to Deer Isle photographer Darwin Davidson, who, late in the game, graciously stepped forward to expertly grasp the last few outlying works. We also wish to thank Anne Lozier, the talented and generous archivist at Deerfield Academy, for her enthusiastic assistance, as well as Dorita Berger, a former collaborator of Dan's, with her answers to questions about the multimedia work. To Elena Kubler, Dan's longtime gallerist, friend, and champion, we do not even know what we owe. She has ever been our rock in hard places.

It is with great appreciation that we acknowledge Leslie Pell van Breen, executive director of The Artist Book Foundation, and ringleader of all that went into this volume. Tremendous thanks as well are due the collegial and talented staff of TABF, with whom it has been a delight to work—most particularly, Deborah Thompson, senior editor and wordsmith, who ushered the project along so efficiently, and David Skolkin, book designer, who so beautifully drew together the prose and the images that grace this book.

Ultimately and oddly fittingly, this is a publication born of the COVID-19 pandemic. At a time when we were all holed-up in our individual homes and apartments, fearful of human contact, these remarkable former students of Dan's moved this beautiful project forward. Dan—a man who was *all about* creativity, human connection, and nurture—would be astonished at how thoroughly his students absorbed these, his ultimate lessons, with this tribute. Nearly 25 years since his passing, it is exhilarating that Dan's oeuvre and life are reinvigorated in this extraordinary volume. The Hodermarsky family extends our heartfelt appreciation to all involved in its creation.

Elisabeth, Maria, and Nancy Hodermarsky

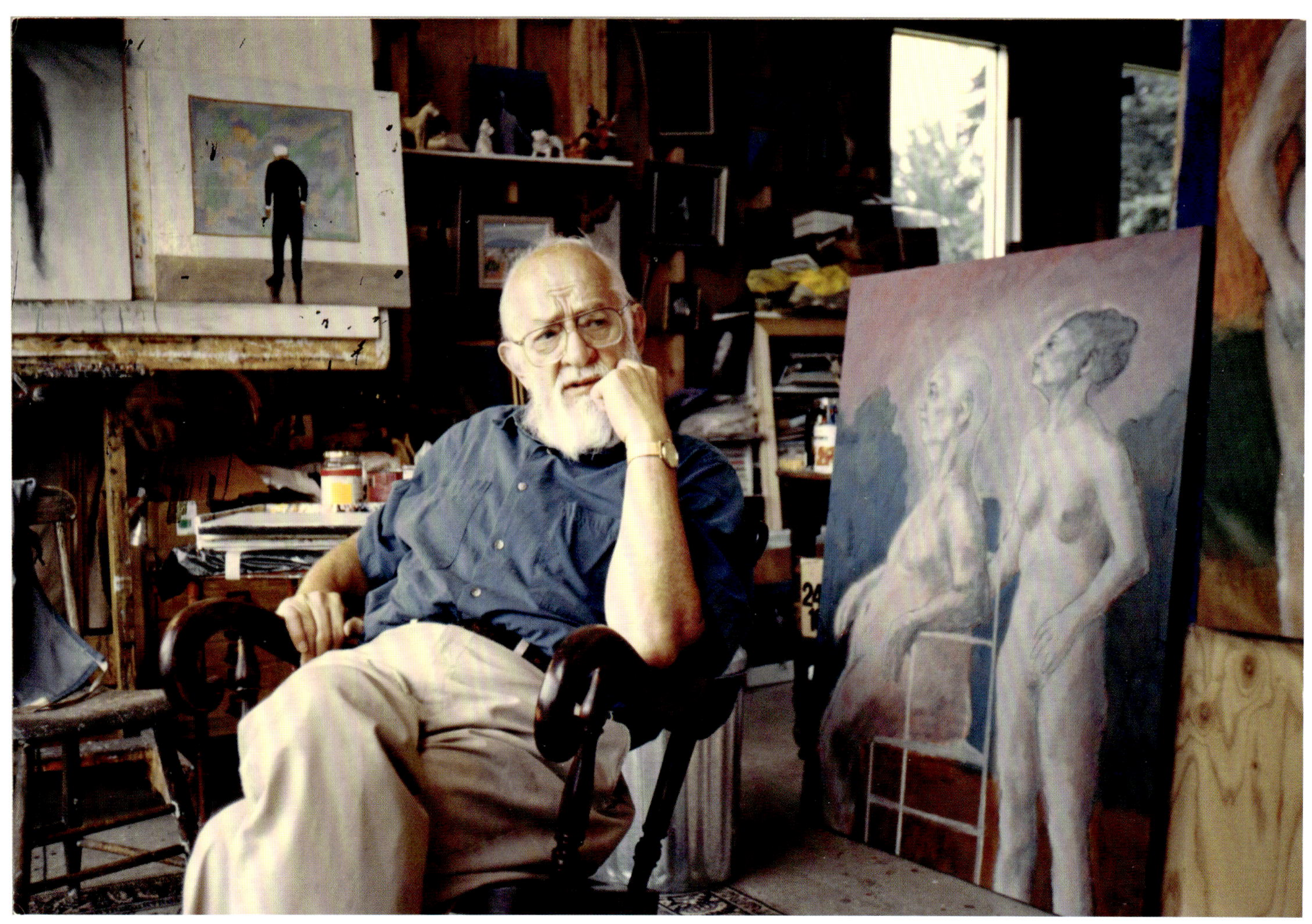

Dan in his barn studio, August 1996

1924 Daniel Hodermarsky is born in Horning, Pennsylvania, on July 2nd, the twelfth child (ninth surviving) of Slovak immigrant parents Mary Kolesárová Hodermarsky and Daniel Hodermarsky, Sr., who were born in Hačava, Slovakia, and had emigrated to America over a decade before. His father works in the West Virginia and Pennsylvania coal mines as his mother raises the family. While a young boy, the family moves to Cleveland, Ohio, where his father works in the woolen mills and older brothers secure positions in the automobile industry.

1942 Graduates with honors from West Technical High School in Cleveland, Ohio. Earns a full scholarship to study at the Cleveland Institute of Art. His studies during the winter of 1942–1943 are interrupted when he is drafted into a three-year tour of duty with the United States Army in Europe.

1943–1945 Serves in the Army's the Armored Artillery Battalion and faces combat in France, Belgium, Luxemburg, and Germany. He witnesses many of the major battles of the Second World War on the Western front, including the Normandy landings, Saint-Lô, the Battle of the Bulge, the Battle of Hürtgen Forest, and the Battle of Remagen Bridge. He is awarded a Presidential Citation, a Croix de Guerre from France, a Croix de Guerre from Belgium, one silver and five bronze combat stars. He returns home suffering from undiagnosed but severe and persistent post-traumatic stress disorder.

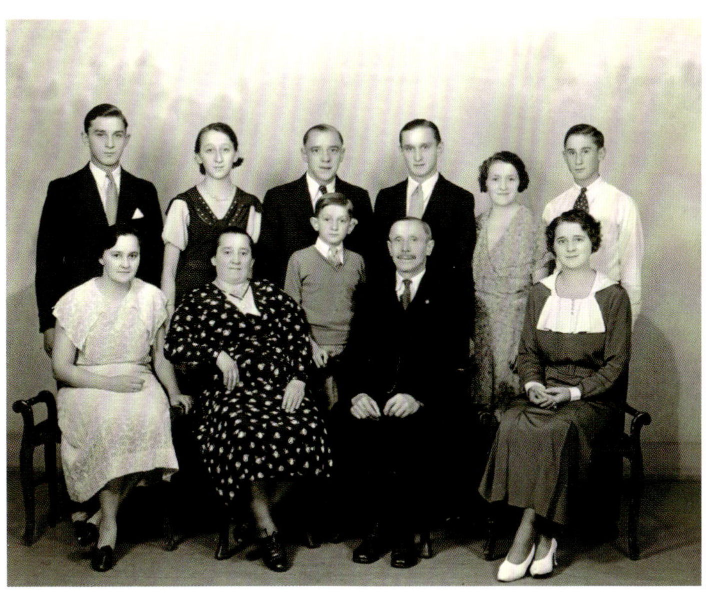

Daniel Hodermarsky and Mary Kolesárová Hodermarsky Family Portrait, ca. 1930. Bottom row, left to right: Mary Jr., Mary Sr., Daniel Jr., Daniel Sr., Julia; top row, left to right: John, Elizabeth, Michael, George, Verna, Paul

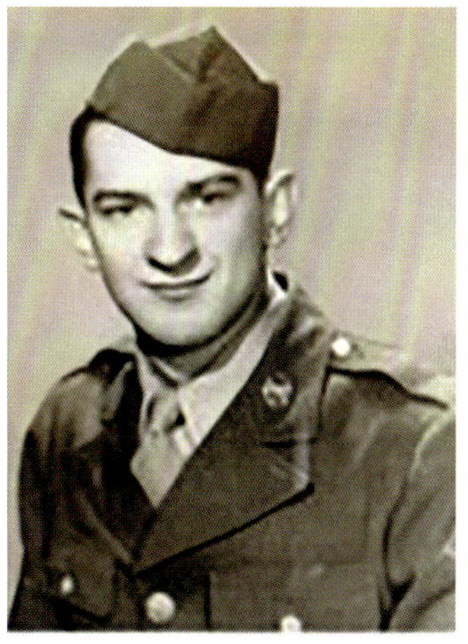

Daniel Hodermarsky, age 18, official WWII U.S. Army portrait

1947–1949 One year after the end of the war, he returns to his studies at the Cleveland Institute of Art and receives a BFA in Painting with honors.

1950 Earns a B.S. in education from Kent State University in Kent, Ohio.

1950 Exhibits work in *The Human Equation*, Akron Art Institute, Akron, Ohio, and wins a Purchase Award.

1950–1955 He works as a chartist and display designer at the Cleveland Diesel Engine Division of General Motors Corporation in Cleveland, Ohio.

1955–1963 Teaches studio art and art history at Lakewood High School in Lakewood, Ohio.

1956 He attends Cranbrook Academy of Art, Bloomfield Hills, Michigan, completing its Special Studies in Painting course.

1957–1969 Teaches figure drawing, painting, and advanced painting, as well as evening school and Saturday classes at the Cleveland Institute of Art. During this time, and throughout the rest of his career, he regularly volunteers to local causes at art and community fairs to create pencil sketches and pastels of children.

1960 Earns an MFA in Art History from Case Western Reserve University, Cleveland, Ohio.

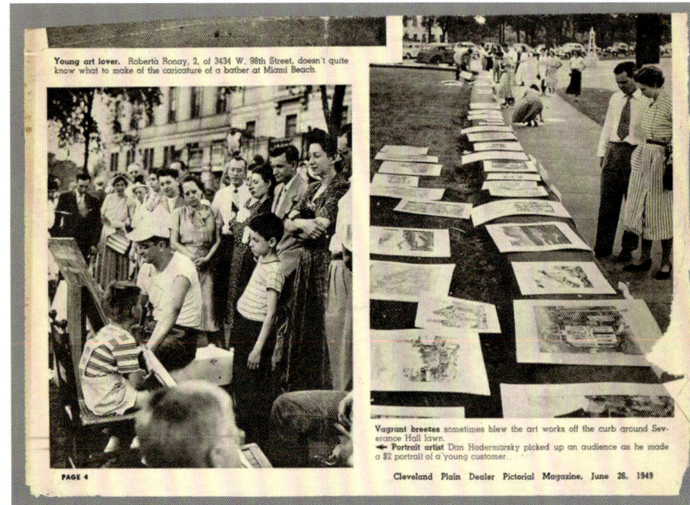

"Portrait artist Dan Hodermarsky picked up an audience as he made a $2 portrait of a young customer," *Cleveland Plain Dealer Pictorial Magazine*, June 16, 1949; photo by Edward J. Solotko

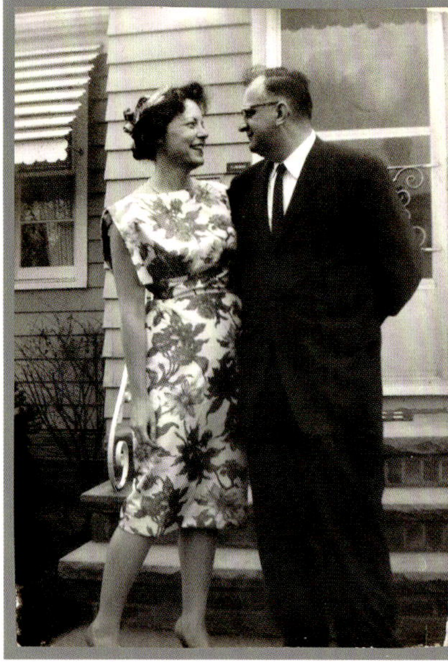

Wedding Day photograph of Daniel Hodermarsky and Nancy Louise Burt Hodermarsky, April 9, 1960

1960 He marries Nancy Louise Burt, of Cleveland, Ohio, a teacher of English and Latin who has spent many of her early adult years living and teaching in Athens and Rome.

1961 Daughter Maria is born.

1963 Daughter Elisabeth is born.

1963–1965 His work appears in group exhibitions at Circle Gallery, Cleveland, Ohio.

1963–1967 He is an instructor in studio art and art history at Shaker Heights High School, Cleveland, Ohio.

1964–1969 His paintings are exhibited annually in the *May Show Exhibition* at the Cleveland Museum of Art. He also earns a Juror's Mention in 1968 and a Special Juror's Mention in 1969.

1965 Wins first prize at the Cleveland Institute of Art's Alumni Exhibition.

1966–1968 Begins to work in an Op Art mode, creating acrylic paintings and manipulating found commercial objects such as mannequins, hand cranks, and carburetors.

1967–1969 He becomes the Coordinator of the Bussed-in Arts Program (a federal Title III–funded program for students throughout the greater Cleveland area) at the Cleveland Supplementary Educational Center. He designs the Center for Multimedia Production, offering after school and Saturday programs in film, dance, and the visual arts.

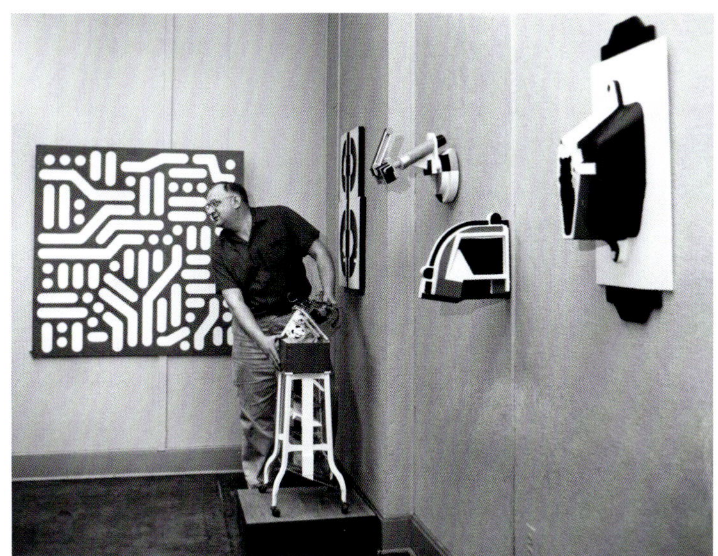

Dan at his exhibition *Industrials*, 1967; press photograph,
© William A. Wynne, Cleveland Plain Dealer, Cleveland, Ohio

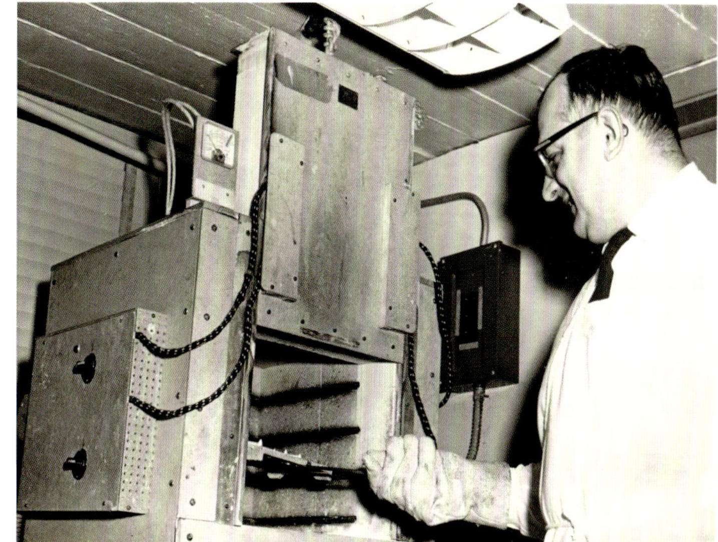

Dan at a kiln, ca. 1960s

1968 He directs the Art Segment in the made-for-television film, *The Circle*, produced by the University Circle Development Foundation, Cleveland, Ohio.

1968–1969 He teaches art history at Cleveland State University.

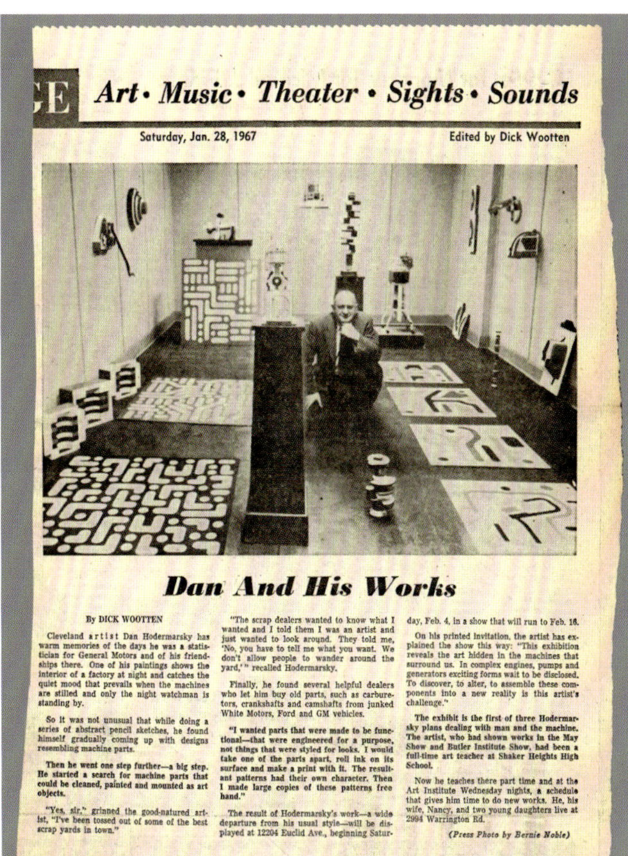

Dick Wootten, "Dan and His Works," *The Sun*, Cleveland, Ohio, January 28, 1967; photo by Bernie Noble

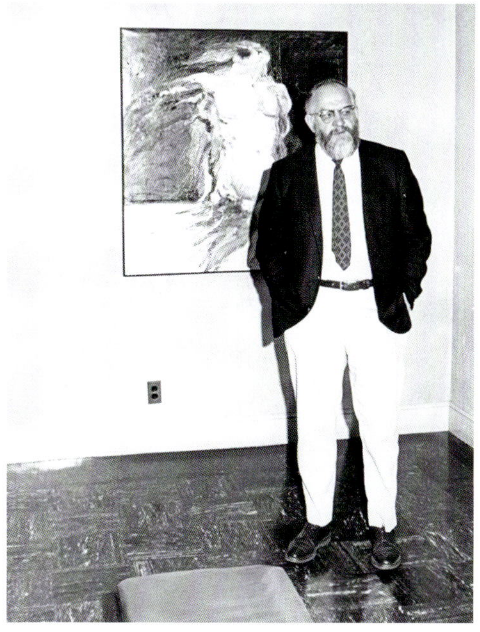

Dan standing in front of *Dismembered Bleeding Man (War Series)*, 1970, at the Agra Gallery, Washington, DC; Deerfield Academy Archives, Deerfield, Massachusetts

1968–1971 Collaborating with composer Donald Erb and choreographer Larry Berger on a series of multimedia performances, he creates all visuals for the productions, including painted-slide light and costume projections, and set designs. Productions include: *Wrap-Up* (1968), *Kinematica* (P.A.C.E. Association, Cleveland, Ohio, 1969), *Fission* (92nd Street Y.M.C.A., New York, 1969; Cleveland Institute of Music, Cleveland, Ohio, 1970; Akron Art Institute, Akron, Ohio, 1970; Hunter College, New York, 1971), *Kyrie* (Hartt College, University of Hartford, Hartford, Connecticut, 1970; Oberlin College, Oberlin, Ohio, 1970), *Interplay '71* (Cuyahoga Community College, Cleveland, Ohio, 1971), and *Pipe Dream* (Hunter College, New York, 1971; Cuyahoga Community College, Cleveland, Ohio, 1972). A Rockefeller Foundation Grant in Multimedia is awarded to Erb (in collaboration with Berger and Hodermarsky), 1969–1970.

1969 He moves with his family from Cleveland to Deerfield, Massachusetts, to establish the arts program at Deerfield Academy.

1969 After summers of vacationing on Deer Isle, Maine, in the 1960s, Dan and Nancy purchase a hundred-year-old farmhouse on Northwest Harbor. They later build an adjacent barn with a painting studio. The property will become their summer home and where they will retire in 1989.

1969–1989 He serves as instructor in studio art and art history at Deerfield Academy and continues to build the Arts Program. He is appointed chairman of the Art Department for the years 1969–1980 and director of the Hilson Gallery at Deerfield, 1970–1986; he serves as the John J. Louis Chair in the Humanities, 1970–1984; and is a member of the Trustee-Faculty Committee, 1975–1980.

1970 Directs "Put a Little Love in Your Heart," an Art Segment in the made-for-television film, *A Child Went Forth*, produced for the American Association of School Administrators, 1970. An exhibition of his paintings is shown at the Hilson Gallery, Deerfield Academy.

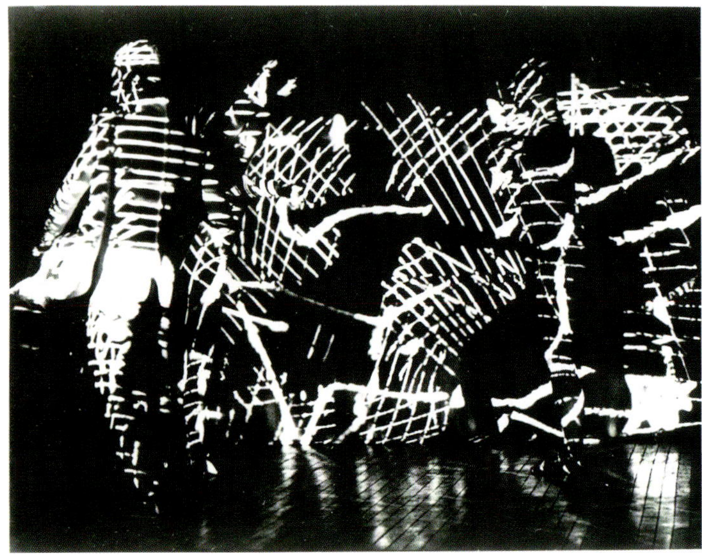

Performance still from the multimedia production, *Pipe Dream*, 1971

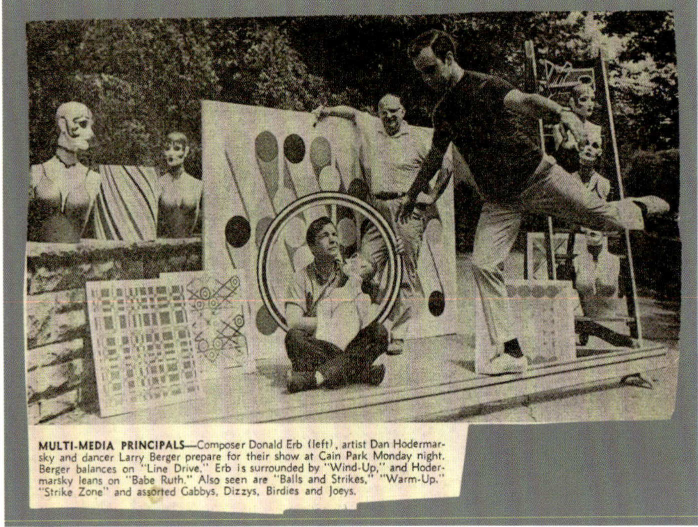

Dan (center) with composer Donald Erb (left) and dancer Larry Berger (right), ca. 1970

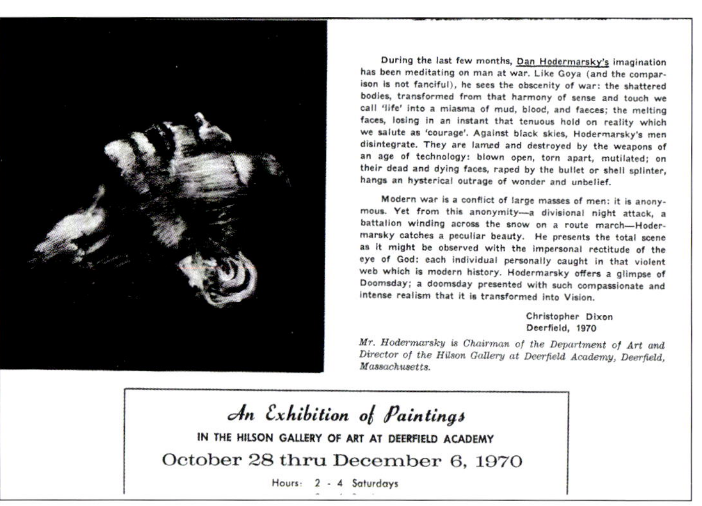

During the last few months, Dan Hodermarsky's imagination has been meditating on man at war. Like Goya (and the comparison is not fanciful), he sees the obscenity of war: the shattered bodies, transformed from that harmony of sense and touch we call 'life' into a miasma of mud, blood, and faeces; the melting faces, losing in an instant that tenuous hold on reality which we salute as 'courage'. Against black skies, Hodermarsky's men disintegrate. They are lamed and destroyed by the weapons of an age of technology: blown open, torn apart, mutilated; on their dead and dying faces, raped by the bullet or shell splinter, hangs an hysterical outrage of wonder and unbelief.

Modern war is a conflict of large masses of men: it is anonymous. Yet from this anonymity—a divisional night attack, a battalion winding across the snow on a route march—Hodermarsky catches a peculiar beauty. He presents the total scene as it might be observed with the impersonal rectitude of the eye of God: each individual personally caught in that violent web which is modern history. Hodermarsky offers a glimpse of Doomsday; a doomsday presented with such compassionate and intense realism that it is transformed into Vision.

Christopher Dixon
Deerfield, 1970

Mr. Hodermarsky is Chairman of the Department of Art and Director of the Hilson Gallery at Deerfield Academy, Deerfield, Massachusetts.

An Exhibition of Paintings
IN THE HILSON GALLERY OF ART AT DEERFIELD ACADEMY
October 28 thru December 6, 1970
Hours: 2 - 4 Saturdays

Brochure for an exhibition of Hodermarsky's paintings at the Hilson Gallery, Deerfield Academy, October 28–December 6, 1970

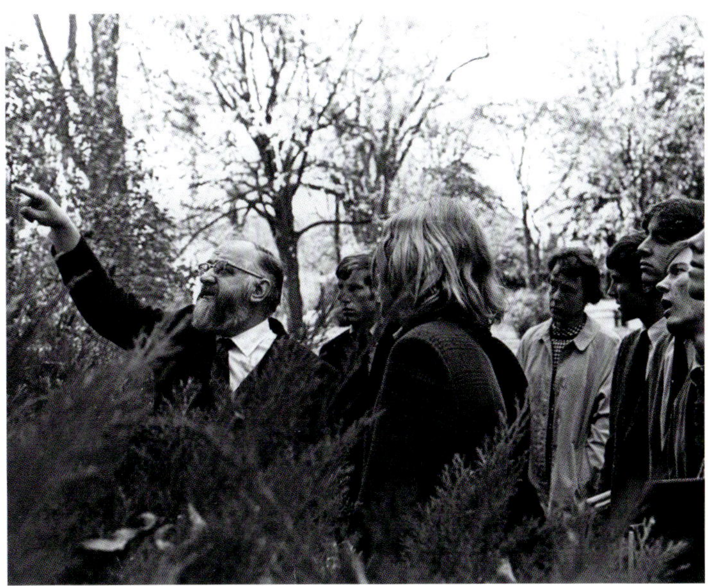

Dan conducting an outdoor class at Deerfield; Deerfield Academy Archives, Deerfield, Massachusetts

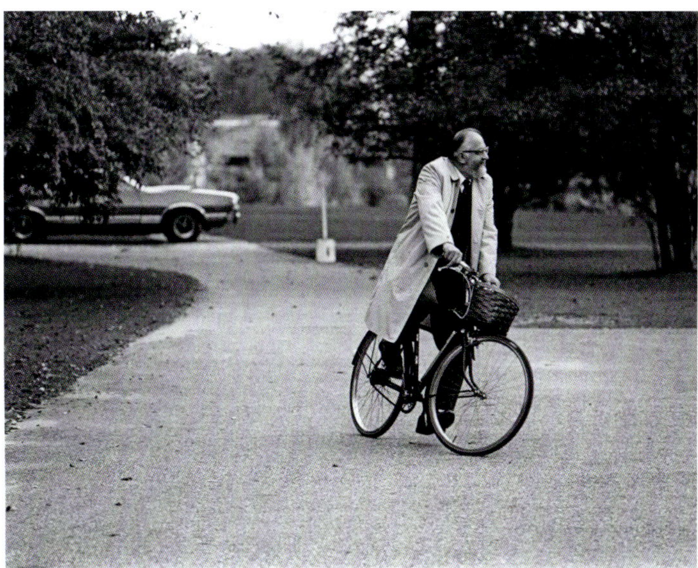

Dan on his Raleigh, ca. 1973; Deerfield Academy Archives, Deerfield, Massachusetts

1973–1974 He becomes the Founding President, Deer Isle Artists Association, Deer Isle, Maine.

1973–1975 Serves as a trustee of the Ballet Arts Regional Repertory Ensemble (B.A.R.R.E.), Greenfield, Massachusetts.

1975–1976 Attends Special Studies in Drawing at the University of Massachusetts–Amherst.

1987–1988 Takes sabbatical leave for Professional Growth in Painting, Deerfield Academy, Deerfield, Massachusetts.

1989 Retires with Nancy to Deer Isle.

1989–1993 Serves as trustee for the Island Medical Center, Stonington, Maine.

1991 He is awarded a sculpture commission for *Fishermen Lost at Sea*, a public monument sponsored by the Island Fishermen's Wives, Deer Isle. His *War Series* paintings are shown in Artists on War, an exhibition at the Ellsworth Public Library, Ellsworth, Maine, and the Bangor Public Library, Bangor, Maine.

1999 Dan passes away on a bright January 24th day while painting in his studio.

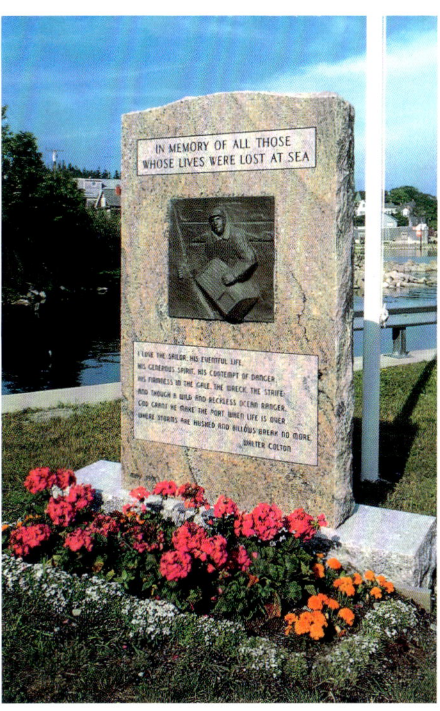

The *Fishermen Lost at Sea* monument, 1992

AWARDS, COLLECTIONS, AND COMMISSIONS

1991 Sculpture Commission for *Fishermen Lost at Sea*, a public monument sponsored by the Island Fishermen's Wives, Deer Isle, ME

1987–1988 Sabbatical leave for Professional Growth in Painting, Deerfield Academy, Deerfield, MA

1970-1984 John J. Louis Chair in the Humanities, Deerfield Academy, Deerfield, MA

1969–1970 Rockefeller Foundation Grant in Multimedia awarded to Donald Erb, composer in collaboration with choreographer Lawrence Berger and visual artist Daniel Hodermarsky

1969 Special Jury Mention, May Show Exhibition, Cleveland Museum of Art, Cleveland, OH

1968 Juror's Mention, May Show Exhibition, Cleveland Museum of Art, Cleveland, OH

1965 First Prize, Cleveland Institute of Art Alumni Exhibition, Cleveland, OH

Charles R. Keller Award, granted by the John Hay Fellowship, New York, NY

1950 Purchase Award, *The Human Equation*, Akron Art Institute, Akron, OH

1942 Full scholarship to the Cleveland Institute of Art, Cleveland, OH

Solo Exhibitions:

2009 *Daniel Hodermarsky: Abstract Paintings*, Turtle Gallery, Deer Isle, ME, August 2–22

2008 *Daniel Hodermarsky: Landscapes*, Turtle Gallery, Deer Isle, ME, July 6–August 2

2008 *Daniel Hodermarsky: Figure Paintings and Deerfield Watercolors*, Charles P. Russell Gallery, Deerfield Academy, Deerfield, MA, May 1–June 14

2007 *Daniel Hodermarsky: Figure Paintings*, Turtle Gallery, Deer Isle, ME, July 8–August 4

2006 *Chautauqua Paintings*, Kendal at Oberlin Gallery, Oberlin, OH, May 6–June 19

Daniel Hodermarsky: A Selection of Paintings on Panel, Turtle Gallery, Deer Isle, ME, August 6–26

2000 *Paintings on Panel*, Turtle Gallery, Deer Isle, ME

1999 *Hodo: A Celebration of the Life and Work of Daniel Hodermarsky*, Hilson Gallery, Deerfield Academy, Deerfield, MA, October 2–November 19

1999 *Into a New Century*, Turtle Gallery, Deer Isle, ME

1998 *Daniel Hodermarsky: Watercolors*, Bar Harbor Bank and Trust, Deer Isle, ME, March 2–28

Seascapes and Figures, Clark House Gallery, Bangor, ME, October 1–28

1998 Deer Isle Artists Association, Deer Isle and Stonington, ME

1997 *Embodiments*, Turtle Gallery, Deer Isle, ME, August 3–17

1994 Deer Isle Artists Association, Deer Isle and Stonington, ME

1991 Deer Isle Artists Association, Deer Isle and Stonington, ME

1989 *Figures: Women*, Turtle Gallery, Deer Isle, ME

1988 *The River and the Sea*, Geissler Art Gallery, Stoneleigh-Burnham School, Greenfield, MA

1987 *Daniel Hodermarsky: Watercolors*, Turtle Gallery, Deer Isle, ME, July 5–25

1986 *Maine Landscape*, Turtle Gallery, Deer Isle, ME

1984 Deer Isle Artists Association, Deer Isle and Stonington, ME

1980 *Dan Hodermarsky: A Retrospective Exhibition*, Hilson Gallery, Deerfield Academy, Deerfield, MA, April 27–May 7

1978 Arts East, Boston, MA

1978–1979 Baracca Gallery, Hadley, MA

1975 Deer Isle Artists Association, Deer Isle and Stonington, ME

1970–1986 Solo yearly exhibitions of figure paintings and landscapes, Hilson Gallery, Deerfield Academy, Deerfield, MA

1970 *Recent Paintings and Sculptures*, Agra Gallery, Washington, DC, February 21–March 10

War Paintings, Hilson Gallery, Deerfield Academy, Deerfield, MA, October 28–December 6 (and subsequent yearly solo exhibitions of figure paintings and landscapes)

1968 *Ballgame*, Cain Park Gallery, Cleveland Heights, OH, August 12–17

1967 *Springtronics*, Women's City Club, Cleveland, OH, May 26–June 22; Hixon's Flower Barn Gallery, Lakewood, OH, June 30–July 6

1967 *Industrials*, Gandola Monument Works, Cleveland, OH, February 3–16

1965 Cleveland Playhouse, Cleveland, OH, January 9–31

1965 Thwing Hall, Case Western Reserve University, Cleveland, OH, March 2–31

1964 Toguchi House, Cleveland, OH

Thwing Hall, Case Western Reserve University, Cleveland, OH, March 2–31

1963 Thwing Hall, Case Western Reserve University, Cleveland, OH

1963 Intown Club, Cleveland, OH

1963 Great Lakes Shakespeare Festival, Lakewood Civic Auditorium, Lakewood, OH, summer

1962 Women's City Club, Cleveland, OH, May

1960 The Cleveland Orchestra, West Shore Concerts, Lakewood Civic Auditorium, Lakewood, OH, January

Group Exhibitions:

2007 Deer Isle Artists Association, Deer Isle, ME

2005 Élan Fine Arts, Rockland, ME

2004 Élan Fine Arts, Rockland, ME

2003 Élan Fine Arts, Rockland, ME

2000 *Maine Mountain*, The New O'Farrell Gallery, Brunswick, ME, October 13–November 18

1998 *Sex and Gender: Who's Who & What's What?* Union of Maine Visual Artists, Blum Gallery of the College of the Atlantic, Bar Harbor, ME, January 5–January 31

Harbor Square Gallery, Rockland, ME

1997 Harbor Square Gallery, Rockland, ME

1996 Harbor Square Gallery, Rockland, ME

McGrath Dunham Gallery, Castine, ME

1995–1996 Park Avenue Atrium Gallery, New York, NY, December 12, 1995–March 1, 1996

1995 *Artists on War*, Union of Maine Visual Artists, Ellsworth Public Library, Ellsworth, ME, March 8–April 3; Bangor Public Library, Bangor, ME, April 10–May

Harbor Square Gallery, Rockland, ME

McGrath Dunham Gallery, Castine, ME

United States Department of State, Art Bank Program

1993 Munson Gallery, New Haven, CT

Two-Dimensional Art, University of Southern Maine Gallery at Gorham, ME

1992 Hilson Gallery, Deerfield Academy, Deerfield, MA

1991 *Artists on War*, Ellsworth Public Library, Ellsworth, ME, March 8–April 13; Bangor Public Library, Bangor, ME, April 10–May

Frick Gallery, Belfast, ME

Gallery Sixty-Eight, Belfast, ME

1990 Gallery Sixty-Eight, Belfast, ME

Leighton Gallery, Blue Hill, ME

1990 *Downtown Downeast*, Maine Coast Artists, Rockport, ME

1990 *Friends and Family: A Figurative Collective*, Sync Gallery, Northampton, MA

1990 Plevin Gallery, Chautauqua, NY

1989 Sync Gallery, Northampton, MA

1988 *Drawing, Paintings, Prints by Daniel Hodermarsky, Timothy E. Engelland, David Ames Dickinson, and Robert Moorhead*, Karen Sprague Cultural Art Center, American International College, Springfield, MA

Plevin Gallery, Chautauqua, NY

1987 Congress Square Gallery, Portland, ME

Hilson Gallery, Deerfield Academy, Deerfield, MA

Leighton Gallery, Blue Hill, ME

1986–1987 Turtle Gallery, Deer Isle, ME

1986 Congress Square Gallery, Portland, ME

Hilson Gallery, Deerfield Academy, Deerfield, MA

1984 Hilson Gallery, Deerfield Academy, Deerfield, MA

1982 Hilson Gallery, Deerfield Academy, Deerfield, MA

1969 Art Faculty Yearly Exhibitions, Cleveland Institute of Art, Cleveland, OH

May Show Exhibition, Cleveland Museum of Art, Cleveland, OH

1968 Art Faculty Yearly Exhibitions, Cleveland Institute of Art, Cleveland, OH

Beachwood Fine Arts Festival, Beachwood, OH

Cleveland Artists Against the War: In Memoriam of Martin Luther King, Jr., Cleveland, OH, April 25–May 26

May Show Exhibition, Cleveland Museum of Art, Cleveland, OH

1967 *Art Faculty Yearly Exhibitions*, Cleveland Institute of Art, Cleveland, OH

May Show Exhibition, Cleveland Museum of Art, Cleveland, OH

Park Synagogue Art Festival, Cleveland Heights, OH

1967 *Art Faculty Yearly Exhibitions*, Cleveland Institute of Art, Cleveland, OH

1966 *Art Faculty Yearly Exhibitions*, Cleveland Institute of Art, Cleveland, OH

May Show Exhibition, Cleveland Museum of Art, Cleveland, OH

1965 *Art Faculty Yearly Exhibitions*, Cleveland Institute of Art, Cleveland, OH

Circle Gallery, Cleveland, OH

50 Artists of Northern Ohio, Mayfield Road Gallery, Cleveland, OH

Great Lakes Shakespeare Festival Art Exhibition, Lakewood, OH

May Show Exhibition, Cleveland Museum of Art, Cleveland, OH

National Exhibition of Small Paintings, Purdue University, Lafayette, IN

The 30th Midyear Show of Contemporary American Painting, The Butler Institute of American Art, Youngstown, OH, June 27–September 6

The 29th Corcoran Biennial Exhibition, The Corcoran Gallery of Art, Washington, DC

Watercolors and Drawings, Pennsylvania Academy of Fine Arts, Philadelphia, PA

1964–1966 Cleveland Museum of Art Traveling Exhibition, Cleveland, OH

1964 Art Faculty Yearly Exhibitions, Cleveland Institute of Art, Cleveland, OH

Artists of the Western Reserve, Cleveland Museum of Art, Cleveland, OH

Circle Gallery, Cleveland, OH

Great Lakes Shakespeare Festival Art Exhibition, Lakewood, OH

May Show Exhibition, Cleveland Museum of Art, Cleveland, OH

National Exhibition, Butler Institute of American Art, Youngstown, OH

Small Paintings, Purdue University, Lafayette, IN

1963 Lakewood Art Faculty Exhibit, In-Town Club, Lakewood, OH, June 6–26

Cleveland 30—Thirty Artists Working in the Cleveland Area, Y.W.C.A., 85th Street, New York, NY, October 22–31

Art Faculty Yearly Exhibitions, Cleveland Institute of Art, Cleveland, OH

Circle Gallery, Cleveland, OH

Cleveland Institute of Art Alumni Association Exhibitions, Cleveland, OH

Great Lakes Shakespeare Festival Art Exhibition, Lakewood, OH

Student Union, Case Western Reserve University, Cleveland, OH

1962 Art Faculty Yearly Exhibitions, Cleveland Institute of Art, Cleveland, OH

Brill Gallery, Cleveland, OH, January 13–February 28

Cleveland Institute of Art Alumni Association Exhibitions, Cleveland, OH

1961 Art Faculty Yearly Exhibitions, Cleveland Institute of Art, Cleveland, OH

Cleveland Institute of Art Alumni Association Exhibitions, Cleveland, OH

National Exhibition, Butler Institute of American Art, Youngstown, OH

1960 Art Faculty Yearly Exhibitions, Cleveland Institute of Art, Cleveland, OH

Cleveland Institute of Art Alumni Association Exhibitions, Cleveland, OH

National Exhibition, Butler Institute of American Art, Youngstown, OH

1959–1963 Cleveland Institute of Art Alumni Association Exhibitions, Cleveland, OH

1959 Art Faculty Yearly Exhibitions, Cleveland Institute of Art, Cleveland, OH

Cleveland Institute of Art Alumni Association Exhibitions, Cleveland, OH

1959–1964 Cleveland Institute of Art Faculty Shows, Cleveland, OH

1960–1961 *Artists of the Western Reserve*, Cleveland Museum of Art, Cleveland, OH

1957 *Artists of the Western Reserve*, Cleveland Museum of Art, Cleveland, OH

1959 *Artists of the Western Reserve*, Cleveland Museum of Art, Cleveland, OH

Multi-Media Productions

Performance-piece collaborations: set designer Daniel Hodermarsky, composer Donald Erb, and choreographer Lawrence Berger

1971 *Pipe Dream*, Cuyahoga Community College, New York, NY, ; Cuyahoga Community College, Cleveland, OH

1971 *Interplay '71*, Cuyahoga Community College, Cleveland, OH

1970–1972 *Kyrie*, Hartt College, University of Hartford, Harford, CT, ; Oberlin College, Oberlin, OH, 1972

1969–1971 *Fission*, 92nd Street Y.M.C.A., New York, NY, 1969; Cleveland Institute of Music, Cleveland, OH, 1970; Akron Art Institute, Akron, OH, 1970; Hunter College, New York, NY, 1971

1969 *Kinematica*, P.A.C.E. Association, Cleveland OH

1968 *Wrap-Up*, Alma Theater, Cain Park, Cleveland Heights, OH, August 12

BIBLIOGRAPHY

"Abstract art exhibition by instructor Hodermarsky shown in Student Union." *Tribune* (Case Western Reserve University, Cleveland, OH), February 14, 1963.

American Psychiatric Association. *Diagnostic and Statistical Manual of Mental Disorders*, 5th ed. Arlington, VA: American Psychiatric Association, 2013.

"Art Show May Gross $15,000." *Plain Dealer* (Cleveland, OH), September 10, 1965.

Blampied, Phil. "Maine's-eye art." *Compass* (supplement to the *Castine Patriot*, *Island Ad-Vantages*, and *The Weekly Packet*, Castine, ME), August 2, 1990.

Borsick, Helen. "It's Abstractionism." *Plain Dealer* (Cleveland, OH), February 3, 1967.

———. "It's Abstractionism, Australian Style." *Plain Dealer* (Cleveland, OH), February 5, 1967.

———. "Show Opens Today at Butler Institute." *Plain Dealer* (Cleveland, OH), June 17, 1965.

———. "*Springtronics* Light Up Hixon's." Plain Dealer (Cleveland, OH), June 30, 1968).

———. "30 Artists' Bring Show Back Home." *Plain Dealer* (Cleveland, OH), December 8, 1963.

———. "Tiny Galleries Helping to Bridge Gap in Art." *Plain Dealer* (Cleveland, OH), Sunday, March 15, 1964.

———. "Works from Butler Show Displayed." *Plain Dealer* (Cleveland, OH), September 19, 1965.

"Deer Isle Artists Association opens exhibition season." *Compass* (supplement to the *Castine Patriot*, *Island Ad-Vantages*, and *Weekly Packet*, Castine, ME), June 4, 1998.

"Exhibits at Local Galleries." *Plain Dealer* (Cleveland, OH), January 9, 1965.

"Found Objects' Fun at Beachwood Festival." *Plain Dealer* (Cleveland, OH), March 10, 1968.

Friedman, Matthew. "The Soldier's Heart. *Pbs.org.* October 7, 2004. https://www.pbs.org/wgbh/pages/frontline/shows/heart/interviews/friedman.html (accessed March 22, 2023).

Frankl, Viktor E. *Man's Search for Meaning.* Boston: Beacon Press, 2014. First published 1959 by Beacon Press.

Freud, Sigmund. "The Uncanny." In *On Creativity and the Unconscious*. Translated by Alix Strachey. New York: Harper & Row, 1958. First published 1919 by Imago, Vienna.

Gibson, Teddi. "This House Goes Round and Round." *Cleveland (OH) Press*, March 2, 1964.

Gold, Donna. "Fifty years later, terror and pain of war lives in art." *Maine (Augusta) Sunday Telegram*, April 30, 1995.

Hammond, Anna. "Memorial Lecture for Dad." Lecture given at Deerfield Academy, Deerfield, MA, 1999.

Harrison, Judy. "Solitude Sitting: Daniel Hodermarsky, Figures and Seascapes." *Maine Times* (Portland), October 22, 1998.

Herman, Judith. *Trauma and Recovery*. New York: BasicBooks, 1992.

Hodermarska, Maria. "For My Father." *Island Ad-Vantages* (Stonington, ME), May 24, 2007.

"Hodermarsky exhibit at Turtle Gallery." *Compass* (supplement to the *Castine Patriot*, *Island Ad-Vantages*, and *Weekly Packet*, Castine ME), July 31, 1997.

"Hodermarsky shows figures, seascapes in Bangor." *Compass* (supplement to the *Castine Patriot*, *Island Ad-Vantages*, and *Weekly* Packet, Castine, ME), October 1, 1998.

"Hodermarsky's work featured at Bangor Gallery." *Compass* (supplement to the *Castine Patriot, Island Ad-Vantages,* and *Weekly Packet*, Castine, ME), September 24, 1998.

Ketwig, John. *Vietnam Reconsidered: The War, the Times, and Why They Matter*. Walterville, OR: Trine Books, 2018.

Kirkwood, Marie. *Sun Press* (Cleveland, OH), August 8, 1968.

———. "Chinese Fans and Album Paintings Score Big." *Sun Press* (Cleveland, OH), March 26, 1964.

———. "Gallery International Show Has Off-Beat Charm." *Sun Press* (Cleveland, OH), February 2, 1967.

———. *"Museum of Art Travelling Show to Open Here Tomorrow."* *Sun Press* (Cleveland, OH), June 10, 1965.

———. "Renaissance of Drawing Called Reaction to Nonobjective." *Sun Press* (Cleveland, OH), October 10, 1963.

———. "Shaker Teacher's Art Is Philosophy of Mingled Irony and Metaphor." *Sun Press* (Cleveland, OH), January 1965.

———. "30 Cleveland Artists' Show Opens Sunday at Circle Gallery." *Sun Press* (Cleveland, OH), December 9, 1963.

———. "22nd Yule Carol Program Sunday at Museum." *Sun Press* (Cleveland, OH), December 12, 1963.

———. "Works of Western Reserve Artists Off on 37th Annual Tour." *Sun Press* (Cleveland, OH), September 3, 1964.

Metzler, Paul B. "Trio at Women's Club." *Plain Dealer* (Cleveland, OH), May 13, 1962.

Mayor, Christine. "Trauma as White Property and the Erasure of Black Victims: The Critical Trauma, Anti-Black Racism, and Whiteness." PhD. diss., Wilfrid Laurier University, 2022.

Morris, David J. The Evil Hours: A Biography of Post-Traumatic Stress Disorder. Boston: Houghton Mifflin Harcourt, 2015.

Nolan, Joy. "Pioneer Valley Colors Brought to Life in Greenfield Show." *Recorder* (Greenfield, MA), April 14, 1988.

Norman, Susan B. and Shira Maguen. "Moral Injury." United States Department of Veterans Affairs. https://www.ptsd.va.gov/professional/treat/cooccurring/moral_injury.asp (accessed November 29, 2022).

O'Brien, Tim. *The Things They Carried*. Boston: Mariner Books, 2015. First published 1990 by Houghton Mifflin.

Park, Crystal L. "Trauma and Meaning Making: Converging Conceptualizations and Emerging Evidence." In *The Experience of Meaning in Life: Classical Perspectives, Emerging Themes, and Controversies*. Edited by J.A. Hicks and C. Routledge. New York: Springer, 2013.

Relihan, Cecil. "Philosophy in the Round." *Plain Dealer* (Cleveland, OH), February 29, 1964.

Salisbury, Wilma. "Instant Psychedelia." *Plain Dealer* (Cleveland, OH), December 8, 1968.

"Show a Delight for Varied Tastes, Budgets." *Cleveland (OH) Jewish News,* November 20, 1964.

"A Smith with an Uncommon Touch." *Plain Dealer* (Cleveland, OH), February 12, 1967.

"Springtronics' Did It!" The Women's City Club of Cleveland (OH) Newsletter 52, no. 10 (June 1967): 2.

Turner, Victor W. "Betwixt and Between: The Liminal Period in Rites de Passage." In *Reader in Comparative Religion*. Ed. Evon Z. Lessa. New York: Harper & Row, 1979. Quoted in David J. Morris: *The Evil Hours: A Biography of Post-Traumatic Stress Disorder* (Boston: Houghton Mifflin Harcourt, 2015).

"Turtle Gallery Mounts New Show." *Ellsworth (ME) American*, August 3, 2006.

"Unveiling—Dan Hodermarsky of Deer Isle unveils the Fishermen's Memorial." *Island Ad-Vantages* (Stonington, ME) 62, no. 21 (May 23, 1991): 1.

Vonnegut, Kurt. *Slaughterhouse Five*. New York: Dial Press, 2009. First published 1969 by Dial Press.

White, Katherine. "The New Hodermarsky Gallery." *Fine Arts* 13, no. 66 (February 20, 1967): 3.

"Who's Who and What's What?: At COA, Maine Artists Explore Sex and Gender." *Ellsworth (ME) American*, January 15, 1998.

"Why Not Take in Show Today?" Art Notes, *Plain Dealer* (Cleveland, OH), January 10, 1965.

Wootten, Dick. "Dan and His Works." *Plain Dealer* (Cleveland, OH), January 28, 1967.

Catalogues

Burkhart, the Reverend Roger, Anna Hammond, James Marksbury, and John C. O'Brien. *HODO: A Celebration of the Life and Work of Daniel* Hodermarsky. Deerfield, MA: Deerfield Academy Press, 1999.

Daniel Hodermarsky: Abstract Paintings. Exhibition catalogue. Foreword by Elena Kubler; essay by Kate McNamara. Deer Isle, ME: Turtle Gallery, 2009.

Daniel Hodermarsky: Figure Paintings. Exhibition catalogue. Foreword by Elena Kubler; essay by Anna Hammond. Deer Isle, ME: Turtle Gallery, 2007.

Daniel Hodermarsky: Landscapes. Exhibition catalogue. Foreword by Elena Kubler; essay by Arthur Hardigg. Deer Isle, ME: Turtle Gallery, 2008.

McNamara, Kate. "Above and Below." In Daniel Hodermarsky: Abstract Paintings. Foreword by Elena Kubler. Exhibition catalogue. Deer Isle, ME: Turtle Gallery, 2009.

Articles, Essays, and Public Lectures on Daniel Hodermarsky's Work

Berger, Dorita. "Multi-Media: A Contemporary Fusion of the Arts." *Fine Arts: A Weekly Guide* (Cleveland, OH) 15, no. 740 (August 12, 1968).

Hammond, Anna. "Memorial Lecture for Daniel Hodermarsky," Deerfield Academy, Deerfield MA, October 2, 1999.

Hodermarska, Maria. "For My Father." Guest Column, *Island Ad-Vantages* (Stonington, ME), May 24, 2007.

Hodermarsky, Nancy B. "Simple Gifts: Remembering a Great Teacher and Artist." *Deerfield: The Publication of Deerfield Academy* (Summer 2008): 30–33.

Wicks, Lee. "Breathing Room: Deerfield's Visual Arts Program." *Deerfield: The Publication of Deerfield Academy* (Summer 2008): 34–35.

Articles, Essays, and Public Lectures by Daniel Hodermarsky

Hodermarsky, Daniel. "Looking Backward to the Future." Graduation Address, Deerfield Academy, Deerfield MA, May 1987.

Hodermarsky, Daniel. "Memorial Day Address to the Deerfield Community," May 30, 1989.

Hodermarsky, Daniel. "Six Senses Toward a New Art, or—Each Child Shall Learn Through New Adventures." *TOPICS: The Junior League of Cleveland* (OH), Spring 1969, 17–20.

First Edition
© 2023 The Artist Book Foundation
All rights reserved under International and Pan-American
Copyright Convention.

Except for legitimate excerpts customary in review or
scholarly publications, no part of this publication may be reproduced
or transmitted in any form or by any means, electronic or mechanical,
including photocopying, recording, or information storage or
retrieval systems, without permission in writing from the publisher.

Published in the United States by The Artist Book Foundation
1327 MASS MoCA Way, North Adams, MA 01247

Distributed in the United States, its territories and possessions,
and Canada by National Book Network, Inc.

Distributed outside North America by National Book Network, Inc.

Publisher and Executive Director: L. Pell van Breen
Art and Production Director: David Skolkin
Design: David Skolkin
Editor: Deborah Thompson
Proofreader: Nicole Barone
Indexer: Barbara Smith
Printed in Italy

Library of Congress Cataloging-in-Publication Data

Names: Rudnick, Allison. Humanist vision.
Title: Hodermarksy / foreword by Duncan Christy ; essays by Allison
   Rudnick, Kat Lee, PhD. ; artist interviews by Anna Hammond.
Description: First edition. | North Adams, Massachusetts :
   The Artist Book Foundation, [2023] | Includes bibliographical
   references and index.
Identifiers: LCCN 2023031483 (print) | LCCN 2023031484 (ebook)
   | ISBN 9781732986466 (hardback) | ISBN 9798987228005 (ebook)
Subjects: LCSH: Hodermarksy, Daniel, 1924-1999—Criticism and
   interpretation.
Classification: LCC ND237.H6625 H63 2023 (print)
   | LCC ND237.H6625 (ebook) | DDC 759.13—dc23/eng/20230726
LC record available at https://lccn.loc.gov/2023031483
LC ebook record available at https://lccn.loc.gov/2023031484

ISBN: 978-1-7329864-6-6
eISBN: 979-8-9872280-0-5

COVER AND FRONT MATTER CAPTIONS

FRONT COVER:
Ambergris 24, 1996
Oil on wood
15 x 12 in. (38.1 x 30.5 cm)
Collection of Ethan Jones

PP. 2–3:
Quiet Shore, ca. 1977
Oil on panel
4¾ x 8⅜ in. (12.7 x 14.3 cm)
Private collection

P. 4:
Veterans Day, ca. 1967
Oil on canvas
47½ x 47½ in. (120.7 x 120.7 cm)
Estate of the artist

P. 7:
Dan in his studio, ca. 1995; gelatin silver print, © Anna Hammond

P. 8:
Reclining Man, 1982
Pen, ink, and charcoal
8⅛ x 10⅞ in. (20.6 x 27.6 cm)
Estate of the artist

BACK COVER:
Self-Portrait in Russian Hat, 1978
Pen, ink, and wash on paper
13¼ x 11 in. (33.7 x 27.9 cm)
Estate of the artist